Business lending

institute of
financial services
School of Finance

Business Lending
3rd edition

Peter Lyons

Institute of Financial Services
IFS House
4-9 Burgate Lane
Canterbury
Kent
CT1 2XJ
United Kingdom

T   01227 818649
F   01227 479641
E   editorial@ifslearning.com
W   www.ifslearning.com

Published by the Institute of Financial Services (*ifs*). The *ifs* is the official brand of The Chartered Institute of Bankers, a non-profit making registered educational charity.

Typeset by Kevin O'Connor
Printed by Antony Rowe Ltd, Wiltshire
© The Chartered Institute of Bankers 2005
ISBN 1-84516-285-4

Contents

Acknowledgements

Grateful thanks are acknowledged to Tottel Publishing Limited, Haywards Heath, for permission to reproduce material by the author published in *Financial Planning for the Small and Medium-sized Enterprise*, second edition 2002 ISBN 0-7545-1785-3.

One

Business strategy

1.1 Introduction

Whether or not a business is commencing to trade or is an established concern it should have researched and adopted in advance a strategy for trading. This can be broken down into four basic components.

1. An internal strategy, which the company can manipulate;
    the internal strategy would decide answers to questions such as what products will be promoted. In what markets and locations will they be traded? At what selling prices? Which customers will be targeted and for what profit?
2. An external strategy to which the company can react;
    the internal strategy can then be married to external situations: what is the competition and how is it likely to affect business? How will customers react to the products on sale and their pricing?
3. There will be a strategy of timing;
    over what future time period will the company assess the success or otherwise of its current trading decisions before considering a change.
4. Finally, there should be a recognition strategy;
    what aspects of trading, be they internal or external, may change in the future? Will the typewriter be replaced by the computer keyboard and, if so, should the business have recognised the advent of the new technology in advance?

The bank will perceive its lending risk in accordance with the trading strategy adopted by the borrowing company.

1.2   Why a strategy should be adopted

A strategic overview must always be present regardless of the size of a business. The aim will be to keep the objectives of the business constantly in mind and prepare for changing circumstances should they arise. Even private companies of very modest size should always maintain a strategic overview of their trading options. Take the case of a small manufacturing business operating in a very competitive environment whose two principal customers account for the majority of turnover. On the one hand, so long as these strategic customers remain, the business has a firm turnover foundation. Should either or both customers change their buying preferences to a competitor supplier, the fixed cost base of the company will be undermined and there will be little time to replace the lost business. The company objective should be to rely less on these customers, so that if circumstances change adversely the business can remain a viable unit.

1.3   What are the strategic variables?

An optimum business strategy embodies several variables:

◆ the perceived needs of the owners/shareholders;
◆ the management's task to steer the business to its adopted target;
◆ the continuing success of the business itself;
◆ the time period(s) over which all variables are evaluated.

The owners will judge their investment by the income (dividends) and capital (share value) that is achieved. The management may be offered incentives to provide successful (share options; salary progression and reputation) and will be judged how they react to changing operating circumstances. The business itself must show added value in the market it is trading through higher earnings and greater market share. It should be noted that higher earnings is not the same as higher dividends; the former does not necessarily lead to the latter. The time taken to attain these objectives will itself judge whether the business is better or worse than its peers

1.4   Batelle's six inputs

How should these variables be evaluated in practice? Dr Stephen Millett (Battelle) identified six inputs, each of which could be declining, staying constant, or expanding, at any one point in time:

1. future demand for the company's services/products;
2. changes in market conditions for these services/products;

3. the opportunities to offer new services/products;
4. the changes in technologies affecting those services/products;
5. the changes in competition and/or substitute services/products;
6. the flexibility needed to account for the surrounding uncertainties.

To draw an analogy with bank lending, Interest rates (input 2) may be increasing and this is likely to lead to a reduced lending demand (1). New services (3) are being offered via the Internet (4) but will take time to become established (6). Meantime, other banks may be quicker to adapt to these circumstances (5). By how much will these factors affect future earnings of the bank relative to its peer group?

1.5   Porter's five forces

A simplified and earlier analysis of this type of external corporate strategy was undertaken by Porter to determine the profitability of an industry relative to its cost of capital through the interaction of five principal sources of competitive pressure. This is usually demonstrated as follows.

Figure 1.1: Porter's five forces

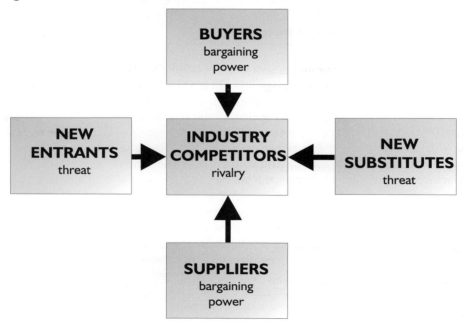

Buyers' (ie customers) and suppliers' bargaining powers will affect the pricing structure of the products and the pricing policy of the company. Their relative bargaining strengths will determine the profitability of the company: if there is dependence on one major supplier, the bargaining power (or choice) of the buyers will affect the profit margin attainable on the product. If the company relies on one major buyer, its profitability will rely on the bargaining (pricing) power of the supplier(s).

Buyers potentially have the power to substitute their choice of provider or there may arise the threat of a choice of substitute products. New entrants may have excess production capacity and/or more modern equipment, enabling them to reap the benefit of economies of scale that would give them cost advantages leading to a more competitive pricing structure. All these factors will determine the extent of competition in the industry and how it will affect individual companies.

The aim for the company would be to compute in financial terms its own strengths of Porter's five forces relative to its competitors and translate that into a strategy to enhance its own return and counteract the effect of the competition. There are some omissions in the analysis: the reading is usually at one point in time and must be repeated for any underlying changes. Also, it does not take into account the time required to effect a strategic change in direction. Some companies take as long as a period of three years for the full results of their new strategy to be achieved.

1.6   Competitive pressure

The work done by Porter in the 1970s and 1980s outlined the five principal sources of external competitive pressure to affect the profitability of an industry relative to its cost of capital.

1.6.1   Perfect market equilibrium

Perfect market equilibrium exists when the quantity demanded of a product equals the quantity supplied. No trading company can improve their position once equilibrium has been reached. Equilibrium for the price of a product is always equal to its value. This will ensure profit maximisation in a perfectly competitive market, when buyers and sellers have no incentive to change the status quo. The equality of demand and supply (the demand curve) will alter according to changes in customer preferences. Buyers will tend to pay more if there is excess demand and sellers will tend to lower their prices if there is a lack of demand.

But markets are very rarely perfect. The effect can nearly reach perfection if there is one overpowering market provider who can dictate the extent of production and the price of the product. The customers will be buying at identical prices and only their efficiency in selling on to the end-user will determine the relative profitability of one customer to another. In practice, this works less well if there is an overpowering customer buying from multiple sources. The buying price initially will be uniform to the providers but some providers will operate on a lower cost base than others and can accept a lower price for their product. The pricing equilibrium is disrupted and will cause ongoing changes in supply and demand.

1.6.2   Trading in an imperfect market

The key to successful trading where market demand fluctuates is a matter of timing and placement. In the first case it will be ideal to be 'ahead of the game' and dictate the take-up of one's product(s) to the optimum speed of production and optimum profitability. This is usually achieved with a new product offering a new technology or 'sales gimmick' that the market will love to purchase. After a period, the newness wears off and competitive products may appear. Competitiveness can be retained, however, through reducing the selling price and the profit margin, hoping that sufficient goodwill has been earned to retain existing customers.

The second key, that of placement, is to offer the market what it requires, rather than raising a product and then trying to create a demand and thereby sell the product in the market. The two most prevalent reasons why start-up businesses fail is that they are undercapitalised at outset and wish to develop a product (or idea) rather than satisfying existing demand for a known product line in an established market.

Additionally, the business may be placed in the right environment at a time when market demand appears. There is the example of a freeholder wishing to build a golf course. The land was flat and barren. Features were needed. The owner hired out the land initially as a waste tip. In time this created the landscape features. The owner gained income from tipping at a time when there was little land available for this use. Thereafter the new pay-and-play golf course proved a boon, placed as it was in an area wanting this facility.

1.6.3   How to combat competition

A company has many choices of fighting competition, such as on pricing, product quality, niche services, marketing, rapidity of supply, after-sales service and strength of market share.

Pricing is easy to re-arrange and can be adopted for only a limited period, especially if the lower margin(s) will increasingly affect the ultimate profit. The business can publicise recognised 'sales periods', following on from when the product(s) were sold at the original, higher, prices. Different prices may also be chosen for different markets or locations.

Product quality has to be recognised for it to take effect. When it does, the selling price may be put at a premium to similar competitive products. Quality is often synonymous with low quantity sales markets: what the business loses in quantity of sales it can make up through higher profit margins. The danger is that quality may deteriorate and the market be lost, or that an insufficiently high selling price will not generate sufficient profits.

Niche services hold several favourable characteristics: they have few competitors by definition, their selling prices are little affected by changes in demand and the market for the product or service is not subject to geographical limitation. There may be a risk that technological developments may adversely affect the business.

Marketing is used extensively by large businesses as a tool to raise awareness in the market for the company's products and thereby gain market share. Some retail businesses use increased marketing to trade themselves out of a poor sales patch. Marketing should not be confused with advertising: the former has a formal budget and programmed expenditure guidelines and monitoring procedures, whereas the latter is aimed at a reactive market and is just informatory.

Rapidity of supply can be an important attribute and many services concentrate on this feature to gain sales. If the consumer has a demand for a service or product, it will be an immediate requirement and it will be important for the business to ensure that production is maintained and machinery is operated efficiently. The service is not particularly sensitive to pricing but the market can still be competitive.

After-sales service, and its quality, will be important if the product(s) sold require regular maintenance. Many manufacturers try to tie in the initial sale with a maintenance agreement or recurring parts replacement (often at very high profit margins, such as branded motor car spares) to increase turnover. Warranty or maintenance contract cost risks may arise in this instance.

If the **strength of market share** is significant this in itself will add to a growth in a company's turnover, as it can afford to undercut competitors' prices due to economies of scale and partially or wholly eliminate competitors' products from public display. Competitors may have to rely on brand loyalty to retain their demand, intermixed with marketing campaigns.

1.6.4   Evaluating the strategic variables

How is an evaluation done? Multinational companies would be assessing the scenario along the following steps (Batelle):

1. Defining the issue (time frame/measuring unit/scope/key drivers).
2. Identifying the areas of influence (the impacting events).
3. Analysing the environmental factors (calculating probabilities).
4. Estimating the cross-impacts (and running the model).
5. Analysing the results (for further study).

6. Introducing sensitivity analysis ('what-if' changes to the variables).
7. Preparing forecasts (and studying the implications).

Small businesses would have to rely on a more simple analysis of the variables affecting trading and consider a much shorter time scale. An example might be the situation of a corner shop business that has just been made aware of a planning application by a supermarket chain to build a new superstore close by. The steps shown above might be interpreted along the lines of:

Steps	Assessment examples
Defining issues	How will profits be affected by the new store opening.
Influential areas	Selling prices; turnover; loss of customers; products.
Calculate factors	What drop in selling prices is needed to retain sales etc?
Cross-impacts	Can product emphasis be changed to maintain margins?
Analysing results	What are the best practical options to adopt?
Sensitivities	Re-assess the options and choose the best one to adopt.
Forecasting	Calculate the revised turnover and profit forecast.

1.7   The Boston measurement matrix

The measurement of business profitability relative to its investment requirement led to the directional policy (business portfolio) matrix (shown below) as drawn up by the Boston Consulting Group. This model compared the market growth (by value) to the market share held by a business.

Figure 1.2: The Boston measurement matrix

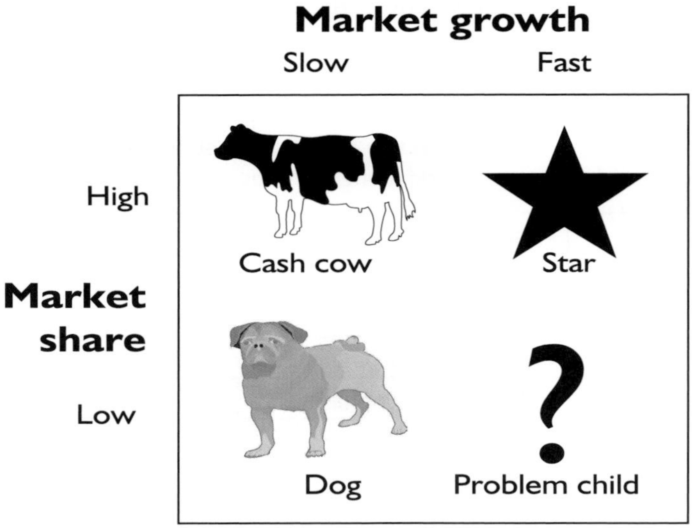

Market growth

| Slow | Fast |

Cash cow   Star

Market share

High

Low

Dog   Problem child

For example, a high market share attained by a business when the value of the market overall is growing slowly should enable it to accumulate value steadily (a cash cow); but it would not be an attractive business if it held a low market share and one would expect it to show a poor return. A high market share in a fast growing market enables the business to capitalise on this expansion through good profit growth, yet if it holds a low market share the expansion in profit will be commensurately less. Its objective should be to gain in market share and 'promote' itself into a star, but can it achieve this metamorphosis?

1.8 McKinsey's 7-S framework

McKinsey found it could apply a 7-S framework to analyse a business' internal strategy. These are summarised as follows.

1. **S**trategy   the allocation of the business's resources.
2. **S**tructure   an organisation chart how departments are related.
3. **S**ystems   the adoption of routine processes and reports.
4. **S**taffing   the categories of personnel and their qualifications.
5. **S**tyle   how the managers perform to achieve their goals.
6. **S**hared values   relationship of the organisation to its members.
7. **S**kills   the capabilities of staff and the business as a whole.

It was discovered that businesses performing well had a bias for action; there was autonomy and entrepreneurship shown by the staff who could identify themselves with the business; there was a belief in productivity; the working approach was hands on and value driven; the business had a simple operational structure and was efficiently staffed in numbers and could operate flexibly.

Another theme leading to business success was termed 'thriving on chaos'. It employed constant innovation, a partnership between all sections of the workforce with a leadership built on change and vision, an obsession to be responsive to customers' demands and with proper control of the business through its support systems measuring the right operating factors.

1.9 PEST analysis

PEST analysis defines and measures the effects of external variables outside the control of a business in order to reduce the operating risks. A weighting is given to each variable similar to benchmarking. Probabilities are assigned to each according to the likelihood of their occurrence and, if so, their quantitative effect on business operations. They are then ranked according to their expected individual impact on the business. Low rankings are discarded, leaving the business to concentrate its strategy on reducing its vulnerability on the remaining factors. There are four principal variables:

◆ **P**olitical;
◆ **E**conomic;
◆ **S**ocial;
◆ **T**echnological.

Political intervention at both national and international levels can be frequent and the effects severe. Banks may be nationalised or have exchange controls imposed. The lending environment may be restricted and there may be political preference given to indigenous lenders.

Economic risks relate to fiscal and monetary policy of the central authorities. They range from control on interest rates, money supply and taxation to more indirect influences such as on the disposable incomes of the population and the imposition of means to stimulate competition.

Social influences may concern the ethical grounds of business operations. Examples are the outsourcing of jobs overseas, social attitudes to established practices (such as 'unacceptably high' lending rates), demographic changes and the propensity to save or spend as it affects bank lending, and overseas nationalism against foreign businesses.

Technological change can have a big impact on businesses that have had a large reliance on staffing branch networks (eg banks) but can now adopt the latest computer systems and offer programmed (lending) products.

Measurements of any strategy are only as good as the accurate recording of inputs and the underlying assumptions on which they are based. The misstatement of oil and gas reserves held by the Shell group of companies that was made public in 2004 would be significant enough, if substantiated, to change the strategy of the group in reallocating resources to boost exploration to find or purchase more reserves in future years.

1.10   Business strategy

1.10.1   The objectives of a business strategy

For a trading entity the owners (or delegated directors and/or managers) of a business should have a continuous concept where they wish their business to be placed in the market(s) they are trading; how profitable they wish the business to be; and how they are best able to achieve these objectives. The concept has to be continuous and ready to react to changing circumstances.

The strategy to meet these objectives may embody a number of options. The examples given below are not exhaustive.

◆ To grow to a strategic size for better control of trading in the business's chosen markets.
◆ To grow and become a public quoted company for ease of raising (cheaper) finance.
◆ To expand into new markets overseas to gain advantage of better trading margins.
◆ To expand into new markets to dilute the risk of a trading downturn in one area of the business.
◆ To diversify into other products for the same reason.
◆ To gain better reward for the owners of the business, be it in higher dividends, greater remuneration or capital value improvement.
◆ To remain at the forefront of technological change and thereby safeguard the business's future trading interests.

1.10.2   Where is the business to be placed in its trading market(s)?

In order to answer this question it should be established where the business is in its life cycle:

1. at the embryo or start-up stage;
2. at the survival stage;
3. at the expansion stage;
4. at the mature life stage;
5. at the declining end of life stage.

1st   The embryo/start-up stage

It should be determined whether or not the business is a 'niche' player, where competition is modest and the skills of management are sufficient to exploit the product(s) or services offered. The business otherwise may be about to trade in a very competitive environment where the marketing prowess or existing contacts of the management will have to be relied on heavily to ensure success. The business strategy for each case will be different: The former example will have the characteristic of an aversion to risk whereas the latter will be relying more on marketing and a wish to trade out of poor demand.

With the former case, the lending banker will be asking whether it is likely that competition will materialise in future, whether there is a risk that the business will not achieve the results expected due to a lack of demand or failings in the product when it is produced or whether the goods or services are likely to be copied. In the latter case, the strength of the competition will have to be assessed. For example, how many similar service companies are offering an identical product within the company's trading area relative to the demand expected for the service? The answer will affect the degree of profitability to be expected.

2nd   The survival stage

The great majority of small start-up businesses fail within the first two years. The business strategy in most cases has not been properly planned and the entrepreneur is relying on the three 'H's' – **H**appiness in the type of occupation, **H**ard work to establish the business and **H**ope that it will be a success. It is critical that a proper business strategy is employed to make the most of the (probably) limited capital invested in the venture and that this capital is adequate and spent wisely.

Survival may be the requirement of the established business that is suffering from poor trading. In this case there will be an immediate need to conserve cash and extend the time that the company can remain trading without becoming insolvent. The strategy will be to cut costs and concentrate on those products or services that are selling well and offer the best financial returns. There may also be scope to raise additional capital to help trade out of the difficulty and, over a longer time period, to sell some peripheral activities to release capital for investment elsewhere. The lending banker will frequently be asked to assist with this reorganisation and it will be necessary to examine closely the business strategy offered to determine whether this will achieve a recovery in its fortunes.

3rd   The expansion stage

Many businesses look upon the lending service of a bank as being akin to that of providers of permanent capital. It is an incorrect strategy, of course, on which to base and run the business and sympathy must go to an overworked lending officer who will, in effect, be monitoring the account and, ipso facto, acting as the business strategist. This may, or may not, be related to the question of borrowing to expand the business. Care must be taken to ensure that the bank debt can be repaid within the agreed period.

Management can plan expansion internally or it may arise through external factors occurring independent of the business. By definition, planning expansion organically will mean the business will have faced the questions that their banker will want to ask: are there sound reasons behind the strategy? Have all probable trading scenarios been assessed correctly? Are the financial projections reasonable? External factors affecting growth may have a positive or negative impact on expansion plans, such as changes in fiscal regulations or natural supply and demand within the national economy, a major competitor closing down or marketing a new product, or a price war.

4th   The mature life stage

This is generally the most lucrative period in a product or service life for the business. No further investment should be needed in plant or specific marketing for expansion. The business should be mindful to maintain its overall profit margin and market share. Strategy will be largely defensive and ready to combat any trading moves by any competitor. The bank should be looking to the business to reduce gradually any outstanding loans specific to the product or service over this period out of the profits being earned. The bank has its own strategy to consider: as the customer is a good credit risk should it be looking to increase its exposure?

5th   The end of life stage

At this point in the development of a product or service there will have built up a customer following and perhaps even an aversion to change. The strategy should be to concentrate on promoting the brand name to retain sales and use the now greater profitability on the product(s) sold to invest in research and development of the next generation of goods and thereby stimulate a continuing growth in turnover. This is after having written off the initial marketing costs and depreciated fully the plant and machinery necessary for production, thus lowering the current cost of manufacture per item. The lender will be wishing to assess how long existing product sales can remain, at what level, and whether there will be a gap before new product(s) make an impact after this expected rundown.

1.10.3   How profitable should the business become?

Many small and medium-size businesses fail to address this operational area properly. Ideally, a target net profit after taxation should be set sufficient to reward the proprietor(s)/shareholders(s) and leave adequate capital in the business to finance future operations. Working back from this base, allowance should be made for the indirect costs attributable to the business and this in turn will set a gross profit target figure. The turnover target will be calculated by taking the gross profit percentage margin that is attainable when trading.

Example	£'000
Profit after tax target	600
Indirect fixed costs of the business	1,200
Resultant gross profit	1,800
Average gross profit margin assumed on sale	60%
Turnover target	**3,000**

The management now have a yardstick by which to plan their trading strategy. Can the business earn sales of £3m? What is its present capability? In order to earn £3m what changes have to be made operationally? Will a reduction in costs be sufficient? If not, what else must be done? If the answer is to increase production this may lead to higher indirect costs and the whole example will have to be calculated afresh. In all probability part of the optimum solution will devolve around the interaction of average selling prices between products or services and the relationship between selling prices and turnover. This is a very important strategy that constantly arises for business.

Example	Product A	Product B	Combined
No of products expected to be sold	1 million	1 million	2 million
Selling price per product	£1.30	£1.56	
Turnover (£'000)	1,300	1,560	2,860
Direct costs (£'000)	520	780	1,300
Gross Profit earned (£'000)	780	780	1,560
Gross Profit margin on sales	60%	50%	

Problem: The company wishes to earn a gross profit of at least £1.69m to achieve the required shareholder reward after tax.

One solution	Product A	Product B	Combined
Increase the price per product by	10%		
Reduce the price per product by		7%	
The selling price becomes	£1.43	£1.45	
Expected sales are now forecast at	0.9 million	1.3 million	2.2 million
Turnover (£'000)	1,287	1,885	3,172
Direct costs (£'000)	468	1,014	1,482
Gross profit earned (£'000)	819	871	1,690
Gross profit margin on sales	63.6%	46.2%	

The pricing changes may have a more limiting effect if costs can be pared. The direct costs will change in proportion to the number of products sold. Many other strategies can be worked to obtain a similar end result, always bearing in mind that they must be achievable.

1.10.4 How is the business best able to achieve its objective(s)?

Management must examine each part of the business critically for acceptable performance. In the event of the business applying for a borrowing facility the bank will apply the same tests in its credit assessment. The list following is not exhaustive but provides some idea of the questions to answer.

◆	Sales:	Are sales regularly analysed by source? Is it known which are the most popular products? What is the relative profitability of different products?
◆	Production:	Is the existing plant efficient and adequate? Can any production beneficially be outsourced? Is there spare production capacity and is it needed?
◆	Labour:	Is the workforce under/over-manned? What percentage of productive time is charged out? Are there adequate training programmes in place?
◆	Selling:	What is the track record of the marketing team? How are they controlled and monitored? What is the proportion of repeat to new business? Are selling incentives doing their work?
◆	Development:	How much R & D is being done? Are the projects realisable? When are projects likely to be marketed? How much additional finance is required?

◆	Financial:	Is the current level of working capital sufficient?
		Are existing borrowings appropriately structured?
		Are debtors being collected promptly?

The bank will be looking overall to assess the following internal characteristics of its lending and the mnemonic is the word 'PREMIER':

Profitability of the lending.
Regulatory procedures to uphold and their cost.
Economics of the trading outlook affecting the company and the lending.
Monitoring of the individual loan and the bank's portfolio generally.
Internal management of banking ratios, staffing and public relations.
External exposure to competition and any offsetting marketing costs.
Risk analysis of the lending portfolio as a whole.

1.11   Financial strategy

In its broadest sense the financial strategy of a business will be aimed to keep the business operating in the way that its management has laid down. This may mean adopting a borrowing policy both on a short and long term view and to ensure that the business does not run out of funds. The financial strategy must be flexible and adaptive to changes in internal policy and external events. It must also embody a risk scenario in case the unexpected occurs. It is inter-related to the business strategy.

1.11.1   For whom is a financial strategy designed?

The **management** of the company (the board of directors for a limited company and the principals/owners/trustees for non-corporate entities) will have adopted an annual Business Plan. This plan will indicate a monetary requirement for the business to achieve the operating goals that have been laid down, such as a certain growth in turnover and profits. The monetary requirement will be sub-divided into what is generally termed 'working capital' (but more accurately defined as the net total of current assets less current liabilities of the company, not being capital that is required to be permanently employed in the business for it to trade) and 'fixed capital' (the capital that is invested in more permanent assets of the business that are necessary for it to trade). The financial strategy will lay down how these different requirements are to be satisfied.

The **staffing** of the company will be critical and will have a large bearing on the financial strategy finally adopted by management. Their cost is usually a large component of overall expenditure and will comprise a mixture of direct and indirect expenditure: direct wages will relate to the staff needed to produce the company's end products and indirect wages relate to the support staff employed in administration, marketing and central overhead divisions. The number of staff employed to achieve productivity will determine the efficiency of the business. The skills of the workforce will affect quality of the product(s) or service(s) offered.

Depending on the type of business, ongoing staff costs may be considerable as will their accruing pension entitlement. The company may operate its own defined benefit scheme or offer employees a defined contribution scheme. The former is an open-ended cost to the company whereas the latter is not. Finally, if staff have to be made compulsorily redundant or laid off for whatever reason, the costs can be significant, so that this should never be the first remedy to choose to improve profits.

The **shareholders** of the company are its owners and, legally speaking, the company should be run by the directors for the shareholders' sole benefit. In practice, the operating responsibilities are delegated extensively to the directors they appoint. Nevertheless, the shareholders have rights to vote at the company's annual general meeting, on adoption of the financial statements and what dividends are to be paid out. The financial strategy of the company should be to provide ongoing enhancement of shareholder value in the company through a mixture of declared dividends and capital growth of net worth (as shown for public companies through their share value).

Where non-corporate entities are concerned it is the owner(s) who will decide the operating objectives and deploy a financial strategy to match this aim. Unfortunately, it is frequently the case that liquidity takes second place to sales growth and marketing, with the result that the financial strategy, at often too late a stage, restults in the bank lender taking strategic decisions that may lead to the liquidation of the business.

1.11.2   How is a financial strategy laid down?

The steps to complete a financial strategy are suggested below.

- Raise and adopt a business plan for implementation.
- Project the trading results based on approved assumptions.
- Forecast future profit and loss accounts and balance sheets.
- Calculate a cash flow picture from the forecasts.
- Re-appraise the assumptions and compare with target returns.
- Revise any forecasts, as necessary.
- Review the future cash requirement to ensure attaining these forecasts.
- Decide how the cash requirement is to be met.
- Provide a sensitivity analysis of the final model.
- Incorporate a risk assessment to account for the unexpected.
- Consider reducing risks through financial derivatives.

◆ Finalise the cash amount to be raised and decide on its timing.
◆ Constantly monitor the result.
◆ Be ready with alternative options should events so demand.

1.12 Business goals

1.12.1 A case study comparison of two public companies

Publicly quoted companies usually announce in their annual reports what strategic and financial goals have been set. The following examples have been taken from the 2002 published results of two nightclub operators and their words have been paraphrased.

Company 1:

...a strategy focused on three key objectives: to continue to develop our successful large capacity lead brand situated in primary population centres in the UK; to launch a smaller capacity format in smaller UK markets; and to build on our London West End presence mainly through acquisition...

Company 2:

...following four years of outstanding growth we have experienced difficult market conditions necessitating a degree of retrenchment and consolidation. We attribute the downturn to an unexpected decline in (participants) when trade did not expand to take up the substantial increase in capacity that has been coming on stream. (The company) has also been hampered by a lack of capital to finance the redevelopment of the acquisitions made during the year ...

Not surprisingly, Company 1 increased pre-tax profits by 10% whereas Company 2 reported pre-tax profits lower by 31% compared with the previous year. Company 2 overstretched itself financially for both internal and external reasons. It reported a small increase of 7% in borrowings at the end of 2002 and total gearing (borrowed debt to tangible net equity worth) was also reasonably modest at 130%. On the other hand, Company 1 increased its borrowings during the year by 95% and had a gearing exceeding 400% at the end of the year.

The table below features some financial data taken from their published annual reports. It may be useful for readers to suggest at this point (before reading further) what other conclusions may be drawn from the results.

Year 2002 (continuing operations)	Company 1	Company 2
Turnover (£ million)	59.9	32.3
Pre-tax profit (£ million)	7.90	3.00
Change on previous year (%)	+ 10	- 31
Pre-tax profit return on turnover (%)	13.2	9.3
Cash flow (£ million)	9.25	4.24
Capital expenditure (£ million)	14.55	12.3
Total borrowings (£ million) (A)	32.38	36.85
Borrowings: margin cost (average % pa)	Libor + 0.75/1.25	Fixed 7.0
Tangible net worth (£ million) (B)	7.78	28.31
Gearing (%) (A)/(B)	416	130
Tangible fixed assets (£ million)	32.8	65.4
Sites capacity (per capita)	26,437	51,018
Turnover per sites capacity (£ pa)	2,265	633
Number of employees (average pa)	1,127	1,024
Cost per employee (average £ pa)	11,096	6,881

Note: Company 1 converted £20m into 2 yr fixed rate of 4.94% pa by the year-end.

Note: Company 2 had a forward up to 2 yr hedging cap and collar arrangement on £12m debt.

It is clear that both companies have identical basic goals: to grow by expanding the number of operational sites. The capital spending of each business was more than its annual cash flow. Both companies partially safeguarded themselves from higher future interest rates that would otherwise increase their borrowing costs. Company 1 achieved a turnover double that of Company 2 and potentially could be less flexible financially and susceptible to a trading downturn in profit terms greater than that of the smaller company. This was not so, however, and the key may lie in the fact that Company 1 runs a greater proportion of sites in London bringing in 3.5 times the turnover pa per capita capacity whereas Company 2 is more provincially located.

Each company's corporate goals should not interfere with its business strategy and action should have been taken earlier to have standby borrowings agreed in case liquidity faltered and to have measures drafted to counteract any drop in turnover. Neither company has matched its long-term assets with long-term debt (although Company 2 aborted an equity issue during the year) and is relying on future trading from a greater number of sites to repay its borrowings.

Company 2 may have benefited from utilising SWOT analysis to spot any trading weaknesses before they occurred.

1.12.2 S.W.O.T. analysis

The aim of SWOT analysis is to highlight the **S**trengths, **W**eaknesses, **O**pportunities and **T**hreats to a business. The first two are generally internal measurements of the company and the latter two are external factors. From the known facts (not all shown by the table above), an analysis of Company 2 would raise the following comments:

Strengths	An established company building up market share by acquisition.
	A substantial amount of property is held for development.
	Many sites are leasehold (not tying up cash resources).
	There is a diversity of sites being operated in the UK.
	The company has built up a strong group trading cachet.
	Operating leasehold sites offers easy closure if unprofitable..
Weaknesses	A reliance on quality and service rather than per capita growth.
	Relatively low earnings led to no dividends being declared.
	Poor cash flow could not support capital expenditure plans.
	Many sites are leasehold (affecting security of tenure).
	Many venues are not sited in prime public locations.
	Free/leaseholds included £15m surplus on revaluation in 2002.
	The group's bank temporarily financed acquisitions in 2002.
	The group is undercapitalised in terms of risk (equity) capital.
Opportunities	Leisure activities including nightclubs continue in popularity.
	Good management strengths can beneficially affect turnover.
	The market for selling/buying venues is buoyant.
Threats	The company does not chase discounting by lowering margins.
	Local Authorities can revoke nightclub registrations.
	Competition in the more popular 'growth' areas remains strong.
	The company is in danger of overtrading #

Definition: expansion of the business without adequate financial support

It should be noted that there are two factors common both to the company's strengths and weaknesses – the leasehold interests and the locations of the nightclubs. If most of the leaseholds held are on relatively short-term tenancies they will be liable to frequent rent reviews affecting profits but, conversely, unprofitable sites can be closed with less liability than exiting from long leaseholds that may also be subject to frequent rent reviews. Secondly, a good spread of locations will safeguard against a drop in usage in some areas, but will not benefit from the potentially high throughput achieved by nightclubs well situated in London.

In the event, the trading of Company 2 in the first half of 2003 sadly deteriorated to a pre-tax loss of £0.6m compared with a profit of £1.4m for the comparative period of the preceding year. This was before allowing for an exceptional loss of £1m due to the effect of losing trading licences in one city. A forthcoming property valuation is expected to raise a significant and material impairment charge in 2003. A substantial number of properties awaiting disposal are incurring onerous carrying costs. A severe downturn in trade continues. The chairman has retired in order to maintain the continuing support of the company's bank, with which discussions are in train to secure a long-term credit facility.

Two

The principles of business lending

This chapter discusses how a lending proposal is approached and evaluated and how a reasoned decision is reached whether to lend or not. There follow sections on the lending terms and conditions that may be set. Further chapters discuss the characteristics of particular industries and the management skills that should be present for the business to meet its growth targets and satisfy the lending obligations laid down.

2.1   The initial meeting

The managing director of business X Limited has asked for a meeting to discuss with you, a lending relationship manager of your bank, the possibility of a loan. At this stage, the amount and period of the loan has not been mentioned and you only vaguely know of the business. A search of your (computer) records may reveal one of the following:

- ◆ no prior contact has been made with the business;
- ◆ the business and/or the owner(s)/management currently have no account relationship with the bank;
- ◆ the business is on the marketing list for possible future business and some details of its trading interests are on record;
- ◆ there has been earlier contact with the business and its management, but without success.

Depending on the answers that are applicable, you will judge how best to conduct the initial part of the meeting. This may suggest referral to earlier contact records to discover why the bank was not able to assist the business previously if no current note on file answered this point. As the managing director has approached you, some direct, but tactfully put, questions to him (or her) would probably be expected. The answers should lead into a description of the present trading position of the company and why a credit line is required. Each banker will have his/her own style of interviewing, an important part of which is to take a listening stance, aided by promptings to obtain more specific information when areas of particular relevance to the banking assessment are broached.

Where no earlier contact is evident on file, the principal aim should be to give the managing director relatively free rein to describe his business while you will be noting down points as they occur that will require further enquiry. As the managing director may assume that you know the basics of the business, it would be wise to acquire in advance some knowledge of its operations, as well as have in hand a pertinent question or so if required.

2.2   A new relationship

As lending banker the following aspects will have to be evaluated:

- whether the loan proposal has been put together in a succinct manner and properly researched;
- why has the business reached the point of requiring credit?
- what is the trading outlook at the present time?
- have other lenders been approached with the same proposition?
- has a cash flow problem occurred before? Of a similar nature?
- how urgent is the borrowing request?

Regarding the first of these points, the loan proposal may be put to you as a marketing opportunity with its attendant risks, or a balance sheet refinancing, or a seasonal borrowing need, or the financing of capital equipment, or to ease general cash flow problems. In each case, you need to be ready to assess the application accordingly.

The potential borrower may not mention the second point and specific answers may have to be requested. These answers will also touch on the third point concerning the trading outlook. It will be of relevance to see to what degree the proposition is backed up with trading forecasts, what assumptions support the financial forecasts, and how these relate to the track record as shown by the historic financial accounts of the business.

If the accounts are produced, a glance at them will show whether the business is borrowing from other sources at the time of the last balance sheet date. This will be an entrée into an enquiry on the fourth point above. In particular, if information can be obtained on the size of the existing bank facilities drawn during the year, it will indicate to what degree there is any 'hardcore' borrowing by the business and will provide a clue to the extent and need for additional finance.

The last two points are of particular relevance. It can indicate the capability of the management in running the business, their speed of reaction to adverse trading trends and the susceptibility of the business to external influences adversely affecting turnover and hence cash flow. If the management has not been properly prepared to forestall a cash flow problem in the past, then is it capable of doing so after new borrowing has been raised?

2.3   A potential target business

Where the business is already targetted for a future lending relationship, the conduct of the interview should be more approachable and, in a sense, at this stage the proposition could be viewed on the merits put forward by the managing director. Any negative features should be brought up at the time of conducting due diligence tests at a later stage of the banking assessment, otherwise the momentum to build a good working relationship may be negated or lost.

As the banker being approached, it is your judgement whether to ask for financial data to be sent to you in advance of the meeting, or received at the meeting, or requested for delivery to you afterwards. Which option to choose will depend on your forethought whether the prospective customer will expect an immediate indication from you of the success or failure of the credit application and the cost of the amount to be borrowed. For example, if the company is substantive and undoubted as to risk, then an immediate, if conditional, decision may have to be indicated straight away to the customer.

Depending on the internal procedures of your bank, you may already have a good idea of the borrowing margin that will apply and/or know what margin has been set for that type of business and size of company. It may be necessary, in difficult cases, to gain a more firm insight as to the lending margin acceptable to the bank in the absence of other guidance by clearing the credit standing of the potential customer with regional or head office prior to your visit. Nowadays, lending managers usually have quite a high independent discretion of the size of facility that can be granted, although subsequent ratification may still need to be obtained.

2.4   Collection of data

At this stage of the meeting, you should have collated answers to most of the questions required to formulate an early opinion of the merits, or otherwise, of the lending request. An example of a general and fairly comprehensive 'check list' of items for consideration to obtain a proper 'feel' for the business is listed hereafter. It is immaterial in what order any points are discussed and it would be unrealistic to try and raise every listed item in the time allowed. The list should be viewed only as a broad guide from which to choose those features of particular relevance, apart from any specialist aspects relating to the business in question.

a) *Financial background*

- turnover, pre-tax profit and retained earnings;
- analysis of turnover and earnings by products/services;
- gross profit as a percentage of turnover;
- the break-even turnover figure;
- the number of times interest payable is covered by pre-tax profit before interest payable;
- stock/work-in-progress held as a percentage of net current assets;
- a comparison of the totals of trade debtors to trade creditors;
- gearing (total borrowings as a proportion of shareholders' funds);
- capital expenditure incurred during the year;
- borrowings analysis by maturity, fixed/variable interest rates, etc.

b) *Trading outlook*

- forecasts of turnover and pre-tax profit;
- doubtful/bad debts levels, obsolete stocks;
- capital expenditure and replacement programme;
- cash flow projections;
- gross trading margin(s);
- expected external trading influences;
- internal trading policy adopted;
- productivity expectations.

c) *Future strategy*

- turnover: pricing, gross profit margins, marketing;
- turnover growth: how is it to be achieved?
- customer relations, mix of new to repeat business;
- staffing levels, wage awards, training programme;
- production utilisation per cent compared with optimum;
- technical development(s) internally and externally;
- is there a financial fallback scenario?
- what will be the effect of the additional borrowing?

d) *Operational management*

- changes in key personnel;
- internal reporting structure and meetings schedule;
- responsibilities and chain of command;
- decision-making procedures;
- operating risks evaluation;
- updating of budgets and regular review of strategies;
- benchmarking;
- reaction time scenario.

It is suggested that the minimum **financial information** necessary to conduct a pertinent business meeting will be some idea of the

- turnover – ie size of the business;
- pre-tax profit – is the business profitable?
- why is the money required – is funding required for expansion or for recovery?
- gross margin – is it varying significantly and can it be compared with a benchmark for that type of business?
- borrowing ratio – is the business heavily geared with debt?

The remaining information listed earlier will provide more detailed data on which to judge the background to the credit application. If the proposal is to replace or add to another lender, this situation should be clarified at an early stage.

The **trading outlook** for the business described by the management may be supported by verbal figures or with the aid of analysis sheets. The entries should be clear as to their understanding, including how all assumptions have been arrived at. The reason for any significant deviations from past trading 'normal' trends should be enquired about. At this stage, the banker should accept at face value the forecasts prior to evaluating them at a later date, at which time the management will be expecting questions to be asked about the business.

The **future strategy** for the business put forward by the management will provide a valuable insight as to the reasoning behind the request for additional credit. For example, finance may be required to boost production to satisfy market demand for existing products or to market a new product. The former could be a less risky proposition than the latter. The purchase of new equipment may be behind a request to increase the overdraft when leasing or hire purchase could be a more suitable option.

Probably the most important point of this section is to discover whether the management has thought out a fallback scenario should the credit request fail or the take up of additional finance be approved, but not have the expected trading result. How will the business fare with the burden of additional debt to service and repay if earnings fail to improve? Is there a fallback plan to counter any loss of expected cash flow?

The lending banker must be satisfied that the **operational management** is competent enough to make and put into effect the decisions incumbent on taking up additional bank debt and using these funds in the manner proposed. A key feature will be the reaction time for the management to identify when an administrative judgement or change of policy is called for, as well as the time needed for any change to be put into practice.

The calculation of **break-even point** at which the annual turnover of a business generates sufficient income to recover all its costs without making a profit or a loss is given in the example following:

Trading assumptions: (£ millions)

Turnover		20.0
Less Direct costs varying with turnover	3.6	
Other direct costs	1.4	5.0
Gross profit (being margin of 75%)		15.0
Less Indirect costs	12.6	
Interest payable	0.4	13.0
Pre-tax profit		2.0

Calculation of present break-even position:

Percentage of costs varying with turnover is 3.6/20 = 18%.

Break-even point for turnover is at 18% x 20 + 1.4 + 13.0 = 17.56.

Turnover may therefore drop by 2.44 (12.2%) before a loss occurs.

Proposed additional financing:

Say 4.0, at an annual cost of 0.2 (5% pa).

Revised break-even position:

The break-even point becomes 18% x 20 + 1.4 + 13.0 + 0.2 = 18.2.

Turnover may drop by 1.8 (9%) before a loss occurs.

Note: the new money invested in the business may earn an identical or a different gross profit margin on sales but the break-even position will remain as before because the cost of these funds does not vary according to the turnover achieved, viz

>Assumption: that new money earns a gross profit margin of 50%.
>Target turnover is raised to 20 + 50% x 4 = 22.0.
>Percentage of costs varying with turnover becomes 3.6/22 = 16.4%.
>Break-even point stays at 16.4% x 22 + 1.4 + 13.0 + 0.2 = 18.2.

2.5 Submitting the proposition

At this stage, the evaluation process will have been partially completed, subject to a detailed analysis of the figures (historic and forecast) supplied by the management and any outstanding queries raised by this information having been resolved. A reasoned judgement of the application can then be made and submitted internally under the procedures laid down by the bank. Different banks may require the proposal to be approved either by 'ratification' or via a 'second opinion' and this may be done by 'computer acceptance' or by a separate personnel credit or management section of the bank.

Where computer ratification is undertaken, the input is done on a set form that allows a concluding summary to be added. The bank software will 'vet' the proposal to ensure that it corresponds with existing general internal guidelines and meets the internal view of the bank of that potential borrower. This will take account of the existing facility limit set for that customer, how valuable the customer is to the bank in terms of present profitability and potential future business and how the additional credit meets the bank's present guidelines on exposure to that business sector. The account manager submits the proposal internally even if he/she holds adequate personal lending discretion to accept the request.

The latter form of approval, via a second opinion, is usually required where the application exceeds any existing facility limit and is of sufficient size to warrant approval from the bank's regional or head office. There is a general trait at the present time for bank managements to disperse decisions as much as possible to their commercial branches and let the local managers build up a more meaningful on-going relationship with their customers. Several years ago, this trend was reversed and decisions were centralised, bank managements taking the view that greater control of risks would ensue. The present trend for decentralisation probably has come about through increased computer usage giving more control of lending operations from a distance and the perception that lending is, after all, a personable skill welcome at a time of increased competition.

2.6   Evaluating the lending proposition

Subsequent chapters of this book will describe in depth how the management skills of the customer are so important (Chapter Three), how the bank approaches its management of risks both in respect of lending to different sectors of business (Chapter Six) and the bank's own loans portfolio (Chapter Seven) and the relevance of security and other lending conditions (Chapter Eight). The basic principles of lending have stood the tests of time well: this has been mnemonically translated as CAMPARI, where the letters remind the banker they stand for:

- the **C**ommitment by the borrower:
- the borrower's **A**bility to manage the business;
- the quality of the key **M**anagement of the borrower;
- the **P**urpose of the borrowing;
- the **A**mount of money the borrower is committing to the business;
- the ease of **R**epaying the debt; and
- the **I**nsurance provided through the security taken in its widest sense.

27

These headings provide the bare bones of an evaluation and if a more detailed definition is required it may be useful to remember that a good lending proposition should have 'street cred(ibility)', viz:

- there is a sound **S**trategy to support the borrowing;
- a forecast of future **T**rading profit and cash flow is evident;
- the borrower has done sufficient **R**esearch on the proposed market;
- the forecast **E**arnings make the borrowing viable;
- the **E**ffect of borrowing is described and understood;
- there is a satisfactory **T**rack record shown by the borrower.
- the borrowing is of a **C**haracter that can be supported;
- there is a feasible plan for **R**epayment;
- the borrowing offers **E**ase of mind for the lender;
- there are well-**D**efined risks that can be managed by the borrower.

Commercial propositions can fail to gain acceptance because the basic **Strategy** behind the borrowing is flawed or, quite simply, no strategy has been planned or fully thought out. To answer that the borrowing will increase turnover and hence earnings misses the point of the assessment. How will turnover increase? What will competitors do to counteract their reduced share of the market? If the additional finance is to be used to recover from a bad trading year, what other options are there to adopt? Is the business under-capitalised? Is the business over-trading where there are insufficient resources to support the current rate of expansion?

Where a **Trading forecast** is provided, is it realistic? Is a **cash flow forecast** evident? The lending bank will be monitoring the business account daily (by computer) and therefore it will only be prudent for the business management to do the same. Has the management explored the benefit of delaying paying creditors for a short period to assist cash flow? Have overdue trade debts been chased up for payment to improve cash flow? If the business is expanding rapidly and requires to increase its gearing, has the management considered invoice discounting as an option?

If the financing is for **Research** purposes, it will be vital to ensure that the product, whether new or a reborn item or service, will meet operational requirements (does it work?) and be acceptable to the market for which it is intended. These criteria will usually demand a pilot marketing scheme and reliability testing, followed by a trial selling pitch. Has the management taken into account that for ease of success a new product should preferably fill an existing customer demand rather than creating its own demand, probably through initiating an expensive marketing campaign?

The lending banker will be looking for quality of business **Earnings** when assessing profit forecasts and ease of repaying the debt. Ideally, turnover and gross profit should be analysed between different products and/or markets, with account taken of new compared with repeat orders, as well as any seasonality to demand. It may be that the business is relying for future growth on just one or two products that will shortly have a limited shelf life and require replacement. If so, by how much will the gross profit margin fall until the replacement products are fully integrated into the product line? Have the earnings forecasts taken account of this expectation? Why is the business still putting significant resources and productive time into selling poor margin products?

If the bank approves the lending request, the business will be accepting a future servicing charge and repayment commitment. If the loan interest is calculated at a cost varying with base rate (either the Bank of England base rate or tied to LIBOR – the London inter-bank offered rate) there will be an open-ended commitment should interest rates rise during the period the loan remains outstanding. Has the management allowed for this **Effect** on its earnings forecasts and the risk that is involved? This is important for the bank where the business appears to be relying on continuous credit, that is, by repaying an earlier loan with proceeds from a further loan. There is a definite risk to the bank that at the renewal date of the loan the circumstances of the business may have changed sufficiently for further credit approval not to be appropriate.

A distinction should be made between the granting of a term loan and short/medium-term continuous credit facilities in the event of repayment difficulties occurring prior to maturity of the debt. The term loan should have clauses of default attached thereto and adequate security to support the debt, whereas a credit line that is being used on a continuous rollover basis, being of a short-term nature, may be unsecured or have diluted security in place. An example of this would be where assets are pledged to other lenders and there are preferential creditors to be accounted for.

The **Track record** of the business is a useful, but not infallible, guide to the expertise of the management to continue to meet profit forecasts and in managing debt. Changes to the basics of the business should be viewed critically. These may include management personnel changes, new acquisitions and material expansion plans, the sale of part of the business, upheaval due to a factory fire, adoption of a different business strategy, or external trading influences likely to remain for some time. Track record is really about confirmation of the capability of the management to adapt successfully to changes in trading circumstances.

The borrowing request may not be in **Character** for the business to undertake. A company that has published religious books for many years, for example, wishing to borrow funds to promote men's magazines would appear to be out of character and would raise the questions: why this form of diversification? What will happen to the present business? Is there previous experience of this type of new venture? Will the existing wholesaler contacts accept the new publishing line? On what grounds have the management taken this decision?

Every lending request must have an acceptable answer to the questions: what is the debt **Repayment** plan and is it soundly based? The form of borrowing proposed by the management may not be ideal from the bank's point of view. A typical example would be where the business expects to repay all the debt at maturity of the loan, whereas the bank would prefer to have more flexibility built in through an overdraft renewable annually or a programmed medium-term loan with regular monthly payments made up of interest due and part repayment of the loan principal that can then be available for the bank to on-lend to other customers.

It will be natural for **Ease** of mind for the lender to think of some form of shared risk and security for the loan. Sharing the risk would entail the borrower to advance some of the required finance, perhaps on a permanent basis by introducing additional capital into the business, followed by the bank providing a further credit facility. The acceptance of security by the bank will offer several coincident aims: it will assist the retention of the business fixed assets in the balance sheet, the conditions laid down will safeguard the loan during the course of trading through the adherence to stated operating covenants and, in the event of a default, it will assist the recovery of the outstanding loan balance.

The bank will not wish to be put in the position of having to manage the business if it defaults on a loan agreement, not least for two reasons: first, the bank may not have the experience to act as a trader and, secondly, management of the business and its borrowings will be time consuming. The **Defined risks** of operating the business should be left to the appointed management and the banker should be concerned with evaluating whether the management can deal with these risks. To take one example, the business may rely for three-quarters of its turnover from one customer source. This is risky if the customer is lost. Will the management be able to replace the customer easily (or at all) by sales orders arising from other sources? Should the management dilute this potential risk through building up additional customers now?

2.7   Banker and customer

Bank lending to a customer marries two different outlooks: what the customer would like and what the bank is willing to grant. How the two match determines whether the transaction is successful or not. Their different viewpoints are exemplified in the following table:

Customer's view	Lender's view
The amount should be met in full	Is it affordable?
Its purpose is sound	Is the purpose valid?
It must be relatively inexpensive	Is it sufficiently profitable?
It should be recurring or renewable	It must be repayable
It must be easy to access	Access must be controllable
It should be without onerous conditions	Security may be required
It needs minimum supervision	Is it easy to monitor?
The request must be granted	Assessment is called for
The business is a good risk	Is the business viable?

Consider the lender's position to each view taken by the customer.

2.8   The amount should be met in full

The lender will first check that the calculation by the customer as to the amount requested fits the facts of the case. Is the forecast of trading by the business sound and are the assumptions of the parameters to forecast turnover and profits valid and accurate? Has the customer provided a correct cash flow from the profit projections and does it match the maximum shortfall that the borrowing will meet, as well as leaving a margin for error? Is the amount requested overstating the financing requirement? If the sum requested is borrowed, will the repayment terms be met easily out of profits and cash flow? Can the lender suggest a better alternative borrowing structure?

2.9   Is the borrowing purpose sound?

The lender does not wish to advance 'good' money after 'bad' that the customer cannot repay. If the company is in temporary liquidity difficulties, the bank will test this validity and consider lending the necessary sum with conditions to tie the advance into the reasons for the additional help. An example would be a factory strike preventing completion of near-finished products; the advance would be short term with repayment tied to the proceeds of sale of the finished goods. If the liquidity difficulty is more structural, say a lack of equity investment in the business or due to a downturn in trading, the lender should examine the business in greater detail to be satisfied that future trading can be profitable given a reasonable time and that the additional advance can be repaid out of future earnings (or in some cases the sale of fixed assets).

2.10   Is the cost of borrowing relatively inexpensive?

The customer will expect to pay for the privilege of the additional financial assistance and, depending on the size of the business and whether it has more than one bank to request a loan so that competitive quotations can be obtained, it is frequently the case that 'beggars cannot be choosers'. The additional risk taken on by the bank supports the view of a higher lending margin and it should also be the occasion when the terms of all the bank's facilities can beneficially be reviewed.

2.11   The bank advance should be recurring or renewable

Many smaller-sized businesses are undercapitalised and have limited means to repay all debt that is borrowed. The bank should continually monitor the recurring nature of the lending in case future trading prospects turn adverse. Larger businesses, by reason of gearing up their profit return, count on renewable facilities as a permanent feature of trading and the lender(s) will have default conditions included in the borrowing terms as part of their security. At all times, the lender should remember that the bank must not take the place of the business owner/shareholders and become the prime holder of risk. That is why borrowings should not normally exceed the value of equity investment.

2.12   The borrowing(s) must be easy to access

The customer would like nothing better than to have access at all times to more finance without resorting to a formal request to the bank for more credit. The bank will accept the commercial need for an overdraft facility within a stated limit when cash demand fluctuates from day-to-day, but can control any abuse of this acceptance through making the overdraft subject to immediate recall. Otherwise, to ensure that the business remains viable and worthy of support, the bank usually annually adopts a regular review and renewal of facilities. If the business runs into difficulties, more control will be necessary to keep the bank in touch with the situation, including segregating wages from the main bank account and requesting for weekly or monthly performance figures.

2.13   The bank facility must be without onerous conditions attached

As has been seen from the last paragraph, the conditions to set on the conduct of the customer's bank account will be determined by the degree of difficulties the business has incurred and the estimated time required to resolve the problem(s). The bank's 'security' in these cases may be one, or a mixture, of trading covenants and formal charges on assets. Examples of the former might be restrictions on the payment of dividends and subordinating other debt in favour of the bank advance. An example of the latter would be a fixed and floating charge on the business assets. The conditions are laid down to prevent future happenings damaging the bank's interests rather than to affect the daily trading of the business.

2.14   The bank facility requires minimum supervision

The business does not want to spend a lot of time checking to see if it is breaking any bank lending covenants or to have the need to refer to the bank each time it has, or might have, a liquidity problem. The bank would much prefer the customer to conduct the account within the conditions already agreed, but to refer in advance to the bank of any potential problem area if it is likely to affect the existing agreed lending terms. Monitoring accounts, particularly problem accounts referred to a specialist section of the bank, is a costly business even if it can mostly be accomplished through the use of sophisticated computer software.

2.15   The request for an advance must be granted

The simple answer is that it should not be granted until due assessment is made of all factors affecting the business and the borrowing. The bank should take the position that it would like to assist the company, notwithstanding there is a financial problem, but needs to know the complete underlying situation to make a valued judgement on the merits of the request.

2.16   The business is deemed a good risk

Business entrepreneurs are born optimists and even the largest companies and banks can turn a blind eye at times to factors known to exist, but perhaps cannot be easily quantified. Asbestos claims were known to exist for many years, but this did not deter companies that were affected to continue to ask for financial support from their established bank syndicates, presumably on an accepted 'risk to reward' basis. Lending banks operate in a very competitive market and it can be hard at times to turn away profitable business.

The balance between what is a good risk and what is not is a constant, important judgement that has to be made by a bank. There are ways the bank can partially mitigate the effects of risk internally: accessing forecasts of the economy preceding a change of lending strategy, emphasising certain industry sectors to lend to over others' offering programmed lending based on the probability of failure, raising lending margins to dampen demand and/or improve the bank's reward margin, and taking additional formal security.

2.17   What determines good lending?

The first determinant is a well-structured preparation of the application by the borrower that gives the lender all the facts that are essential on which a risk assessment can be based. The smaller business may have only a rudimentary idea how to put together a proposition and it may be helpful for a questionnaire to be issued to the prospective lender up to a certain size of credit application to complete and return to the bank, preferably in advance of the initial interview, if it does not put the applicant off applying. The larger business will already have done its sums and perhaps even assumed some of the answers, eg the type of advance.

The lender will expect the borrower to explain the strategy behind the borrowing request. Many commercial propositions fail to gain credit because the strategy is flawed or has not been well planned. A request for additional working capital to promote a new product without having test marketed the product first would be potentially flawed. A projection of future trading turnover without first checking that the required number of widgets can be produced for sale to meet the sales forecast would not be a well-planned application.

The borrower must have distinguished properly between 'turnover', 'profit', 'cash flow' and 'timing'. Turnover only becomes unrealised profit when the sales invoices are accepted and profit is only realised as cash when the sales invoices are paid. Good management of the debtors' ledger is required. The timing gap between a sale and receiving the cash requires (working) capital to pay for production, wages and other costs.

The borrower must also distinguish between 'sales', 'profitability' and 'mix of products'. Increasing sales do not necessarily equate to a higher profit or even a profit at all if the pricing of the product(s) or service(s) is too low to recover the costs of production. The business will be inefficient if it concentrates on selling low margin products when it could just as easily and more profitably sell higher margin goods.

Thus far, we have concluded that the prospective borrower must understand the key variables behind successful trading, has raised a well-prepared application, has managed the business well to date, and has recognised and accurately incorporated into trading projections the earlier points raised. It is now time for the lending banker to exercise his/her skill and judgement on the lending proposition detail.

2.18   Safety

Will the advance be repaid on time? What risk attaches to the advance? What risks attach to the business? What formal security is required?

The business cash flow will indicate whether the advance can be repaid over what period of time. A sensitivity analysis on the trading projections will indicate the margin of error to be allowed in the calculations before repayment is jeopardised. The type of business and the characteristics of the trading market will suggest what business risks to assess. The extent of free (equity) capital held in the business will determine the unsecured element of security and the extent of assets that are to date not pledged will denote the scope for taking a legal charge.

A typical sensitivity (variation) analysis will amend the borrower's forecast turnover, profit margin and costs to see the effect on net earnings and how the revised projection(s) will affect the servicing and repayment of the proposed loan. For example, turnover may be reduced by 10% and 20% and profit margins (or selling prices) may be similarly reduced. Materials and labour costs are likely to be reduced by smaller figures and the least likely change may occur for indirect costs. Care should be taken to make the changes inter-actively compatible: for instance, if selling prices are lowered, this may stimulate sales demand and raise turnover.

2.19 Liquidity

The lending banker will wish to turn over the bank's cash resources as quickly as is practicable. A loan having an early repayment date will in most cases generate more fees quicker than a longer maturity loan with annual refresher fees. It will also have the benefit of being susceptible to the company's trading risks over a shorter period. Larger, medium-term loans tend to have a fee structure lower at commencement and higher after the early years. This reflects the greater exposure risk over time. Conversely, companies that can draw funds from several sources may well repay the loan early before the higher margin kicks in. The banker should also be aware that funds set aside, but not drawn, are unproductive.

2.20 Profitability

The bank has an armoury of loan charges to levy on the borrowing customer to cover certain lending costs and to raise income, in addition to the 'profit turn' on the cost of funds itself when the interest margin is added to the money lent. In the European market, the interest margin will in most cases be based on the Bank of England base rate, the London inter-bank rate (LIBOR) or the European inter-bank rate (EURIBOR). There will also be added a fee to cover the mandatory costs of borrowing ie the cost to the lender of complying with the Bank of England's deposit rules and fees payable to the Financial Services Authority.

There is usually a standard front-end fee payable on the whole facility, either on signing the loan agreement or when it is initially drawn. A utilisation fee may be added if the facility is not drawn above a certain percentage and is payable on the average size of loan drawn and outstanding over set periods. The aim of this will be to act as an incentive for the borrower to use the facility more. There may also be a commitment fee payable on the undrawn part of the facility over set periods, also acting as an incentive for the borrower to use the facility. Both these fees will be smaller than the basic lending margin, typically up to 1/8% pa (ie 12.5 basis points where 100 basis points equates to 1%).

Large loans syndicated between banks will have one-off lead arranger and manager fees, participation fees and underwriting fees. The lead arranger(s) will pilot the syndication and be paid for the work involved. Manager banks will be taking a larger share of the loan onto their lending book and will receive an additional fee for this exposure. If the loan is underwritten as a guarantee that the whole amount of the facility will be taken up by the banks making up the syndicate, then there will be a fee due to the underwriting banks for their potential risk of having to take up a greater share of the loan in the event that the syndicate will not subscribe to the whole amount of the loan.

2.21 Pricing

Each bank will have its own pricing policy guidelines. For smaller credit facilities, the fixed or variable interest rate pricing will be agreed privately between the bank and the borrower at the time of signing the facility agreement. Some banks make their general lending rates available to the public by publishing their standard rates in set bands and revising these bands each time there is a change in interest rates set by the Bank of England. Major companies, however, may wish to negotiate fees privately with their bank(s).

Large credit facilities will be priced at a fixed or floating interest rate margin over either bank rate or inter-bank rate as described in the preceding section. The lending agreement may have options for the borrower to change between a fixed and a floating rate at each renewal date of the facility. Where loans are based on money market inter-bank rates, the most frequent period taken for drawings is three months, with interest being paid at the end of each period. Conversely, if the facility is drawn by way of acceptance credits (bills of exchange), the interest cost is fixed at the start of the borrowing period. The interest rate margin is mutually agreed between the bank and the company and is determined by the credit standing of the company, competition for the company's business, and the bank's propensity to gain the lending business.

The bank will be weighing up the loan application and its pricing in a number of ways: how will the loan fit in with the bank's existing perspective of country and industry exposure? What is the risk of a company default? What perception is held of retaining the company's business? What is, or will be, the total potential earnings from the company as a bank customer? It is worth remembering that it is easier to retain a customer than to gain one and often a fine profit margin is accepted by the bank if it is judged that the fees being, or to be, earned on peripheral business will outweigh any shortfall in the loan margin. All the above points are covered in greater depth in subsequent chapters.

2.22 Bank regulations affecting lending: Basel 2

The European Commission's original Basel Capital Accord laid down a capital adequacy framework for regulated banks by way of a non-binding agreement, having the twin aims of strengthening the soundness and stability of the international banking system and applying a high degree of consistency and fairness in the regulatory treatment of banks across countries.

Its two concepts were, first, to adopt an agreed categorisation of bank capital between core capital (tier 1) and supplementary capital (tier 2). In essence, tier 1 consisted of equity capital plus retained earnings. Tier 2 included reserves, hybrid debt/equity capital instruments and subordinated debt. Secondly, risk weightings were added to reflect the relative risks carried by different classes of counterparties. The aim was to assess capital in relation to credit risk that the borrower would not repay its loan. Minimum target ratios of capital to risk were laid down, ranging from 0% to 100%, effective by 1992. A later amendment in 1996 added additional capital requirements relating to market risks of losses in outstanding trading positions arising from changes in market prices.

The standardised and foundation levels of Basel 2 are scheduled to come into effect from January 2007 and the advanced system one year later even though precise terms have still to be agreed by all participants. The intention is to improve the treatment of sovereign debt (where previously members of the OECD – the Organisation for Economic Co-operation and Development – were effectively classed as risk free, but non-members had a 100% weighting) and to amend different private sector lending exposures that had been previously treated identically from a risk view.

Basel 2, in its present format, adopts a credit rating approach by introducing new methods of measuring and rewarding economic profitability and accurately allocating capital. There is more emphasis on operational risk and a revised assessment of credit risk. Banks adopting their own advanced internal ratings based (AIRB) approach for measuring credit risk or the advanced measurement approach (AMA) for operational risk will have a minimum capital base to meet. There is a more basic (foundation) revised standard approach (RSA) for credit risk and a basic indicator approach (BIA) for operational risk as an alternative choice. Market risk will be internally monitored in the advanced case, but a standardised approach applies in the foundation case.

The effect will mean a re-pricing of products (by banks and all other credit institutions and investment firms, as defined) to reflect the capital charge involved. The current market risk assessment is expected to remain unchanged. The aim will be to create a level playing field for participants. Its effect will mean that banks will have to improve their management controls to assess risk, have much greater data on which to judge risks (given the implementation of suitable IT programmes) and encourage the use of what may be termed 'economic profitability models'.

Each bank will start with its own risk portfolio profile. It is believed that a lower regulatory capital requirement through a reduction in risk weights will apply to uncommitted and unsecured (retail) loans such as overdrafts and credit cards, mortgages, investment grade (safe) corporate loans, and loans to small- and medium-sized businesses. Fee/service-based operations (asset management and specialised private banking) and un-rated (sovereign) or non-investment grade loans will require increased capital.

Implementation of Basel 2 will be through three so-called 'pillars'. The first has been broadly explained and concerns minimum capital requirements. The second covers the supervisory review process to ensure that banks have good monitoring and risk management methods. The third involves market discipline and disclosure requirements to allow each bank's capital adequacy to be compared one with another.

The new regime is hoped to lead to a reduced risk of (a world) financial crisis and its effect on overall capital requirements to be broadly neutral. Because lending to the retail sector and high-quality corporate borrowers will demand less regulatory capital requirements, the theory is that their cost of borrowing will fall. It may be more likely that borrowing to these sectors will be stimulated. If this increases competition to provide loans to a market showing static demand to borrow, then this might be so, particularly at a time of sluggish economic growth generally. Otherwise, during a period of a booming economy, it may overheat these sectors that could lead to bad debt troubles further ahead.

2.23 Matching lending to the corporate structure of the borrower

The **smaller company** will be looking to borrow broadly at the cheapest rate that can be satisfied by the cash flow of the business. In most cases this will put the onus on the structure of the proposed borrowing on the bank. The bank lending officer will have the opportunity to satisfy both parties: the borrower as to the terms of the proposed deal and internal bank policy as to the type of advance made (or is wished to be 'promoted' by the bank) and at what lending rate. This is where the experience, knowledge and skill of the lending officer should be paramount.

The lending banker may have to advise the business on the structure of its borrowings. What steps should be invoked in order to advise the company? The factors to consider will be:

- the overall future annual cash flow estimated for the business for several years ahead;
- for those years, whether there will be any significant monthly fluctuations to the expected cash flow;
- confirmation that all new projects have been incorporated in the projections in respect of capital investment and operating revenue expenditure and trading income;
- a forecast of the profit and loss account and balance sheet at the end of each trading year;
- separate forecasts relating to any subsidiary undertakings;
- analysis of all existing group borrowings and repayment profiles;
- an assessment of the tax implications of trading and borrowing;

◆ an understanding of company policy on the use of derivatives for hedging purposes, cash management and (any) dividend payments.

The company should have already provided the lending officer with its up-dated business plan wherein most of the above points would have been set out. Possibly not in evidence will be cash, etc, forecasts of each subsidiary. This will be required if the subsidiaries are autonomous financially and have to borrow locally rather than from the holding company. The tax implications will be important if public debt is raised in a country having a lower tax charge than the parent company's domicile or where cross-border trading is made intra-group. In this latter respect, the company will not be able to shield profits arising outside normal commercial considerations to a low tax-bearing country. It will also be wasted effort if the lending officer puts up suggestions that are contrary to the policy of the borrower.

Some of the more common lending structures that may be suitable for the bank to consider offering, subject to the particular borrowing circumstances of each company, are given in the table. This is very much a simplification and individual cases relating to different types of borrower are discussed in Chapter Six and different forms of lending in Chapter Eleven:

Borrowing type	Borrowing structure to cover
Overdraft	Daily/periodic/seasonal cash flow swings.
Debtor and stock finance (factoring/ invoice discounting)	Expanding businesses with low net worth/equity capitalisation/property assets.
Produce finance (L/Cs, bills)	Imports/exports. Seasonal crop financing.
Asset finance (HP, leasing)	Plant/machinery/vehicle financing.
Medium-term loan	Term to match the life of the asset.
Medium-term rollover (multiple option facility)	Expanding businesses, but undercapitalised and wishing to gear up by borrowing.
Long-term loan	Property assets and trade investments.
Syndicated, sizeable loans	Quoted companies. To spread banks' risk.

The **larger company** will be sufficiently well versed financially to be able to raise a full business plan to support the proposed borrowing together with the reasoning behind the proposal. This will include how the terms and the structure of the new loan will fit into the existing debt portfolio of the business in respect of maturity, currency and cost. To this extent, the lending bank will be asked to accept the proposition from the company rather than having to raise a solution from scratch. It will be up to the bank to offer and suggest better alternatives to those put forward by the company.

Three

Management skills

'A poor business can exist with a good management but a poor management cannot co-exist with a good business.'

Is this a correct statement? Certainly, a good management should be able to ensure that a poor (ie relatively unprofitable) business can be turned round and show improved profitability, but a good and profitable business would frequently find that poor management decisions could ultimately lead to financial deprivation and worse. This relationship can apply to large companies as much as smaller business units. Take the cases of Volkswagen and Rover cars.

Volkswagen was 'saved' through the management rationalising production into one model that proved to be very successful, enabling the company to diversify later into a range of models once sufficient financial resources became available. Rover Group, on the other hand, after its release from the BMW stable, attempted to continue to manufacture and sell a range of increasingly outdated models with the obvious end result of insolvency when cash ran out. There was one good management in place, matching resources to opportunities, and the other a management in control, but making, in hindsight, poor strategic decisions.

What aspects of business management should the banker have awareness when making a lending assessment?

- Is there evidence of good leadership in decision-making? Does this apply to human resources?
- Is the leadership cognisant of teamwork or led entrepreneurially?
- Is the business controlled by an owner/manager or is the management reporting to a group of shareholders?
- How much strategic planning goes into critical decision-making?

◆ What is the objective of the company and is it put into practice, ie to maximise share value over time or earn and withdraw profits?
◆ Is management succession in question?
◆ What motivation does the management have in running the business?
◆ What are the individual skills of the management and how do they interact when running the business?
◆ What is the track record of the management to date? Financially? Risk-averse? Human resources? Customer-related? Externally influenced? Sensitivity analysis? Having fallback scenarios?
◆ Is the business being actively managed or is it operationally self-sufficient?

Each of these potential management traits, or lack of them, is discussed in turn.

3.1   Good leadership

Good leadership revolves around taking business decisions, overseeing their implementation and monitoring the result so that trading strategy can be amended in good time. Probably the best way for an outsider to discern and measure this is to discover where a significant change in the management process has occurred, find out what business decision the 'leader' (the chief executive officer) made and determine whether that decision was successful or not. In practice, there are many ways to pick up an earlier business decision and 'test' the decision for success or failure.

◆ The advent of a new product or diversifying into new business markets of geographical areas. What was the trading result?
◆ Lower profitability or losses occurring due to prior poor action by the management. Did this lead to over stocking, inappropriate sales price changes, lower sales demand, a less-profitable sales mix, lower plant productivity, a loss of key staff and so on.
◆ Lack of any prior action implemented by the management in the face of changing business circumstances that could have been known in advance. Examples would be a recession being felt in the industry, an adverse trend materialising in interest rates and emerging adverse currency movements affecting the value of sales proceeds.
◆ Lack of any subsequent action by the management once an adverse business trend had been established causing the business to suffer from increased competition, technological innovation, a drop in market share, a higher level of outstanding trade debts and so on.
◆ Internal changes to working relationships. Were they easily adopted and a success? Examples would include sideways job movements by staff and/or changes to job responsibilities, an increase to the labour force, the purchase of new plant, the adoption of new production practices and amending existing costing procedures for new orders.

◆ External changes to the business, such as implementing a new marketing strategy, opening a new depot or branch, increasing the geographic area of operations and commencing to sell products abroad.

When considering the management of human resources, different tests should be applied to discover how well this responsibility has been executed.

◆ What proportion of the workforce leaves each year? Are there valid reasons for workers to give notice that do not reflect on the specific business environment or on particular management decisions eg redundancy?

◆ Are labour relations satisfactory? Has the management adopted a regular programme of training for staff and initiated individual career assessments and proper grievance procedures as required by law?

◆ Have 'sensitive' personnel decisions and procedures been adequately clarified to staff? This would include benefits, bonuses, wage awards policy, promotion opportunities, pensions, leave, sickness and absenteeism and seniority.

Re-structuring costs can have a sudden and significant impact on the profitability and cash flow of a business. Frequently the first operating 'solution' to put into effect when cash flow reduces significantly will be to ask for more credit and, following that, to prune both direct and indirect operating costs. The greater impact will be to reduce indirect costs or, in other words, to reduce production and initiate a redundancy programme. This is an expensive procedure since it causes a loss of morale, work upheaval and the crystallisation of liability payments due to staff that are laid off.

The lending banker should be aware of management thinking in this area and be warned of such a decision at the earliest juncture. There may be other preferred solutions to consider. It has been known for a company wishing to make redundancies in order to continue trading not to have the financial resources to do so, with the result that the company was served notice for an outstanding debt by a creditor, was unable to pay, and became insolvent to the detriment of all its creditors, including its bank.

3.2   Teamwork or individuality

The business may be entrepreneurially driven by the chief executive, in which case management decisions will be based more on the personal preferences of the entrepreneur rather than the choice of the combined management team. The risk is that the implementation of poor judgement in choosing an unsuitable strategy may be greater where it is not based on the consensus of management. The banker will have to judge whether business decisions of a single person will affect unduly the lending proposal.

3.3 Structure of the business

The business may be managed differently according to whether it is 25%; more than 50%; or 75% controlled by an individual person or party. Companies are controlled where a person or related parties hold a simple majority of the voting rights amounting in total to 50% plus one share. Under the ruling Companies Acts, if the shareholding comprises at least 25% of the voting rights this is sufficient to block changes that have to be ratified through a formal extraordinary or special resolution of the company. The changes can include any dilution proposed in the present shareholdings, for example, through the issue of additional shares through a 'rights issue'. The converse applies in that where at least 75% of the voting rights are held otherwise, the blocking effect of the 25% holding is negated. If the shareholding amounts to at least 90%, then a compulsory takeover of the remaining company shares can be made. A more minor point is that holders of at least 5% of the voting shares can prevent a general meeting being called without proper notice.

The importance of voting control becomes evident where decisions can be made detrimental to banks as creditors if the terms and conditions applying to loan facilities are insufficient to safeguard the amount outstanding through the subsequent actions of the controlling shareholders. A company may be a 51% subsidiary of a larger group, as an example, and the group management may decide to transfer significant assets or operations or declare dividends out of the retained profits of the borrowing company, thus leaving the company as a 'shell' business, but with sizeable bank debt. The lending covenants should be drafted to make such action a cause for default and repayment of the loan.

3.4 Strategic planning

Even modestly-sized businesses should be operating within a strategic plan laid down to meet the objectives of the shareholder/owner(s). If a plan is not formalised, the question can arise whether there has been enough thought behind the request for a bank loan by the company, including how the debt is to be regularly serviced and repaid. The banker should ask for a plan incorporating these points and attentively test all the assumptions therein. Where a plan is in existence, the operating history of the business achieved should be compared with what has been forecast and this comparison will add to or detract from the forecasts currently put forward by the company in support of the loan application.

3.5 The company objectives

The reasons for the loan application may or may not be pertinent to the business, its future success or to the repayment of any borrowing. If a loan is granted, one condition should be that the money when received must be used for the purpose claimed. This purpose may be to take out another bank loan and/or provide further working capital for the business. The banker should be very clear of the reasoning behind such a request and why a new bank will gain a worthwhile customer whereas the old bank failed. What additional risks attach to the substitution of lender? Are the risks acceptable to take?

The management may have as its objective the withdrawal of capital through the replacement of bank debt. The lending terms should prevent this action by putting a minimum value covenant on the amount of capital to be left in the business while the loan remains unpaid. The bank should not be left in the position of acting as 'risk equity' provider.

3.6   Management succession

The banker may overly rely on the personal business acumen of the chief executive officer when approving the loan application, with the result that if this person no longer fills that position, for whatever reason, the business may lack leadership and trading may suffer. It will be important to have the question of leadership succession satisfied in advance and the choice of leader acceptable to the bank for continuation of the business. Succession may be internally promoted, where the person(s) eligible will have built up adequate experience of the many facets of operations, or it may be an external choice, when a time delay and acclimatisation period will be inevitable, perhaps causing some disruption to the working environment before the new entrant has learnt the operational characteristics of the business.

A pecuniary loss on succession may be incurred by the business where the chief executive suddenly departs: there are 'top hat' assurance schemes that pay out on the death or incapacity of key executives. This will be particularly relevant if the key person owns a majority or large holding in the business and the remaining owners have to pay out in cash to the estate of that person the capital he/she has invested in the business. Without a policy of this type to provide a lump sum, any business loan outstanding may not be repayable on the due date until future profits are earned or, worse still, the business may have to be re-capitalised through a further commercial loan.

3.7   Motivation for management

The banker should be conversant with the long-term objectives for the business. Examples are the acceptance of a long-term loan having a repayment date extending beyond the retirement date of the principal shareholder(s) holds the risk of how full repayment will be accomplished or settling any external pension fund liability could prove to be a large additional burden on cash flow that in turn could affect the servicing of the bank loan. Answers to these questions will assist the structure of future credit facilities to be offered to the business.

3.8   Management skills

The lending banker must judge the qualifications and experience of the management team to run the business as a part of the credit risks. A high technological company having no suitably qualified person on the management team will be operating at a disadvantage if constant research and development and new design work is required to maintain its market competitiveness. Existing experience of running similar businesses, production lines and sales forces will be very relevant, but may lead to a lack of insight and innovation for the business and a loss of opportunity by not taking up new ideas in favour of maintaining the status quo.

3.9   Track record

It is too sweeping a judgement to say that a poor track record will fail a loan application, whereas a good record automatically grants acceptance. Take the case of a manufacturer that has made the decision to replace an old product to maintain market share and profitability. The gestation period is two years from designing to marketing. After eighteen months, a competitor announces their own new product that is virtually identical to yours, but at half your proposed selling price. What do you do?

If you abandon your product, there will be a large cost item to write off against profits. If you persevere in putting your product on the market, to obtain sufficient bulk sales, a large price reduction has to be made. This will lower your profit margin and profits will fall. You might make your product 'exclusive' at a higher price and accept lower sales than once forecast. You could spend more money and try and advertise your way out of the predicament through generating sales. The risk is in not meeting the revised sales target and spending more capital than envisaged. Your track record will be put in jeopardy in any event. Can this situation be put down to poor management?

The company banker, if not knowing the problem in advance, should be asking (at a later stage) why the business plan forecast was reduced or why the gross profit margin dropped over that trading period and what is the operating forecast for the future. A request for an additional loan facility should be able to be formulated and discussed between the management and the bank based on a new well-founded proposal, notwithstanding the dip that will occur in the business's track record. Which solution is chosen will depend on further factors to be considered: what will be the size of the cash loss if the product is abandoned? Will the business remain competitive by continuing to sell its old product? Are the new sales forecasts robust enough and will the profit envisaged be acceptable? How will these options affect the risks to the bank?

3.10   An active or inactive management

All company managements should be sufficiently active to maintain growth and profitability and to counteract any adverse events affecting trading. An inactive management will assume that the business can support itself with the minimum of action. What has been good enough in past years should suffice for the future. The track record (sic) on this theory should show a good, constant earnings trend. Unfortunately, trading is never in a constant state of equilibrium. There are too many external influences that can change the trading balance of power.

A classic case of change arose when the supply of oil was adversely affected by the producing countries and caused a shortage of supply leading to the wholesale price rising dramatically on world markets. Businesses budgeting for static oil prices in their product costing have had to change significantly their forecast assumptions. An active management may have operated a strategy of buying oil partly under long term contract, the critical supply, and partly by buying 'spot' in the open market. An inactive management selling oil derivative products will have contracted long term at a set selling price and was thereby unable to increase its prices in line with market rates, although having to buy at these higher prices. The banker to the business adopting an inactive management should have been aware of this potential risk element to its trading and should have chosen a more conservative lending posture.

3.11   Business assets

The management skills of running a business extend to the management of the assets underlying that business. The lending banker may not fully understand the technical side of the products that the business manufactures, services or advises customers, but will be speaking the same language with the management where the administration of the financial assets is concerned. The banker should be acquainted with the choices facing the management in the usual course of business and be ready to advise on the best options accordingly.

3.12   Management of excess liquidity

The timing of income receipts can vary materially from business to business and the payment of debts can vary depending on the traditional credit period allowed within that sector of industry. There will be occasions when the cash flow is in credit unless the hard core borrowing element is so ingrained that the business is always in debt to the bank. If this positive balance is continuous, there will be a choice whether or not to withdraw the funds surplus to trading needs. Two questions then arise: how much of the surplus funds will not be required in the business in the foreseeable future and, secondly, what to do with the surplus.

Surplus funds not required may be used to repay existing borrowing unless early repayment incurs an onerous penalty, as might be the case with a long-term, fixed-rate facility where the market (variable) interest rate has diverged from the fixed rate agreed and would cause the bank a loss on early redemption. This penalty charge may be calculated as so many additional months interest due on the debt or, in the case of a fixed interest term loan, the penalty more likely would be the additional cost to the lender of unravelling the loan that will, of course, be passed on to the borrower. An example of this type of calculation is given here:

Example of redemption cost	Original position	Current position
Cost of money to the lender	7% pa	5% pa
Bank's lending margin	<u>3% pa</u>	
Term loan cost to the borrower	<u>10% pa</u>	
Borrower wishes to repay early		
Bank wishes to retain its income margin of		<u>3% pa</u>
Investment yield required by the bank		<u>8% pa</u>
Repayment required from the borrower		
per £100 of original loan: £100 × 10/8 =		£125

The bank can take the early repayment of £125 and re-lend the money at the current interest rate of 5% plus the same margin of 3% to receive an overall return of £10, which is the same as the original gross return accepted when the earlier loan was made. For simplification, the bank's administrative costs and the money market buying/selling 'turn' have been ignored and it has been assumed that the bank wishes to retain its 3% lending margin. This is not an exhaustive list, but the business will be contemplating a strategy along the following lines.

3.12.1   Financial options

- ◆ Deposit the excess money temporarily at short notice of withdrawal.
- ◆ Negotiate a fixed margin account setoff (debt v surplus) with the bank.
- ◆ Repay existing loans early (penalties?) if interest rates have fallen.
- ◆ Possibly match any fixed-rate term loan with a fixed-rate term deposit.
- ◆ If trading abroad, consider buying trading currency early to gain an advantageous exchange rate if this is available.

3.12.2 Trading options

- ◆ Pay outstanding bills from suppliers early to obtain cash discounts.
- ◆ Order extra trading stocks early, negotiated at advantageous prices.
- ◆ Replace capital plant earlier than planned to achieve cost savings.
- ◆ Embark on an additional marketing programme to boost sales.

3.13 Financial options

Money on **temporary deposit** is probably the least beneficial method to adopt when current rates of interest available for short-term deposits are relatively low. The investment should be a readily-realisable, fixed-interest deposit account offering the minimum risk to the depositor. If the business is likely to incur large swings in cash balances into and out of overdraft, the bank may agree to accept a set margin on the daily net balance (**setoff**) over successive trading periods. This can be particularly advantageous if the period in overdraft is lengthy, or the amount when overdrawn is large or where there is a seasonal surplus that is gradually whittled away by running costs over the ensuing twelve months.

If the business has a variable rate loan with some years remaining and interest rates generally have risen since it was negotiated, the loan may beneficially be **repaid early** to save on interest charges. Care should be taken to check that early repayment is still worthwhile after allowing for administration and penalty charges. If the loan was at a relatively high fixed interest rate and interest rates generally have since fallen, it may be beneficial to repay the loan early regardless of redemption penalties or, conversely, if interest rates have risen, the cost of continuing the (by now cheaper) fixed-rate loan will have to be weighed against using the surplus funds in other ways to gain a greater financial reward.

The bank may be able to use the funds that are put on deposit to greater advantage through lending to another customer, depending on the differential in lending margin that can be earned. In this case, there will also be the opportunity of earning an initial lending fee. Front-end fees wholly credited by the bank at the time of initiating a loan now have to be accounted for over the period of credit granted under proposed standard accounting proposals. This will be applied in the instance of revolving credit loans only over the initial term of the loan and the change in accounting may well see a resurgence of this form of lending in future.

If the loan was taken out at a variable interest rate and early repayment could only be done by incurring stringent penalties and if the fixed rate currently available in the market for deposits of a term matching the remaining period of the loan at least equals the loan rate (because interest rates in the meantime have risen), the future cost of the loan could be negated by the business **matching the loan** amount with an equal deposit.

Where a business **trades overseas** and has an ongoing currency requirement, rather than dealing in forward foreign exchange contracts the currency may be purchased in advance to benefit not only from accruing some deposit interest, but also to hold for the opportunity to gain on any favourable future currency exchange rate movements should that currency appreciate against sterling. An incorrect reading of currency movements will give rise to a loss of potential profit rather than an actual monetary loss, as the currency will eventually be used to settle the overseas creditors.

If the business buys stock or raw materials in other currencies, a matching currency deposit account (possibly offshore) will counteract any currency risk when later paying in currency for the supplies. The interest received on the currency may or may not be preferential to a sterling equivalent deposit, however, and this benefit or loss of interest should be weighed against the attraction of holding a currency trading account for easy collection and payment purposes.

3.14   Trading options

Suppliers' discounts offered are usually between 2.5% and 5%. If an account is settled in, say, 60 days and a 5% discount is accepted, the benefit to the business payer is equivalent to (5% x 60/365 =) 0.82% pa of the amount outstanding for that particular early repayment and this should be compared with the use of 95% of the amount outstanding (being the sum tendered early as payment less the discount) as a deposit for 60 days. If a particular supplier is in known financial difficulties, then a higher discount rate may be able to be negotiated.

Special deals may also be arranged for the **supply of stocks** of raw materials prior to the required date for their use in production. There are several risks involved: the stocks will need to be securely stored, without deterioration, and take into account any future change in production requirements or quality controls. If the stocks are standard commodities of suitable volume acceptable to the trading commodities market, then 'paper' futures (see Chapter Eleven) may be bought rather than physical shipments.

Replacing plant and equipment early may enable greater efficiency of production, lower (maintenance) costs and increased plant usage. Purchase of the equipment for cash is likely to be granted a worthwhile discount on the selling price. There may even be the opportunity to acquire peripheral equipment to manufacture ancillary products to enhance the business's selling range.

Surplus cash may be used for an extended **marketing programme** to try and open up new sales avenues or enable greater penetration of products into existing markets. Funds may also be used on a regular advertising basis to raise a general 'awareness' of the products to the public. In each case, the potential risks and rewards should be carefully assessed in advance before a decision is made.

Perhaps the underlying decisions to take when managing excess liquidity should be to ensure that surplus funds arising in the course of business are used principally to improve their financial performance rather than just lying idle in a current account (to the detriment of the bank's earnings) and, above all, the funds are spent prudently and set against the projected future cash flow requirements of the business.

3.15 Balance sheet management

The balance sheet is an image of the state of the business at one point in time. Being an historical document based on the book values of assets and liabilities, its use as a management tool tends to be overlooked compared with turnover and profit projections and cash flow forecasts. Three valuations of a simplified balance sheet are illustrated hereafter, each being observed from a different viewpoint after making some necessary valuation assumptions.

3.15.1 Fixed assets

The historic book values reflect (intangible) **goodwill** and (tangible) **premises and equipment**, all shown net of depreciation that has been charged annually in the profit and loss account and accumulated prior to being deducted from the acquisition value of the assets at the end of each accounting year. These values can differ markedly from their (higher) current replacement values if new assets are soon to be acquired, but the values may understate their current selling value where, for example, the freehold of the site has appreciated from the date it was originally purchased many years ago or the plant is specialist by nature and has held its value in the second-hand market. In each case, the lending banker will judge the balance sheet values according to the reasons for which they are being examined, ie replacement cost, forced sale, etc.

Current assets should hold their historic balance sheet values well compared with their current replacement values, subject to raw materials' prices changing and possible bad trade debts. On a forced break-up sale, however, their book values are most unlikely to be attained. In this situation, trade creditors will try and obtain the full value of their debts and the bank overdraft will usually be supported by security to obtain full repayment, whereas it may prove difficult to recover the full value of trade debtors, eg the excuses may range from faulty goods through to non-delivery. In the example shown hereafter, the future break-up value of the business is negative (-25) compared with the historic balance sheet value of 130:

Balance sheets (£'000s)	*Historic net book values*	*Current replacement values*	*Future break-up values*
Goodwill	10	0	0
Freehold	100	70	0
Leasehold	15	20	5
Plant/vehicles/fixtures	75	150	25
Fixed assets	200	170	100
Stocks/work in progress	60	60	20
Trade debtors	45	45	30
Current assets	105	105	50
Trade creditors	55	55	55
Other creditors	10	10	10
Bank overdraft	30	30	30
Current liabilities	95	95	95
Net current assets	10	10	−45
Employment of capital	210	180	55
Capital	100	70	−55
Undistributed earnings	30	30	30
Long-term liabilities	80	80	80
Capital employed	210	180	55

3.15.2 The banker's view

The banker will be looking at certain key features shown by the historic, traditional, balance sheet and will not necessarily be privy to more detailed management returns until the business becomes a customer of the bank. Several years' figures are preferred so that comparative trends can be highlighted, but if only one year is made available, the following facets would invoke attention.

◆ Capital employed totals £120k (after deducting goodwill) and borrowings total £110k, giving a gearing of (110/120 =) 92%. Most businesses would be starting to become uncomfortable were the gearing to exceed 100%, implying that its lenders are investing the greater share of the business. Ignoring other factors, the business may have difficulty in persuading its bank to increase the credit facilities.

◆ The net current assets position is positive, inferring that the business could stop trading, sell off its stocks, run down its debts and still have funds in hand before considering a sale of the fixed assets. This is referred to as the current ratio, being current assets divided by current liabilities (= 1.10). It does not mean that a ratio of less than unity shows the business to be insolvent. To be solvent, the business must be able to pay its liabilities as and when they fall due. Re-arranging the current assets and current liabilities for a solvency test would indicate the following.

Time period	Solvency test	Current assets	Current liabilities	Net position A	Net position B
30–60 days	receive debtors	45,000			
30–60 days	pay creditors		55,000	– 10,000	– 10,000
60–90 days	realise stocks	60,000		+ 50,000	Ignore
90 days +	pay deferred creditors		10,000	+ 40,000	– 20,000
annually	review overdraft		30,000	+ 10,000	– 50,000

In practice, the trade debtors and creditors would be analysed probably under weekly bands when the receipts were likely to materialise and the bills paid. Other creditors would be taxes and non-trade debts, again with specific times for payment.

The **Net position 'A'** assumes stocks are realised for cash within a 60 to 90 day period. If the management wished to remain within the overdraft exposure shown of £30,000 and a projection of trading for the next three months, for example, gave an exact balance of receipts and payments from future business, the table indicates a requirement of £10,000 working capital to settle all trade creditors and at least to maintain a future overdraft of £20,000 on renewal of the facility. In the circumstances, the management would, no doubt, defer paying some £10,000 worth of trade creditors and ensure that the overdraft renewal was agreed.

Stocks, however, may consist of worked raw materials or work-in-progress not yet sold and therefore not readily realisable. It would be prudent to ignore this figure in the solvency calculation and this is shown in **Net position 'B'**. The financing need has doubled in the example to £20,000 before assuming that the overdraft facility will be continued. Again, a projection of future cash flow from forecast trading may indicate that there will be no cash problem to resolve in the months ahead, but do all businesses check and control this position on a regular basis?

Many businesses can operate showing a net current liabilities position for part of their trading year. This can be due to a number of factors: the day taken for the year end balance sheet may be during a period when the overdraft is close to its peak, whereas during the remainder of the year the cash position is much improved. The stocks held may also not be representative of trading throughout the year. If a net current liability is shown, the shortfall may be made up through drawing additional bank credit where it is available.

There are few alternatives: reducing stocks or accelerating the receipt of debts will improve the cash position, but not alter net current liabilities overall. Only an injection of cash will do this, either from increased profits on sales that are paid for or from additional working capital that is either retained or injected into the business.

Long-term assets shown in the original example have a tangible book value of £190k, which compares favourably with (matching) long-term liabilities of £80k. Sometimes a debt ratio is quoted, being long-term debt divided by the sum of long-term debt and capital (= 0.40). The important points from this comparison are that, first, long-term debt is classified as capital invested long term in the business and not short-term working capital. Secondly, it brings into prominence the gearing (or leverage) factor. Adjusting the figures from the original example once more, the effect of gearing would be as follows:

Balance sheet	With gearing	No gearing with the same capital	No gearing with increased capital	Adding gearing to improve earnings
Fixed Assets	200	120	200	200
Net Current Assets	10	10	10	30
	210	130	210	230
Long-term Debt	80 (a)	0	0	100 (a)
Capital & Reserves	130	130	210	130
	210	130	210	230
Earnings		(48 x 130/210=)	(40 – 8=)	(29.7– 10 + 100 x 22.9%=)
(say)	40	29.7 (c)	48 (b)	42.6 (d)
Return on Capital	30.7%	22.9%	22.9%	32.8%

Column one of the table shows pre-interest earnings assumed of £48k, less interest on debt (*reference note (a)*) at 10% pa = £8k, leaving £40k to add to the capital invested in the business. The return on equity capital employed is 30.7% pa. Had there been no long-term debt invested in the business, less money would likely have been spent on fixed assets (machinery) and the production capability would not have supported the same level of sales or profit, hence the lower earnings calculated pro rata of £29.7k shown in column two. The return on equity capital has reduced to 22.9% pa and the profit earned has reduced by £10.3k.

If the management decides to repay the long-term debt (column three) and have surplus funds available to do so, the business will generate higher earnings through eliminating interest payable on the debt, although this will not improve the investment return on equity capital straight off. The management has a decision to make whether present earnings on the surplus funds of £80k that is currently invested elsewhere would be greater or less than the £8k interest saved. Taxation has been ignored but will constitute part of the decision assessment.

Finally, the effect of increasing the gearing by £20k is shown in column four. Earnings have risen by £2.6k and the return on equity capital has risen to 32.8%. Debt as a proportion of equity capital has risen from (£80k/£130k =) 62% to (£100k/£130k =) 77%. The earnings cover to meet the interest payable on the debt has reduced from (£48k/£8k =) 6.0 times to (£52.6k/£10k =) 5.3 times.

3.15.3 The management view

The management should be viewing the balance sheet as shown by its current replacement values. The aspects to consider in this case are:

◆ to replace the existing assets, the business would require additional finance of £30k. The questions to answer are over what period must the replacements be purchased and how will the money be raised for this latent liability;

◆ the (short-term) lease is due for renewal and a possible premium might have to be paid, say £5k, if alternative premises have to be found;

◆ The freehold owned holds the option for the business to consider a 'sale and lease back' to raise funds. Alternatively, the property may be sold to benefit the owners financially and additional premises leased so that the business can in future be accommodated under one roof at a more advantageous site.

3.15.4 The bank view

The bank may have monitored the debt to equity capital ratio and for prudence would have noted the possible break-up value of the business. On the figures shown, there would be negative equity of £25k and, as part of the continuing relationship between the bank and the business, the bank should be enquiring how the business is trading and what its plans are for replacing plant and continuing the business when the current lease expires.

Three very disparate pictures of the business have been drawn up. In conjunction with profit and cash flow forecasts (not shown) the management should already be aware of the strategic necessity to plan ahead and ensure that future balance sheets convey a more acceptable depiction of the state of affairs of the business. Each main asset heading is now examined in greater detail.

3.16   Fixed assets

It is presumed that all businesses wish to trade at a profit and the accrual of fixed (working) assets is a necessary feature of this aim. A business in its most basic form would outsource or contract out any pre-sales work, use agents to sell the product and act purely as administrative manager. Virtually no capital would be required and no fixed assets, apart from a personal computer, would be necessary to operate the business. At the other extreme, considerable financial capital will be necessary to trade if the business is capital asset intensive and an environmentally friendly site needs to be acquired with specialised plant and equipment. Every business should regularly appraise its needs for investing in and maintaining fixed assets. A sample check list template is given below:

Type of fixed asset	Action check list
Intangible	Generally amortise under accounting recommendations. What controls limit research and development costs?
Freeholds	Is it necessary to own property? If so, who should be the owner? Consider taxation and owner pension options.
Long-term leaseholds	Can any part be sub-let for additional income? Is there a premium receivable on relocation? Would the freeholder be willing to sell?
Short-term leaseholds	Is there a policy laid down for renewal? Would longer lease terms be preferred?
Plant and machinery	Is there a replacement programme in place? Is maintenance better done in-house or externally?
Motor vehicles	Should they be owned or leased? Can the transport fleet be outsourced?
Equipment/furniture/ Fixtures/fittings	Have refurbishment costs been budgeted? Can any equipment be leased?
Patents	Are they fully safeguarded? What strategy is planned for when they expire?
Trade investments	Are they necessary? Would it be preferable to own the company outright?

An ongoing plant and machinery register should be maintained to indicate the cost of using each piece of equipment, the proportion of time it is in use and when it could most beneficially be replaced. Some of the data will only need to be updated occasionally. Headings to consider for each major item of plant and machinery are:

- date purchased, the purchase price and age (if second-hand);
- any attached financing (eg hire purchase, showing terms and period of repayments);
- any contracted maintenance terms (eg renewal date and cost);
- operating costs per hour, including the above indirect costs (note: the employment of specialist operatives is a direct expense);
- work sheet details downloaded to give a usage time analysis.

The last two items will provide the financial information necessary to cost out the machinery when tendering for customer contracts and will show how frequently the machine is used. In this latter respect, the percentage of use to idle time will assist in answering the questions: is the machine being used efficiently? When (or not) should it be replaced?

There is a school of thought that it is good policy for a business to own freehold premises, taking the view that the asset can easily be borrowed against for security purposes and it is an appreciating asset. The purist answer is whether the company is in business to hold assets for eventual depreciation or to trade at a profit where leased premises are sufficient and offer the easy option to relocate or expand into larger buildings.

Financially speaking, discounted cash flow (see Appendix 8) should be used to compare the cost of future rent payments against the cost of buying premises and the loss of earnings through using capital to buy the freehold. On the one hand, there are rent reviews to consider and, on the other hand, there is the upkeep of the owned freehold. Business rates may apply to both options.

3.17   The labour force

It may appear incongruous to the management that one form of 'fixed' asset is never shown on the traditional balance sheet, that of the valuable labour force that is needed to maintain trading. This is because the 'purchase' cost of employing staff is rarely significant in amount and staff turnover can vary considerably. The nearest to a mention, and that occurs in company accounts, is the statement in the notes to the accounts describing the pension commitment of the business and the overall cost and number of staff employed.

At any time, the business would have a liability to pay staff on compulsory redundancy and this should be a negative addition when evaluating the break-up value of a business. For an ongoing business there would be agency and advertising costs associated with appointing new staff and, for high earners, perhaps a 'golden hello' payment. The 'investment' of the business in its staff will be the annual costs of training, providing for staff amenities and pension commitments.

The management should review, on a regular basis, its labour force incorporating a check list of:

- 'key' operatives and other personnel, listing their responsibilities;
- the number of years each employee has been employed;
- any training commitment approved and is outstanding;
- current pay/overtime rates, review dates and annual cost plus benefits;
- productive hours worked and the cost per hour for the business;
- work sheet details downloaded to give non-/productive time split;
- the liability of redundancy payments were employees given notice.

3.18   Current assets

3.18.1   Stocks

Efficient control of raw material stocks held should be a key feature of all balance sheet management skills. Until sufficient experience has been gained of trading and until adequate finances are on hand to allow for any build-up of stocks, conservative principles should be the order of the day: that is, gear production only to firm orders and preferably receive cash on delivery or, if services are offered, accept the payment in full up-front or at least a partial down payment with regular stage payments thereafter. Many ongoing contracts set out customer specifications and prices but no firm delivery times or quantities. The full negotiation of terms should lead to mutual agreement satisfactory to both sides.

3.18.2   Finished goods

The management should be conversant with retention of title agreements, where a contract for the sale of goods can include a clause stipulating that the property in the goods is not to pass until payment has been received by the seller (Romalpa clause: *Aluminium Industrie Vaassen BV v Romalpa Aluminium Ltd* [1976]). The exact wording of the clause will be important to convey the security of retention of title.

If the sales contract(s) is ongoing and dependent on end-user demand, the supplying business or subcontractor should discuss with the customer (who may be a wholesaler main contractor) what stock is needed as a strategic minimum to satisfy normal demand for the product(s). The cost of raw materials for this element of finished stock and the direct costs of manufacture can then be calculated and the customer asked to subsidise or provide credit to the supplier up to this amount.

If individual sales contracts are one-off, of a reasonable size (say, £20,000+) and the customer is an established name, it may be possible for the supplier to finance the contract commercially to obtain sufficient raw materials to produce the goods. In this case, stocks can be purchased to fulfil the whole contract rather than jeopardising delivery dates through purchasing stocks piecemeal having the attendant risk of a market shortfall.

Where the stocks are standardised finished products and the type of trade demands immediate deliveries, say, of perishable goods, it may be possible for similar suppliers, close to one another, to agree to help each other out in supplying raw materials and selling the packaged goods. There would be netting out of balances owing at agreed intervals, but no intervening cash payments and receipts.

The question frequently posed is: how much finished stock should be held for any given level of sales? Clearly, there is a strategic level of stock that is needed to maintain production or selling capability. This may be adjusted for specific orders or for seasonal demands. Retailers operating a stock control system can discern quickly what selling lines are getting low and previous ordering experience will show what lines sell more rapidly and what products do not sell well. Manufacturers need more sophistication with their calculations both for raw materials and finished stocks unless a complete computerised stock control system is in place. Consider the following forecast example:

(£'000)					Forecast months:				
Profit and loss:	*1*	*2*	*3*	*4*	*5*	*6*	*7*	*8*	*9*
Sales invoiced	100	100	100	120	140	160	180	200	200
Materials delivery	20	24	28	32	36	40	40	40	40
Labour cost	40	40	40	48	56	64	72	80	80
Cost of sales	60	64	68	80	92	104	112	120	120
Gross profit	40	36	32	40	48	56	68	80	80
Cash flow:	*1*	*2*	*3*	*4*	*5*	*6*	*7*	*8*	*9*
Sales receipts	100	100	100	100	120	140	160	180	200
Materials payments	20	20	20	24	28	32	36	40	40
Labour payments	40	40	40	48	56	64	72	80	80
Cash inflow, net of other costs	40	40	40	28	36	44	52	60	80
Cash expectation:									
Change		−	+ 4	+ 8	− 12	− 12	− 12	− 16	− 20	0
Cumulative		−	+ 4	+ 12	0	− 12	− 24	− 40	− 60	− 60

The table shows that sales progressively increased and doubled over months 4 through to 8. Materials (comprising one-fifth of the value of sales invoiced) for production had to be delivered two months in advance. Customers were given one month's credit and suppliers were paid after two months. The management can make two assumptions from the table.

◆ It is indicated when, and by how much, raw materials should have been ordered.

◆ Cash flow is expected to dip in months 4 and 5 and therefore sufficient cash should be available at that time to meet the direct costs shown, otherwise creditors may have to be deferred for payment until a later date or other cash savings made.

3.1.8.3 Work-in-progress

Management of work-in-progress of a sub-contracting business such as in the construction industry, for example, will largely centre around the accurate estimating of tenders, full evaluation of performance risks, prompt accounting for progress payments and regular site monitoring.

The costing of job expenditure is only as good as how recent and accurate are the underlying charge-out rates for plant, materials and labour. Performance risk evaluation is only as good as the research into, for example, soil conditions for a construction contract. Cash flow will devolve on the rapidity of billing and collecting progress payments. Quality control will be dependent on the efficiency and regularity of site inspections. At the outset, an estimate of the labour requirements for each contract should be calculated and, if the present workforce is not sufficient, allowance should be made for the time needed to employ additional temporary employees or outsource the work.

Where work-in-progress consists of manufacturing products or selling a service, any sizeable sales contract should be broken down into several deliveries with separate billing for each. The management of contracts may require the allocation of plant time and staff depending on the size of the labour force. A wall chart of available employees' names (after allowing for holiday dates) with their allocation to jobs could greatly assist forward planning. Some customers may ask for prototypes of a new product to be made in advance of placing an order. If the cost of these would be significant and the supplier has to bear the risk of failure, the work should be billed as a separate consultancy or the customer asked to make stage payments, thereby ensuring that as work progresses, the risk of loss through aborting the product lessens.

3.19 Trade debtors

The collection of trade debts has become almost an industry in its own right ('credit management'). The best way to safeguard against losses from debts becoming irrecoverable is to take added care when agreeing trade credit. The effect on a business of a bad debt may be judged from the following example:

(VAT ignored)		**Sale**	**Loss**
Debtor invoiced		£1,000	£1,000
Cost of sales: materials, say	£150		
Labour, say	£450	£600	£600
Indirect costs, say		£100	£100
Net profit on sale		£300	£700
Future sales required to recoup the expenditure			£2,333
Future sales required to recoup the lost profit			£1,000
Future sales required to offset the total loss			**£3,333**

From the example given, it will be easier to achieve sales of £1,000 than £3,333 and it would be preferable to invoke caution in allowing trade credit to new customers where there is any doubt over payment or no knowledge of the new account. Equally, it is better and easier to nurture long-standing repeat customers since they are unlikely to require persistent marketing or 'special terms' to gain further orders. The lending banker should enquire what system of credit management over sales debts is in force, ie what checks are given before new credit is allowed? How frequently is the debtors ledger monitored and overdue debtors contacted for payment? What action is done when debts become significantly overdue? Is the management always in touch with the situation?

The management of trade debts should include the following characteristics:

◆ adopt a system of verifying the account risk before allowing credit;
◆ monitor the debtors' ledger constantly and keep running records of the ages of each debt;
◆ record the date when each debt was chased for payment, by whom, to whom and answers given by the debtor when contacted;
◆ the management should review overdue debts individually at least on a monthly basis;
◆ have a formal notice procedure of appointing debt collectors or, if collection is done in-house, when this stage is activated;
◆ decide when an approach 'without prejudice' for partial settlement of an overdue debt should be made and by whom it should be authorised. Small debts are usually not worthwhile to pursue above a 50–60% recovery proportion;
◆ consider whether quick payment should be encouraged by discounts;
◆ agree when a customer withholding payment should be notified of revised trading terms, eg future trade subject to cash on delivery.

The banker's security in respect of book debts and the merits of fixed and floating charges with particular reference to the Brumark Case [*Agnew v Commissioner of Inland Revenue* (2001)] is discussed under 'security' in Chapter Nine.

3.20 Current liabilities

There is a clear financial advantage to pay business creditors later than receiving business debts. This must be weighed against the legal right for interest to be added to debts once they have been deemed late for payment (which is either after the agreed credit period has expired or otherwise after a default period of 30 days) and the possible damage to the business' reputation in being brought to court and a loss of purchasing power through becoming a payment 'laggard'. The interest that can be charged on the outstanding debt is 8% pa above the ruling Bank of England base rate on the day that settlement should have been made.

If the business situation does not give the option of making a choice, then it could not be the best strategy to have one or two large creditors outstanding, since if a voluntary arrangement for settlement is pursued, these creditors may well hold and exercise the power to close their business, whereas a more widely spread list of smaller creditors may not be so active. Before this situation is reached, however, it will be found that most creditors will be willing to listen to some form of deferred settlement. Care should be taken by the company not to create a fraudulent preference in advance of becoming insolvent.

A business borrower in default to their bank may expect to be treated somewhat differently. First, the bank should show understanding for the adverse financial situation, especially if it has not been exacerbated through mismanagement. The bank will be looking to have the debt repaid by some means and the choices are usually two: by letting the business trade profitably out of its predicament (if possible) or by recovery of the debt through realising the security held.

The type of security in force and its ease of conversion into cash will play a major part in the bank's decision about how to treat the errant account, as will the customer's past account record. A well thought out proposal by the management to repay the bank over time should be welcomed and put to the bank for their consideration. It will be important for the bank to have been forewarned by the management that trading difficulties were becoming apparent so that remedial action could have been mutually agreed and implemented before the situation became more difficult to resolve.

3.21 Recovery procedure

Every bank of size will have a specialist recovery unit that is skilled in close monitoring of business accounts in difficulty and in deciding what remedial measures may best be adopted in the circumstances. Responsibility for the account will be removed from the relationship branch and experienced assessors will be put in charge. The recovery unit will be in a strong position to control future trading of the business and safeguard the bank's interests. Probably the first action will be to freeze all accounts and raise a separate account for the payment of business wages (see Chapter Nine and *Clayton's case*).

3.22   Long-term liabilities

Long-term liabilities of a business should not be forgotten when managing the balance sheet. There may be the option to convert into less onerous debt, particularly if a loan has commenced at a variable interest rate and the borrower can convert into a fixed interest rate. If the terms of the borrowing do not allow this choice, a matching deal (for the remainder of the period of the original loan) may be possible to convert the liability from fixed into floating rate, or vice versa, or a similar exercise in currencies. A further alternative that is always available is to replace the debt with a new credit line on more preferential terms. This may lead to a change of lender. Before doing so, consideration should be given to all the ramifications of such a move.

The situation of the bank taking security in the form of a personal guarantee before allowing money to be borrowed is an emotive one. When managing the balance sheet, it should not be an oversight on the part of the borrower to discuss with the bank whether the (presumed) greater net worth of the business warrants the elimination of this security. If this is unavoidable (and it should be avoided if possible in favour of other forms of security), then it is well to remember that the liability can be 'capped' as to the maximum amount and may not have to be 'joint and several' in scope, ie when the bank can approach one guarantor in preference to another for the whole debt. Of course, a sole trader always holds personal liability, a partnership may do so and a company shareholder does not.

3.23   General considerations

The balance sheet provides the viewer with the (historic) state of that business at one point in time. More strict accounting and legal regulations in the UK over the years have largely eliminated any 'massage' of the entries to show a position that may not be totally relevant to what occurred during the accounting year since the date of the previous balance sheet. There are extensive tax regulations to prevent a re-arrangement where it is for the purpose of avoiding the payment of tax. Companies are still allowed to hide their ownership by registering abroad.

3.24 Managing the business assets: other considerations

When a business has been built up successfully over a number of years and is expected to continue as such, with all borrowings repaid and future cash requirements to trade allowed for, the management will have other considerations to take decisions on, probably the principal one being should the business expand or not. If expansion is chosen, the house bank may be asked to part finance the acquisition of another business and therefore should be aware of the factors affecting the decision-making process, including the basics of how to value another business to be acquired.

Let us assume the major shareholder of a trading company has to make a decision whether to continue trading as before and withdraw surplus earnings annually to invest in a retirement pension fund or whether to expand the business so that, by retirement, the company can be sold at an enhanced value. The first point to make is that building up cash and leaving it as such in the business will not offer enhancement because any prospective purchaser will only pay like cash for cash. Secondly, if investment in a pension fund is chosen, it may be in-house (such as a self-administered pension fund) or external (investing in a fund(s) managed commercially and set up through an independent pension broker) and there are valuable tax benefits applying to each.

Pension fund investment is beyond the scope of this text and is a specialised area where professional advice should be taken. Two examples are outlined hereafter of the use of funds surplus to business needs that the management can come across. Example A compares the return of reinvesting the surplus back into the business with an investment made externally. Example B takes this a stage further and outlines factors that may arise that the management should consider when making its decision.

Example A – the theoretical case

Surplus business earnings after personal tax thereon	say,	£30,000
Present rate of return on capital invested in the business	say,	10% pa
Expected additional earnings if re-invested in the business		£3,000
Current average return on quoted shares after tax	say,	4% pa
Annual investment return on invested surplus earnings		£1,200
Net benefit if reinvested in the business rather than shares		£1,800

But the questions not answered are:
◆ will the additional £30,000 invested in the business for stocks generate the equivalent additional sales and earn the equivalent gross profit?
◆ will the business be able to sustain these surplus earnings?

◆ what are the chances of achieving a capital gain on the external investments?
◆ how will this gain change the reward calculation?

Example A shows that worked on the given assumptions, the business would have earned an additional £1,800 by re-investing the surplus earnings in the business. Taking into account the extra costs of £3,500 in earning a profit on the re-investment in Example B following, however, the additional profit of £3,000 is lost and the business would have incurred a loss of £500 on this particular management decision.

Example B – the practical case:

The business trades on a gross profit margin on sales of, say	50%
The additional turnover generated will be	£60,000
But the business suffers higher direct labour costs (overtime) amounting to 5% of turnover	£3,000
And the new customers increase the average bad debt experience of the business by, say, 2%	£1,200
And there is a small increase in indirect costs of, say	£800
That would reduce the additional profit by	£5,000
or after allowing for taxation at the rate of 30%, say	£3,500
Compared with the Example A, additional profit of	£3,000
It suggests a loss of	£500

3.25 Acquiring a business

The skills of the management do not usually extend to valuing a potential business acquisition, whether the company's shares are quoted or not. The bank relationship manager should have some idea of what is involved when the management of a customer company wishes to expand in this manner, particularly if there is the likelihood that the acquisition may be (part) financed through a loan or the potential acquisition will have a material effect on the financial standing of the purchaser. Comment on business valuations is given in Appendix 8.

Four

Why businesses fail

The common reason behind a lack of survival is running out of money to continue to trade. Up to this time, the trading may or may not have been profitable and the owner-manager may or may not be to blame for the cause. The management of the business has shown a lack of foresight to account for the factors behind the change in fortunes. It may have been in respect of not allowing for changing trading patterns, the business may have overstretched its financial resources or, simply, the working directors may have retained insufficient working capital for the business to survive. In each case, warning signs have usually been evident, but the management has not counteracted the portents.

The frequent assumptions made, quite erroneously, are that the business could trade out of its predicament and therefore there was no immediate need to cut expenditure, or that the business would ask its bank to come to the rescue with more finance. Delving deeper into the reasons for failure, one may be able to discover situations less immediately obvious:

- product failure and warranty liabilities;
- technological advancements;
- a failure to market the product(s) properly;
- too rapid expansion (over-trading);
- excessive marketing expenditure;
- not establishing a viable market presence;
- a lack of price competitiveness;
- inadequate selling prices;
- extending too much credit to customers;
- long overdue debtor balances leading to bad debts;
- a lack of liquidity due to a high level of asset investment;
- operating costs running too high for the turnover being achieved;
- overstaffing;

◆ over-stocking;
◆ a failure to promote the strengths of the business.

4.1 Product failure and warranty liabilities

The problems associated with marketing a new product, spending much launch money and initiating a good reputation can be immediately dashed if the product soon shows a flaw, causing many items to be returned under warranty or otherwise recalled for remedial reworking and losing any goodwill from hard-won customers.

There have been so many examples of good ideas leading to implementation failure, for instance, the infamous gadget to make doughnuts that worked perfectly, except that when a different mix of dough was used it clogged up the works and the mix shape failed to materialise. Or the IT company that 'guaranteed' to improve any company's performance on the strength of implementing software to one successful niche customer. When other companies operating in the same field took up the offer, it was found that their methods of working were not as compatible with the software product being offered and the resulting considerable additional work led to losses and ultimate insolvency.

Many product failures show themselves in one of two ways: either the strength of part of the assembled components is not robust enough to work for an extended period of time or the inventor has failed to test the product under sufficiently diverse working conditions. The remedy is to extend the testing period and to build in a greater margin of safety with the components, even at the expense of a higher unit cost.

Warranty insurance should be taken out whenever possible although it is not easy to obtain cover for a new product or in a market, such as North America, where litigation is frequent and costly and the claims can be astronomic in amount. The business may have to limit the number of different risks covered to obtain initial acceptance, although where the product is to be partly manufactured by a larger business, a sharing of the insurance cover and costs may be possible.

4.2 Technological advancements

If the product is dependent on using specialised technology and needs to remain at the forefront of future developments in the field, then the management should consider appointing a consultant to assist with ongoing research and development to retain competitiveness. The extra time spent on research should be built into the marketing model. The consultant may be a university professor or research graduate specialising in that type of activity. Otherwise, valuable time will have to be set aside by the management for constant updating of knowledge through regular trade contacts, reading journals and maintaining contact with the relevant trade organisations. Turnover forecasts should take into account the effect of competition arising in due course if the product cannot be patented.

4.3   A failure to market the product(s) properly

A business can have a good product that fails through inadequate marketing and a bad product that is a success through good marketing. The former case is not necessarily the fault of the management, at least initially, but it should have been recognised at an early stage that success was exceeding expectations and the marketing plan adjusted accordingly. There has been the example of promoting the characterisation of animals through songs, where the first album was a great success, but no back up had been planned, resulting in marketing failure of the follow up album when it eventually appeared. The public appeal had been lost.

Poor (or perhaps better words to use are 'lower quality') products can sell in great quantities if they are promoted well. Jewellery and electrical goods have been examples in the past, but the list is far more extensive. The general thread to look for in this case is 'value for money'. Either the product is marketed at too low a price to ensure a good enough quality product or the profit margin required has been marked too high, causing a lowering of quality in the manufacture to meet a target selling price. For the retailer, having to suffer a relatively low margin set by the manufacturer, the risk is doubled; the profitability will be sub-standard and the product quality may lead to lower sales and unwanted stocks.

An example may be given of a major motor car manufacturer that reduced the quality of its car bumpers (fenders) at the last moment to save costs and preserve profitability without increasing the selling price of the model for competitive reasons. After the model was marketed to the public, it was found that the bumper was strong enough to withstand quite an impact, but even a minor impact caused the undamaged bumper to move into the bodywork with disastrous repair consequences.

Marketing is also a matter of timing. Does one first display Christmas goods in September, October or November? Similarly, if the new product is to be ready in July, does one advertise the goods for August sales, when many customers are on holiday and work staff will also be taking leave themselves? How should the marketing be done? It may be in-house, through a consultancy, via the web or other media. Is there time to build up a clientele gradually or should effort be spent in outsourcing selling through a business on a joint venture basis that already has the necessary sales contacts and sales force?

The critical tests are: what level of sales are required for the business to achieve so that it may continue in business and will the implementation of the proposed marketing plan from the date it is scheduled to commence be able to attain those sales on time?

4.4   Too rapid expansion

It seems inconsistent that too rapid an expansion of sales may lead to the demise of the business through over-trading. This occurs when the rate of expansion is such that there are insufficient financial resources available to support this growth, notwithstanding that the business may still be operating at a profit. The shortfall in resources may arise through:

- the incorrect supposition that the sales being achieved will generate sufficient cash to pay wages and raw materials from suppliers to ensure, in turn, that more products can be produced and sold, thus allowing the business to trade out of any potential cash shortfall. Unfortunately, sales take time to be converted into cash, raw materials have to be purchased in advance and wages have to be paid weekly to manufacture the goods;
- the high growth has led to an expansion of trade debts that are proving difficult to collect in due time;
- the rapid expansion has outrun the administration of the sales ledger and efficient ordering of supplies;
- the commercial borrowings of the business may have reached their prudent maximum and the cost of servicing becomes prohibitive;
- the capacity of the business may have been allowed to expand to such an extent that capital expenditure on plant and operating overheads, particularly production wages, to meet the increasing demand for more products to sell has become too sizeable to manage;
- resources of the business have been diminished through the withdrawal of cash by way of excess salaries, pensions or dividends.

It is very important, therefore, in addition to monitoring cash flow and the payment dates for outstanding current liabilities, to check regularly the trend of two ratios:

- a comparison of the total of trade debtor balances against trade creditors to discern to what degree those creditors may be supporting the credit given to trade debtors and whether this support extends to the operational cash flow in general;
- the trends shown by the value of stocks and work-in-progress maintained and the cost of direct labour. If these cost items balloon without a commensurate increase in turnover, the business may be over-extending itself financially.

Yet sales expansion is always limited by the capacity available to produce goods for sale in a number of ways:

- the physical number of resale items that can be produced with the existing production and labour resources;
- the physical number of goods that can be stocked;
- the number of coincident consultancy assignments that can be undertaken by a professional business;
- the financial resources required in supporting the degree of business infrastructure necessary to continue the sales expansion.

When any of the above limitations arise, the shortfall that is occurring will have to be resolved through the business having more working capital (ie cash that is used to continue trading on a day-by-day basis) invested to prevent a business collapse or otherwise having to curb sales to a level that can be readily accommodated. This may mean extending delivery times and/or outsourcing some production. As over-trading, for what this is, may be a frequent problem with the small to medium-sized business, it will be useful to have a handy rough check that can be applied to see whether there is such a problem in the offing.

4.5   Handy over-trading check

4.5.1   Manufacturing

1. What is the maximum capacity of the plant (number of units produced)?
2. How many units have been produced recently (say, over weekly periods)?
3. During these weeks, has production been abnormal? If so, adjust to a normal basis.
4. In the next few weeks, will production be abnormal? If so, use this abnormal capacity.
5. What is the forecast level of sales (number of units) in the coming weeks?
6. How much finished/near-finished stock is held? If so, add the value to item 5.
7. Take item 2, as adjusted by 3 and 4, and compare with item 5, as adjusted by item 6.
8. Ask the question: can the expected unit production level meet the expected unit sales targets?
9. If not, can production be increased through taking up this slack capacity (and re-arranging production)?
10. If not, for how long can the timing of sales deliveries be extended and accepted by customers?
11. If not, what future expenditure is required to increase production to meet the unit sales targets?
12. Does the business have this financial resource?
13. If not, and the finance cannot afford to be borrowed, the business will be over-trading.

(Note: if it is not practical to work in (average) product units, then values should be substituted – see below.)

4.5.2   Services

1. What has been the weekly turnover, on average, recently achieved?
2. What is the future forecast of weekly sales that is expected?
3. What has been the weekly goods purchased for stock, on average, recently achieved?

4. Will stocks purchased in future be subject to seasonal variations?
5. If so, adjust item 3 to allow for this variation.
6. Adjust the amended total for item 3 by multiplying it by item 2 and dividing it by item 1.
7. Compare item 6 with the amended total for item 3.
8. Ask the question: can the business afford to spend this greater sum on additional stock?
9. Does the business have this financial resource?
10. If not, and the finance cannot afford to be borrowed, the business will be over-trading.

4.6 Excessive marketing expenditure

It may seem strange to non-business persons that so much money can be spent on promoting a product(s) in advance of getting any reward through sales receipts (the emphasis being on 'so much' rather than 'any'). Of course, a new product must be advertised to the customers targeted, otherwise they will have little immediate likelihood of knowing that the product is available for purchase. The type of product will determine to a degree how much money can prudently be spent on marketing. Where the business and the product is 'national', the marketing may be split between 'specific products' and 'general awareness of the company'.

Take the dot.com start up businesses as an example. The accepted marketing points are that there is a market to be tapped for business and expenditure has to be undertaken in advance to bring to the potential customers the knowledge of the benefits of using these services. The unaccepted points are that it is easier and less risky to sell a product that is already in demand and been seen to be accepted in this manner by the public than to create a demand from scratch. It is also a high-risk venture to start trading with a known time limit before the venture will halt due to lack of funds, brought about by poor customer utilisation. Excessive marketing, insufficient financial resources and a lack of public acceptance therefore contributed to the downfall of so many theoretically well thought out businesses.

4.7 Not establishing a viable market presence

Following on from the preceding paragraph, in order for a business not to fail, it must reach a strategic size. This means its continuing turnover must be sufficient to cover its variable direct costs and its fixed indirect costs so as not to suffer a trading loss. For example, if a business operates from an expensive base with high running costs, but has low direct costs that vary with the level of turnover, it may be difficult to sustain turnover at a sufficient level (its 'strategic size') to cover all these costs if the trading environment deteriorates and less business is won. The number of pay-and-play golf clubs going into liquidation is an example, because the high cost of buying land and the number of players using the facilities could not support building an expensive clubhouse with borrowed money.

4.8   A lack of price competitiveness

Extending the preceding example of the financially overstretched golf club, an ancillary reason for failure was the increase in competition as too many clubs sprang up around the same time because of the pressure to change the use of unproductive rural land and a perceived view that the market held unsatisfied demand. In the event, each club had to compete for a slower growth in the number of new golfers taking up the sport and this led to a watershed in the value of green fees and membership subscriptions that could be charged. There was no flexibility to boost trading through price competitiveness without damaging the income return necessary to earn a profit.

4.9   Inadequate selling prices

Continuing the golf club example yet further, because the green fees were below break-even point for the club(s), the annual income they generated was inadequate to meet constantly increasing operating costs. These costs could not be reduced further because staffing was at a minimum level to meet regular grass cutting and other maintenance chores. Some clubs survive through a mixture of exclusivity and subsidy and others through an established reputation, but inadequate turnover has caused the downfall of many other clubs.

4.10   Extending too much credit

A business may concentrate too much on gaining orders and sales to the detriment of a proper credit control on its trade debtors. All new potential customers should have their credit references checked through one of the recognised agencies (eg Dun and Bradstreet) before any credit is granted to them for settlement of the debt. Particular attention should be paid on the most recent up-to-date information available and whether the business being reviewed has had a change in credit rating.

If necessary, time should be taken by the management to visit the potential customer and discuss future credit terms. The sales invoice should have written thereon the terms of trading, including any interest penalties, etc when the debt is overdue. A regular monitoring of the ages of each debtor account from month to month will show whether a more firm credit attitude and chasing of overdue debts are warranted. Failure to retrieve debts on time may lead to poor liquidity and, perhaps, eventually irretrievable business difficulties.

4.11   Bad debts

These are the bane of the hard-working business owner. If a bad (ie irrecoverable) debt occurs, the loss to the business can be made up only by creating new sales of circa three times the loss, subject to the gross profit margin the business is working to (see Chapter Two, trade debtors). Particular care should be taken where the business relies on one or more significant customers for a majority of sales and the total amount due from this/(these) major customer(s) is increasing and would cause a liquidity problem for the business if the account(s) defaulted in payment.

To prevent a situation like this occurring in the first place, the business should agree a maximum credit limit per account that would not cause the business a liquidity crisis if the debt did prove bad and then to stick to this limit. Among the measures to take to prevent a bad debt loss when a customer is consistently late in payment and/or 'settles' the account partially with lump sum payments, both occasions highlighting the likelihood of further difficulties, are to put new sales to that customer on a cash payment at delivery basis and agree with the customer an unequivocal schedule of repayment on the old outstanding debt balances.

4.12   A lack of liquidity due to asset investment

Instances have occurred where the business has been good at replacing plant and equipment before they become obsolete or cost too much in repairs or, for example, has correctly deduced that the purchase of a colour printing machine to replace a black and white machine will keep the business competitive and lead to additional customers. Unfortunately, although the purchase may have been negotiated at a reasonable cost, the expenditure has been of sufficient size to reduce the day-to-day working liquidity of the business and the bank has had to be approached in retrospect for an emergency loan. This may, or may not, be forthcoming. The failure could have been prevented either by ensuring that the borrowed funds were available before the equipment was ordered, or cost savings introduced to offset the planned capital expenditure or other less critical expenditure programmes deferred until all the costs could be met.

4.13   Too high operating costs

Managements, as a rule, should be conversant with knowing how their operating costs in total compare with their income, if only to measure the changes in the cash balance (or overdraft) at the bank. What they may be less inclined to monitor regularly is whether all the operating costs are being recouped by sales in the form of an adequate profit margin and hence in selling prices. When asked how they pitch their selling prices, many give the answer that the sales value is the maximum the customers will pay. This explanation may hide the fact that selling prices are too low to cover operating costs. If selling prices cannot be raised then operating costs must be pruned for the company not to go out of business.

4.14   Overstaffing

During the past few years, it has become proportionately more expensive to employ staff over a period when inflation (and annual wage increases) historically has been at a very low rate. This is because there has been the introduction of the minimum wage, compulsory working breaks, greater maternity leave and higher employer National Insurance contributions. It is now even more important for the business to utilise its staff to the maximum benefit possible and to employ the minimum number of staff that can do this in practice. If a business is overstaffed, it can be expensive to incur redundancies and even more expensive if, a while later, an upturn in trading requires staff reinstatement.

Paying employees is a regular expense whether or not they have a job to fulfil, whereas mechanisation is an immediate expense, but it costs little to let machines stand idle and even outsourcing tasks offers the flexibility to be called on only when the job(s) has to be performed. Keeping staff employed for too long when there is little work for them to do, hoping that trading will pick up shortly, has been the cause of many business failures, particularly in the building services trades.

4.15   Overstocking

A business can overstock with raw materials used in the production of goods and overstock with finished goods that have either been bought in or have been self-produced and are ready for sale. In the first instance, the management should have knowledge of the quantities of what materials (or goods) will be required to manufacture (or sell) the products and when these stocks will be required. If ordering is left or decided at the last minute there may be a risk of non-delivery on time, causing production to stop.

Larger businesses like to have more than one source of supply to alleviate this potential problem. If the materials are specialist or self-manufactured to be assembled into a product, the supplier(s) may, on request, hold the stock themselves at their cost in order to ensure an eventual sale and maintain the custom of the purchaser. This will tie up cash resources and the stockholder may suffer liquidity problems if the purchaser cancels future deliveries due to changing the product or if future trading deteriorates and does not warrant the original quantity of deliveries.

The second instance of overstocking that may occur is when a business stockpiles finished goods that cannot immediately be sold. The reason for doing so may be to maintain production and keep key staff employed, knowing that the goods in time will be bought, and/or to enable a longer production run to be accomplished. This assumption may cause a terminal problem for the business: will the goods be sold and, if so, at what price? If the eventual selling price to move the excess stocks is pitched below the cost of manufacture, a trading loss will be incurred.

Adopting sub-normal selling prices may adversely affect the sale of new goods in the pipeline waiting to be marketed. The business hopes that sales of 'old' stocks will be at the expense of its competitor(s) products rather than other products of its own, otherwise a potential liquidity problem can still arise.

4.16 A failure to promote the strengths of the business

In this example, the business is profitable, but only just. It is well established with a good reputation, but sales have remained stagnant for some years. The management is finding it increasingly more difficult to match cash receipts with expenditure and is spending a lot of time in trying to do so. In short, the business is in a rut. The management by now should have recognised the downward trend in fortunes and decided on a remedial course of action. A decision where the management wants the business to stand in a few years time has to be made: either expanding turnover or increasing profitability from maintaining turnover?

If increased profitability from **maintained turnover** is to be the objective, all facets of the business should be examined for improvements.

- ◆ If it is to maintain turnover, what actions should be implemented immediately to capitalise on the current worth of the business?
- ◆ Will these actions cost money and is this finance available? If not, is it feasible to borrow?
- ◆ Do not contemplate investing new money or borrowing money to achieve the objective unless increased profitability is the result.
- ◆ Look for small modifications to existing trading that can be done with current staff/finance resources.
- ◆ Introduce these modifications without affecting the current trading pattern.
- ◆ Raise a revised business plan. Assess and monitor the result.
- ◆ Each of the above options will have their own solutions to promote the existing strengths of the business.

If **expansion** is contemplated, a SWOT analysis (strengths, weaknesses, opportunities and threats) should be produced to include a re-assessment of the current trading outlook of the business to review decisions on:

- what must be done in respect of improving buying, production, selling, financing, employment, etc?
- estimating the financial effects of the proposed changes: are they worthwhile? After putting into effect, will the business improve viability?
- deciding what other resources (human, machine, money, etc) are necessary to put the expansion plan into action;
- assessing whether these resources can be raised;
- looking again at the business assumptions and forecasts, will the sales targets be met? Are all costs included?
- if the projected net earnings return is adequate over the period in question, then the revised business plan can be adopted.

A translation of the options given above would be as follows:

Strengths	**Translation**
The business is profitable	Build on the most profitable business sectors
It is well established	Use the existing clientele to gain more turnover
It has a good reputation	'Advertise' the fact to others

Weaknesses	**Translation**
The business is loss making	Find the source of losses and rectify
The business is not growing	Has the sales product or customer mix changed?
The business has cash a flow problem	Analyse the reasons why

Opportunities	**Translation**
What products/service sell best?	Promote these more
What could be expanded?	Compare the profit return pre/post-expansion
What could be promoted?	What cost can new products/areas be developed?

Threats	**Translation**
What can affect profitability most?	Leave no stones unturned
What can adversely affect turnover?	Consider internal and external influences
What is the trading outlook?	Get each director/manager to list the possibilities

Each problem will have its own danger signals enabling early remedial measures to be implemented by the management. The table following indicates in broad terms the warning signs met and some of the preventive measures to take to counteract the problems. Their causes and their solutions can be inter-related.

The failure	Warning signs	Preventative measures
Money		
Lack of starting capital	Difficulty to raise money	Raise a viability appraisal
Lack of growth capital	Reducing cash, higher sales	Forecast future cash needs
Lack of contingency capital	Lower cash, higher creditors	Agree standby credit line
Excessive capital drawings	Reducing net asset base	Plan management strategy
Products		
Lack of competitiveness	Falling sales	Check market sales price
		Review competition
		Review product range
		Conduct customer survey
Trading operations		
Loss of profit	Reduced cash resources	Check profit margins

4.17   A lack of initial capital

Before any business start up commences or an existing business embarks on a new venture, a realistic assessment of the turnover that is to be expected should be completed and the cash requirement needed to generate these sales forecast, at least on a monthly basis, over the ensuing one to two years. For new ventures, the cash requirement, of course, will incorporate the acquisition of equipment, staff and the working capital to trade before sales build up and receipts flow into the business.

Frequently, start up businesses forget the ongoing cash needs and this, allied to over-optimistic sales forecasts, immediately indicate financial difficulties ahead. With an established business, what can be forgotten is how the existing trading set up can help finance a new venture, either directly through providing money from existing cash flow until the new project is fully established or by providing collateral for additional commercial borrowings to support the new venture.

4.18   A lack of capital for growth

The business may already have adopted an expansionary theme, bought additional equipment, stocks of raw materials and appointed key staff. If the cost of this is not properly reflected in the business's present cash flow forecast or is not fully recovered through a realistic gross profit margin, then the growth forecast may already be fatally based on incorrect financial assumptions and the profit expectation never achieved in spite of intensive marketing that may initially boost sales. The qualification 'initial' is important because, as cash resources reduce, it will become increasingly apparent that there is inadequate working capital on hand to maintain the early rate of growth in turnover.

4.19   A lack of contingency capital

Few small businesses build into their financial plans a deliberate contingency policy in the event that cash resources, for whatever reason, unexpectedly drop in future. This policy may be either 'active', 'passive' or perhaps both.

An **active policy** will plan for a cash surplus each year and set aside, after all expenditure and dividends/proprietors' drawings have been met, a portion of this to be held in reserve in the business. How it is held will also be important: it should be cash or assets easily converted into cash as and when the occasion arises. Examples of the latter being raw materials in excess of immediate short-term needs acquired at a cheaper cost through bulk buying, by paying creditors early to gain discounts, or by spending some of tomorrow's planned costs in advance through accelerating an equipment replacement programme.

It will invariably be better financially to repay borrowings with short-term surplus funds rather than to leave the money on deposit earning interest (unless the borrowing is at a low fixed interest rate and deposit rates generally rise thereafter higher than this cost). It could be beneficial to purchase stocks or equipment before expected price rises, rather than putting the funds on deposit. A cash surplus each trading year, after allowing for the business's capital equipment replacement programme, should always be the first aim.

It should also be remembered that although sole traders, partnerships and companies are all taxed on the profits that they achieve, the remuneration of owners/directors of companies is classified as employee earnings and is a deduction before corporation tax, whereas for sole traders and partnerships, tax is payable on all profits earned regardless of any drawings by the owners.

A **passive policy** will adopt in advance the setting up of a commercial lending facility to be available for the business to draw on in case of need should day-to-day cash flow fall unexpectedly. One method of doing this is to set up an 'evergreen' or continuous credit facility, where the bank respectively allows automatic annual extensions to the existing (medium-term) credit limit or allows the re-drawing of loan repayments previously made, in each case to enable the business to tide itself over any temporary trading downturn.

4.20   Excessive withdrawals out of the business

Many businesses go through three phases of capitalisation in their life. The first is where the entrepreneur decides to make a business out of an invention, idea, hobby interest, training skill and specialist knowledge. Start-up money is invested to bring the idea into play. The second stage comes when the initial pot of funds starts to run dry and the entrepreneur realises that external capital needs to be raised. Usually, all the local and national grant schemes are tapped and approaches made to the agencies that offer these advisory services.

The third stage arises when money has to be searched for, possibly on payment of a fee to an intermediary, for the provision of additional capital. By this time, the entrepreneur can offer a working model of the original idea and much heartache, but little else. There is frequently no comprehensive market assessment on the commercialisation of the idea and no realistic financial assessment as to its viability. Meantime, development expenditure and probably personal drawings out of the existing capital will have reduced the business capital further and what financial plan there is indicates that a proportionately high percentage of any new capital injection will go to repay the entrepreneur for the work done on the idea to date. This is not a re-capitalisation of the business.

The established business, conversely, may be earning a reasonably regular, but rather static, income for the manager/owner. If the earnings are adequate, there will be limited incentive to change this status quo. The danger is if the balance sheet is not sufficiently strong to withstand a downturn in trading and/or a re-equipment programme. Either money must be re-invested or the bank asked to refinance the business.

The bank will look at the capital that remains invested and the new advance applied for, compare this with the projected cash flow requirement according to the business plan and make an acceptance or rejection judgement accordingly. If the business is a private company with the major shareholder looking to retire in the medium term, the banker should take into account if there has been years of passive management neglect, whether this will change and to what extent past withdrawals of capital have limited a proper value of the business for a future sale.

In each of the situations stated, above an effective management strategy has not been planned in advance and implemented. If a sale is likely, the assets employed in the business should have been regularly renewed and maximum profits earned in the years prior to a sale so that the best selling price could be obtained. If a disposal to other family members is contemplated, additional questions arise over the quality of the new management in terms of experience, skills and technical knowledge and the extent the business will benefit through retention of the sale proceeds as additional capital.

4.21   A lack of product competitiveness

Falling sales may be due to seasonal trading variations, changing fashions or an external general market malaise. If it is internally generated then lower sales may be due to too high selling prices, a product(s) that is not popular, inadequate quality control, poor delivery times, a product(s) that has been outmoded due to technological advances, what may be termed 'market unattractiveness' or just a lack of concentrated marketing effort.

The priority will be to find out the causes for the deterioration in sales. Better still, a regular review should be conducted of the business's own market penetration and customers' needs, the effect on sales of competitive products and how the market might be changing. The management should check whether there is scope to launch a special marketing campaign or reduce margins on some products (or tender for contracts on more fine terms) without damaging regular future business or profitability.

4.22   A loss of profit from trading operations

Not specified within the annual turnover and profit figures can be a loss on one or two contracts, or bad debts, or a change in mix of product sales, or a gradual deterioration in operating margins through costs having increased without this extra expense being mirrored in tender prices or a deterioration in the business's terms of trade (eg allowing more credit to customers). A regular monitoring of several key financial components should be maintained to warn of any pending difficulties or inefficiencies:

Monitoring area	Warning signs	Action required
Turnover	Reduced gross profit %	Check sales mix
		Check contract profits
		Check sales margins
Direct costs		
Materials	Higher stocks	Check ordering system
	Slow moving stocks	Confirm future use
Wages	Loss of chargeable time	Monitor work sheets
	Increased ratio to sales	Consider subcontracting

Monitoring area	Warning signs	Action required
Indirect costs	Higher expenditure	Consider outsourcing
Net current assets		
Cash	Deteriorating balance	Analyse in/outflows
Short-term borrowing	Hard core evident	Check facility options
	Returned cheques	Re-assess cash needs
Debtors	Increasing age	Improved recovery
	Increasing balances	Better collection
	Bad debts	Modify credit approvals
Creditors	Increasing balances	Check cash projections
		Check orders procedure
Finished goods	Higher stocks	Check sales orders
	Increasing returns	Check quality control

Little or no change in the gross profit percentage on sales can hide large compensating changes in trading. For example, the sales margins on some lines may have been eroded by higher direct costs, but compensated by higher sales of larger margin products. The table earlier mentioned higher (raw material) stocks and slow moving (finished product) stocks. If the former is reduced, it will free cash for more efficient use in the business. If the latter is recognised early enough, it may be possible to sell the products at reduced prices and recover at least some part of the production costs. It will also show what products are susceptible to lower demand and should not be produced or bought for resale in such quantities in future.

If a check is maintained on the broad mix of sales and an adjustment made to the expected overall gross profit margin, a better forecast of future profit will be possible and a more permanent expectation of the future gross profit margin on sales will be forthcoming. Retailers can take the main sales splits of their turnover, allocate the gross profit margin for each and take an average margin in total on the many product lines. The importance in this respect of operating a cash register with a sales analysis capacity is obvious. Manufacturers will have a more sophisticated costing procedure related to the content of each individual product, including the gross profit percentage built in, but this should be changed every time the cost of purchasing a component or the hourly pay rate of employees changes.

Where the direct labour force works at sites rather than on the business premises, it is not easy to gauge whether the operatives are working to full capacity or not. The usual method is to take the tender estimate of work required for particular jobs and monitor this against the weekly time sheets for the number of workers employed on each task. If the direct labour is employed on the factory floor, management observation may be more appropriate and a rolling production line would be better still to view inefficiencies.

Indirect costs may not appear to have much scope for improving profits but there could be areas for significant benefits to arise. There is now more opportunity to choose the best competitive supplier of energy, telecommunications, cleaning and deliveries. Vehicle fleet management is a more obvious candidate for consideration. The leasing and maintenance of vehicles will be a fixed cost over the lease period and will enable the full cost to be offset against taxable profits. It will also release cash that would otherwise be needed to spend or to borrow to purchase vehicles. The disadvantage is that the lease cost will be borne for the full period of the lease otherwise early cancellation penalties will be imposed (see also Chapter Eleven).

4.23   A lack of management implementation

Behind all business failures is a shortcoming in management skills. The list can be extensive and this is by no means exhaustive:

◆ a lack of trading foresight leading to having the products marketed at the wrong time in the wrong areas to the wrong customers;
◆ a failure to foresee how the market will respond in future;
◆ inadequate pricing policy on sales products;
◆ underestimating the effects of competition;
◆ a failure to monitor the business properly on a day-to-day basis;
◆ inefficient staffing levels;
◆ inefficient production methods and under-utilisation of plant;
◆ slowness in effecting remedial measures when problems occur;
◆ over-expansion without the necessary resources in place;
◆ too high gearing with borrowings and the attendant servicing costs;
◆ simply not acting when the business goes into recession.

Five

Business recovery and financing growth

5.1 Business recovery

5.1.1 Introduction

When a company becomes insolvent, the directors must not knowingly continue trading otherwise they will be personally liable for the debts of the business subsequently incurred. This may be countenanced as intent to defraud the company's creditors and refers only where the liquidator applies to the court in the course of winding up the company (Insolvency Act 1986, para 213). There are legal formalities to adhere to and the insolvency managers appointed will be looking to raise as much money as possible for their appointees, the creditors. This may entail letting the company continue to trade until it recovers, is broken up and sold piecemeal or sold en bloc, in each case to realise the highest value for the creditors.

Prior to reaching the stage of a compulsory liquidation, the company may endeavour to reach a settlement by way of a legally binding voluntary arrangement with its creditors. Again, there are strictures as to what can be achieved and this will depend on a sufficient percentage acceptance by all the creditors to the proposed arrangement. Where a private limited company is involved, the usual arrangement offered involves an estimated minimum repayment of the outstanding debts of so many pence in the pound sterling on a graduated settlement basis over a set period of time as the assets of the business are realised. There may also be an immediate up-front payment. If an arrangement cannot be reached, then an application for a compulsory winding up is to be expected (see also Chapter Nine).

Non-corporate traders that cannot pay their debts as they fall due have the spectre of bankruptcy to face. There is still the choice of attempting a voluntary arrangement with the major creditors of the business and, with their prior agreement, satisfying all the smaller creditors. It will only require one creditor to refuse to accept the proposed arrangement and press legally for settlement for the whole deal to fail.

The key is to show that if the business is allowed to continue to trade, the creditors will receive a greater sum in settlement of their debts through accepting a deferred repayment period than if the business were closed down immediately. In all cases, professional assistance is recommended at the earliest stage.

This chapter is concerned with a business, corporate or otherwise, that is having or is expecting financial difficulties shortly but believes that a recovery in fortunes is possible. A list of the actions required by the management is set out:

1. accept at the earliest juncture that there is a financial problem to face;
2. build up a balance sheet of assets and liabilities from the accounting records as at the present day. A reasonably accurate stock take will be required;
3. incorporate any expected changes not shown by the balance sheet. These may be deferred expenses, contingent liabilities, capital commitments that cannot be cancelled or will otherwise incur penalties, a taxation assessment on the current year trading to date, forthcoming professional help fees and deferred debts now likely to become due;
4. appraise the trade debtors outstanding for possible defaulters should the news of financial difficulty escape to the business customers;
5. make a calculation for a possible diminution in the value of assets owned in the event of a business closure. Reduced values will probably have to be put on the fixed assets and stock-in-trade in the event of a forced sale.

Steps 2 through to 4 will show the latest estimated current book worth of the business. Step 5 will indicate how the net worth will change in the event of forcing a closure.

Actions (£'000)	Step 1 historic	Step 2 current	Step 3 adjusted	Step 4 bad debts	Step 5 closure
Assets: (abbreviated)					
Plant and machinery	45,000	45,000	55,000	55,000	40,000
Office equipment	5,000	5,000	5,000	5,000	1,000
Stocks: materials	10,000	15,000	20,000	20,000	15,000
Finished goods	2,000	2,000	2,000	2,000	1,000
Trade debtors	18,000	23,000	23,000	20,000	15,000
TOTAL	**80,000**	**90,000**	**105,000**	**102,000**	**72,000**

Actions (£'000)	Step 1 historic	Step 2 current	Step 3 adjusted	Step 4 bad debts	Step 5 closure
LIABILITIES:					
Trade creditors	29,000	43,000	48,000	48,000	48,000
Other creditors	6,000	7,000	19,000	19,000	19,000
Bank overdraft	25,000	30,000	20,000	20,000	20,000
Capital introduced	0	0	10,000	10,000	10,000
TOTAL	**60,000**	**80,000**	**97,000**	**97,000**	**97,000**
NET WORTH	**20,000**	**10,000**	**8,000**	**5,000**	**- 25,000**

5.1.2   Notes to the various steps

Step 1

The figures shown have been taken from the most recent prepared accounts. The problem is that creditors are pressing for payment and the overdraft is at its limit. Sales (not shown) are dropping and trading is believed to be unprofitable.

Step 2

Present day figures are taken from the trial balance that has been compiled. The balance sheet shows that net worth has halved.

Step 3

New machinery costing £10m has been ordered (increasing other creditors by the same amount). Additional raw materials costing £5m have been ordered and are in transit (increasing trade creditors by the same amount). Other creditors have allowed for £2m fees for forthcoming professional help. The shareholders have introduced additional capital of £10m to reduce the overdraft at the request of the bank.

Step 4

The proprietor believes that trade debts of £3m will be difficult to recover if news gets out that the business is asking for financial relief.

Step 5

A realistic valuation of the assets is shown on a forced sale.

The next task should be to evaluate the possibility of adopting a recovery programme. The management plans the following to put before the bank.

Step 6

Take the cash (or overdraft) in hand figure from the compiled balance sheet and set out, for each succeeding week, the expected income and expenditure. At the bottom of the sheet, show a cumulative cash total.

Step 7

Compare the cumulative (cash deficit) figure with any new cash resources that are available to be injected into the business, either from personal funds or possible additional borrowings. The latter figure has to be realistic.

Step 8

Examine all expense items for pruning costs. Notate in the margin why and how this was calculated; at a later stage, these reductions may have to be substantiated.

Step 9(a)

Examine the order book and the sales ledger by customer for any possible increased business based on current experience and selling prices.

Step 9(b)

Alongside these potential sales make another entry with the assumption of selling to customers at a reduced or discounted price.

Step 10

Re-run the projected weekly cash flow after allowing for the changes given by step 7 through to step 9a and again for step 7 to step 9b.

Inspection of the result of step 9a will indicate whether the cash flow trend is more or less positive and step 9b will show whether it is viable to adopt the strategy of lowering prices to generate additional sales.

The next table summarises the recovery programme assessment:

Assessment (£'000)	Week 1	Week 2	Week 3	Week 4	Week 5	Week 6	Etc
Step 6:							
Overdraft b/fwd	- 20,000	- 21,000	- 21,000	- 22,000	- 20,000	- 22,000	
Expected income	15,000	17,000	16,000	18,000	19,000	18,000	
Expected costs	- 16,000	- 17,000	- 17,000	- 16,000	- 21,000	- 19,000	
Cash forecast c/f	**- 21,000**	**- 21,000**	**- 22,000**	**- 20,000**	**- 22,000**	**- 23,000**	
Step 7:							
New resources	0	0	0	0	0	0	
Step 8:							
Costs reductions	1,000	0	0	0	0	0	
Step 9:							
(a) More sales	0	0	1,000	0	1,000	0	
(b) Discounting	0	0	-100	0	-100	0	
Step 10:							
Step 6 Overdraft b/f	- 20,000	- 20,000	- 20,000	- 20,100	- 18,100	- 19,200	
Step 6 net income	- 1,000	0	- 1,000	2,000	- 2,000	- 1,000	
Steps 7 to 9 adjustments	1,000	0	900	0	900	0	
Cash forecast	**- 20,000**	**- 20,000**	**- 20,100**	**- 18,100**	**- 19,200**	**- 20,200**	

5.1.3 Notes to the various Steps:

Step 6

The expected income and costs have been shown in the table as totals only. In practice, each total will comprise a number of different items.

Step 7

The shareholders have no new cash resources to inject into the business.

Step 8

An immediate cost reduction of £1m is believed to be possible, thereby enabling the business to remain within its overdraft limit.

Step 9

Additional sales are forecast at the expense of allowing a 10% discount.

Step 10

The revised cash flow indicates (for this example) that the business is not expected to recover in the next six weeks from its immediate financial problem.

At this point, a judgement should be made as to the depth of the problem. Is a business recovery feasible? It must not be assumed that the problem will go away of its own accord just because trading has had a 'bit of bad luck' and it is felt that the corner has been turned. Neither must the result of the assessment be so dismal that the decision is to 'close the eyes to what is happening and walk away'.

Action must be initiated and a decision made to:

- ask for professional help to confirm the findings (is there time?);
- try and raise additional temporary finance from known sources;
- pursue the internal measures proposed to reduce costs, etc;
- understand the cause(s) of the business failing;
- consider negotiating a voluntary arrangement with major creditors;
- review the longer-term trading and financing strategy (ie make a revised business plan);
- put in place new monitoring and management practices.

5.1.4 Professional help

A legal or accountancy insolvency practitioner must be called in straight away if the trading position is deemed hopeless for a recovery. Otherwise, the business's external accountant can be asked to check the calculations, assumptions and forecasts made to lend weight to any application for additional commercial funding or other form of raising finance. If the projected weekly cash flow (step 10 above) indicates that the cost savings and income producing measures proposed will lead to a recovery, even if additional funding is still required, then the steps outlined will have already given a base for a revised business plan to put to advisers and the bank as a potential additional funder.

Perhaps the saddest case met in practice was an agricultural wholesaler whose directors raised a workable business recovery plan to exit from some services and products, close some depots and make some staff redundant so that the resulting reduced operating costs could be met by a lower turnover of the remaining business interests. Unfortunately, the cost of the redundancy payments proved too sizeable to meet unless the company's bank provided more funds. The directors could not prove within the time at their disposal that their measures would succeed and the bank was asked to review its decision not to increase the overdraft. That decision took too long to resolve and a major preferential creditor forced the company into liquidation before the (viable) recovery plan could be implemented.

5.1.5   Raising temporary finance

As speed will be paramount to achieve a successful financial recovery, the business's existing bank(s) must be informed at an early stage what actions are proposed. Depending on the severity of the problem(s) the bank may already have deduced that there are difficulties for the business to keep to its agreed overdraft limit as seen by the day-to-day operation of the business account(s). There may be abundant goodwill built up over the years between bank and client for the bank to endeavour to assist the client as much as possible over a temporary business downturn.

The bank will be pleased to see the extent of what has already been done by the management to rectify the trading situation, together with firm ideas of what further moves it would like to implement. This will be even better received if there is an element of own additional funding (say, from personal resources of the shareholders) in the rescue package. Raising money by re-mortgaging the current value of the equity in the residential home is a typical solution for the family business because it shows a personal commitment to succeed by the owner/proprietor.

5.1.6   Pursuing cost savings/income producing measures

Each business will have its own characteristics and opportunities to reduce operating costs and to generate additional sales. The management may wish to review this list of actions with its advisers to see if further measures should be considered. Priorities will then have to be set as to which actions are best pursued. Generally speaking, internal measures are better to adopt than ones that affect external customers and a few significant measures are easier to action than many smaller changes. A contingency plan should also be adopted in the event that the cost savings and income producing measures are more successful than envisaged. In this case, it will indicate what cost limitations are to be shelved or stopped.

There is also a question of scale: by concentrating on fewer product lines the business may better be able to control stock levels and profit margins and staffing. This has been evident in department store retailing. The charging of peripheral services such as 'postage and packing', 'carriage outwards' and 'repair insurance' on catalogue retailing can greatly increase profit margins. These charges may be more easily acceptable to the public than an increase to the basic selling price of the product. Frequently, a loss on manufacturing or distributing a product has been converted into a profit through the simple expedient of banning overtime or changing outdated labour practices.

A business rescue is more likely to be based on reducing the expenditure for a known level of turnover rather than trying to increase turnover to improve income. This is because a higher turnover cannot be assumed to succeed in advance, whereas reducing internal costs are more easily controlled. An assumed higher turnover may not be possible where the cause of the business failure lies in lost sales that cannot be easily replaced. A higher turnover will also raise the direct cost of manufacture tied to the level of sales, as well as causing some increase in indirect selling costs.

5.1.7 The reasons why a business has to be rescued

Chapter Four has discussed the reasons why businesses fail. The reasons why a business is in the predicament of needing a rescue to survive is a somewhat wider question and may not at first become apparent. Two common failings are when a business concentrates on serving one large customer to the detriment of others or when it is not realised that the nature of the business requires a growing need for additional capital.

An example of the former was a business selling a single basic product to the building trades and to individual house owners. There was one large repeat customer and many single sale individuals. Sales to the former were easily won as the product was in demand. The customer was a very prompt payer. Sales to the latter by comparison were showing only a modest annual rise and had long credit periods to contend with. The gross profit margins on sales to the repeat customer were squeezed down to half that achieved on sales to individuals. Turnover overall was increasing substantially, but profit and cash flow were not. The management discovered just in time that concentrating too much on selling at a low margin to the repeat customer and not enough at the higher margin to individuals was reducing profits and cash flow to the extent that the business had nearly foundered for lack of capital.

An example of the latter was a business in the vehicle hire trade. Turnover was increasing and the immediate strategy was to build up the fleet of vehicles to meet hire demand. It was then found that cash was haemorrhaging severely. The fleet was cut back and the capital profit made on the subsequent sale of these vehicles hid until later the fact that turnover would be more difficult to maintain unless the retained vehicles were hired more frequently. There was also the situation of purchasing the vehicles on hire purchase, so that the business would never achieve the position of having usable vehicles already paid for to earn hire charges that would then be mostly bottom line profit. The fleet needed to be cut back to a level that cash resources could cover expenditure.

5.1.8 Negotiating a voluntary arrangement with creditors

Just one creditor can cause difficulties to a business by lodging a small debt claim at the local court, causing damage to the business's creditworthiness and raising public awareness of the financial predicament that its debts cannot be settled in due time. Some creditors, such as the Inland Revenue and Customs and Excise, are in future to relinquish their preferential rights of payment. Staff wages outstanding will still have preferential rights according to current law. Creditors holding good title to individual assets as security, such as a bank, will have to act as soon as possible to safeguard their preferential interests, particularly if only a floating charge is held over assets of the company. This aspect is commented on in Chapter Nine.

Trade suppliers owed relatively large sums will be looking to see that they get paid and the debt reduced as quickly as possible. Some would prefer not to lose a good customer if the adverse trading circumstances delaying settlement could prove to be temporary. There will be a greater chance of coming to a mutual agreement if a possible working proposition that the current cash flow of the business can accommodate has been thought out beforehand. This proposition may incorporate repaying part of the debt over a period of time, perhaps with interest added for the privilege and settling future invoices within shorter credit periods and/or paying cash for future goods deliveries. Some creditors will accept security, informal or otherwise, should it be available as an inducement to agree to payment on deferred terms. The security should be readily realisable.

By way of examples, creditors may agree to write off their debts in return for an interest in the business that may take the form of ordinary (equity) shares, preference shares or a loan (debenture) with a stated repayment date(s). Depending on the type of business undertaken, the creditor supplier or bank may accept repayment from the proceeds of sale after the company has sold its stock of finished products. The problem associated with this situation is whether the supplier or lender can be assured that the sale proceeds will be paid over on receipt and not be spirited away elsewhere to satisfy other creditors. As with any negotiations, the greatest care should be taken not to exacerbate the existing situation of the business before it is too late for the business to recover while trying to negotiate a solution.

5.1.9 Review of the long-term strategy

The management should not consider just immediate measures for implementation to ensure that the business trades out of its difficulties. It should be demonstrated at the same time that a long-term strategy is being put in place to ensure that the financial difficulties, whatever they are, do not recur and that the management is capable of resolving all the adverse issues. In particular, some remedial actions will take time before they are fully achieved, through cost savings or the receipt of additional income.

The long-term strategy should set out the financial return that is expected from the immediate, emergency actions, as well as a forecast of the profit to arise from more substantive changes. In the latter case, working assumptions will have to be laid down and the management should be prepared to argue that they are reasonable and attainable. Some examples of substantive, long-term changes in strategy would be:

- concentrating on selling more ancillary or new product lines;
- changing marketing policy and selling procedures;
- outsourcing component manufacture and closing one's own plant;
- changing labour pay from hourly rates to piecework;
- becoming a processor and distributor rather than a manufacturer;
- accepting longer-term contracts with regular progress payments;
- reviewing existing finance arrangements to gain more beneficial terms;
- entering a manufacturing/marketing joint venture with a known trading partner.

An example of a business requiring a strategic rescue relates to a quoted supermarket chain. The company had been very profitable and had increased turnover for many years. The decision was made to expand nationally through acquiring an existing, larger chain that had lost market share and was suffering from a competitive squeeze on sales margins. After the takeover, the administration and management system of the buyer was adopted for all the store outlets and a number of key managerial posts were declared redundant.

The acquired business continued to suffer from competition, lose turnover and did not benefit from adopting the identity of its new parent company. The costs of integration continued to mount. Profit margins on many selling lines were cut to try and regain sales. Cash flow of the whole group was greatly reduced. A larger number of store outlets than was originally envisaged at the time of the acquisition were sold to generate cash. In its efforts to expand the company had strategically over-stretched itself, lost its proven trading model and required a significant financial retrenchment from a lower base, together with revised management implementation, to return to its former profitability and growth tack.

5.1.10 Monitoring and good management practice

Once the immediate 'rescue' moves for the business have been implemented and a long-term trading strategy is in place, the management must ensure that adequate and regular monitoring procedures are adopted. The procedures will be particular to each type of business, but will have a common thread comprising a mixture of adequate bookkeeping and returns compiled for the management on a daily, weekly and monthly rota:

Frequency	Task	Reason
Daily	Handling/recording cash/cheques	Security
		Improve cash flow
	Sales orders/near orders	Marketing response
		Plan future production
	Purchases requisitions	Production efficiency
		Minimise stock levels
	Deliveries	Invoicing purposes
		Customer satisfaction
	Returns and queries	Quality control
		Customer satisfaction
Weekly	Debtor collection	Cash flow benefit
	Bills for settlement	Cash flow planning
	Cash flow forecasting	Working capital needs
Monthly	Production and sales achievements	Plan operating strategy
	Trial balance	How the business is operating
	Profit return	Compare with budget

To summarise, good management will incorporate a review of operating areas apart from just the accounting and financial aspects of the business of budgets, forecasts, profit margins and cash flow, including:

◆ employee manning, responsibilities, performance, contracts and pay;
◆ production systems, capacity, machinery efficiency and supply buying;
◆ selling procedures, customer base, marketing strategy and debtors;
◆ product or service quality;
◆ quality controls, health and safety, environmental and other regulations;
◆ management responsibilities, reporting and personnel relations;
◆ external influences such as competition, market trends and future costs;
◆ relationship with creditors and banks, level of stock and controls.

Much of the management questioning and the bank interest will be fundamental and include the following.

◆ Why continue with customers that are bad or poor payers?

◆ Are poor payers charged more for the extra credit period incurred?
◆ Is there a concentration on low profit margin product lines?
◆ Are product pack sizes standardised to market and display better?
◆ Are display products rotated regularly to generate public interest?
◆ Is there a system to receive workers' ideas to increase efficiency?
◆ Does the management know what it costs to produce/sell each product?
◆ At what stage will the equipment/vehicles be uneconomic to run?
◆ Is a new machine needed if it will be idle for much of the time?
◆ Can processes be mechanised to save labour manning and costs?
◆ Why is overtime allowed if it is expensive and not recovered on sales?
◆ Has the potential demand for a new product been fully assessed?
◆ How much business capital is tied up in non-core activities?
◆ Have costs/benefits of leasing or buying assets been fully explored?
◆ Would it be advantageous to factor/invoice discount the sales ledger?

The working brief for the management will be to consider one or more of the following actions. Which options will be appropriate will depend on the present health of the business; if it is a 'rescue' that is required by a creditor, then it is unlikely to incorporate at this stage any new investment or funding plans or a review of management practices. Conversely, a 'recovery' turnround by the management to improve profitability or lay down future plans for growth when the business is only suffering operational stagnation rather than a liquidity crisis will emphasise different alternatives to accept. The usual options will be to:

◆ stem losses;
◆ raise profitability;
◆ reduce operating costs;
◆ increase business turnover;
◆ use only the present resources of the business;
◆ consider re-capitalising the business;
◆ negotiate additional borrowings;
◆ propose a new investment programme;
◆ review present management operating practices;
◆ realise non-core assets;
◆ prepare a new business plan.

5.2 Financing growth

It would be unwise to promote an employee into a position of greater responsibility if the person were not capable of making a success of the tasks that went with the new appointment. Likewise, a business should not attempt to attain objectives that are beyond its capabilities. Perhaps the most common failure for a business is to try and expand its operations without having the right form or size of resources to back up the intent.

The resources of the business in this context will be a mixture of:

- fixed assets   tangible buildings, plant, equipment and motor vehicles;
- living assets   the management and staff employed;
- disposable assets   stocks, debtors less creditors and cash held;
- intangible assets   goodwill, brand name and reputation of the business;
- convertible assets   the capital and creditworthiness of the business;
- asset earning power   that is self or independently generated.

Each of these assets should play their part in promoting future growth. Unfortunately, a financial balance sheet only shows part of the business resources, and these are on an historic value basis. This shortfall becomes more noticeable when the business reaches a time of change. For example, if the major shareholder is considering a sale, what is the real worth of the business? It will then be too late to 'groom' the business balance sheet to obtain the best price.

When planning for growth, two basic scenarios should be examined: whether the business strategy is to expand its capital value (ie the net worth of the business to the owner/s) or its earnings. The latter is accomplished through retaining profits and thereby enhance the former. Equally, the former can be used as a springboard to expand earnings by gearing up investment (through borrowing) or saving resources until it is judged they can be spent on acquiring new business interests. The difference is essentially a matter of timing; growing earnings are received immediately and, if not distributed, will add to the capital value of the business and be available to be spent at some future time.

5.2.1   The characteristics of growth

If a business is pursuing in the main an earnings or capital value growth strategy, it should have regard to the following options that are shown in the table. Some of these points are discussed in greater detail thereafter.

Resources	Earnings	Capital value
Fixed assets	Rent/lease	Ownership
Living assets	Sub-contract labour	Retain core staff long term
Disposable assets	Minimise stocks	Positive net current assets
	Minimise debtors	
	Maximise creditors	
Intangible assets	Less important	More important
Convertible assets	Minimum necessary	Retain critical mass
	Consider gearing up	Important to enhance

Resources	Earnings	Capital value
Asset earning power	Profit margin	Reputation
	Competitiveness	Long-term market outlook
	Demand	Fixed rate long-term loans

5.2.2 Fixed assets

The business property may be leased or owned. High-growth businesses that may rapidly outstrip their initial floor area needs are best advised to rent in the short term so that future expansion can be easily accommodated. The preferences of staff should be noted, as a change of address may lead to resignations due to the travel time to work and cost of transport. The best location of a retail outlet is vital to success if this depends on easy car parking access, a regular passing trade and minimal competition. If the business is high-tech, it may be more appropriate to lease equipment if it is likely to get rapidly out of date. Regular office tasks such as road fleet management can be delegated to specialised rental organisations to save costs.

5.2.3 Living assets

Employing staff is becoming increasingly expensive, so the greater the opportunity for the business to contract out jobs or to pay for piece work, the less likelihood there will be of having to pay staff in unproductive periods. For continuity in the long term, however, some key personnel should be retained either in a supervisory/ training role or to act as trouble -shooters to ensure that quality control and delivery deadlines are met.

5.2.4 Disposable assets

Major (valuable) stock items should be controlled at all times in respect of ordering, delivery, safe custody and issue out of stores. Minimum quantities of raw materials stocks based on future production needs should be approved. If expensive items have to be bought for resale, it should be laid down in advance how much can be purchased monthly. More credit should try to be obtained from business suppliers than is allowed to customers so as to maximise earnings growth.

5.2.5 Intangible assets

Business reputation is probably more important for a business than being long established and identified with a particular sales brand. This is certainly true for service businesses where the customer objective is to get a reputable firm to do the job acceptably. Retail selling is likely to depend more on accessibility, price and choice: if brand X is not in stock, then a substitute may suffice.

5.2.6 Convertible assets

By this term is meant the ease and extent that the business can convert its credit rating into raising finance for investment or working capital or convert its net worth into liquid funds for reinvestment elsewhere in the business. The credit rating will be determined by the track record of the business (as demonstrated by its financial results) and the quality of its management. The second definition may be given by a notional example.

Freehold assets			£200,000
Other fixed assets at written down value			£80,000
			£280,000
Current assets: debtors		£10,000	
Less Creditors	£30,000		
Bank overdraft	£100,000	£130,000	(£120,000)
Total net assets			£160,000
Long-term borrowing			£30,000
Shareholders' capital			£130,000
			£160,000

The net worth of the business is the shareholders' capital of £130,000. The business would like to purchase a new machine for £40,000. Where will the money come from? Debtors are insufficient to factor. The existing borrowings are high relative to the net worth of the business (the gearing is 100%). Note that some banks will look at the gearing and ignore a relatively high ratio if the risk of lending is acceptable in all other respects, particularly where future trading is forecast to provide earnings that can rapidly reduce the debt level. Hire purchase may be a possible finance option. The fixed assets mostly consist of freehold premises that, for this example, are not suitable for a sale and lease back. If earnings (not shown) are poor, the business has a problem without more equity capital being invested. Its convertibility factor is low.

5.2.7 Asset earning power

To maximise earnings sales demand for the business's products and the resulting profitability must be high and competition must not be critical to affect these factors. The interaction of these influences will be self-generated: sales demand may be beneficially affected by a good marketing scheme and it may be possible to pitch profit margin(s) to what the market can afford. Taking a longer-term view will suggest different alternatives dependent on external influences: the overall market may be entering a period of recession; the business may wish to operate on a non-growth tack until the market improves, meanwhile, its reputation and standing should be nurtured for the future. If finance is being considered, a standby borrowing facility may be arranged as a precautionary measure and converting an existing loan into a fixed interest rate (if appropriate) to stabilise the annual borrowing cost may be prudent.

5.2.8   The gearing (leverage) factor

To attain increased earnings quickly, excess capital should not be locked away in long-term assets not directly related to trading, but invested in more labour, machinery and stocks to enable, in due course, more production to be sold. This may demand additional funds to be invested through gearing up the profit return by borrowing, as shown by the table below. The situation where a company diversifies its trading interests would be an exception, but the assumption would have to be made that the diversification added greater earnings on capital employed than the original trading assets.

(£'000)	**Without gearing**	**With gearing**
Capital employed	100	100
Borrowing	0	40
Overall capital employed	100	140
Return on capital employed	20%	20%*
Net profit	20	28
Less borrowing cost, say, 5%	0	2
Revised net profit	20	26
Net profit margin achieved on sales	6%	6%
Sales implied	333	433
Sales and profit growth		+ 30%

* *Note*: the critical assumption is that an identical profit return can be achieved on the increase in sales.

Some types of business are more favourably placed to achieve earnings growth than others. The table below offers some common characteristics of earnings intensive and capital intensive businesses:

Business situation	Use of earnings growth to	Use of capital value growth to
Mature sector	Retain current earning power	Retain for future use
	Improve distributed rewards	Consider new investment
	Consider product diversification	Prepare for a future sale
Developing	Reinvest to expand	Obtain critical mass
	Develop the markets	Achieve good asset base
Cash generator	Offer competitive margins	Possible diversification
	Accelerate the number of sales outlets	Consider other investment
Labour intensive	Consider more mechanisation	Build an optimum team
Plant intensive	Minimise labour costs	Plan a replacement programme

Most small and medium-sized businesses opt for **earnings** growth. This is understandable when profits today may change into losses tomorrow. The shareholders will look to the whole of their annual profits as just reward for their capital investment over the past year, with minimal retention of profits in the business. If the business runs short of funds, the shareholders may have to invest new capital or the management may have to borrow commercial funds. The potential catch is that if the capital value of the business is not retained at a reasonable level, the latter option may not be possible and if the shareholders do not or cannot invest additional money, the business could have a problem to expand.

It is interesting to compare the change in financial outlook over the years: businesses previously had relied on raising long-term capital through 'rights issues' asking shareholders to purchase more shares in the business with the encouragement of pricing the new shares at a discount to their pre-rights listed market price. Nowadays, companies are very willing to release surplus capital by initiating share 'buy back' programmes for cash and to finance acquisitions through an offer of shares and/or cash.

The reasons for this change are to reduce the future cost of dividends, improve the earnings return on shares remaining in issue, take advantage of the present relatively low cost of raising commercial debt should the situation arise, and release surplus capital that otherwise would only go on short-term deposit. There is greater awareness now that companies have to improve their earnings return on the capital invested in the company.

Non-corporate businesses are taxed on their full annual profits and if they withdraw their business earnings to invest elsewhere, it will be to spread the risk of loss or to gain a better return net of tax. Company earnings are taxed at the profit stage and again when distributions (dividends) are declared, although the latter is offset when the recipient is taxed later on the dividend income received each year. The executive shareholders alternatively may award directors fees instead of dividends and be taxed accordingly.

An accurate comparison of returns net of tax, therefore, is fraught with many variables, including the applicable current rates of interest and the personal tax rates that apply to particular investors, to consider before an equivocal answer can be relied on. If the business places surplus cash (ie earnings) on deposit with its bank, it does not necessarily follow that a more rewarding alternative would be to use the cash in the business as working capital. The table that follows broadly shows the effect of these options:

Businesses	Corporate	Non-corporate
Assumptions:		
Pre-tax profit return on capital	10%	10%
Tax rate	30%	22%
Deposit rate (gross)	5%	5%
Deposit return net of personal tax	3.90%	3.90%
Capital employed	800	800
Borrowings	200	200
Borrowing cost	8%	10%
Earnings for retention	20	20

Comparison A: Surplus placed on deposit

Businesses	Corporate	Non-corporate
Profit before interest and tax	80.0	80.0
Borrowing interest cost	16.0	20.0
Pre-tax profit after interest	64.0	60.0
Taxation (at rates assumed)	19.2	13.2
Earnings after tax	44.8	46.8
Earnings retained in the business	20.0	20.0
Earnings withdrawn placed on deposit	24.8	26.8

Businesses	Corporate	Non-corporate
Interest 3.9% net earned on deposit	0.97	1.05
After tax profit on earnings retained	1.40	1.56
Total income est'd for next year	2.37	2.61
Investment in business next year	820	820
Return on investment net of tax	2.89%	3.18%

Comparison B: Surplus used to part-repay borrowing

Businesses	Corporate	Non-corporate
Assumed borrowings are repaid instead	20.0	20.0
Borrowing cost reduced by	1.6	2.0
Profit before interest and tax	80.0	80.0
Borrowing interest cost	14.4	18.0
Pre-tax profit after interest	65.6	62.0
Taxation (at rates assumed)	19.7	13.6
Earnings after tax	45.9	48.4
Earnings retained in the business	20.0	20.0
Earnings withdrawn placed on deposit	25.9	28.4
Earnings used to part-repay borrowing	20.0	20.0
Earnings withdrawn placed on deposit	5.9	8.4
Interest 3.9% net earned on deposit	0.23	0.33
After tax profit on earnings retained	1.40	1.56
Total income est'd for next year	1.63	1.89
Investment in business next year	820	820
Return on investment net of tax	1.34%	2.30%

Where a business is under-capitalised and has difficulty in not remaining so, it should adopt the strategy of minimising the distribution of its annual earnings and instead try to build up the **capital value** of the business to obtain what might be described as 'critical mass'. A banker would define this as trading with sufficient capital permanently invested in the business to support its current and future trading aspirations and service any commercial borrowings. Where commercial borrowings exceed its capital investment, the financial question may be put: for whom is the business trading? The bank will be taking the greater (equity) risk of supporting the business for the reward of its lending margin. In the short term, until the business re-capitalises itself, this may be an acceptable banking choice providing the trading problem and the borrowing are both temporary and the bank has good collateral to fall back on for repayment.

5.2.9   Planning for growth – a check list

◆ To enable a business to grow there must be a suitable infrastructure (ie capital base) on which to build a larger unit.
◆ Expansion will require investment in advance before the reward from that investment through sales receipts will be received.
◆ The cost of investment tends to increase in steps: as full capacity is reached from one step, so investment for the next step arises.
◆ If the immediate planned growth is not likely to be as profitable as present trading, reconsider why the expansion should be attempted.
◆ Review the growth prospects held by the type(s) of product/services the business is wishing to invest in before making a decision.
◆ Is expansion to be in a niche market expected to suffer less from changes in demand?
◆ Does the product(s) have a relatively short 'fashionable' life?
◆ Is it a mature product having to be replaced in the near future?
◆ Could the product be classified as a high-tech item where competition, new developments and consumer acceptance are significant factors?
◆ Will the new product be marketed in the vanguard of demand?
◆ Does the product have a ready-made market?
◆ Can the product compete on price/quality/quick service/availability?
◆ Will the (new) product be adaptable to react to changes in demand?
◆ Have the risks and rewards of investment been calculated?
◆ Have any limiting factors to the expansion planned been recognised?
◆ Have the special capital or labour intensive characteristics been noted?
◆ Has the project been planned objectively to offer growth, proved financially viable and vindicated on a projected cash flow basis?

Six

Risk management at portfolio level

Risk management in a bank can take a variety of forms: there will be the legal and regulatory steps to fulfil correctly, the internal operating procedures to maintain satisfactorily when dealing with money, the conditions laid down that must be upheld when promoting specific customer services and products, the steps required to safeguard the assets of the business, and the regular review of, and improvement to, procedures necessary to ensure that the business is best managed through changing circumstances.

This leaves the management of specific financial risks associated with market movements, both in a micro and macro sense, and risks relating to the future performance of counter parties, the balancing of liabilities with assets, the use of certain financial instruments to perform required tasks and the transference of risk to other parties. Each of these points is discussed in the following paragraphs. In summary, one is considering the management of risk through the adoption of a financial strategy laid down as part of the basic operating structure of the business.

An offshoot of risk management will be how the financial institution expects to develop its business: whether this will be through organic growth, by acquisition, an expansion in other geographic or product areas or a mixture of these options. In most cases, these options will lead to different risk strategies to assess and adopt. This section discusses the types of financial strategy to be raised and how they are carried and developed in the lending portfolio of the institution.

Finally, lending to specific sectors of industry is analysed.

6.1   The types of portfolio risk

6.1.1   Market movements

A bank (or financial institution) offering a variable interest rate facility, be it an overdraft or a term loan, where the interest is calculated on a daily balance, will have the greatest flexibility in raising the funds necessary to lend to the customer. The funds may be bid for in the inter-bank money market on a matching basis or may be provided out of existing cash resources held by the lender. As future market movements in interest rates occur, a similar movement will arise for the borrower and the lender's gross lending margin will remain the same. In this case, the bank will have no need to modify the transaction internally for risk purposes regardless of the reason for the change in the interest rate.

Compare this position with the situation where there is a perception that market interest rates will change in future. In this case, the interest rate has not changed yet, but the bank may wish to 'take a view' of what might happen shortly. This can be done through the bank accepting a term deposit at a fixed interest rate to 're-finance' the loan if the perception is that interest rates in general will be increased. The bank's original variable interest rate deposit may be 'swapped' (see Chapter Eleven) in the inter-bank market for a like amount of fixed interest money so that the interest rate risk is eliminated or the bank may decide to run with the mis-match and so gain a higher lending gross margin.

In practice, unless the particular deal is large, the mis-match will not be tied to any particular loan, but will be part of the internal dealing strategy of the bank. Each bank will be allowed to deal with a certain sum set internally on its own trading account in an endeavour to maximise the return from this part of its overall lending portfolio. The Bank of England regularly reviews, monitors and can control the maximum exposure of all banks on their own account dealing.

6.1.2   Counterparty risks

Each bank will maintain and update daily the risk attached to lending to other bank and non-bank institutions and where the risk relating to a particular lending transaction has been transferred to another party, unless the transfer has been on a non-recourse principle. An example of the latter deal would be in the derivative 'swaps' market, where a variable interest rate might have been exchanged for a fixed interest rate by the bank. A default by the counterparty taking the variable rate and offering the fixed rate will constitute a potential loss for the lending bank if the cost of replacing (or abandoning) the deal exceeds any profit made.

6.1.3   The balancing of liabilities and assets

In an absolutely no-risk financial environment the value of each group of assets will be matched by groups of liabilities holding similar characteristics. This would mean that shareholders' permanent capital would be matched by the value of assets required to operate the business, the life of long-term assets would be matched by the maturities of long term debt (borrowings) and so forth.

This is not wholly possible in a practical world since the life of some assets cannot always be ascertained with accuracy and there is a limit to how much the market or counterparties will undertake to offset very long term commitments. For instance, a bank may wish to raise 30-year debt in the market and use these borrowed funds to offset some 30-year loans on its books. The market may not wish to accept the bank's 30-year paper to match the deal or make the deal profitable to be worth pursuing.

6.1.4   The use of financial instruments

The financial risk to a transaction can be 'hedged' (see Chapter Eleven), ie the risk of loss can be reduced or eliminated by entering into compensating transactions. It may not always be possible, however, for a bank to match assets and liabilities with identical maturities. An interest rate, for example, may wish to be 'capped', ie have a maximum limit set for a long period, at a time when the financial market would only deal in that cap for a much shorter period. Ignoring cost considerations, successive capped deals may be entered into, one after the other, for the length of the period in question, but the cost of the future caps would not be known in advance and could turn out to be uneconomic for the desired transaction. In this case, the bank may decide to run the risk in its own portfolio, notwithstanding the problem in having to value the market risk regularly.

A bank usually carries some mis-match of risk at any one time, especially if the economic view of the management supports the bank taking a 'short or long position' of interest or currency rates. This imbalance cannot be taken to excess and, for this reason, the Bank of England also regularly monitors each bank's exposure, together with a joint 'agreement' stating how much this exposure can amount to. In the past, there have been occasions when even this monitoring has not proved effective in curbing a bank's portfolio or dealing risk. An example of this was when a deal covered two different world time zones and there was a time gap in closing the exposure, as it happened, too late to prevent loss.

6.1.5   The transference of risk to other parties

A bank's lending portfolio may become over-endowed with one category of loans after an assessment of the future outlook for that business sector has been made.

The immediate and easier option is to cease to accept loans within that sector for a temporary period until the proportion of lending becomes a smaller part of the whole portfolio. A permanent and immediate remedy would be to 'securitise' (see Chapter Eleven) those loans in excess of deemed requirements and sell them en bloc to another lender.

The inherent risk in this mini-portfolio may also be sold or may remain to some degree with the selling bank, but the rights of ownership will be released to the buying bank. A further effect of the securitisation will be to reduce the value of the lending portfolio of the selling bank and free up its capital tier ratios to accept new business, probably in other business sectors. The sale may or may not be disclosed from the underlying borrowers, depending on the lending conditions previously agreed. This type of offsetting of risk has been more prevalent in the retail sector with mortgage portfolios since commercial borrowers may view a change of lender detrimental to their banking relationship.

6.1.6   Development of the business

Of all the changes that a bank is likely to put into effect with some frequency is the different strategic emphasis placed on the mix of business interests. Together, they amount to the individuality of each bank's operational portfolio of services. Here is a representative list of changes by UK banks over the past few years:

- ◆ significant minority holdings taken in indigenous banks overseas;
- ◆ acquisitions of financial institutions overseas, where allowed;
- ◆ accumulation of relatively small, niche, banking interests;
- ◆ purchase of specific interest lending portfolios;
- ◆ build up of fee income from investment services;
- ◆ acquisition of non-banking groups in ancillary fields;
- ◆ joint banking ventures with major non-banking retailers;
- ◆ outsourcing of certain internal administrative tasks;
- ◆ closure of uneconomic bank branches and reductions in staffing;
- ◆ executive recruitment with skills/contacts in investment banking;
- ◆ expansion of various services in the personal banking area;
- ◆ (de-/)centralisation of risk assessment and customer liaison.

The overall theme to these changes has been to improve profitability and increase the return on shareholders' funds, while providing a better base for improved trading results in the future. A number of banks, in attempting this, have not been successful in the short term due to poor judgement of timing with acquisitions, overpayment for new acquisitions, not making sufficient allowance for changes in external influences (eg a market recession) and over-emphasising certain lending sectors in their portfolio. It is the risks involved in this last area that are now considered.

6.2   Farming

Agricultural businesses will be dependent for profitability on crop yields, the vagaries of the weather affecting the growing seasons and market prices when selling the harvested produce. There is a constant seasonality to income and the financial resources of the farm will have to meet prior expenditure of tending the ground, planting, fertilising and harvesting before market income is received. Milk quota receipts offer a more regular income and, as such, are a valuable asset to hold, but sales are subject to market prices and the quota must be economically sufficiently large to earn a realistic return. Many grants/subsidies are available to augment farm productivity.

There are some 90,000 farmers trading in the UK, most of whom are what might be termed relatively small operating units, but farming activity, taken as a whole, comprises an important sector of the business community. It is guided by ongoing policies and directives agreed by the European Union (EU) for its member states and these are then put into effect by department(s) within the UK government after amalgamating them with their own supplementary legislative programmes covering the national interest of the time.

The farmer, therefore, and consequently the lending banker, has to be constantly pre-disposed to the market effect of regular intervention in the areas of crop and livestock pricing, the availability (or non-availability) of direct grant and subsidy support, the use to which farm land is put, safety regulations pertaining to the food chain, diversification of usage opportunities with farm assets and taxation.

For example, the Common Agricultural Policy of the EU was originally introduced to provide stable food markets through a universal pricing support mechanism adopted by member states, but this has now been largely reformed and is being phased out to reduce the growing food stockpiles created at artificially high prices that it has encouraged. The effects are likely to be more pronounced now that the most recent enlargement of the EU has been accomplished and brought in the largely agricultural-based economies of Eastern Europe.

The new subsidy regime set out by the EU members to operate from 2005 now devolves on providing cash support to farmers based on land area in use rather than through pricing subsidies. The 'Simplified Area Payments Scheme', as it is called, provides cash according to the land used as crops, grazing, pasture, orchards and even vineyards. There are enhanced schemes subsidising land cultivated under 'Environmental Stewardship' practices for the maintenance of wider field edges, hedges, woodlands and public access. The land must be in good order and there are many minimum standards to meet. A 'higher level' environmental scheme subsidy is available where land is not in use for farm production.

As has been mentioned, the different types of subsidy offered by the EU to governments has now been reduced to one, the Single Payment Scheme, although settlement of awards remains at twice per year, usually in January and April/May.

The subsidy approximates to about £50 pa per eligible acre and, for the UK, will be received in decreasing proportions over a ten-year period. How will this affect the lending risk of banks that financially support farming? Banks will, in future, have to put more emphasis on certain operating risks when assessing the overall creditworthiness of farms:

- ◆ future trends in crop, livestock, milk and cultivation selling prices;
- ◆ the valuations of stocks held at each accounting year end;
- ◆ the use to which farm land is put year by year;
- ◆ the eligibility for land subsidy support under new EU directives;
- ◆ the viability of farm operations proportionate to other activities.

To this list should be added the traditionally important aspects to consider when assessing farm lending:

- ◆ crop and livestock production seasons vis-a-vis accounts years;
- ◆ the seasonality of cash flow: the buying and cash receipt months;
- ◆ the extent to which the farm is asset rich, but cash poor;
- ◆ the regular monitoring needed to determine future profitability.

6.2.1   Production seasons and accounting years

Consider a farm that is growing mixed produce of arable cutting crops (such as wheat and barley), root crops (such as potatoes), horticultural crops (such as cabbages) and also includes an orchard of apples. Appendix 9 outlines the general programme of work to be expected throughout the farming year for arable harvesting and another for livestock. In each case, a two-year period is covered to indicate more appropriately how periods of production and non-production can overlap.

6.2.1.1   Arable farming

The activity of some of the principal farm operations by quarter years, subject always to weather conditions and the chosen mix of produce, may be summarised as follows:

Quarters ending:		31 Mar	30 June	30 Sept	31 Dec
Arable	**– Spring cereals**	being sown	growing	harvested	receipts
	– Winter cereals	growing	growing	harvested	receipts and sowing
	– Potatoes	receipts and sowing	growing	early harvest	late harvest
Cabbages		growing	harvested	receipts	sowing
Apples		receipts	growing	picking	receipts
Cultivation work		sowing	some sowing	harvest	harvest and sowing

Growing produce at the date of each farm's accounting year end would require a valuation of work in progress and direct costs spent to date (ie cultivation labour, seeds, etc), reduced if necessary to the lower value of cost price or the expected realisable value of the produce when sold. Harvested produce would be similarly valued. Some unrealised profit may be accounted for in the profit and loss account in advance of sale if the receipt is known with clarity and will shortly be invoiced.

The income from produce sold may be received either soon after harvest if marketed independently or when released from store if sold under contract for delivery over a time period of several months, as with the case of apples from cold store marketed through a co-operative venture under contract to supermarkets. A specified percentage of the contracted income expected from specific crops may be agreed between the farmer and the intermediary wholesaler and advanced early to the farmer. Temporary overdraft facilities may be agreed on a similar basis where the crop is to be marketed independent of a wholesaler.

It is important for the banker to realise that the farmer has three options to dispose of his crop. He may:

♦ keep the crop in store and sell at the rate offered by the buyer;
♦ sell the crop immediately once it is harvested at market price;
♦ sell the crop 'forward' for future delivery at the market rate.

By keeping the crop in store, he will incur storage costs and be subject to the buyer's rates when the buyer takes delivery. The settlement rate will be subject to rates available in the market at the time of delivery, but the buyer will fulfil the contract. Supermarkets do not usually guarantee a buying rate in advance. If the farmer sells his crop immediately for cash, the price received will be market driven. He may be missing a higher price by holding onto the crop for a period of his choosing or, conversely, the market rate may soften further.

Where the crop is sold forward, the farmer knows what price he will receive at the date the forward contract matures for delivery. There will be a cost involved in selling forward that will reduce the profit margin to be received and possibly there may not be a forward market available, particularly for odd tonnages and sub-quality crops. Few farmers are sophisticated financially to 'cover' their crop forward under an option contract that can be lapsed at maturity if the market rate exceeds the striking price of the forward contract or realised in the forward market if the market selling rate drops below the strike price.

A recent study by *Cass Business School* published in 2005 estimated that only 11% of producers use derivatives to manage risk.

6.2.1.2 Example of crop sale options

Sale value today	Forward sale strike price	Future market sale value	Decision on forward	Profit/loss *
100	105	110	lapsed	+ 10
100	105	95	taken up	+ 5

* Example excludes dealing costs.

The banker monitoring the account, and perhaps providing credit to the farmer based on the value of the crop(s) post-harvest until the sale proceeds are received, should have discussed with the farmer his marketing strategy in advance in order that a (credit) risk assessment can be built into the business forecast. This will mean the banker needs to have a good understanding of farming and is a reason why most banks have a specialised department dealing solely with advances to this sector.

Farmers have three variables to take into consideration when setting out their farm strategy from year to year for their arable interests. Best management of these variables will maximise the farm worker's activity throughout the year, fit the crops into the planned rotation programme and decide on the likely most profitable crops to grow. They are:

◆ the different growing and harvesting periods;
◆ the necessary rotation required between fields to ensure the best crop yield can be obtained;
◆ the expected trading outlook for different types of produce and therefore what crops can be grown in preferences to others.

6.2.1.3 Livestock farming

This is much easier to manage and account for since the dairy or fattening herd of beef or pigs or the sheep or poultry flock will remain as a fixed asset. In these cases, the farm will have different strategic questions to answer:

- how to ensure a constant production flow, be it milk or eggs;
- when to time the sale of animals in the open market;
- how best to correlate the land usage to achieve the highest income.

A regular production flow to meet contractual obligations will become less critical as the herd expands. Achieving the best time to sell animals requires a careful matching of weight with the cost of feed. The use of available land may be more difficult to change, depending on the geographic contours and quality of the soil. The banker should obtain a broad outline of how the farm is being managed in these respects.

There are two aspects of fiscal import that the banker should be aware: HM Customs and Excise offers an 'Agricultural Flat Rate VAT Scheme' alternative to normal VAT registration where the farm would otherwise lose input tax on purchases. When the farmer sells produce or services to VAT registered customers, a flat rate charge of 4% is added as compensation for the VAT incurred on the farm's purchases. There are conditions to meet, such as non-eligibility if the farmer's non-farming activities exceed the VAT registration threshold set in the Budget.

The second aspect is tax accounting for farm animals on a 'herd basis'. Generally, animals kept by a farmer for the purposes of farming are treated as trading stock. The farmer can elect instead to have the herd treated as a capital asset. The general rules are:

Accounted for in profit & loss account	**Not accounted for in profit & loss account**
Replacement stock	Initial purchase of the herd
Sale of stock	Additions to the herd
Replacement of whole herd:	
Stock sales and purchases	Additional stock if new herd is larger
Old stock if new herd is smaller	
	Non-replacement of whole herd:
	Herd sale if no replacement within 1yr

The effect on the profitability of the farm from the banker's point of view is that building up the herd through normal purchases and sales will be a trading cost deductible from profit earned at the time of the purchase, whereas, on the herd basis, the benefit arises when the whole herd is eventually sold and no tax liability occurs. There is also a more immediate impact on the cash flow of the farm where the herd is 'turned over' frequently and the herd basis is not chosen. The farm valuation will also be affected as the herd will be entered in the balance sheet either 'non-herd' under current assets or 'herd basis' under fixed assets.

6.2.2   Farm accounts

Apart from the statutory requirements to fulfil when the farm is a limited company, there is no set proforma to show the annual trading results of a farm. Broad outlines are adhered to, however, the most common of which is to set out the profit and loss of each crop/livestock showing receipts (sales, subsidies, etc) and direct expenditure (labour, sub-contracting, seeds, fertilisers and the difference in stocks between the beginning and the end of each accounting year). To obtain a figure for the overall turnover of the farm, therefore, receipts from each crop/livestock account will have to be added together. These separate activity accounts are then transferred to the profit and loss account from which is deducted the analysis of indirect costs, depreciation and non-farming income (rents received, wayleaves, etc), followed by taxation and the balance of profit or loss transferred to the capital account of the owners.

Of special importance to the bank will be the regular cash flow of the farm. This can be judged by examining the capital accounts of the owners for profit accrued less personal drawings. One final adjustment remains, to add depreciation to the earnings (as it is not an item of cash outlay) and any sum of cash introduced into the farm and to deduct the cost before depreciation of all capital expenditure. The resulting figure will show the cash input or output sustained by the farm over the year subject to any changes in accruals of debtors and creditors made when preparing the accounts. These items are usually relatively minor amounts.

Since farm cash flow has wide swings due to the seasonality of the crops, the lending bank should be careful to estimate at the outset the likely high point of drawings under the proposed facility and this usually occurs when money has to be spent on seed, fertilisers and cultivation costs before any crop receipts and subsidies are received. Apart from winter feed, livestock costs will not vary as much as to timing and the herd can be managed over a period so that receipts such as milk sales can occur throughout the year. The bank should be informed in advance what crops will be cultivated during the forthcoming year, on what acreage, and what crop yield and pricing the farmer expects to attain. This can be converted into a projection for cash flow and profitability purposes.

Many farms are 'asset rich, but cash poor' as a result of families handing down the fixed assets to younger generations while suffering farming losses due to low market prices and other problems such as disease quarantine and inclement weather. The lending bank, like the farmer, has to ride out these adverse times through giving additional facility support, in the knowledge that the farm assets can be realised as a last resort to repay the indebtedness. Often, the first asset realisation is done by the farmer by selling land that may be surplus to requirements or perhaps renting out fields for grazing if the return is large enough. When farm land itself suffers from a decline in value, diversification into other activities may be appropriate, eg converting barns to offices or tourism.

6.3 Property

The bank may be asked to lend to a builder contracted to repair properties or complete a development, a business wishing to develop and market a site, or a business established to invest in completed developments. The property may be residential or commercial under contract for the private or the public sector. Each type of property has its own characteristics and lending risks.

6.3.1 The building contractor

Construction and building businesses need to have sufficient capital to finance the work before completion, notwithstanding the receipt of regular progress payments. There should be an accurate tendering system in place to ensure profitable trading. In cash flow terms, the profit is not received until near the end of the construction cycle with the final sales of individual properties, the latter being an important factor to consider where residential housing is concerned. The contractor may also act as its own developer or work under instructions from a developer. Where a contract is drawn up, the banker should check the following clauses to ascertain the potential lending risk.

- ◆ The potential cost variations that might arise to increase the financing requirement. It is rare for a contract to be agreed at a fixed price without an escalation clause included to allow for wage awards and increases in raw materials prices.
- ◆ Liability clauses in the event of defective workmanship and/or overrunning the agreed completion date.
- ◆ Planning permission restrictions and covenants.
- ◆ If the contract is for a local authority, indemnities may have to be given for pre-building work to provide infrastructure services such as drainage and access roads.
- ◆ There may be a reinstatement clause requiring the builder to make good any site damage or upheaval once the building work has been completed.

Apart from the contract terms other potential lending risks will have to be considered.

6.3.2 Failure of the builder to complete the development

The bank should already have covered a possible default of performance as one of its lending conditions so that it is automatically assigned the development for continuation until it is completed to minimise its losses on the deal. The occasion when default occurs should be made clear in the conditions and the time taken for change of ownership to the bank should be minimised where sub-contractors are involved, otherwise the building team may be disbanded or move to another development.

6.3.3   How the builder will repay the bank loan

If the development is to build on a single plot, the profit element will arise on completion and the bank must ensure that the final payment is used to repay the borrowing. One method of achieving this is for a separate bank account to be raised, having the twin aims of facilitating monitoring the work being done and ensuring that all receipts are paid into this development account. Day-to-day site expenditure will be drawn from this account and, if the original budget is adhered to, the resulting overdraft will remain within the agreed borrowing facility.

If the development comprises a new residential estate, the profit from selling the first tranche of houses for preference should be factored into the resources needed to build and complete the remaining houses rather than being withdrawn by the builder. If the money were withdrawn at the earliest opportunity, it may be used by the builder to finance other developments that would be outside the terms of the advance. There could arise an added risk in that the builder may suffer from over-trading through accepting too many building developments at the same time.

6.3.4   The sub-contracting risk

Many smaller builders operate through calling on a pool of self-employed workers when a development contract arises. Alternatively, the builder may employ a few 'key site managers' to oversee the work and, if necessary, call on labourers as and when required. The terms of employment should be confirmed: that the labourers will be available when asked and they have self-employment tax clearance, otherwise their statutory pay-as-you-earn and National Insurance liabilities can devolve on the builder. Larger-sized building firms with their own workforce potentially hold the risk that if new orders do not occur to keep the employees fully occupied, then the builder will be incurring wage overheads without any corresponding profitable work to pay for them.

6.3.5   Financial history of a building development

The risk of financing a building development will always revert to the creditworthiness of the building firm and the terms of each individual deal. The financial steps of a typical development are set out hereafter and shown as a proportion of an overall cost of 100:

Assumptions: the borrowing terms agreed are for the bank to finance 60% of the sale proceeds, including a 75% share of the cost of the land. The builder's funds are to be otherwise used first in priority over the remaining bank facility.

The project:	Value of development	Builder's proportion	Bank's proportion
(base 100)			
Land cost	20	5	15
External build cost	44	35	9
Internal work cost	32	0	32
Retention money	4	0	4
Total	**100**	**40**	**60**
Budgeted profit	25	25	0
Share of proceeds	**125**	**65**	**60**

The exposure of the bank in this example will be:

Bank exposure Month	Project cum value	mthly cost	Work done to date	Certified work	Bank cumulative paid	blce	as % of PV	Builder cum've paid
Outset	20	20	0	0	15	45	75	5
1	42	22	22	0	15	5	36	27
2	64	22	22	22	24	36	38	40
3	80	16	16	22	24	36	30	56
4	96	16	16	16	40	20	42	56
5	25	4	0	16	60	0	48	65

The example shows how the exposure of the bank, after initially assisting with the land purchase, reduces by half and thereafter does not exceed 50% of the budgeted project value until repayment. On this basis, the risk is relatively modest, particularly as the market value of the land is not expected to fall by 25% after purchase to erode the money advanced.

6.3.6 Non-specific financing

The bank may be requested by the builder to provide a credit facility not tied to any particular project, usually by way of overdraft, but sometimes in the form of renewable drawings constituting continuous credit. The bank looking at this proposition will be relying on the covenant of the borrower in the normal manner, including the merits of taking suitable security.

6.4   The developer

The bank will be asked to part-fund the purchase and sale of a single property or an estate. Effectively, this will be open-ended bridging finance without a contracted purchaser of the completed development. Sometimes, finance will be requested to acquire a land bank to be available for future development. The security for the bank will lie in good title to the property, from the start of building to completion, and the creditworthiness of the developer's business as a whole to finance its part of the deal and ensure that the assets are put in a suitable state to sell in the market. In turn, the risk of lending to the developer will incorporate the risk that the building contractor will complete the contracted development satisfactorily to pass to the developer to market.

Where the building contractor and the developer are separate entities and the property is to develop a residential estate for sale, some properties will be completed early so they can be marketed early (with the remaining properties perhaps sold 'off plan'). At this stage, the pricing of the units will have been accomplished. When property selling prices are moving quickly, the developer stands the risk of losing some profit in a rising market and vice versa. The bank should allow for a shortfall in the profit margin if it is likely that the latter will occur.

If the development comprises commercial units, the demand for this type of property will be more specialist and rental or sale dependent largely on the size of the units being constructed. There will be greater demand for smaller units, so that many developers resolve this problem by partitioning a large building according to how demand proceeds. There will also be a greater effort to pre-sale or pre-let the units in advance of their completion to reduce the risk of ending up with empty units generating no income. The development of a residential estate or commercial complex will generally have the following characteristics:

1. acquisition of the land (and any buildings thereon for demolition or partial reinstatement);
2. planning of the development;
3. marrying the budgeted financial cost to the expected future yield;
4. monitoring the work done and commencing marketing;
5. completion of unit sales or transfer to an investment company.

By way of example, stage 3 may show the following result:

Bank borrowing (cost 7% pa)	£600,000
Developer's own resources	£400,000
Budgeted financial cost to completion	£1,000,000
Gross yield (excluding corporation tax liability)	10% pa
Expected rental income per annum	£100,000
Less interest on bank borrowing	£42,000
Profit per annum	£58,000
Net profit return	5.8% pa

The bank may judge that a 10% void factor for the units would be appropriate, bearing in mind the location of the development being contemplated, and the state of the commercial letting market suggests that the market rental for this type of unit would be closer to 9% pa gross.

The budget calculation would alter as follows:

Expected rental income @ 9% pa	£90,000
Deduct suggested void units @ 10%	£9,000
	£81,000
Less interest on bank borrowing	£42,000
Amended profit per annum	£39,000
Amended net profit return	3.9% pa
Bank interest cover (ie 81,000/42,000 =)	1.93 times

Assuming the bank lending terms include equal annual repayments of loan principal over 15 years, the project viability calculation at the outset would become:

Amended profit per annum	£39,000
Less loan repayments per annum	£40,000
Income shortfall initially	£1,000

At first glance the project would not prove viable on the assumptions stated, but three factors may change this decision: first, there will be rent reviews upwards every three years (it is common to have reviews every three or five years), secondly, the bank loan may be able to be obtained at a fixed interest rate, thereby preventing an increase in this part of the project cost and, thirdly, the developer may be able to provide additional security to the bank in addition to the first fixed and floating charge on the property. The floating charge would be taken to cover rent debtors.

6.4.1   The property investor

Property investment companies will be retaining a portfolio of assets for the long term to generate rental income and eventual capital gain. They will also be developing existing buildings or new sites. Where a bank provides a long-term loan, this may be tied to a particular development or property, the quality of the tenant(s) should be assessed for risk and the overall rental yield compared with the cost of the money lent. A development that has as yet no firm tenants should be supported by additional security. Market demand for office accommodation at the time determines the rental that can be obtained on the property. Residential property will frequently be acquired for resale and, again, current market forces will influence the selling prices that can be realised.

A key area for property lending will be the value attaching to the property in the event that recourse has to be made to this asset should default occur in repaying the underlying loan. There are two aspects to the valuation: how much is the flow of rental income per year and what is its 'bricks and mortar' value if letting has not occurred or is incomplete. The investor will be looking for long-term finance to enable some enhancement to be attributed to the property over a period of time. If the loan is repayable in full at the end of a stated period, this gearing effect will allow the investor to build in value through rent reviews and achieve a capital gain before the property is eventually sold to repay the debt. As with any investment, property yields can rise and fall according to demand. Advantage can be taken of good opportunities to sell when values rise (and yields fall) and reinvest in new developments.

6.4.1.1   Property valuations

The portfolio may consist of residential and/or commercial properties developed or bought for subsequent sale over the short/medium term or to be retained long term, principally for income and capital gain. In respect of the former, the lending banker will be expecting to be repaid from the sale proceeds, whereas the latter policy will be for the income from the property(ies) at least to service the loan (with a safety margin built in) until the debt can be repaid out of future rental earnings with/without any proceeds arising when the property(ies) are sold.

There are a number of valuation bases in use, according to the circumstances to which they will be put. These are summarised and listed in overall terms (the full definitions as laid down for professional valuers by the RICS would run to several pages) in the following.

- ◆ Open Market Value (OMV). The value assumes prior marketing of the property will be required before a sale under open market conditions (a willing buyer and a willing seller).
- ◆ Estimated Realisation Price (ERP). The sale is scheduled for a specified future date and a future selling price is estimated.

◆ Estimated Restricted Realisation Price (ERRP). In this case, the sale is scheduled with the minimum delay, the restriction being the lack of time allowed for the sale.

◆ Estimated Market Value (EMV). A market value is placed on the property at arm's length, but arranged privately between the parties.

◆ Estimated Use Valuation (EUV). This valuation accords with the existing use of the property.

◆ Replacement Cost (RC). As the name implies, the valuation corresponds to the replacement cost of the property.

◆ Forced Sale Valuation (FSV). While strictly not a recognised form of valuing a property, as it is similar to an OMV, bankers may use this description to incorporate the deduction of any prior security charges to be accounted for, as well as any costs of realisation.

◆ Cost Valuation (CV). This valuation would apply if the purchase cost of the property were lower than the OMV for lending purposes.

6.4.3   Prior charges are evident

The following guidelines are usually adopted when valuing a property where a prior charge(s) is evident:

Valuation at OMV (or CV if lower)	1000
Deduct the value of the prior (first) charge (say 70% of 1,000 =)	<u>700</u>
Value available for second charge	<u>300</u>
Value of the (second) charge held (say 45% of 300 =)	**<u>135</u>**

The additional valuation margin of 165 (ie 55%) is to allow for the realisation costs and delay in receiving value in the event the first charge holder claims on the property as security on default in repaying the prior loan. Depending on the type and quality of the property and the covenant of the borrower, a loan secured by a first charge would expect to be offered up to a maximum 70% +/- 10% of the OMV. Where it is agreed, a loan secured by a second charge would have a more variable maximum value attributed according to the individual circumstances of the application, but a figure of 45% as shown above would be a reasonable supposition on average.

6.4.4   The effect of Value Added Tax (VAT)

There are complicated rules governing the imposition of VAT on construction activities. It is relevant to know the broad liability to VAT in judging the cash flow and profitability of a proposed development. The more important conditions are listed below.

- Zero rating will apply to the costs of new construction of a qualifying (ie non-business purpose for less than 10% of its use) dwelling(s) on bare land, whether or not an existing building thereon has to be demolished.
- Standard rating will apply to ancillary work such as attendant professional services, management services, plant hire, site investigations, landscaping and internal fitments.
- Reduced rate construction services applies at 5% on the installation of energy saving materials on non-commercial buildings or household dwellings that have been empty for at least three years.
- Otherwise, other services including commercial and civil engineering works, are standard rated at the current VAT rate of 17.5%. This also applies to the self-supply of construction services at their OMV where the services value is at least £100,000.
- Freehold land and buildings that are let, leased or sold in the course of business and lease assignments or surrenders are generally classed as an exempt supply for VAT purposes (except where the sale is new residential property when residences are zero-rated as stated earlier).

6.4.5 Leasehold property

Short-term leases having only a few years to run should be considered akin to trading stock when valuing these assets for security purposes. There is no security of tenure beyond the present expiry date and therefore the property is a wasting asset. Long-term leases have a value as security for a loan providing their unexpired life is at least 20 to 25 years. They are still a wasting asset, but there could be value enhancement in the early years depending on the outlook for the property market generally. If the lease expires in 20 to 25 years, the underlying loan granted by the bank is likely to be repayable within 15 years.

6.4.6 Assessment of property companies

A common ratio to compare the status of (investment) property companies is to measure their net rental income with the gross interest cost of borrowings. A ratio of less than unity will suggest that the net worth (yield) of the company's property portfolio relative to its gearing (borrowings) is poor.

6.5 Professional firms

Businesses classed under this category would be solicitors, accountants, architects, estate agents, independent financial advisers, doctors, dentists and other firms operating in the public and private sectors and being taxed under self-assessment and self-employment Schedule D regulations. Self-assessment carries the obligation of settling annual tax dues in equal halves by 31 January and 31 July each year for late penalties not to arise. There is the equal obligation to pay the estimated tax due for the current tax assessment year (ending each 5 April) in two parts by the identical 31 January and 31 July. The lending banker is likely to see a call on cash flow of the professional business to meet the partners' tax liabilities at these times, particularly at 31 January.

The issue of when to take into account revenue recognition in the accounts of firms and businesses is still being discussed (Urgent Issues Task Force Abstract 40 – UITF 40), but part performance of contractual obligations is likely to require recognition of the attached revenue to reflect partial performance as work-in-progress on the contract progresses.

6.5.1 Taxation

There is no mechanism for the non-incorporated business, unlike a limited liability company, to defer some distribution of profits to the members of a privately-owned 'close company' and retain this in the business without being personally taxed at the standard rate of 22% up to the current top income tax rate of 40%, compared with a company's corporation tax rate of up to the current 30% rate (or 19% for small companies, as defined). When speaking of rates 'up to' a top percentage this is because individuals currently have a starting tax rate of 10% on the first £2,090 of income (for the tax year 2005/06), whereas companies have a nil start rate for the first £10,000 of assessed profits. A 'close company' is principally one where there are five or fewer controlling participants, in which event more stringent tax liabilities may ensue.

6.5.2 Limited liability partnerships

Some practices have become limited liability partnerships (LLP) under the Limited Liability Partnerships Act 2000 and have to be registered as such with the Registrar of Companies. The LLP is a separate entity with the individual partners acting as its agent and not being directly responsible for its debts. The laws relating to partnerships under the Partnership Act 1890 (where all partners are liable for one another's actions) and the Limited Partnerships Act 1907 (where there must be a general partner fully liable for the partnership's actions) in this instance do not apply. The lending banker, therefore, should be aware of this liability demarcation where security for lending is being requested.

6.5.3 Solicitors

There are stringent regulations controlling the acceptance, retention and release of clients' money. The total of money held on behalf of clients, in 'clients accounts', whether for short or long periods, must always mirror the liability in the accounts of the solicitors' firm to pay away these funds at some future stage and at no time will this sum be included in the net worth of the business. The running total of clients' funds held is a useful general indicator of the progress of the firm in accruing business.

The method of determining the value of work-in-progress and analysing its make up will be an important part of the risk assessment of the business. The internal measurement of work done, comprising the number of hours booked per member of staff multiplied by the clients' charge-out rates, may bear only a limited resemblance to the actual sum finally agreed and received by the firm from the clients. A breakdown of work-in-progress showing the period over which the work has been collated and the likely future time taken before its completion, will provide the banker with data on which to judge the risk, or otherwise, of the firm receiving full payment. For example, a case that has taken over one year to date and with the prospect of another year's work, may give rise to a sum (if judgement is not favourable) that will be hard to recover.

Payments made on account by the client will mitigate the risk of full settlement by the solicitor. The banker should enquire whether this practice has been adopted by the firm and should also examine the age of outstanding accounts in the debtors list. This will also suggest the degree of good financial management that is prevalent within the business. Work may be divided between regular activities, such as property conveyancing and singular litigation. The former may not be always as profitable as the latter per hour worked, but it may prove easier to facilitate, enable a great number of similar cases to be ongoing at the same time, and more constant in the accrual of instructions.

All but the smallest of firms are expected to offer a wide range of law services: corporate, matrimonial, criminal and so forth. It will be useful to the banker to have background knowledge of the specialisations of the firm and how it supports them. If a large proportion of gross fees arise from one working section and/or one partner, the risk of that partner leaving, voluntarily or due to ill health, may prove a burden on the firm as a whole to continue at its former profitability.

Solicitors, like accountants and other financial advisers, have been classified as good business for banks, in that they may pass on client leads for future lending business. Through their client accounts, they can provide money deposits. Their technical skills suggest to the banker that should the firm suffer a poor year in profit terms, this can be overcome relatively rapidly through the introduction of suitable remedial measures and 'trading out' of the problem. It is rare nowadays to find a firm of size that does not hold adequate professional indemnity insurance to guard against the occasional lapse in professional expertise. Both insurance cover and the qualifications and experience of the partners should be factors to be examined by the bank in viewing new professional client relationships.

6.7 Accountants

Accountants and other professional firms share many common business aspects with solicitors. A representative list would include the following.

- ◆ The mix of firm's income (and whether it is a predominance of repeat work, singular assignments or peripheral services).
- ◆ The adequacy of professional indemnity insurance cover.
- ◆ Partnership agreements, their terms and possible limited partnerships.
- ◆ The effect of debtors and work-in-progress on cash flow.
- ◆ The fixed cost of qualified staff to be paid for out of business won.
- ◆ The value of client leads.
- ◆ How changes in partners will affect the partnership financially.

Taking some of the above statements in greater depth, one important facet is ownership of the business assets and profit shares. If one partner owns the office freehold, what will happen when he/she retires? Will this mean that the remaining partners have to ask for finance to purchase the property? Will this put the bank in a good position for more business or will it cripple the partnership with an onerous annual repayment liability?

The partners may be divided between equity partners and salaried partners, the latter receiving a fixed salary plus perhaps a yearly bonus depending on performance, but not a share of the earnings residue of the partnership. Some partners may not bank personally with the firm's bank and therefore their full financial standing will not be immediately evident. There may be a greater preponderance for salaried partners to leave the partnership, perhaps taking clients with them if they are not made up to full equity partners, especially if they first joined with a client nucleus that was incorporated into the firm.

The ratios of the number of other qualified and non-qualified staff to gross income and the client fee earned per member of staff as a proportion of their cost (including benefits and pension commitments), when compared with their trends and as against a national or regional benchmark (if available) will tell the banker the state of financial health of the business. Is the firm growing? Are the numbers and cost of staff employed relatively high and therefore is there an inherently greater credit risk? Can the invoicing of work being done be accelerated to improve cash flow? The larger the total value of repeat audit/accountancy/tax assignments as a proportion of gross fees and the extent by how much they exceed the firm's fixed operating costs will imply how financially sound the business is based.

6.8 Architects

A business is said to require the services of an accountant regularly, that of a solicitor occasionally, but not often to require the services of an architect. This is on the premise of the infrequency of building work, unless building and construction is part of the nature of the trade being undertaken. The type of work will be a critical factor in judging credit risk. For instance, speculative investment building projects may be highly profitable to the developer when sold or they could be a term liability if depressed property prices subsequently arise due to the state of the market as a whole. In the latter case, the architect may have difficulty in fully recovering the fees charged and may not easily gain further work until the demand for architectural services improves.

Most architects work on a fee structure that is either a fixed percentage of the value of the project in hand or on a time basis at an agreed rate per hour. The former is more frequent than the latter, particularly where the work requires regular site visits of an unknown duration. The lending banker should enquire to what extent the firm of architects relies on specific builder firms for their future assignments. To rely for regular business on long-standing builders/developers will be less risky than accepting one-off assignments from occasional small builder firms.

A further risk element is where architect work is reliant on tendering for business. At worst, no business arises or the work is not very profitable. Reputation is important to gain commercial work, whereas pricing may be more important with private work. Similar financial considerations apply when judging lending proposals as for other professional firms.

6.9   Estate agents

Risks pertaining to estate agencies are higher than for other professional businesses. Competition is perceived to be greater, if only for the plethora of different agencies having shop windows facing the public. The vagaries of 'boom and bust' times for private house sales and the 'hit-or-miss' element in gaining new business that is largely price driven, when added to the high proportion of fixed operating costs (setting up offices and paying staff wages), make this type of business a greater lending risk. This is not assisted by the fact that anyone can open and deal as an estate agent, with or without qualifications. The track record of this type of business and the number of years it has been operating (and therefore in building up a knowledge and 'feel' for house prices in the areas of working) will be material to the risk judgement.

6.10   Doctors and dentists

Doctors' practices may be wholly public sector (National Health Service) based, wholly private sector oriented or, becoming more common, a mixture of both. In terms of the public sector, general practitioners are independent contractors to the NHS with their earnings subject to annual review. The pay is a mixture of fees, calculated according to the number of patients on their books, and allowances, determined by the different services practised and seniority of the doctor. Doctors may also be employed on a salaried basis by the Primary Care Trusts (PCTs) responsible to dispense NHS services in each geographic area. Specialist consultants are likely to be employed by the PCTs as well as having their own practice.

Practice income allowances from the NHS may arise through meeting (audited) preventative medicine targets such as the extent of child immunisation, pre-school boosters and women cervical smear tests. Service fees will arise from NHS minor surgery work, the training of students and anaesthetic duties. Other NHS-derived income will come from service fees in the areas of night visits, maternity work, contraceptive advice, vaccinations and immunisations and dealing with temporary (holiday) residents. Non-NHS-derived income may arise through medical examinations, cremation fees, insurance reports, corporate doctoring, hospital appointments and other certifications.

State allowances are available to assist with surgery ownership through a cost rent allowance to match the loan interest charges of the building development. The aim has been to provide for NHS patients the best possible care from modern premises. Alternatively, a notional rent assessment allowance may be made, periodically revalued by the District Valuer, if premises are not being acquired or modernised by the practice.

Bridging finance and mortgages at variable or fixed rates may be negotiated with commercial sources at the choice of the borrower. The lending banker will be in the position of having the loan (at potentially 100% value to cost) serviced by the state through annual cost allowances given to the practice. This may, however, lead to negative equity being incurred in the early years of the mortgage advance. The partnership agreement must be examined for the financial effect of a change in the partnership as, under NHS regulations, no goodwill is allowed on 'selling' the practice (this differs in the cases of dentists and doctors in private practice).

Where a building (or improvements) loan has been negotiated on a 100% value to cost basis, the build costs may still exceed the market value of the property and the net worth of the practice and/or the share of the practice value to the outgoing partner. The options are:

- the mortgage may have to be repaid (with a loss to the shared owner?); or
- renegotiated (probably by extending the value of the loan to book value unless other partners' assets can be pledged as security); or
- deferred (until property prices improve); or
- the outgoing partner may pay the partnership the share he/she is relinquishing; or
- the debt is retained in the partnership for the time being.

The partnership agreement may not allow all these options and neither may it take into account the basis of valuation of the partnership assets in the event of one partner leaving. The lending bank may find itself with limited room to manoeuvre on any renegotiation of the facility.

The partnership may be run as a dispensing practice, in which event stocks of drugs and related goods will have to be maintained. These will require financing with good stock control. Separate accounting records should be upheld and a trading agreement raised with the practice. The banker should view this activity as a separate profit centre.

The partners will wish to draw money monthly from the partnership as part of their annual profit share to cover living expenses. The partnership should provide, in advance of each operating year, a budget worked out as follows:

- calculating the expected net surplus of income to arise less expenditure (including any drawings to pay for personal tax liabilities);
- deducting a proportion of this net surplus as a contingency fund;
- deducting a further amount as may be necessary to maintain an adequate cash flow for the business throughout the year (particularly if capital expenditure is envisaged and there will be a period of time elapsing before the corresponding NHS allowances are received);
- dividing the balance of the surplus between the partners in proportion to their agreed shares;
- dividing these individual sums by twelve to give the monthly drawings to be made.

As part of the monitoring of the business, the bank should ask for a copy of this calculation and compare the data with actual results. Similar budgeting should be applied to other types of professional partnerships.

The government has recently announced proposals to increase the fees that dentists earn for non-complex treatment: band 1 will cost up to £15 per patient (currently costing around £6) for a general check-up; band 2 costing up to £41 will cover fillings and extractions; and band 3 up to £183 for crowns and dentures. These rates will replace more than 400 existing charging rates and in future provide dentists offering National Health Service treatments (and banks lending to dentists) greater security of income. However, it does not allow for the public deciding to have dentistry less often than before in view of the increase of charges.

6.11   Retailing

The retailing sector spans businesses ranging from the corner shop to the large store. There are lending risks that apply to both, but also some prevalent to each individually. Retailers will be selling to the public who will, in most cases, be price conscious unless ease of location of the shop(s) determines custom. Profits will depend on rapidity of turnover and the size of stocks on show of good selling lines. Higher stocks will also require more working capital for their purchase. The bank should check that stock turnover and the overall profit margin, after allowing for any change in the mix of sales, are maintained and that losses from unsold lines and pilferage are kept to a minimum.

6.11.1   Retail shops

The critical factors determining trading success or failure will relate to the following questions.

◆ What are the type(s) of products sold?
◆ How good is the proprietor at purchasing? And at stock control?
◆ Are the profit margins allowed sufficient to make a living?
◆ Is there local demand for that type of goods being met?
◆ What is the competition?
◆ Does the business offer a niche product?
◆ Is the property in occupation owned or rented?
◆ What is the business strategy? To withdraw earnings or expand?

The products sold may be basic needs (eg foodstuffs), fashion led (eg dresses) or collectables (eg books). Basic needs will incur a regular turnover, but are susceptible to quality and competition restraints. Fashion articles may change rapidly, leading to unsold stocks. Collectables will be subject to a lower demand that should be offset through higher profit margins.

Purchasing skills are a mixture of product knowledge, where to source the best goods and experience of what goods might sell best. Good stock control is to maximise the stock turnover and earn as much profit as possible from the selling prices set and limit as much unsaleable stock as possible. Working capital should be used to purchase stock lines that can be sold rather than tying up capital in non-moving stock, hence the need for periodic cut-price 'sales'.

The risk of achieving a poor turnover is reduced if the shop can cater for an indigenous customer base (eg selling newspapers next to a major railway station). The location and type of competition is important when judging how a retailer might be successful in trading. The risk of a grocery store being placed next to a supermarket is clear cut since the latter can sell at lower profit margins due to its purchasing power. If the shop is a pharmacy, as a measurement of trading risk, the bank could set a limit how close a competitor should be placed before agreeing to lend.

Where a niche product is being sold, the risks relating to location, competition and inadequate profit margins are muted, since the business can set out its own trading parameters. If the business is too successful, there is the risk that competitors may arise on seeing the potential in this trading area, but good management of the customers through attentiveness to their needs and the quality of the product should retain their custom without too much of an erosion to the profit margin.

Many small retailers, particularly in urban areas, have to lease their premises. This should be accepted as normal by the lending bank, but any liability for the reinstatement of the premises laid down by the lease and rapid timing to rent reviews could cause a marked effect on the profitability of the retail business. These possible effects should be borne in mind when viewing the retailer's profit forecasts supporting a lending request. Forecasting sales demands a special form of approach for the best results for any size of retail business.

6.11.2   Forecasting retail sales and profit

A example is provided in Chapter Ten.

6.11.3   Stock control

Where the retailer's books of account provide an analysis of purchases and sales by gross profit margins, it will be possible to estimate the stock movement each month. A rough calculation of stock would be:

- ◆ value at cost prices of stock at the last stocktake = (A);
- ◆ value at cost prices of stock purchased during the 'month' = (B);
- ◆ value of sales during the 'month' at selling prices = (C);
- ◆ adjustment of sales (C) to cost price = (D);
- ◆ value of stock at end of the present month = (A) + (B) − (D).

Stock calculation (£'000)	At last stocktake	Purchases month 1	Sales month 1	Stock cd/fwd
Goods A	40	+ 10	− 12	38
Goods B	20	+ 6	− 4	22
Goods C	10	+ 2	− 2	10
Total	**70**	**+ 18**	**− 18**	**70**

If the retailer does not operate a stock control system (which is quite likely) and does not know the book value of stock held until the date of the end of year accounts are prepared, it may not be possible to calculate with accuracy the value of stock at the end of each 'month'. Note that each month end will be at a weekend when the shop is closed for business and the month will comprise a period of either four or five weeks. In this case, the most recent gross profit margin will be taken from the historic annual accounts on which to base profit forecasts. The monthly forecasts will then be compared to actual as they occur:

Gross profit margin achieved in the previous accounting year	60%
Forecast sales for the current year as calculated	£900,000
Gross profit expected for the current year (= 60% x £900,000)	£540,000
Monthly average gross profit: per four-week period =	£41,538
per five-week period =	£51,923

6.11.4   Department stores

Many stores spread their operating costs through leasing areas within the building to retail supplier groups. This provides a regular income and lowers the risk to the lending bank should day-to-day turnover from the public fall in times of recession or changes in fashion lead to unsold stocks. As the store will be sited in a prominent position in the high street, its asset valuation should be attractive and prove good security for a commercial loan unless the building is leased. When stores suffer from cash flow difficulties, the management often initiates a 'sale and leaseback' with another institution, thereby reducing its security value.

When assessing the profitability of department stores the calculations are based on turnover per square foot of available space with overall costs apportioned accordingly. In turn, this may be sub-divided into sections to gain a better idea of the sales and profit return, eg mens, ladies, catering, etc. Direct staff costs are allocated to specific sections, where possible, with general administrative staff overheads being shared over all sections.

6.12   Wholesaling

The critical factors to determine profitability and risk in respect of wholesaling are:

◆ the certainty of sources of supply;
◆ the reliance of customer demand;
◆ the skills to match supply with demand;
◆ the availability of financial resources to complete the supply chain.

Retail customers are likely to switch allegiance to another wholesale supplier if the goods ordered are not delivered as ordered on time. This is particularly true for goods manufactured and imported from overseas. Even a contract with the manufacturer will be of little use to ensure a continuation of supply as the only recourse the wholesaler will have is for legal indemnity against loss. If the jurisdiction for legal redress is overseas this may add to the problem and certainly extend the period before compensation is achieved. Risk can be mitigated through using two or more suppliers so that if one supplier fails to deliver, the order(s) can be quickly switched to the other supplier.

If the wholesaler's customers are not contracted to take up definite quantities of goods and demand for the goods falls, the wholesaler will be left with unsold stocks. Recovery of the value in the wholesaler's purchases will depend on finding new customer outlets or markets and/or selling the goods at 'sale' prices. The lending banker should ensure that the financial position of the wholesaler is adequate to suffer the loss of cash flow that, perhaps, a temporary fall in customer demand will cause. It is not usual to have perishable goods sold under a supply contract specifying firm dates, prices and quantities of supply. Supermarkets, however, may lay down strict quality controls and agree in return for wholesalers to supply some goods off-season up to a certain quantity, for example, out of cold store.

The business skills of the wholesaler will be decisive in judging the level of risk to accept when trading open-ended in accepting goods/products that he/she may have little or no previous dealing knowledge for selling on to customers without advance orders with whom little or no trading experience is known. In this situation, the bank should build in a large financial margin for safety and not rely overly on the underlying value of the goods whose title may be taken as security, as the bank will not wish to be put in the situation of having to sell the goods to repay any loan. The extent of business resources (financial backing) of the wholesaler will be especially important to support the deal and the period of the loan should be short term, particularly where perishable goods are dealt in.

6.13   Manufacturing

Different categories of risk apply to different types of manufacturing. The manufacturer may build the product(s) from raw materials to the finished article, or manufacture a small amount of the finished product while buying in other components ready made or supply the labour to tailor a bespoke article with a minimum of manufacturing content. Examples would be where the base structure of the product is manufactured in-house, but the motors it requires may be bought in from a supplier or where an air conditioning system is designed that requires only the ducts to be fitted on-site after the manufactured sheeting has been supplied from another source.

Engineering covers a wide field and may consist of heavy and light engineering work. The work can be very competitive and relatively unskilled, as with the small 'metal-bashing' business, or be highly skilled involving large contracts completed over a long period of time for which there may be few competitors. The market(s) in which the company is trading should be examined for movements in demand (ie seasonality and cyclical trends) and how they might affect the business. It would also be pertinent to benchmark the company's profitability to its peers. Contracts of significant size may be adaptable for self-financing, particularly if the work is situated overseas, otherwise general lending options will apply.

6.13.1   Manufacturing the complete product

The lending banker should be aware of the characteristics of the production line operated by the manufacturer. Specifically, an assessment should be made of any potential risks that might cause production to be halted or delayed.

- ◆ Are there any raw materials whose delivery could be open to doubt?
- ◆ Are adequate quantities of raw materials stocked to ensure production is not delayed?
- ◆ Has due regard been taken of any planned management programmes, eg plant stoppage for maintenance or the training of operatives?

- ◆ What is the operating efficiency of the production line, eg is there capacity slack or can increased/overnight plant working satisfy demand?
- ◆ What is the efficiency of the plant layout, eg all under one roof?
- ◆ Is production adequately supervised and quality control evident?
- ◆ Are individual machine records maintained for replacement purposes?
- ◆ Are finished product stock levels monitored where standard products are manufactured for stock prior to receiving sales orders?
- ◆ Are the financial records satisfactory to calculate accurately the costs of production when tendering for new production contracts and setting selling prices of the finished articles?

It will be quite likely that when more than one machine is used for production, each will vary as to their age and their operating efficiency. Monitoring of stoppages for maintenance and repairs will provide an indication of the future useful life of each machine. Individual calculations should be evident what it costs to operate each machine for each production contract job undertaken, eg the cost of basic materials used, the labour and other indirect costs involved. In turn, these estimates will provide the basis of tendering for future contracts and the expected profit.

The most frequent measure of costing will be based on the time taken for each operating machine run. A notional example is given:

Typical production steps required to manufacture a 'widget'

Step 1:

Cost of raw materials (listed individually)	£120
Cost of labour (20 hours x 2 persons x £12 per hour =)	£480
Total direct costs	**£600**
Indirect costs apportioned (£4 per hour =)	£80
Total direct and indirect costs	**£680**
Number of widgets made	100
Production cost per widget	£6.80
Add estimate for non-productive time (15%)	£1.02
Adjusted production cost	£7.82
Add profit mark-up (25%)	£1.96
Production price for step 2 (rounded)	**£9.78**
Step 2:	
Finishing stage (calculations similar to step 1) say	£2.22
Final standard selling price	**£12.00**

6.13.2   Buying in other components

The risks involved with this aspect of manufacture are twofold: first, that delivery of the items may be interrupted, leading to temporary close down of the production line and, secondly, a possible loss of know how where the bought-in article has been based on specialist design work that could be copied. In the first case, either the manufacturer has at operate with at least two sources of supply or retains sufficient stock to meet delivery interruptions, eg when the supplier factory closes for staff annual leave. Having an exclusive supply agreement with a confidentiality clause included, or having the design patented, can reduce the second risk.

6.13.3   Tailoring an existing product

The greatest risk attaching to a manufacturing product requiring a high input of installing labour and a minimum of exclusive own-build will be from competitors who can offer an identical service. Quality and speed of workmanship and competitive tendering are key attributes to win business. Where the size of jobs being tendered is modest, frequently a fixed price contract may be requested. It will be important for the manufacturer to keep a close control at regular intervals on costs and the time required to complete the contract, otherwise the potential profit to be earned may quickly disappear. Each facet of the contract should have been allocated the number of hours it will take for the work to be completed.

Manufacturing, for the most part, comprises the construction, fabrication and/or assembly of specialist products. Each product as such may hold risks indigenous to that service and the lending banker should be aware of these. The common questions to ask in an assessment are the following.

- ◆ If the product or service proved flawed, what would be the liability?
- ◆ Can the liability be determined in financial terms?
- ◆ What measures can be taken by the manufacturer to limit this liability?
- ◆ Regardless of moves by the manufacturer, what can the bank do to limit its own risk?

6.13.4   Forecasting manufacturing sales and profits

An example is provided in Chapter Ten.

6.14   Technology-based businesses

This sector can include a business having a sound and profitable product that will require marketing and constant research to remain at the forefront with its peers or a business that has an idea that should prove successful, but will require financing and development. The lending banker will be looking to see that the management has the technological skills to develop the product(s) successfully, that a robust business plan is evident, that the financial resources are principally equity led and the business is not susceptible to requiring 'top up' financing in future to remain operating.

Computer companies may be involved in hardware or software development. The speed of technological change has been evident for several years and what might be a good chip development marketed in one year could easily be overtaken by a more sophisticated product the next year. The business may have a long-term contract production run, however, and this can give the company time to stay at the forefront of market demand, continue to expand and be increasingly profitable.

Electronics companies have characteristics similar to those mentioned for computers. They may be trading at the 'heavy' end of the market and be subject to the same risks as large contractors/suppliers of equipment or they may be more specialised at the 'light' end of the market situated in a niche product area. If the latter, it is more likely that the company will be relying on just a few main products, so an assessment of their individual, continuing viability to sustain business turnover should be carried out.

6.14.1   Developing a new product

Many high tech businesses that have not yet commenced trading and are developing a product will have applied for a government grant to assist with research and the building of a prototype ready for commercial exploitation. A business plan will have had to be provided and technical assessors introduced to test the theory supporting the product before a grant will have been approved. These submissions will be available for the lending bank to view and assist in the interpretation of what may otherwise be a difficult exercise.

There should still be evident a summary of projected expenditure and cash flow for the period until the product becomes 'marketable', even if no business plan has been raised. This is acceptable because the management may not yet have decided whether to manufacture the product in-house or give it to an established company with the financial and marketing resources in return for a royalty on sales. When this point in development has been reached, the bank should enquire at an early stage whether it will be asked to finance the manufacture of the product or whether the lending made to date will be taken over by the marketing joint venture company. If the answer is no, the bank should assess its risk for what now might be seen as short-term lending and how repayment is expected to be effected.

As the risk of failure of the product is high until it is proven, the bank should ensure that it is fully covered with a large margin for error by easily realisable security that will retain its value, together with the personal guarantee(s) of the developer(s). The reason for this is because it is usually found that the early investment has been partially paid away in drawings and therefore the capital value of the product at this stage is purely intangible know how.

The investment already made in the product by the developer(s) ideally should be disregarded when new capital is being raised. Therefore, if it is agreed, for example, that the bank will provide 30% of new money, the developer(s) must provide the remaining 70% in cash and not say that their earlier funding comprises part of their 70% share. The bank should be careful that its loan amounts to a minority share of the new finance being injected and that the conditions for financing lay down that equity investment should be used in priority to loan money and be drawn for specific working capital purposes relating to the project, not as drawings.

The developer(s) will be looking for risk finance until the project becomes commercially viable. There are many types of risk money in the market to finance speculative projects, rather than traditional bank finance: venture capital funds, individuals (so-called 'business angels') and larger, established commercial enterprises that are willing to provide money, each for a package of equity and roll-up loans.

Typically, the equity element initially may comprise 20% to 30% of the company's shares (reducing in time to 5% to 10%) and the loan portion equivalent to a compound 10% to 20% pa return on the finance amount, payable on a deferred basis, plus a seat on the company's board of directors. Business angels may additionally have the knowledge to play an executive part in the business's development. The 'exit route' is usually short term (three to five years), except for a joint venture with a commercial enterprise when the interest can be long term. There may also be a ratchet condition: if the company meets its forecasts, the venture capital portion of equity rights will reduce as the loan is repaid; if the forecast is not met, the venture capital portion will increase to a majority shareholding to safeguard the investment made.

Where the new high tech project is part of an existing business being run successfully, there may be sufficient security already in the balance sheet to raise finance from the bank as part of an overall package. In this instance, the part of finance that relates to the new development should be ignored at the outset by the bank in capital value terms (since the money will be used as working capital) and the complete facility viewed on a risk basis relative to the overall net assets of the entire business, including any value that may be separately attributable to the new venture.

6.14.2   Marketing a finished product

The developer(s) should embark on a pilot marketing exercise and a 'test to destruction' prior to commencing manufacture. This will establish, or otherwise, whether the product is ready for commercial exploitation and what market demand is likely to be met. In turn, this will give some credence to the projected turnover figures to target on which bank finance will be judged. Once knowledge of the product reaches the public domain, the chance to acquire patent protection will be lost. Not all new products can be patented: they must hold some unique 'additionality'. The bank should be made aware of the patent application outcome.

Comments given in the previous paragraphs relating to the choice of marketing, financing, the adoption of a suitable business plan and security conditions to set for a loan apply equally when the product is marketed.

6.15   The leisure industry

There are many different types of businesses operating in the leisure field. The principal activities, in no special order, are restaurants and hotels, public houses, travel firms and agencies, hire transport, sports and games, music and films.

6.15.1   Entertainment

Entertainment is a wide field and can encompass music, shows, films, radio and TV media to external events and bookmakers. Each depends on participation of the public for revenue and requires capital spending to upkeep their assets to provide this service. The advertising income generated has to be adequate for the activity to provide a satisfactory cash flow. The difficulty arises in that money has to be spent before the profit return can be realised. If this is overdone, a loss will ensue. Competition can be fierce but pricing limitation is muted since the public would prefer to pay to see or hear its choice rather than not at all. Long-term investment is mainly tapped through equity capital backing.

The lending banker must be fully acquainted with all contractual rights and obligations under which the borrowing vehicle operates. This may include cross-border agreements with complicated legal drafting. The bank should preferably advance monies short term within the period of the expected receipts arising from the activities and ensure that the long term 'risk' capital invested is adequate for unexpected costs and liabilities. Entertainment can be short lived (eg one-off performances), medium term (eg musicals) or long standing (eg bookmakers shops). In each case, the reason for the borrowing will set the basis for the risk.

6.15.2   Food and drink

Food and drink companies are trading in a relatively stable market and particular brands can have a regular public following for many years, especially if they are well marketed. When a brand gets 'stale' and loses its turnover momentum, they are often re-marketed under a revised or a new label. Finance may be requested to help support a new product launch. This can be risky if the public does not respond well. Unexpected raw material price increases may be difficult to pass on to the public and existing competition will limit the scope to improve selling prices and margins. Having said that, there will always be the need to purchase food and drink. Lending to these companies should take these factors into account.

6.15.3　Other organisations

Leisure activities can embrace hotels and football clubs. Capital expenditure on hotel rooms requires a certain average percentage occupation to be profitable. Tourism is a fickle business and demand can vary widely from year to year. There is an inherent risk when lending to a hotel chain with ample asset value, but poor cash flow. A forced sale of assets may, or may not, be easy. Football clubs, on the other hand, are rarely asset rich, but do have the nebulous benefit of selling players, potentially profitably, but usually as a wasting asset. Many clubs have resorted to paying exorbitant transfer fees and wages to players rather than tying a large element of pay to a bonus scheme based on performance.

The risk is that the attraction of a new signing will not translate into turnstile receipts or cup success. Television receipts can have a limited life if the franchise changes to another sponsor. On the other hand, assisting in financing a new stand should bring in more game receipts, as will diversification into the marketing of team memorabilia. The lending bank may consider its advertising logo on team shirts to be sufficient risk return to take to lend the club money at commercial interest rates.

6.15.4　Travel firms and agencies

The prime risks involved are the pre-chartering of air flights and hotel bookings, foreign exchange exposure that is not hedged (see Chapter Seven) and sudden changes in public demand, either for different holiday locations or competition through the Internet. Travel firms that are ABTA registered have to raise a bond in advance as an insurance that claims from the public for the cost of return flights or non-performance of holidays as a result of agents going out of business will be met. The cost of publishing brochures can be significant and itinerary changes or prices will make these rapidly obsolete. Compulsory insurance taken out at the occasion of booking the holiday should cover part of the risk of late cancellations.

The lending bank will look to see how much deposit money has been collected by customers pre-booking their holidays, the success the agency has had in deferring payment of many operating costs for as long as possible and whether an escalation to costs (eg fuel surcharges) can be passed on to the customer. The break-even point of the business should be calculated, ie the total of booking fees required to meet all contracted outgoing expenditure. Many customers are leaving their booking until the last minute and this does not assist in estimating the viability of the business. Advertising special deals in return for early bookings can be successful. Nevertheless, lending to this sector will be risky unless the capital backing of the agency is sufficient to offset adverse trading periods.

6.16 Financial businesses

Independent financial businesses offering a specialised banking service ('intermediaries') may still require bank finance in the course of their day-to-day commercial activities. This money will be used to expand their capacity to offer credit, to provide more permanent time deposits over short periods rather than relying on the vagaries of on-demand public investment and to reduce the average cost of deposits held (since a bank credit line will be less expensive than offering a competitive interest rate for deposits from the public).

Financial institutions depend on several income streams for their profit: there will be a 'turn' on lending, fee income raised, account management charges and revenue from specialised services such as export/import business. The niche financial institutions will be looking to set up credit (working capital) lines with larger banks. Their risk to a lender will be in the type of business being conducted and the degree of security provided to the lender. This can range from the risk of an unsecured consumer loan to a term advance secured by a first charge on the borrower's property.

The institutions may be local financial intermediaries who are willing to accept sub-prime (high risk) personal and commercial borrowing requests from the public where the borrower has been turned down from other sources. In these cases, the institution might be termed as 'lender of last resort'. Alternatively, they may offer a niche borrowing service backed by the security of a first charge on residential or commercial property. The lending bank will judge each application on:

- the types of borrowing risks undertaken by the intermediary;
- the conditions the intermediary sets out for the customer to sign;
- the typical period of the loans that are offered by the intermediary;
- the quality of security the intermediary will accept;
- the lending margin required relative to the loan outstanding;
- the track record of the intermediary with this type of lending;
- the management capabilities as financial intermediaries;
- previous bad and doubtful debt experience in good times and bad;
- the regulatory controls the intermediary will operate under;
- the stability of profits of the intermediary;
- the ownership of the business and whether there is recourse thereto.

6.17   Other types of business

6.17.1   Chemicals

Chemical companies need to maintain a research capability to remain competitive and provide the products the market demands. New products marketed by competitors may wreck sales forecasts and lead to problems in completing planned capital expenditure programmes. The lending bank should be aware of the principal products of the company that generate the greatest share of profits and relate this to the risk of these products incurring a reduced demand in the future, particularly when the patent period expires.

6.17.2   Conglomerates

Conglomerate companies will comprise a number of major businesses operating in different markets subject to different trading factors and unrelated cash flows. Each separate business should be independently assessed for its own borrowing requirement and risk factors and then examined as to whether all the requirements can be met through raising one universal borrowing facility or by an amalgam of several separate facilities, each considered on the merits of the separate companies. The bank should be aware of the risk involved in lending to a 'shell' parent company rather than to the operating subsidiaries that may own all the group's assets. Cross-guarantees will be essential security in these cases.

6.17.3   Defence

Defence suppliers also have to tender for contracts, usually at fixed prices, subject to a limited agreed price escalation. Much of the specialised work can be sub-contracted and the financial standing of the contract is only as strong as the weakest link, be it meeting performance criteria or accurately forecasting profits when tendering. Cost overruns due to work delays or technical problems can be very expensive due to the size of contracts in this field. The lending bank should enquire about the present status of all major contracts. There is also the risk of suffering from the lack of a continuous order train. Debts from government agencies are not usually accepted for invoice discounting since they are non-transferable and the time taken for settlement frequently is over an extended period.

6.17.4   Exploration

Exploration requires capital funding that may extend over many years before a 'find' is discovered that can be commercially exploited. Meantime, the company will need working capital to support its activities. Income from past discoveries will assist to a degree in meeting ongoing expenditure. Any long-term borrowing should be on a speculative 'equity risk' basis, perhaps topped up through a minority part of long-term debt. The security offered by a mine should be valued in relation to the income flowing from mineral extracted sales and the estimate of known reserves.

6.17.5   Fuels

Fuels such as oil and gas, like exploration companies, rely on sufficient reserves to act as security for current research and exploration work. Where the oil and gas is already being piped out, then the long-term sales contracts are security in their own right, after allowing for variations if the proceeds are dependent on market rates. The cash flow will generate capital to support new developments. The main risks to occur will be in fuel recovery if the wells are situated in territories having an unstable political background and the well prices set. The size of funding required will mean that most corporate borrowing will be through the international money markets.

6.17.6   Investments

Investment companies will also rely significantly on money markets and equity markets to raise new capital. Banks are not in the business to lend money akin to a long-term investment unless it is through their specialised venture capital vehicles. There may, however, be short-term requirements that can be satisfied in the normal course of business, with formal security being taken on the underlying investments. There may also be demand for short-term finance to enable the borrower to take advantage of sudden market investment opportunities. The investment company may use derivatives to safeguard the immediate value of its portfolio or to underwrite guarantees given to investors. If so, the lending bank should be aware of the borrower's investment policy and the maximum risk it is prepared to take in its portfolio dealings.

6.17.7   Non-profit-making organisations

Non-profit-making organisations/entities, depending on their size, may have little or no professional financial management. The lending risk is if they overstretch their expenditure budget and have no clear means to raise further financial resources. Where their rules permit borrowing the lending bank should check how commercialised is the business: what is its objectives? Can income be increased rapidly if it is needed? Is it an association (possibly a company limited by guarantee) where the membership may fluctuate from year to year or a more established, large company having underlying legacies providing a high annual income? It should be noted that a registered charity has no powers to borrow funds.

6.17.8 Clubs and associations

Clubs and associations are usually non-statutory bodies, non-profit-making, with their own operating rules and regulations, including a statement of their borrowing powers that the bank should be conversant with. Where borrowing is allowed, there is usually only a nominal recourse to the members. The committee members may be volunteers with a modest knowledge of financial management. Few of these bodies will hold property as an asset that might be available to the bank as security for an advance. Personal guarantees from committee members are a possibility, but may prove difficult to obtain when management decisions are subject to a majority vote at any time and the appointment of committee members is vested for only short periods, commonly three years.

6.17.9 Partnerships

Partnerships may be limited, unlimited, or have limited partners within an unlimited partnership. The partnership may be a professional business (accountants or solicitors) or a commercial business that has not decided to convert into a limited company. Professional partners will be looking to the annual profits of the partnership to earn a living; nevertheless, this should not prevent the partnership agreement from having a clause stipulating therein that a certain amount of capital should always remain invested in the business. Professional partnerships will have a clients account to hold money on deposit pending payment away under client instructions and this can be additional short-term deposit business for the bank. In terms of risk a commercial partnership should be viewed in a similar way as lending to a commercial company.

6.17.10 Pharmaceuticals

Pharmaceutical companies will have large research and development units and their products can take many years before they are proven for commercially exploitation. Their research projects should be safeguarded with patents. The risk is that much expenditure over many years may lead to abandonment of the project in not meeting its requirements or failing to gain authorisation to be sold to the public. There is also the risk of supplying drugs to the public that are subsequently proved dangerous and raise litigation. Depending on the size of the company, access will be needed to the money market(s) for raising ongoing, long-term capital.

6.17.11 Telecommunications

Telecommunications, now that it is unregulated and open to competition, will be relying for growth on the public paying for new services and products. This will demand a high investment and then active marketing for businesses to achieve 'critical mass' in the sector in a competitive environment. It will be important for the bank to check the accuracy of the cash flow expected by the business on which to base a lending decision. New developments preferably should be financed to a major degree out of existing cash flow or capital raised for that purpose.

6.17.12　Transport

Transport businesses require capital for fleet replacements, acquisitions and operating overheads that will include the payment of fiscal duties and road tolls, both of which are out of the control of the business. Delivery times for the transport of perishables have to be strictly adhered to and a truck's use may be limited to the same type of load once it is used and contaminated (eg cheeses). The lending risk may be lessened where long-term hire contracts are employed, especially if the contract is on a cost-plus basis. Asset security is a problem as the vehicles are always on the move, frequently overseas, and depots are rented rather than owned freehold. If the fleet is leased or being purchased on hire purchase, the value of fleet assets will be diluted as security for another lender.

6.17.13　Utilities

Utilities are now also unregulated and subject to competition. This is particularly evident where a competitor from another geographic area is allowed to sell electricity and/or gas at a unit price lower than the incumbent local supplier. There may be the liability of having to upgrade the infrastructure and/or create new supplies to meet an expected higher demand from the public. These operating risks are somewhat abated through the fact that there is a captive market that cannot do without the services provided. A loan proposition should incorporate an assessment of long-term expenditure needs and compare this with the potential rewards for the company, always taking into account any government restraints on price increases to the public.

6.17.14　AIM-quoted companies

AIM-quoted companies, rather than companies having a full Stock Exchange quotation, will be incurring the benefits of less official regulation and lower costs to have the advantage of access to the public for financing. The great majority of companies will be fledgling businesses, neither achieving profits nor having established a mature market for the product(s) or service(s) being developed. To this extent, equity financing, coupled with some venture (risk) capital from specialised financial organisations, will comprise the bulk of the initial funding package. There can be the modest addition of an overdraft from a traditional banking source or, by choice, a secured short-term loan. The skills and qualities of the management will be of prime importance when deciding whether to advance commercial funds.

6.18   Summary table

Each business will have its own characteristics that will affect the type of loan advanced and the lending risks involved. All types of business will require 'working capital' at some stage. By this is meant current assets that are used in the business to earn a profit rather than being invested in the business on assets of some permanence that are used to earn a profit. A simplified table of the most common types of business with their specialist borrowing needs and particular credit risks is summarised:

Types of business	Typical borrowing need	Typical credit risk
Agricultural	Seasonal working capital	Market prices
Chemicals	Research and development	Market demand/competition
Conglomerates	Expansion	Multiple cash flows
Computers	Research and development	Technical developments
Construction	Working capital	Fixed price long-term contracts
Defence	Contract financing	Fixed prices/technical developments
Electronics	Research and development	Technical developments
Engineering	Contract financing	Contract pricing/demand
Entertainment	Promotion/asset replacing	Lack of profitability/demand
Exploration	Long-term investment	Cash flow
Financial institutions	Working capital	Bad debts/investments
Food	Expansion	Competition/pricing
Fuels	Asset exploitation	External environment
Investment companies	Long term investment	Investment losses
Leisure	Asset investment	Changing fashions
Non-profit-making	Working capital	Financial management
Partnerships	Working capital	Capital withdrawal
Pharmaceuticals	Research and development	Non-productive research and development
Property	Long-term investment	Market demand/rent yield
Retailers	Working capital	Competition/sales demand
Telecommunications	System development	Long lead-in time/competition
Transport	Working capital	Demand/operating costs
Utilities	Supply financing	Regulatory environment
AIM-listed companies	Expansion	Lack of profitability

Seven

Managing risk

7.1 The make up of a lending portfolio

When considering a loans portfolio, there can be significant differences in overall profitability for a bank or lending institution according to the mix of loans and/or sources of deposits held. Some types of lending are inherently more profitable than others and this also applies to deposits received. A lending portfolio can only be entertained if there are funds in hand to lend to customers. These funds may be gained directly from the intake of deposits, through bidding for funds from the (inter-bank) money market, from taking term deposits from commercial or retail sources or, to a lesser degree, as a result of account management and transmission activities by customers.

The use of deposits, and hence the profitability of the lending portfolio, will be set by the interaction of three variables: the basic cost of the money borrowed by the bank, its source and the fixed term (or period) the deposit has been lent. The old adage 'don't borrow short to lend long' still holds true for banks. There is always the risk that a (relatively) short-term deposit may move out of the bank at maturity to be deposited elsewhere in the money market if the interest offered is not competitive or if it was surplus working capital now required to be re-used in the customer's business. Either way, the bank will need to replace the deposit lost with new money or accept a corresponding fall in liquidity.

The basic cost will be market driven, in that commercial competition will determine the rate offered. The size of the deposit will partly determine the rate offered, otherwise the cost will most likely be judged according to ease of placement and possible lethargy on the part of the (smaller business) lender to accept the best rate offered rather than what is available. The source of deposits will also determine their cost: inter-bank interest rates will be 'fine' quotations close to the ruling minimum lending rate set by the Bank of England, but money bid for from commercial companies will be less expensive.

Where the deposit is for a fixed term, its cost will mirror the yield curve for maturities accepted by the money market at that time (after due allowance for the 'turn' or margin offered by the bank bidding for the funds). The yield curve will be the benchmark for dealings having that period to maturity and will be compiled from the individual rates offered by a setting group of major banks for deposits (and loans) for each maturity band, eg commonly seven days, one month, three months, six months, one year, two years, three years, five years and at five-yearly intervals up to 20 years or more. Intervening 'odd' periods will be broadly pro-rata, where available, with the yield taking into account the non-standard singularity of the period.

What have been termed account management and transmission activities by customers relate to the current account balances held by, and necessary for, businesses to conduct their day-to-day dealings, assuming that, at the end of each day, any 'net' balance on the accounts managed will not be transferred automatically to an overnight deposit account and earn interest at the overnight market rate with the bank. These current account balances may only earn 0.1% pa from the bank, although competition is becoming more prevalent to offset the loss of interest with free banking on other services. Transmission balances will comprise items in course of transit between customers' bank accounts that cannot be drawn against or earn interest until after expiry of the transmission period, usually from two to five days, but competition among banks is reducing this time period down to zero in some cases.

7.2 Developing a bank's portfolio

There are three basic options how a bank might develop its lending portfolio: through organic growth, by acquisition or by diversification, geographically or product-led. In many cases, the strategy adopted will constitute a mixture of all these options, with the principal aim being to improve profitability within an acceptable risk framework. Profitability itself has various definitions, the most prevalent being the return earned on capital employed.

7.2.1 Organic growth

Organic growth in one's own domicile is probably the easiest to achieve, as it does not require foreknowledge of new lending markets or the capital cost of raising a presence in new locations. It does require the procurement of new customers and/or selling more existing products to more customers. The latter is easier to accomplish than the former because of its captive audience. The return from marketing for new customers may be initially negative in profitability terms, depending on the incentives offered for a business to change banks.

The portfolio risk for a bank in accepting a new customer from another banking institution should be very carefully assessed. There must be a reason for the request and this may reside in the financial viability of the customer, particularly where the former bank has refused a request for more credit. Equally, it may be due to the customer being dissatisfied with the service of that bank and have nothing to do with the lending risk.

7.2.2   The acquisition

The acquisition of an existing loans portfolio may be through the takeover of another bank or the purchase of a separate loans portfolio. Due diligence as to the risks of accepting bad or doubtful debts must be undertaken in depth. The frequency of takeovers is low in the banking sector due to political reasons and the public sensitivity recognised by the authorities not to remove customer choice. Nevertheless, once accomplished and providing the management(s) of both parties can make it work, it can be a most rewarding strategy, initially through paring common costs and extending the customer base.

If the acquisition occurs between banks operating in the same markets, there may still be a different reason for the amalgamation, as in the case of a former building society since converted into a bank being acquired by a bank with a small personal mortgage section, thereby increasing the acquirer's exposure to this sector. This does not supersede the requirement for balancing lending risk within the bank's portfolio. Another example would be where the acquiring bank is purchasing sub-prime customers and accepting that the higher margin reward has to be balanced by the higher default risk.

7.2.3   Geographic diversification

The diversification may instead apply to the geographic area of operations rather than to the type of borrower. One bank may decide to expand in Asia, while another may choose Africa or North America to be its main thrust to gain business in future in another market. The choice will be determined through a mixture of political acceptance, the traditional image that potential customers perceive for the bank in that overseas market, the importance of local business contacts, the expected profitability of future operations and the type of business that is likely to arise. An example of this portfolio risk will be to determine how business in overseas countries will fit into the bank's global trading picture. This could entail the acceptance of seasonal deposits from customers in one country counteracted by lending seasonally to customers situated in another country.

7.2.4 Comparative analysis

Consider the following proportionate, comparative analysis of two major UK banks' assets, liabilities and returns at the close of business in 2004. The funds figures are shown to a loans asset base of 100.

Selected balance sheet figures only *	Bank A	Bank B
Sources of funds:		
Deposits lodged by banks	22.3	24.5
Deposits from customers	68.7	70.5
	91.0	**95.0**
Application of funds:		
Loans to banks	13.2	14.4
Loans to customers	86.7	85.6
	100.0	**100.0**
Average gross yield on banking monies:		
Interest-earning assets	6.89	5.30
Interest-bearing liabilities	4.59	2.70
Interest spread (excluding interest-free funds)	**2.30**	**2.60**
Proportion of non-interest to total income	48%	59%
Cost to income ratio	51%	40%

Loans portfolio:	B of E #	Bank A	Bank B
Manufacturing	3	2	3
Service industries	4	4	16
Property and construction	9	5	16
Financial	34	16	19
Personal	45	68	44
Other sectors	5	5	2
Total (percentages)	**100**	**100**	**100**

* Figures exclude the capital of each bank, the value of fixed assets owned, and the commercial debt raised on its own account less any debt held as investments.

Figures include lending to UK residents as at 31 December 2004 for all banks.

Source: the Bank of England.

The loans portfolio table figures should be taken as a guide only in the absence of a more accurate comparison. The Bank of England entries include securities dealing advances. If this is excluded from the total, the percentage for financials drops to 26%, that for personal rises to 51% and property and construction to 10%. The conclusion suggested is that the major banks operate according to their individual portfolio characteristics derived from their historic customer base rather than a central guideline. Significant changes to this base would depend principally on winning customers from other lenders. Where a Bank of England directive requests that banks reduce their exposure in certain sectors, eg property lending, this is most likely to affect the influx of new business loans rather than reduce existing exposure.

Banks A and B have been chosen at random for their relative divergent interests and profitability. In these cases, the analysis of their principal working balance sheets is quite similar, whereas their interest margin profitability varies. Comparison of their lending portfolios shows a wide divergence in the categories of borrowing customers. Analysing the figures further discloses that fee income and non-mainstream lending activities are proportionately higher for Bank B and this bank achieved greater success in curbing operating costs.

The marketing of new lending products and services probably offers the greatest reward potential, as well as a high degree of risk element, but it is an area that can soon be copied by competitors and it is also necessary to gain acceptance of the new product(s) or services by customers to succeed. The most opportune way for a bank to satisfy customer demand is to tailor financial products specifically to the customers' needs, if necessary through offering a package of services.

For instance, banks are increasingly offering a mixture of overdraft, loan and leasing/ invoice discounting facilities, each set out to deal with the specific financial interests of the business: the overdraft to meet seasonal credit demand, the loan to provide hard core longer-term finance and the leasing facility to facilitate asset replacements, with invoice discounting to draw on as the business and its debtors portfolio expands faster than the equity capital invested in the business might otherwise warrant.

7.3   Portfolio risks relating to the customer

An analysis of the number of large, medium and small-sized companies having a London market share price quotation in terms of their market prices at mid-May 2005 (see Appendix 1) does not appear to reveal any specific correlation as to their lending risk. An overall price/earnings (P/E) ratio (see Appendix 7) for the market of a fraction under 16 times is similar for most sectors of business except basic industries and cyclical consumer goods (lowly-rated sectors) and information technology (highly rated).

Yet one might argue that the sectors having the lowest lending risk (utilities and non-cyclical services) should be those with the highest P/E ratios. One says 'arguably' on the basis that the consumer will always require water and electricity supplies (utilities) as much as food, drugs and telecommunications (non-cyclical services).

The price/earnings ratio of a share is a recognised, but not the only, guide to the value of that share; it is defined as the share price divided by the distributable annual earnings of the company, each denominated in pence. Put another way, it is the number of years' purchase of the earnings of that company. When earnings are rising rapidly, the growth is built into the share price, so that a company perceived as having double the growth rate of another share would have twice its P/E ratio. The operable word is 'perceived' since the growth rate (and its P/E ratio) will change according to the actual earnings that company achieves each year.

An individual bank may wish to take advantage of the lower lending risk offered by a particular business sector, but there are two other factors to bear in mind: a lower risk sector usually offers a lower lending margin for the bank and, secondly, the bank has to take account of the credit standing of individual companies. The largest company may fall on hard trading times, but this will not necessarily lead to insolvency or a re-capitalisation of debt and consequent loss to the lending bank. Losses may occur more frequently with smaller companies having fewer financial resources at hand and less chance to amend their trading strategy.

7.3.1   Bad and doubtful debts

There is increasing evidence to support the perspective that banks are becoming more reactive to the risk of bad debts rather than passively waiting until a default arises. Aside from the daily update of accounts records via computer printouts, from which hard core lending can be monitored and excesses over facility limits are highlighted, bank relationship account managers typically have up to 80 or so active accounts that are visited once or twice a year, together with telephone contact updates. This does rely on a pertinent two-way dialogue with the customer and assumes that the company spokesperson has up-to-date financial information on which to pass a judgement to the banker. Certainly, greater monitoring prominence should be given automatically to cyclical industries and other sectors recognised as commencing or already being affected by a trading downturn within their industry.

The bank examples given earlier showed the following bad and doubtful debt provisions at the end of 2004. These figures are not too divergent in total, although they could suggest that reduced company fortunes in future in the service industries, property and personal lending would affect Bank B rather more than Bank A, always offset of course by the degree that losses are mitigated through the security held underlying each loan.

As per cent of loans outstanding	Bank A	Bank B
Specific provisions (net of recoveries)	0.89	1.06
General provisions	0.18	0.17
Combined	**1.07**	**1.23**

It should be noted that the 'general provisions' are, in effect, amounts set aside out of earnings not related to specific debts, but reflect the bank's portfolio in general relative to the state of the economy and how this might affect the debts of customer accounts operating in those sectors in future. Reference should be made to Appendix 1 and the tables analysing lending in the banking sector according to industries.

7.4　Risk and the use of derivatives

There are many types of risk. For the lending banker this devolves on the probability of failure or loss associated with a particular course of action that results in an undesirable event. Evaluating the event will take into account the probability that it will occur and the magnitude of its effect should it occur. Banks should not accommodate events that are too risky as a lending proposition, but when does risk reach this state? Every bank must make its own judgement as to what degree of risk it is willing to countenance in regard to each lending decision.

Where companies set up to transact sophisticated treasury functions and wish their bank(s) to take the counterparty risk, the banks would be highly exposed themselves if they did not match their open currency or interest rate positions through the market by transacting offsetting positions in the appropriate derivative instruments. A derivative in its widest sense is defined as something that arises from another source. In banking terminology, it means a financial instrument that is derived from the value and type of trading risk involved. The various financial instruments are explained hereafter, including how they relate to portfolio lending.

7.4.1　Value at risk

The measurement of risk commonly used today by the major banks is called 'value at risk' (VaR for short) and was believed first adopted by JP Morgan in the 1990s. Each bank operates with a changing portfolio of trading instruments that hold different risks and the need was to raise a method of calculating levels of risk that the management would be prepared to accept. The calculations incorporate a mixture of views on interest rates, equity share prices, currency rates, loan creditworthiness, commodity prices and other (macro-economic) factors. The potential loss in currency value of trading positions due to adverse market movements is calculated over different periods of time for assumed different percentage confidence levels.

The most frequent time period taken is one day, on the basis that the bank can reset the risk exposure the next day by trading out of its position, either by closing the open position(s) to realise the loss or possibly by hedging (ie protecting) the exposure forward into another time period and taking the view that the loss position will reverse. This latter option is rarely chosen in practice because major dealing losses have arisen through bank dealers continually carrying forward their (unauthorised) loss positions to enormous proportions without a market recovery being seen.

Having calculated the risk of losses for each time period, the next step is to choose an acceptable confidence level. This may be stated as a 99% (or 95% or whatever is chosen) probability that, under normal market conditions, there is only a 1% (ie 100% less 99% et seq) chance for a loss to occur greater than the currency value proposed as being acceptable to the bank. As might be expected, the higher the VaR currency value, then the greater the risk for the bank to incur a larger loss than if there were a lower VaR. It is important for the bank to monitor its own VaR constantly and the dealing losses publicised recently by several banks have accumulated in size before being discovered largely due to poor internal monitoring procedures and controls.

VaR has its limitations when used to predict future losses: when trading markets are volatile, the risk to reward ratio increases. If a one-day scenario is computed, this will not account for dealing positions longer than one day or, indeed, for dealings in a fluctuating market during the day. The calculations are only as good as the basic programming material being assumed and it is difficult to predict with accuracy by how much, and when, world markets will react to changing circumstances. It has been mentioned that the matching of exposures, be they currency exchange rates or interest rates, is a key measure to adopt to limit risk. It should be remembered that for every bank deal there has to be another market source to take the counter view and that, in itself, is a further risk.

7.4.2   The financing risk

Every company has the risk at any one time of not being able to finance its trading from commercial sources or, if that is possible, of financing at a cost that uses up most of its earnings after tax and provides an inadequate return for its shareholders/ owners. This risk includes the potential inability to refinance existing debt when that matures or is repaid.

From the company's point of view, there is some merit in having more than one funding source, providing the finance required can support the business operating with two banks. The advantages are that there will be a greater likelihood of competition giving the best financing terms for the company and possibly greater choice of financial products. The disadvantages are that having two bank relationships may prove difficult if the company has to offer security and/or requires financial support at a time of need (one bank may be sympathetic and the other bank not so sympathetic). Larger corporations, because of their size of operations will have several banks, usually drawn together in a syndication, providing banking services and each bank will set its own credit limit for that customer as a matter of prudence.

7.4.3   The currency risk

To put risk management into perspective, not all risks relate to trading deals and not all risks have to be covered against loss. When dealing in **foreign currencies**, there will be an economic factor affecting a company's trade generally that could be partially or wholly hedged. How much turnover should be hedged and over what period? To what extent should future profits be safeguarded? A good example is the cross-border motor vehicle industry where a manufacturer (Porsche) exports most of its production to the United States. A majority share of its forward dollar receipts are hedged up to two years in advance to safeguard profit earned from currency fluctuations relative to the euro. Volkswagen similarly hedges up to 75% of its North American earnings in this manner.

Similar questions may be asked when embarking on a long-term project involving other currencies. Assumptions made now may be entirely different when the project comes to fruition. To what extent should tender prices reflect hedged currencies? The construction industry is an example in this case. There are also accounting risk variations that occur: the balance sheet value of a deal from year to year may differ from its risk at both inception and maturity.

Unless the local currency is tied to other currencies or to decisions made by centralised bodies (eg the euro), there will be the risk of fluctuations when cross-border transactions are incurred and have subsequently to be settled in non-local currencies. This will apply to currency borrowings, asset and other liability transactions and trading receipts and payments. Currency swaps and other derivative options can be used similar to the interest rate options available that are described later in this chapter.

Swaps are widely used for hedging currency rate (and interest rate) risks where there is volatility of rates or where companies wish partially or wholly to eliminate the effect of changes in rates on their trading returns. They do not incur an up-front investment of funds and they offer good market liquidity for trading in a competitive environment.

A tenet of all borrowing should be to match receipts and payments as to value and maturity in the same currencies as much as possible to offset any currency fluctuation risk. Trading transactions can be matched by utilising currency accounts for receipts and payments on a daily basis. Single transfers will only be required where the imbalance becomes significant and is of some permanence. The transfer will be done at the spot currency rate available at the time of dealing.

Where there is a permanent imbalance between the overseas and the local currencies, the company may wish to take a view and hold the currency on deposit in that country in order to profit from any future appreciation. If the money being earned overseas is required at home to assist cash flow as it arises, it can be repatriated in due course, again at the spot rate. For these dealings, no currency hedging will be necessary.

On the other hand, if the foreign currency to be received from trading has some regularity of amount and timing and the company wishes not to take the risk that the currency rate will move adversely, the bank can be requested to enter into a forward transaction at today's currency rate calculated on the value of money to be received in future. This sum can be repatriated now as a short-term loan, to be repaid when the currency receipts are duly received.

In essence, a **currency swap** contract involves two different currencies, where the notional principal amounts are physically exchanged on maturity. The swap may also be a combined interest rate and currency deal (interest rate swaps are commented on later in this chapter). A 'differential swap' is where a reference interest rate in one currency is applied to a notional principal of another currency. The two swap parties may be bank-to-bank or corporations with a bank intermediary. The risks of the bank are related to the counterparty(s).

7.4.4   Currency risk example

Taking a simple example, a customer expects to receive US$100 in six months' time and asks its bank to sell the equivalent amount of US$ today for delivery in six months time and to loan it the proceeds in sterling now. The present exchange rate is US$100 = £60. The customer either expects US$ meanwhile to lose value (in which case, conversion of US$100 in six months' time will be less than £60) or wishes to receive the cash now for use in its business. The bank has lent the customer £60 and has a future liability of paying the market US$100 in six months' time. The customer has to repay £60 after six months when it will receive US$100. The risk of the bank is:

◆ that the loan outstanding to the customer of £60 for six months will not be repaid; and
◆ there is a **forward liability** to pay the market US$100 in six months' time.

There is a currency mismatch and in this case the bank does not wish to take this risk. The bank therefore buys US$ 100 for delivery in six months' time from the market (ie another bank) to match the transaction. The cost to the bank will be the supply of £60 to lend plus the two currency deals. The customer will have to pay the borrowing cost and the equivalent currency deal cost. Interest spreads and dealing margins have been ignored.

The bank could have decided that US$ 100 today would be worth (in today's sterling terms) only US$90 in six months' time. It may decide not to buy US$100 forward for delivery in six months' time, but to take the risk of exchange rates moving in its favour to buy dollars at the 'spot' (ie immediate delivery) price ruling in six months' time. This exposure will have to be within the internal limits for dealing set by the bank.

7.4.5 Other hedging choices

What other choices are open to the customer and the bank? Instead of selling dollars forward, an **option** (to deal for forward delivery) could have been taken to sell in six months' time at the prevailing currency rate now. An option has the advantage of being exercised or abandoned by the purchaser. The option will be taken up if a profit ensues and US$ 100 costs less than £60 for the bank, otherwise the converse will apply.

A 'call option' gives the right to purchase currency and a 'put option' the right to sell the currency. If the purchaser is dealing in a volatile currency with significant fluctuations in exchange rates to the home currency, a 'cylinder option' may be taken out. This sets dealing limits up above and below the present spot rate when the option will be exercised (within the cylinder price limits) and limits the attaching risks of a profit and a loss.

Similar to an option is a more recent addition to the derivatives market called a **covered warrant**. The warrant is 'covered' in that no short selling (without the underlying asset as backing) is permitted. The warrant gives the holder the right, but not the obligation, to buy or sell a currency (or asset, share or index) at a predetermined price on or before a fixed (expiry) date in the future. Such warrants are issued by banks and other financial institutions, are negotiable and usually have a longer maturity (up to two years) than options. The underlying asset is the security for the deal and there is a conversion ratio (of so many warrants per single asset). The offer (purchase) and bid (sale) price spreads can be very wide and the possible risk/reward ratio is therefore highly geared.

7.4.6 The interest rate risk

Commercial interest rates are set by dictum and perception. It may be the decision of the Bank of England to raise or lower the structure of UK interest rates as applied through the markets, or it may be the markets reacting in advance of changes or reacting as a result of known or perceived influences that it believes will affect future interest rates. There is a constant risk that changes in the structure of interest rates will upset the commercial strategy of businesses.

For example, company borrowings may be incorporated into the pricing of sales products at, say, 6% pa, whereas unexpected sharp interest rate movements may push the rate up to 8% pa. If the company has not allowed for this change in advance, its profit margin on sales will be eroded due to the consequent higher borrowing costs. Fortunately, there are derivative instruments available that can allow for interest rate changes at a very modest dealing cost compared with the loss that would otherwise be incurred if no interest rate hedging had been done.

7.4.7 Swaps

An ideal instrument for hedging interest rate (or currency) risk is a **swap**. Perhaps the simplest hedge is when a company borrows money at a variable interest rate, but wishes to eliminate any subsequent interest rate movement that would push up its cost of borrowing. A swap of the underlying interest rate is done with a counterparty: the company accepts an agreed fixed interest rate on the borrowing and the provider (bank) intermediary takes over the risk of the variable interest rate element on the debt.

Thus, the swap contract commits two parties to exchange two streams of interest (or currency) payments over an agreed period calculated to apply to a common, but notional, principal amount. One party agrees to remit a flow of cash payments, equivalent to a fixed interest rate on the principal sum, to the other party, who in turn will make cash payments equivalent to a floating interest rate on the same principal sum back to the original party. The dates of the payments swaps need not be coincidental but the maturity dates of the agreement have to match.

A 'basis swap' is similar, except the swap is between two floating rate calculations with different reference rates, eg six-month LIBOR and 30-day commercial paper. Other references commonly used are contracted between 'fixed-fixed' or 'fixed-floating' rates.

There are different ways how a swap can be structured: the debt itself can be transferred, or substituted, by the lender in the inter-bank market if the lender does not wish to take the fixed interest rate loan on its own books or the loan principal can be exchanged notionally (with no principal changing hands) so that, at each interest rate settlement date, only the cash difference between the variable and the fixed interest rate calculations is paid over by one party to the other (according to how the variations in the fixed and floating interest rates have moved during the last settlement period), leaving the company bearing only the amount of the fixed interest rate cost that it required at the outset.

7.4.8 More specialist interest rate hedging variations

Fluctuations can occur in interest rates and there are instruments to counter this risk. A **forward-forward** deal commences on one forward date and ends on another forward date. When a borrowing (or deposit) deal is known to arise in the near future, it can be useful to lock in the interest rate based on the market's current interest rate structure rather than have the uncertainty of waiting until the date the deal commences and be governed by interest rates at that time. The lending bank will incur an interest rate risk exposure up to the time the deal matures.

An alternative instrument to use would be a **forward rate agreement** (FRA). The FRA is purchased now and fixes in advance the cost of the forward borrowing (or the deposit). In this case, however, the deal is done at the market interest rate ruling on that future day and the FRA separately settles the interest rate difference between the FRA striking price and the ruling interest rate on the deal. The FRA is a known, contingent risk in that it is off balance sheet and does not crystallise until activated. The risk is known and can be re-calculated at any time. It is contingent since the agreement, although binding, has yet to materialise. If a bank has surplus funds and expects interest rates to fall, it could buy an FRA and make a profit if interest rates fall below the FRA rate. If interest rates rise above the FRA rate, however, a loss would be incurred.

A **credit default swap** (CDS) is being increasingly used in the bond (refer to the specialist hedging variations section later) and loan markets for the management of risk. As the name implies, should a borrower default on its loan, the bank or syndicated banks to the lending will be repaid in full from the counterparty, usually an insurance company. CDSs are negotiable in the market and have the advantage that the borrower does not know that its borrowing has been underwritten for risk by the lender. They may lead the bank(s) buying CDSs in the knowledge that the risk of default has already been covered. The cost of the cover will reduce the profit margin to be taken on the loan.

Similar to interest rate hedging options, there are alternative methods for companies to adopt to cover risks: group deposits and borrowings (in like currencies) can be netted out daily, bank accounts can be structured so as to minimise surplus balances and overdrafts, assets and liabilities can be closely matched by value, currencies and maturities, cash flows can be matched to production and trade cycles and the terms of trade can be modified by taking advantage of discounts offered for early settlement or settling in local currencies if borrowing terms are more beneficial.

One final point about external currency trading; 'spot' settlement is made two working days in the future, but it is still the base point for forward trades. A 'forward outright' is an outright purchase or sale of one currency for another for settlement on a fixed date in the future other than the spot date. Banks, however, deal with one another in 'forward swaps', that is, the forward outright price less the current swap price.

7.4.9 Other trading instruments to reduce risks

Some trading instruments have a multi-use, be they used for interest rate or currency or commodity dealings. Similar to an FRA is a **futures contract.** This is formalised by having standard specifications and terminology and can only be dealt through a recognised exchange market. These contracts have the benefit of being able to be traded at any intervening time up to their maturity date. The contracts are quoted as an index shown as '100 minus the agreed interest rate'. There is, in most cases, a notional delivery date and when delivery is due, an exchange delivery settlement price is set, eg 100 minus the BBA (British Bankers Association) three-month LIBOR. The calculations are similar for currency deals.

A bank can **hedge** its FRA exposure through using the futures market rather than using a forward-forward deal, because the former will incur virtually no risk of principal, as it will be settled through the relevant market exchange rather than another market dealer. The exchange partly covers itself against risk by asking that all dealers have to put up an initial (partial) margin as collateral (against adverse market rate movements that might give rise to a default). There is also a variation margin that is paid over daily to mirror each day's dealing profit or loss, thereby leaving the original exposure on the deal intact.

There can be a counterparty risk to the bank where it has allowed the counterparty to settle its daily variation margin through a separate credit facility. Note also that if the bank wishes to cover its risk position after having sold an FRA, it must sell a corresponding futures contract, as the sale of the FRA will be profitable if interest rates rise, in which case the price of the equivalent futures contract would fall and the bank would have sold the contract at the higher price.

7.4.10   More specialist currency rate hedging variations

7.4.10.1   Bonds

A bond is a security issued when a marketable loan is raised and it evidences title to the debt together with the issue terms, including interest payments and repayment of the principal sum. Bonds are usually issued in bearer form, where possession confers ownership, or they may be registered, when they are more correctly called a 'bearer debenture'. A bond issued for less than five years may be called a **note** (or a promissory note as defined in the Bills of Exchange Act 1882). Eurobonds are bearer bonds issued on the international market in various currencies, whereas domestic bonds are issued in individual countries. The market prices of issued bonds reflect the credit standing of the issuer, which may be a government or a public corporation.

Certain types of bonds have specific characteristics: a **floating rate note** (FRN) has a fixed interest margin over a variable interest rate that is based on a known quoted market pricing, such as three or six months LIBOR. Regular interest payments are made until maturity of the FRN that is usually issued initially for a longer period than its cousin, the **certificate of deposit** (CD). Both FRNs and CDs are fully negotiable. There is also a market in **bond futures**, where a seller must deliver to the buyer an agreed amount of bond at an agreed time for an agreed price.

A bank may wish to borrow from the market while holding security in the form of government or high credit quality commercial bonds. The security could be sold to realise cash, otherwise the bank may enter into a **(sale and) repurchase agreement** (a 'repo') with a counter-party to sell the security and, at the same time, buy back the same security at a subsequent date at an agreed price. It is equivalent to borrowing cash against collateral and offers a further instrument to improve market liquidity. The borrowing bank's risk is for performance at maturity.

A bank's near-liquid earning assets will include a portfolio of bonds, subject to the risk of changing yields generally, as well as the standing of the issuer. If a government is the issuer, the economic and fiscal policies of that government will influence demand for the bond issue (be they UK gilt-edged securities or USA Treasury Notes). Government bonds have good marketability due to the size of the issues regardless of the ruling interest rate yields, but corporation bonds stand a much greater risk of difficulty of realisation and a capital loss if the creditworthiness of an issuer is lost, as happened to one well-publicised portfolio of high-risk international corporate bonds held by Abbey Bank in 2003 when they were realised in the market.

7.4.11   A summary of available derivatives and their characteristics

The relative characteristics and risks of the various forms of derivatives discussed are summarised in the following table.

Instrument	Maturity (typical)	Negotiable	Risk factor basis
Overdraft	On demand to 1 yr	No	Creditworthiness
Commercial paper	1 to 6 months	Yes	Issuer
Futures contract	Up to 3 months	Yes	Exchange traded
Bond futures	Up to 3 months	No	Counterparty
'Repo' agreement	Up to 3 months	No	Collateral backed
Bill of exchange	3 or 6 months	Yes	Acceptor
Floating rate note	Up to 6 months	Yes	Issuer
Option	Up to 6 months	Yes	Exchange/issuer
Certificate of deposit	Up to 1 year	Yes	Issuer
Forward-forward	Up to 1 year	No	Counterparty
Forward rate agreement	Up to 1 year	No	Contingent/issuer
Covered warrant	Up to 2 years	Yes	Exchange/issuer
Swap	3 months to 10+ yrs	No	Counterparty
Loan	Variable 1–10+ yrs	No	Creditworthiness
Bonds	Can be up to 30 yrs	Yes	Credit standing

7.4.12   Ratings services

There are subscription services available to assist lenders, including banks, and investors in evaluating the risks of individual companies, sectors and countries. A credit rating indicates the likelihood of default on its financial obligations. Three well-known services are Standard & Poors, Moodys and Fitch Ratings. Their evaluation procedures are broadly similar, offering some 20 valuation gradings, and are based on a mixture of public information and personal interviews with corporate managements. A final assessment grades each company and this grade, with subsequent changes, is largely relied on to price the public funding programmes for those companies by investment banks. Fitch has recently introduced a new service, assigning recovery ratings to borrowers that indicate the likelihood of recouping indebtedness in the event of insolvency or bankruptcy (low to high recovery prospects).

The risk evaluation covers an assessment of the corporation's strategy, management, competitors, suppliers, customers, gearing, capital spending programmes, banking relationships and the regulatory environment to build up a medium-term earnings model (say three years) which is then subjected to discounted cash flow value analysis and compared with price/earnings ratios, efficiency valuations and profit margins of peer groups. This is then brought together into a final, single rating.

Since public companies must provide a statement for the public at the earliest opportunity to the Stock Exchange of any news that is share price sensitive, it is not necessarily the case that the ratings services will be evaluating companies in advance of important news or, indeed, that their evaluation will be accurate. Rather, the value lies in their reasons behind a grading change, the benchmarking of companies to their peer groups and, particularly, when assessing sovereign risks.

7.4.13   Bank relationships: Loans syndicates

The relationship between a bank and its customer is contractual, that of (lending) debtor and creditor (or vice versa if taking deposits) and of agent and principal (in collecting and paying cheques). The lending banker may have a primary or secondary relationship with the company: the primary relationship would be where the bank acts as the company's daily transaction bank and is a major source of finance to the company. A secondary relationship would be where the bank joins a **loans syndicate** in a minor role and leaves the management to the principal managers of the facility. In this case, the bank will be relying to a degree on the prime banker(s) for assessing the credit risk and the pricing of the loan deal. For this service, the secondary bank will be earning a lower fee on its facility than that being earned by the prime lenders.

Whether or not a bank is a prime or a secondary source for the company, a risk evaluation is still required and it might be said that the risk position of a secondary source bank is inferior should a default occur. It would have limited input to the terms of any restructuring of debt and possibly access to the available security. The prime source bank will have daily knowledge of the financial conduct of the company through its bank accounts and should be in a better and earlier position to redeem a deteriorating financial situation where that is possible.

7.4.14   Lending attributes when evaluating loan portfolio risks

The bank, through its account managers when evaluating risk, should:

- be knowledgeable of the business of the company and up-to-date with all published news relating to the company;
- be able to ask one or two pertinent questions about the company's trading;
- know the responsibilities of the people that are to be seen;
- have a common outside interest as a talking point;
- be knowledgeable of all current banking products, even if one's own bank does not offer some of these services;
- be knowledgeable of current banking trends, loan pricing and news;
- hold a view on future monetary economics: interest rates, currency trends, fiscal assumptions and recent public news of relevance;
- try and have at least one new product to hand to offer the company with reasons why this should be considered;
- maintain a regular contact with key personnel in the company;
- prepare a (short) list of relevant questions to ask at the meeting;
- ask if the company has a financial problem requiring assistance;
- let the company executive have his/her say in the conversation;
- try and leave with a return commitment to provide advice.

It will be much harder to raise a new customer than to retain an existing banking relationship. The bank representative should:

- not duck the question if the bank cannot deliver;
- be accurate what the bank can deliver (in terms of pricing etc);
- discuss in detail why there have been any changes in bank policy;
- emphasise what bank product is good value now and why;
- provide a speedy reply to questions raised that cannot be immediately answered;
- set up a dialogue with the bank's in-house specialist provider, if appropriate.

As banks try to raise more and more cross-selling opportunities and the risk exposure to each company enlarges, it will be increasingly important to have an in-depth knowledge of what and how the company is doing. A close relationship between bank and company will work towards this ideal. An example of the benefit of a joint relationship is the monitoring of the company's treasury dealings. Questions to answer include the following.

- Are all operating accounts cleared daily, with the net position deposited overnight?

◆ What is the return on average surplus funds and could the money have been utilised to greater benefit in/outside the business?
◆ If currencies are dealt in, how much percentage cash flow risk is hedged?
◆ What instruments is the company dealing in? Could more appropriate treasury instruments be suggested?
◆ When facility rollovers arise, does the company test the market for the best rates and maturities?
◆ What treasury objectives are in place? How frequently is treasury policy revised?

A model treasury policy must incorporate at least the following characteristics:

Characteristics	Action
Objectives	How is the management of risk to be applied?
Responsibilities	Are all relevant management roles defined?
Identification	Risks relating to currencies, interest rates, refinancing, liquidity, counterparty, macro exposure and investment.
Tolerance	How much risk is to be allowed?
Controls	Is the monitoring of controls adequate?
Reporting	Does this include performance measurement?

7.14.15 Simple derivative examples

Appendix 3 provides from first principles some simple derivative working examples.

Eight

Financial statements

8.1 Background

An important part of assessing the success of a business in achieving its financial goals is to interpret correctly and fully its historical trading record. The figures themselves may be historic, but they will provide the means to assess past actual results with the benchmark of what was forecast, as well as to judge the financial acumen of the management. To do this, knowledge is required of what is shown in the financial accounts.

8.2 Historical accounts

A general definition of a company (or corporation, the words are synonymous) is an association of persons formed as a separate legal entity to carry out a business enterprise and with the authority to act as an individual. Where a UK commercial business is concerned, this 'individual' usually takes the form of a private or public limited company, incorporated and registered under the Companies Acts (1985 or earlier). The business may otherwise be unincorporated as a partnership, with or without limited liability partners.

Companies so regulated have to issue financial statements showing the result of their past trading annually (exceptionally for other periods at the commencement or cessation of business or at a change of accounting date) in a certain format. In order properly to interpret these trading results, bankers should have an understanding of the disclosure regulations, what to look for when examining the accounts and where relevant information is displayed.

Apart from showing the necessary regulatory information, the accounts have to conform to general guidelines issued by the accounting authorities or otherwise provide a statement stating why there has been a divergence and what its effect has been on the operating figures being reported. The Accounting Standards Board (ASB) has set UK accounting standards in the past and various additions and amendments have been published over the years. These standards are now being superseded by International Financial Reporting Standards (IFRS) for the consolidated accounts of quoted companies to apply from 2005.

The expectation is that global companies will report under IFRS but the option to remain under UK ASB standards will still be available for smaller companies. This is not to say that there will be two different standards, but rather that the UK rules will be less onerous in terms of providing the quantity of information. In some respects, the IFRS requirements are less strong than current ASB standards.

8.3   Proposals for accounting standards from 2005/06

The IFRS disclosure standards at present recommended for companies to implement shortly, insofar as they may affect bank loan assessments, are:

Aspect	Content
Business combinations	Assets acquired at their purchase cost Goodwill to be written off in year occurring Intangible assets to be capitalised
Discontinued operations/assets for sale	Show separately, not depreciated
Derivative hedge accounting	Fair value definitions allowed
Financial instruments	Presentation and measurement
Retirement benefits gains or losses	Fully recognised as they arise
Post balance sheet events	Disclosure requirements
Earnings per share (listed companies)	Calculation thereof
Related party disclosures	Definition and disclosure

There are similarities between the disclosure requirements of financial information required by private and public companies. In broad terms, public companies have a greater degree of disclosure as befits their public ownership standing.

8.4 Financial information to be published in the accounts

Reference has been made to medium and small-sized companies. These definitions are laid down as:

Defining conditions satisfying at least two criteria in the current and the preceding year	**Medium-sized company**	**Small-sized company**
Turnover not more than	£22.8 million	£5.6 million
Balance sheet total not more than	£11.4 million	£2.8 million
Employees average number not more than	250	50

Note: the base definitions are quoted in euros, therefore currency fluctuations will slightly amend the values.

The content of the **company report and accounts** will vary according to the size of the company reporting its results. The table following summarises how the information differs in this respect. The lending banker should be conversant with what information is made available and where it is shown in the financial statements.

Content of the company report	**Full disclosure**	**Abbreviated** Medium-sized company	**Abbreviated** Small-sized company
Chair and/or chief executive's operating review of the year	Shown	Usually not shown	Not required
Company information: including directors and advisers	Mandatory	Mandatory	Show company number
Report of the directors	Mandatory	Mandatory	Not required
Corporate governance with directors responsibilities	Mandatory Mandatory	Optional Mandatory	Not required Not required
Independent auditors' report	Mandatory	Mandatory	Mandatory if not exempt

Content of the company report	Full disclosure	Abbreviated Medium-sized company	Abbreviated Small-sized company
(Consolidated) profit & loss account	Mandatory	Mandatory	Not required
(Consolidated) balance sheet	Mandatory	Mandatory	Mandatory
(Consolidated) cash flow statement	Mandatory	Not required	Not required
Note of historical cost profits and losses	Mandatory	Not required	Not required
Reconciliation of movements in shareholders' funds	Mandatory	Not required	Not required
Notes (forming part of the accounts)	Mandatory	Mandatory	Mandatory
Other financial information and notices	Optional	Usually not shown	Not required

8.5   Companies requiring full accounting disclosure

The **Operating Report** will summarise the trading highlights of the year and the board of directors' strategy for the future. This will be useful in preparing questions to put at the interview. A comparison with financial results for earlier years may be shown here or otherwise given in the information at the back of the report. Particular note should be made of any drop in returns compared with the previous year and the reasons given for the fall. Is it likely to recur? Was it due to internal or external factors? Why was the company not better prepared to counteract the fall?

The next important search will be to read the **future plans** proposed for the company. Additional information may be given in the report of the directors' and further clues shown in the notes to the accounts under the headings for capital commitments and post balance sheet events. It may be possible to access additional information from public sources about the company. If it is appropriate, a breakdown of turnover, profit before tax and possibly capital employed (net assets) both geographically and for the different divisions of the company will be set out, together with a summary of continuing and discontinued operations resulting from acquisitions and disposals made during the year.

The **company information** pages will state the principal bankers to the company and list the directors, including non-executives. Their shareholdings and share options in the company and holdings of other investors owning more than 3% of the issued share capital will be revealed in the **Report of the Directors**, which is otherwise a summary of the important events that have occurred during the year.

Corporate governance has had some prominence of late and a new code (of best practice) became applicable to listed (quoted) companies with reporting years beginning on or after 1 November 2003. A prospective banker to the company should note that the directors have to report that the business is a going concern with supporting assumptions or qualifications as necessary. The principle is that the board of directors should present a balanced and understandable assessment of the company's position and prospects and, for this objective to be met, there should be supplied, in a timely manner, information in a form and of quality appropriate to enable a proper discharge of these duties.

The **Independent Auditors' Report** should be read for any possible qualification stated therein. Apart from reassuring the lending banker that proper accounting records have been kept, the audit report also gives a true and fair view, after a test basis on the evidence provided, and reasonable assurance that the amounts and disclosures in the financial statements are free from material misstatement. There is now an audit exemption threshold affecting companies having a year end on or after 30 March 2004, who may now opt out of a statutory audit if their turnover does not exceed £5.6 million (previously £1 million) or where their balance sheet total does not exceed £2.8 million (previously £1.4 million).

The **Profit and Loss Account** can be set out in one of two formats to comply with the Companies Acts. The essential difference is in disclosing operating costs, which may be stated either in a more summarised or a more analysed form.

Summarised form	Analysed form
Turnover	Turnover
Less Cost of sales *	Change in stock of finished goods and work-in-progress
= Gross profit or loss	Own work capitalised
Less Distribution costs *	*Add* Other operating income
Administrative expenses *	*Less* Raw materials and consumables
Add Other operating income	Other external charges
	Staff costs separating social security/ pension costs
*including depreciation that is shown separately in the notes to the accounts	Depreciation and other amounts written off assets
	Exceptional amounts written off current assets
	Other operating charges
Add other income and interest received less paid	*Add other income and interest received less paid*
Less taxation	Less taxation
Less extraordinary charges = Profit or loss for the year	*Less extraordinary charges = Profit or loss for the year*

The **Balance Sheet** disclosure requirements have been standardised in successive Companies Acts. Generally speaking, the reporting figures to be shown are identical for all types of company, but publicly quoted companies have to disclose much greater information in their attached **Notes to the Financial Statements** than private companies.

8.6   Companies not requiring full accounting disclosure

Abbreviated Accounts may be filed by choice by medium-sized and small companies. For medium-sized companies, the format is identical to the full accounts shown above, except that no separate turnover, cost of sales and other operating income have to be disclosed. For small companies, no profit and loss account is required and the notes to the accounts are more limited in disclosure. Small companies may also opt for **minimum disclosure** requirements (with less extensive balance sheet notes and without the need for a cash flow statement) or, as a further choice, choose disclosure under the Financial Reporting Standard for Smaller Entities (FRSSE). There are greater non-disclosure benefits through adopting FRSSE rather than minimum disclosure. The present FRSSE has been re-drafted and the new edition will be effective on accounting periods commencing on or after 1 January 2005.

8.7   Specimen layout of financial statements

Profit and loss account

Statutory layout	*Values*	*Comments on the disclosure requirements*
Turnover	x	split between continuing and discontinued operations
Cost of sales	<u>x</u>	or show separately change in stocks, raw materials, staff costs, depreciation of fixed assets and other operating charges.
Gross profit	x	
Distribution costs	(x)	shown as negative (in brackets)
Administration costs	<u>(x)</u>	shown as negative (in brackets)
Operating profit	x	split between continuing and discontinued operations
Fixed asset changes	x	book profits and losses realised
Investment income	x	
Interest receivable	x	
Interest payable	<u>(x)</u>	shown as negative (in brackets)
Profit before taxation	x	on ordinary activities
Taxation	<u>(x)</u>	on ordinary activities profit
Profit for the financial year	x	
Equity dividends	<u>(x)</u>	declared and proposed
Retained profit	<u>x</u>	for the financial year

Balance sheet

Fixed assets

Intangible assets	x	goodwill, patents, development costs
Tangible assets	x	land, buildings, plant, assets in construction
Investments	<u>x</u>	group and other shares and loans
	x	

Current assets

Stocks	x	includes work-in-progress, payments on a/c
Debtors	x	separating trade other debts and accruals
Cash	<u>x</u>	
	x	
Creditors amounts due within one year	<u>(x)</u>	separating trade and other creditors, loans, payments on account and accruals
Net current assets/ (liabilities)	**x**	
Total assets less current liabilities	x	
Creditors due after one year	(x)	items as for creditors due within one year
Provisions for liabilities & charges	<u>(x)</u>	taxation, pensions, other provisions
Net assets	**<u>x</u>**	figure equals shareholders' funds
Capital and reserves		
Called-up share capital	x	
Share premium account	x	
Revaluation/other reserve	x	
Profit and loss account	<u>x</u>	
Shareholders' funds	**<u>x</u>**	

Note: the Net assets figure will be identical to the Shareholders' funds figure.

Cash flow statement
(where required)

Reconciliation of operating profit to net cash inflow from operating activities

(this reconciliation may alternatively be found in the notes to the accounts)

Operating profit	x	
Depreciation charges	x	
Profit or loss on sale of fixed assets	x	a profit will be negative
Increase in stocks	(x)	a decrease will be positive
Increase in debtors	(x)	a decrease will be positive
Increase in creditors	x	a decrease will be negative
Grants released to income	(x)	
Net cash inflow from operating activities	x	carried down to next statement

Cash flow statement

(a detailed analysis of these items may alternatively be shown in the notes to the accounts)

Net cash inflow from operating activities	x	
Returns on investments and servicing of finance	(x)	interest, dividends, rents
Capital expenditure	(x)	sales, grants less acquisitions
Equity dividends	(x)	
	x	
Financing	x	borrowings less repayments
Increase in cash	x	carried down to next statement

Reconciliation of net cash movement to the movement in net debt

(this reconciliation may alternatively be found in the notes to the accounts)

Increase in cash	x	
Cash inflow from financing	(x)	new loans less repayments
Cash spent on finance leases	(x)	capital element only
Change in net debt resulting from cash flows	x	may be positive or negative
Exchange differences	(x)	may be positive or negative
Movement in net debt	(x)	may be positive or negative
Opening net debt in the period/year	(x)	
Closing net debt in the period/year	**(x)**	

Notes to the financial statements

(the following headings relate to a company with full disclosure)

(entries occur only where occasion demands)

Notes:

1	**Accounting policies**	including turnover, fixed assets, leases, stocks, deferred tax, pensions, research and development expenditure, grants, foreign currencies
2	**Analysis of turnover**	by activity and geographical market
3	**Operating profit**	showing depreciation, lease costs, etc
4	**Freehold property disposal**	if applicable
5	**Directors' remuneration**	total only
6	**Staff numbers and costs**	analysed by department etc
7	**Interest payable**	separating bank debt and finance charges
8	**Taxation**	detailed calculations
9	**Dividends**	proposed (in future will be in creditors)
10	**Tangible fixed assets**	analysed by type of asset and depreciation
11	**Fixed asset investments**	details where applicable
12	**Stocks**	analysed by category
13	**Debtors**	showing trade and other debtors
14	**Creditors falling due within one year**	analysed, includes bank, lease debt
15	**Creditors falling due after one year**	analysed, includes bank, lease debt
16	**Provisions for liabilities: deferred tax**	including change in the year
17	**Share capital called up**	analysed by type of shares
18	**Reserves**	analysed, including change in the year
19	**Contingent liabilities**	description
20	**Commitments**	showing contracted and not contracted
21	**Gross cash flows**	shows financing in year with make-up
22	**Analysis of net debt**	shows change in year with analysis
23	**Post balance sheet events**	description with amounts
24	**Related party transactions**	description with amounts

The following text offers guidance on the more important aspects of the declared information as it relates to a corporate lender. In all cases, a comparison with existing benchmarks set down by the lending bank should be made, as well as a comparison with the policies adopted by peer corporate borrowers operating in similar markets. Where these values or policies differ, a judgement should be made of their materiality to the lending risk. The comments supplied offer a broad outline to understand what can lie behind a company's published information and are not intended to be a substitute for appropriate legal definitions or accounting recommendations or exceptions only rarely met in practice.

8.8   Accounting policies

Certain subsidiary and/or related or associated companies may not be **consolidated** in order for the group accounts to reflect a 'true and fair view' and this can override company law requirements. Care is needed to trace back through any cross-guarantees or contractual liabilities whether the lack of consolidation is material and how it may affect the borrowing company. An important example would be where the borrowing company is a 'shell' with its assets being shares in other group companies who trade and have asset substance. Lending to the shell company could be very risky without the security of cross-guarantees. A comparison of the consolidated balance sheet with the parent balance sheet will show how the assets and liabilities are distributed.

A **subsidiary company** is one where the parent or holding company owns more than half its issued share capital or can effectively control the subsidiary company through the exercise of voting powers. These voting powers may be direct or indirect through other group companies and either share driven or having majority control of the board of directors.

A **related or associated company** is one where it is not wholly owned by the parent company. Disclosure of financial information of a related or associated company is governed by the Companies Acts and recommended accounting principles. Disclosure of shares owned, loans and amounts owed, and income attributable from the related or associated company will be shown in a separate note to the accounts.

The company's policy on **research and development** will be described. The carrying forward of expenditure in the balance sheet, rather than charging it to the profit and loss account as it occurs, can materially affect the company's profit (or loss). The lending bank should be aware how the company expects to amortise this amount, by how much is it likely to increase in future years and whether the full amount is expected to be recovered through future sales relating to this expenditure. The standard is to write off this expenditure against earnings arising from the project.

Goodwill is the excess of the cost of an acquired entity over the total of the fair values of its identifiable assets less liabilities. It is currently written off (against profits) over its estimated useful economic life and there can be an additional 'impairment' charge arising at any time if the value of the net assets falls below book value. This is now being changed so that goodwill has to be written off in its entirety in the year it arises. Where a company is requesting finance to acquire another entity, the extent of the goodwill to be created arising from the purchase price (where it is in excess of the net assets being acquired) will affect earnings for that year and perhaps also the acquisition price on the deal.

A valuation shortfall of the company's in-house **pension fund** may give rise to a significant current liability where the annual contributions charged against profits are insufficient to match the long term actuarial pension liabilities. Where the fund is a defined (retirement) benefit scheme, the underlying assets value (and the company's contribution liability) will fluctuate from year to year. This will not have an effect on cash flow, but it is another liability to account for when calculating the net worth of the business. New (IFRS) accounting regulations now require a company to analyse its pension liability annually and if this is not fully funded, to charge profit and loss account with the full shortfall, even though this may not crystallise for many years. The management may adopt a strategy to eliminate this liability, for example, by closing the end salary-based scheme in favour of an externally funded scheme and/ or increasing the employer's percentage contribution the business makes into the fund. There is no standard method to value pension liabilities.

Foreign currency dealings have previously been translated at the rate of exchange ruling at the balance sheet date. The proposed new standard IAS 39, due for implementation from 2005, is still being amended, but it will require companies to measure financial instruments (derivatives) at fair (or market) value and the trade result taken to the profit and loss account, rather than being valued at their original cost at present with any amortisation in value spread over their effective life. In practice it will make company profits far more volatile and will be particularly important for banks' accounting and when they evaluate company earnings. The main proposals currently are:

◆ only items that are assets and liabilities are to be recognised as such in the balance sheet. Hedged items are excluded and their interim changes in value do not have to be calculated and accounted for;

◆ gains and losses from hedging do not have to be allocated across all the individual items being hedged;

◆ any prepayment risks are to be priced based on expected rather than contractual time periods;

◆ fair values are limited to the first date when the counterparty can demand payment.

8.9   Turnover

Depending on the size of the company, turnover will be analysed by activity and by geographical market. Any significant changes to the mix reported should be enquired after. Not necessarily shown, but nevertheless very relevant, will be the profit earned from each activity. Going a stage further, the estimated market share the company enjoys and the proportion of turnover arising from the largest two or three customers will also be important information to judge the future value of the business if this information can be obtained.

8.10   Changes in operations

The profit and loss account or notes to the financial statements must show separately turnover, cost of sales, selling and distribution costs and operating profit/loss for continuing operations, acquisitions made and discontinued operations. When a bank assesses the company's earnings forecasts, it should rely on projections of continuing operations together with an estimate of the full year's contribution attributable to any acquisitions, ensuring that the latter will also include the cost of the acquisition on a full year basis. This may then be compared with the return from continuing operations for the previous year and a judgement made on the acquisition strategy whether the lending risk has increased.

8.11   Staff numbers and costs

The number of production and sales staff divided into the sales achieved will be a comparative guide to the efficiency of operations, as will changes in overall wage costs. The figures will be the averages for the year and it would be advantageous to compare the analysis with end-year figures if they can be obtained from the company. This would reveal the recruitment trend.

8.12   Taxation

Corporation tax will be deferred if the total capital allowances claimed on assets exceed the current tax charge on profits. The reconciliation of current tax shown in the notes to the accounts will reveal the extent of this deferral and also whether there are any group losses set against profits. This will be helpful if the bank is not aware that a part of the group is loss making.

8.13 Tangible and Intangible assets

The specimen financial statements provided earlier mentioned the analysis of items grouped under these headings. The cost of additions will be necessary to include in the calculation of the company's cash flow. There may have been a revaluation of land and buildings or other assets in the past and any surplus arising would also be shown under shareholders' funds as a revaluation reserve. The date and type (eg open market current use basis) of revaluation will be shown. If property values have since fallen there should be a note to this effect, but it will not necessarily indicate a firm revised value, only a directors' opinion thereof.

8.14 Acquisitions

Subject to the size of the company and whether it is publicly quoted, there should be included a summary of the financial effects of any acquisitions or sales made during the year, if material. Any deferred consideration for these purchases may still be outstanding and will affect future cash flow. There may be conditions attaching to the deferral (ie the purchase price being subject to future trading returns of that business) that will be of note to the bank. Full financial information about the acquisition may not be evident, particularly where the vendor has sold a division of its company that does not compile separate financial statements other than management figures.

8.15 Borrowings

It will be of interest to the bank if the company discloses information greater than the statutory requirement of disclosing total borrowings repayable within one year, between one and two years, between two and five years and after five years. Some analysis by type of borrowing will be given, such as between overdraft, bank loans, hire purchase and finance leases and loan stock. Public companies will additionally report on the amounts and cost margins of fixed and variable rate debt, the effect of derivate dealings, the security taken for the borrowings, the extent of undrawn facilities and a statement of risk management.

8.16 Post balance sheet events

The lending bank should not forget to read this section of the notes for up-to-date information valid at the date of issuing the annual report. Now that many companies have their own website, the information included therein will assist the reader to obtain a better understanding of the products sold, historical record and latest financial statements, eg when a profits warning has been issued.

8.17   Cash flow forecasts

The cash flow statement shown in a company's accounts at the end of the year will take the operating profit figure for that year, add back depreciation charges (as these are not payments in cash, but a provision against future diminution in asset values), account for the increase or decrease in net current assets (excluding cash-in-hand and borrowings), deduct taxation, capital expenditure and any dividends declared before adding any money received from new financing to arrive at the increase (or decrease) in cash during the year.

There is no set format to interim management accounts but they should incorporate cash flow forecasts based on future trading projections. Different types of company will each adopt their own preferences to suit their circumstances. Cash flow, of course, must account for income and expenditure inclusive of VAT, whereas the profit and loss account shows net trading figures exclusive of VAT, together with any expense charge for irrecoverable VAT during the year. The overall effect of VAT will be neutral over time, but there will be monthly or quarterly timing differences in money spent and received before the VAT amounts therein are settled with Customs and Excise.

A general proforma of a cash flow forecast sheet is shown hereafter. The assumption is that the lending banker has been provided with a year's management forecasts and wishes to verify their base assumptions. The important task will be to verify that the monthly closing cash balances forecast earlier do reflect reasonably accurately the actual balances attained and, if there are significant discrepancies, to discover the cause.

Trading forecasts	Month 1	Month 2	Month 3, etc
Invoiced sales	note 1		
Less Materials	note 2		
Direct labour	note 3		
Other direct costs			
Gross cash flow			
Less Indirect labour			
Other indirect costs			
+/– VAT settlement	note 4		
Net cash flow before tax			
Less Tax payable	note 5		
Less Distributed dividends			
Net operating cash flow			

Trading forecasts	Month 1	Month 2	Month 3, etc
Asset sale receipts			
Less Asset purchases			
+/– Exceptional items			
Add Capital/loans introduced			
Less Capital/loans repaid			
Net non-operating cash flow			

Overall net cash flow	note 6
Add Opening cash resources	
= Closing cash resources	

8.17.1   Notes to the pro-forma

Note 1

Comparative monthly returns for the previous year should provide an initial basis for forecasting future months, as adjusted for any exceptional returns and allowing for seasonal demand. Future months can then be adjusted for known occurrences (eg estimates of new product income, forthcoming price increases and changed sales mix). If greater accuracy is required, the number of working days in each month can be set out and turnover calculated accordingly.

Note 2

Materials costs as a proportion of sales should not differ materially if the use of future production materials to manufacture goods for resale in the coming year will be similar to the previous year.

Note 3

A check should be made of the average number of operatives employed in the past year and their overall annual cost as a guide to the total cost in the coming year. Wage increases should be accounted for, as well as overtime working, if material in amount.

Note 4

The VAT settlement will most likely be a payment rather than a receipt unless sizeable capital expenditure is incurred on which VAT can be reclaimed. There can be an annual reconciliation of the liability as well as the regular monthly or quarterly settlement dates.

Note 5

The tax liability for companies will be self-assessed; small and medium-sized companies will pay corporation tax (at rates varying according to their profits) due nine months following the end of their accounting period. Large companies (having a corporation tax rate currently of 30% and reporting a profit exceeding £1.5 million) may pay in four instalments, due in months 7, 10, 13 and 16 of the accounting period.

Note 6

Calculated as the sum of net operating and non-operating cash flows.

8.18   Profit and loss account forecasts

Management accounts are typically compiled from monthly accounts postings. These will not mirror the actual profit or loss for each month unless the company is operating an accounting system that includes the provision of monthly stock figures, detailed creditors accruals and apportioned depreciation on fixed assets. The major deficiency to an accurate profit (or loss) estimate will be the lack of a stock figure. The lending banker can mitigate this shortfall by working the following sum:

Stock held at the last stock count	£x
Add materials purchases delivered during the succeeding month	£x
	£x
Less materials used in sales for the succeeding month	£x
Revised stock figure at the end of the succeeding month	£x

The management accounts will show the purchased materials paid for during the succeeding month rather than the value of materials delivered. This value may be obtained from the record of deliveries inwards kept by the company so as to check what deliveries have been made and whether they are what the company has ordered. The company's order book will be a further, partial, check on deliveries received. Materials used in production and sold in the month may be obtained from analysing the sales invoices and deducting the average profit margin earned on materials invoiced.

Where the company cannot easily extract the above materials information, an approximation for stock can be done by taking the percentage historic usage value of materials purchased relative to sales made in each period. This figure is then compared with the cost of materials purchased (which would be two months if the usual credit period allowed by suppliers is 60 days).

Example: *(figures exclude VAT)*

Sales made in the previous year at cost prices, say	£2,420,000
Materials purchased in year	£1,370,000
Percentage of materials to sales	57%
Materials purchased two months ago say	£130,000
Management forecast: month 1	
Sales expected at cost prices	£200,000
Materials calculated therein @ 57%	£114,000
Month 1: opening stock (actual) value, say	£440,000
Add estimated purchases not yet paid for (see above)	£130,000
	£570,000
Less estimated stock used in sales (see above)	£114,000
Revised stock value, end of month 1	£456,000

8.19   Ratio and returns analysis

Calculating a ratio or a percentage trading return (hereafter described commonly as a ratio), by itself, conveys little explanation as to the strength of the business or why it may have sustained a change in fortune. A comparison is required to be made with earlier ratios and returns to find out whether there has been a variance, followed by an assessment why this has occurred. A benchmarking exercise with peer (groups of) companies will be helpful if it is available, as will an enquiry to the management of the return that was budgeted for that trading period with an explanation why this was not achieved.

Benchmark ratios taken from public sources, unfortunately, do not necessarily include important information that would add significantly when assessing a company's trading returns. An example of this would be a business having two principal sales lines, one being labour intensive requiring little raw materials and offering a relatively low profit return, and the other on-selling goods made elsewhere at a high profit return. Calculating an average gross profit return on total sales would not indicate how each part of the business was trading unless figures for each division were available and a comparative ratio analysis done separately.

There are what may be termed 'primary ratios' and 'secondary ratios'. The former provide the analyst with the most pertinent information to conduct a more intensive assessment to judge the health of the company. The latter may be useful supporting data, but their worth will depend on the type of business undertaken and other factors specific to the company. Further descriptions of ratios are given in Case Study 2 in Appendix 10.

8.20 Primary ratios – profit and loss account

Gross profit percentage return on turnover will show whether average sales margins on trading have dropped, been maintained or improved. For greater accuracy, where the company analyses its turnover and gross profit, the return for each division should be calculated separately. There may be several reasons for a variance, such as

- ◆ not passing on higher production costs in higher selling prices;
- ◆ selling goods at reduced margins (old stock or sales reductions);
- ◆ more or less employment of direct labour leading to changed costs;
- ◆ inaccurate tendering for work leading to changed turnover margin;
- ◆ stock losses, for whatever reason;
- ◆ changes in the mix of goods being sold;
- ◆ changes in internal production efficiency (machinery breakdown);
- ◆ changes in delivery charges (own delivery or outsourced);
- ◆ changes in stock valuation (referred to hereafter).

Changes may occur in the valuation of stocks notwithstanding that audit requirements insist that the basis of the valuation must be consistent. For example, raw material replacement costs may increase significantly so that where the company is adopting a first-in-first-out valuation basis, the value of stock at the end of the period will be much higher although the quantity of stock held may be unchanged. This will lead to a higher average production cost figure for the year until the new stock is used in production, or selling prices are changed to recoup the loss of profit.

The **stock turnover** figure will measure the speed of the business in selling its stock of goods for sale during the period of assessment. This may be calculated in one of two ways:

- ◆ the number of times the average value of goods held during the year will divide into the turnover; or
- ◆ dividing the cost of goods sold during the year by the average value of stock of goods held converted into a number of days.

Example of calculating stock turnover

(note: stock is defined as raw materials, work-in-progress and finished goods)

Assumptions:

Turnover for the year	£28,477,000
Beginning of year stock value	£1,125,000
End of year stock value	£1,967,000
Hence average stock value	*£1,546,000*
(Production) Cost of sales (goods sold)	£16,770,000
Calculation 1:	28,477,000/1,546,000 = 18.4 times
Calculation 2:	(1,546,000/16,770,000) × 365 = 33.6 days

Calculation 2 is not directly dependent on the level of turnover and measures how fast stock is shifted into production. It is a direct measurement of the value of stock as a proportion of all production costs. Calculation 1 measures the stock requirement to generate a certain level of turnover. Calculation 1 is used more frequently in practice and it does provide a more direct comparative measure as to how much stock is necessary to support the turnover achieved.

Capacity of production and its utilisation will measure the realised value to the maximum value of production that can be achieved with existing (human and machine) resources of the business. It will be the actual percentage production efficiency of the business measured against full production, after allowing for unproductive labour hours and idle machine time.

The ratio is calculated as the average value of production (or perhaps the number of widgets produced) achieved in the year divided by the maximum production possible and shown as a percentage. This information is not usually available directly from the financial statements although the lending banker may be able to request it from the management. By calculating this ratio companies will be able to assess whether they should:

- employ more staff or use existing staff more efficiently to raise production;
- consider replacing some production machinery to reduce breakdowns;
- estimate by how much turnover can be increased before additional production resources are needed to be implemented;
- evaluate where best economies of production can be made to reduce costs.

The ratio of the value of **trade debtors to trade creditors** will show the efficiency of the company in collecting debtor balances to improve cash flow and in using deferred payment credit made available by trade creditors to expand the working capital employed in the business. It is usually shown as the value of trade debtors divided by trade creditors. Taking this ratio a stage further, by subtracting the end of year trade creditors from the trade debtors and comparing the figure to the calculation one year earlier will show the change in cash flow resources. If this is then divided into the turnover achieved during the year, it will show whether or not the higher level of sales is reflected in an improving trade cash position (as is calculated in the following example):

Example: end of	Year 1	Year 2	Year 3
Turnover (£ millions)	180	200	240
Trade debtors	35	40	50
Trade creditors	17	20	20
Debtors less creditors (net trade balance)	18	20	30
Improvement in cash flow		+ 2	+ 10
Net trade balance/turnover	10%	10%	12.5%

8.21   Primary ratios – balance sheet

Gearing is the measurement of third party debt to the net worth of the business. Different businesses, by their nature, operate with different levels of debt and there is no single ratio by which to judge them all. Bankers most frequently look to a one-to-one basis of debt to net worth as being the benchmark to formulate an opinion whether the business is over-geared or not, working on the principle that if the ratio is higher it means that the bank is putting in more working capital at risk than the owner's equity.

The reasons why a company will request debt may be because the business is under-capitalised and further share (risk) capital cannot be easily raised or it may be because the business is expanding rapidly and/or the profit return being enjoyed is more than the cost of raising debt (ie the company is 'gearing up' its return).

Example of the effect of gearing

Assumptions: (£'000)

Annual earnings available for distribution		375
Share capital (2,000) and reserves (500)		2,500
Total borrowings		2,000
Gearing		80%
Return on share capital and reserves		15%
Cost of dividend @ 10% pa		200
Retained earnings after dividend	(15% x 2,500 – 200)	175
Further borrowing requested		400
Revised gearing	(2,400/2,500 =)	96%
Cost of borrowing @ 6% pa	(6% x 400 =)	24
Additional earnings on new money	(15% x 400 =)	60
Dividend cost of new equity	(10% x 400 =)	40
Net return if debt were raised	(60 – 24 =)	36
Net return if equity were raised	(60 – 40 =)	20
Benefit of gearing up	(36 – 20 =)	16

Note: it is assumed that the new money will earn an identical earnings return to that of the existing capital and reserves.

It is usual to include all borrowings in the gearing ratio (overdraft, bank loans, other loans, hire and lease purchase debt) and not to net out any cash in hand, on the principle that all debt will have prior repayment rights over equity holders. If priority of debt repayment is specifically to be accounted for, then the borrowings figure will only incorporate debt that has a prior charge over the bank indebtedness. In both cases, the definition of share capital and reserves will be net of any goodwill, but not other fixed assets having an ascertainable market value, eg patents.

Akin to the gearing ratio is **debt interest cover**. This is defined as the ratio of earnings (ie profit) before debt interest and tax to the interest payable in the same accounting period, quoted as the number of times covered. In the earlier example given, the profit before tax (at a 30% rate) would have been 536 and before interest (at 6% pa) would have been 656 before allowing for any additional borrowing. The interest cover, therefore, would be $656/120 = 5.5$ times. When the interest cover approaches unity, the bank will be asking itself will the business be able to continue to pay interest on its loans as they fall due?

A supplementary ratio not frequently met is to redefine the interest to include repayments of borrowing principal over the same operating period on the principle that a failure to pay either sum will constitute an event of default. Where a company raises new debt during the year, the interest thereon should be taken as a full year's charge on the principle that this will be the amount to be charged against future profits.

The **return on capital employed** (percentage) is used to measure the value of success the business has achieved in investing its capital. It is the ratio of profit to capital employed over the same period of time. As with some other ratios, there is more than one definition to the terms: 'profit' can be taken as 'profit before long-term debt interest and tax' to be divided by the total of 'share capital and reserves and long-term debt', recognising that long-term debt is as much operating capital as shareholders' funds. It seems illogical only to include long-term debt and ignore all borrowings, since all borrowings are used to generate earnings and some companies exist through the constant use of overdraft finance.

Alternatively, profit may be defined as 'profit after interest and tax that is available for distribution as dividends' divided by 'share capital and reserves', reflecting the purest return available to shareholders of the business alone. This ratio would appear to be more appropriate, since shareholders may wish to compare an investment return from the business (whether or not all available earnings are withdrawn as dividends) with the return offered by other forms of investment. Comparative use of the ratio will be effective so long as the lending bank accepts one method of calculation on a regular basis.

The **liquidity** of a business is important and its foremost balance sheet measurement is by the 'current ratio', current assets divided by current liabilities, on the principle that these assets and liabilities are quickly converted into cash. Sometimes, this is modified and the 'acid test' or 'quick' ratio is used by deducting the value of stocks from current assets before calculating the ratio. This seems rather incongruous, because stocks are turned over several times a year and debtors and creditors can be outstanding for up to 60 days or more. Why should stocks be treated differently from trade balances? As ever, there can be exceptions: manufacturing companies may carry work-in-progress and finished goods in their 'stocks' figure for long periods that are not rapidly converted into cash.

8.22 Secondary ratios

When analysing balance sheets, it is sometimes advantageous to measure the turnover of a company in relation to the use of its **business resources**, both human and assets. The former is calculated through dividing turnover by the average number of staff employed in the business and the latter by the average total book value of fixed assets shown by the balance sheet. A comparison with previous years will indicate the trend whether the company is achieving more or fewer sales from its workforce and investment in assets.

The definition of assets requires care: probably the best indicator is to take just the plant and machinery, equipment and vehicles necessary for production and sales, because to include land and buildings (that is likely to remain a static figure without additions) will rather disguise the operating trend. Furthermore, the assets should be taken before deducting depreciation, since this is a provision to build up book funds for the replacement of assets, whereas the trend being measured is the return earned on the original cost of the fixed assets.

The trends of various **expenditure ratios** (of their individual costs to turnover) may wish to be monitored; marketing costs are one example and labour costs are another. They are most beneficial when the company is going through a period of change or is examining the potential result of a new project and whether its implementation will affect the historical trend. Companies can let labour costs balloon as much as expenditure on equipment and keeping an eye on the relationship between fixed assets and the net worth (share capital and reserves less goodwill) of the business may also be relevant.

The calculation of **earnings per share** (the distributable earnings in pence divided by the number of shares in issue) is more an investment tool than a banking guide, for it gives shareholders and investors the profit earned by the business as relating to the share capital employed. The **earnings yield** (the distributable earnings in pence per share as a percentage of its market price) is the return the company has made on the full value of the company and, where the earnings are partly distributed as dividend, the **dividend yield** (the annual total dividend in pence per share as a percentage of its market price) will show the income return attributable to investment in the company's shares at that time. The inverse of the earnings yield is the **price/earnings ratio** (the price of a share divided by the annual earnings, both in pence per share), which shows the number of years earnings that are required to purchase a share as represented by its share price.

These investment valuation instruments can be useful to a bank in assisting to judge, for example, whether a company is distributing too much earnings by way of dividends, or is about to pay too much money in acquiring another company for which loan support is requested or, in the perception of the stock market through the share's price/earnings ratio, is too highly valued in respect of its future earnings capacity. There are two valuation concepts, however, that are helpful to a bank.

First, the trend of **earnings before interest, tax, depreciation and amortisation** (of fixed assets), otherwise known as **EBITDA**, will show the value of future earnings in cash terms. If several future years projections of this figure are discounted back to a present day value, this can be compared against the present day total of share capital and reserves plus debt. The greater the differential by which EBITDA exceeds share capital and reserves plus debt then, the greater the value of the business and the less risk when lending to the company, other aspects being equal.

Secondly, banks will also be interested in viewing the **enterprise value** of a quoted business. This is similar to EBITDA, but only accounts for long-term debt and the figure for share capital and reserves is substituted by the market share value of the company. The net enhancement of the company arises through the retention of earnings, a factor that banks wish to see as companies grow.

8.23   A comparison of financial trends

The trend is the direction that the company is reporting; it may show an improvement or a decline in financial performance. Sadly, for both income and expenditure forecasting, it is rare for all variables to perform at the same time in an expected manner. Income may reduce due to changes in the weather pattern and stocks of winter clothing are left on the shelves during an unexpected heat wave. The clothes may be mothballed until the following winter season, at risk of being 'out of fashion', or the more likely result is to initiate a sale at reduced prices, thereby lowering the overall trading margin and eventual profit to be earned. While profits may be maintained, unexpected expenditure on infrastructure, perhaps roof repairs due to a leak, will reduce cash flow and create another drain on resources against forecasts.

One benefit of comparing trends is to gauge past results as an indication of possible future performance. An established product that has been on the market for many years is likely to retain its public following unless a dramatic event materialises, such as contamination of food being sold, causing a product recall and adverse publicity leading to lower sales in future for an unknown period. With the former, the sales trend will be a good barometer of future sales; with the latter, the historic sales trend should indicate what future sales might pick up to once the contamination scare is lifted.

There are sophisticated mathematical models to measure and value empirical trends, namely by using probability choice matrices and 'least squares linear regression' modelling. The latter consists of taking an average relationship between two variables (say turnover with net profit) and measuring these historic observations based on the assumption that they will revert to their average values over time, so that they can form a trend line for the future, ie the line of best fit.

8.24   Financial statements and lending propositions

Lending to a company is based on the same principle of lending to an individual; the size of credit may be different and the rules of engagement will not be the same, but the risk to each proposition is as good as the individual(s) that invest the funds for a profit. A company, like an individual, will be measured by the results it achieves: the profits earned, the return to its shareholders and the success in repaying all its debts on time. Measurement of the company is done through assessing the performance of its management and analysing its financial statements, the second part being itself a measure of the first.

When looking at a borrowing proposition from a company, a bank should be aware that its prime consideration will be **security of repayment** of the loan. The company and the management may be top class and the reason for the advance may be fully acceptable, but this will not count for much if the loan is not repaid. Financial statements may be the only firm (ie independently audited or independently compiled) evidence of the security of the company as a creditor to the bank. As these statements have to disclose minimum facts about the business, they are important for the bank in evaluating its credit assessment. Ancillary information in the form of business plans and forecasts are unlikely to be audited unless they relate to the company obtaining a public quotation or a quoted company proposing a sizeable acquisition.

Small and medium-sized companies have now gained exemption, if they wish, from a formal audit. This will put even more emphasis on the bank to conduct a thorough risk assessment of these companies. This trend can only increase the possibility that banks will be more cautious in future when granting credit facilities and will increase their commitment to take formal security for any advance.

Credit repayment risk and **liquidity** are virtually interchangeable; if the company has constant good liquidity, then there are (hopefully sufficient) funds available to repay the bank facility over time. The measurement of liquidity is shown by the company's balance sheet at the date it is drawn up. Future liabilities and their time of crystallisation into immediately repayable debt will be shown either by the balance sheet or by the notes to the accounts. Examples of the former are 'current trade and other creditors' and 'creditors falling due after more than one year'. Examples of the latter are liabilities analysed under time bands when loans, leasing payments and the amount of future capital commitments authorised become due for repayment.

A useful (and conservative) exercise when considering future liquidity is to extract from the balance sheet those assets and liabilities that have to be settled within the next year. In the example following, it is assumed that the value of stock held will be unchanged. The company has not provided any indication of the likely profit (or loss) for the coming year and no earnings value has been entered. It is known that the company is still suffering from trading problems and is relying on its bankers for continuing support. The possible liquidity shortfall can be estimated as follows:

Example (A) (£ '000)

Current assets:		
Debtors	5,702	
Cash at bank	8,726	14,428
Current liabilities:		
Capital commitments	131	
Loans due for repayment	0	
Creditors	27,638	27,769
Liquidity deficit		13,341
Expected net earnings next year	0	
Undrawn bank facilities	9,729	9,729
Liquidity shortfall		**3,612**

A company can be profitable, but still incur (future) liquidity problems. Once again a review of the financial statements can reveal a story. In the next example, the company reported net earnings after tax of £1.3 million but, as a banker with privileged information may gain, the next year disclosed a loss. Given this information, the extent of the short-term liquidity problem is revealed:

Example (B) (£'000)

Current assets:		
Debtors	6,005	
Cash at bank	911	6,916
Current liabilities:		
Capital commitments	0	
Loans due for repayment	1,116	
Creditors	6,362	7,478
Liquidity deficit		562
Undrawn bank facilities	0	
Expected net loss next year	2,494	2,494
Liquidity shortfall		**3,056**

These 'approximate' estimates of liquidity do not take the place of detailed projections that the company has raised, but they do show that financial statements can be made to adapt to future analyses and they do offer a working tool as a guide when more appropriate financial information is not available.

Nine

Security

Security in this chapter concerns lending that is backed by the values of various forms of rights over varying types of physical assets. The aim of the lender in each case faced with a loan default will be to realise the asset backing for monetary value as soon as possible and to eliminate the debt to the bank as much as possible. The situation faced by a lender with a potential lending opportunity is to ask oneself the following questions.

- Is security needed?
- What type of security is available?
- How easy is it to take security?
- How relevant is the asset as security?
- What is the value of the security?
- How can the security be perfected?
- Does the security need monitoring?
- How easily can the security be realised? followed by
- What security should be asked for to agree to the loan requested?

9.1   The need for security

The need for security can be evident when the borrower defaults on the agreed repayments and it is too late to ask for additional collateral to support the loan before the company becomes insolvent. Small businesses can incur a rapid change of fortune that even regular monitoring by the lender cannot foresee quickly enough. Large businesses will have a portfolio of borrowings and attaching to each facility will be the respective rights of the lender over specific or general assets of the business. In this instance, when a large company defaults, there will be little or no room for each lender to change its security position.

An example of the former would be where the bank held a floating charge over company assets with the right to appoint a receiver upon insolvency and thereby remain in control of the assets rather than their title reverting to an administrator appointed by the court. An example of the latter would be where the bank is participating in a syndicated loan and the security obligations and rights are preset in the syndication agreement and the syndication managers would be acting for the consensus of bank participants.

Consider two similar public property companies, each offering business space to let. Salient financial figures reveal the following:

2003 (£m)	Company "A"	Company "B"
Turnover	3.7	5.1
Pre-tax operating profit/loss (-)	0.7	– 3.4
Total bank borrowings	11.4	3.4
Shareholders equity funds	19.8	7.3
Money on deposit	5.3	4.6
Properties	29.2	5.1
Turnover return on equity funds	19%	70%
Gearing: borrowings to equity funds	58%	47%
Asset backing: properties to equity funds	1.47 times	0.70

Company 'A' is profitable, holds the greater asset backing and is not over-geared with debt. Company 'B' is not profitable (reasons to be enquired about) and has the poorer property asset backing. Extracts from the notes to the accounts relating to security taken show:

Company 'A'

> 'All bank loans are secured by first charges on all of the group's freehold and leasehold properties ... by debentures (given by the holding company) and by guarantees given by all companies in the group.'

Company 'B'

> 'The bank loans and overdrafts are secured against legal mortgages over properties owned by the company's subsidiaries and ... other loans are secured by cash deposits.'

The call for security is indicated in several ways.

◆ Each group consists of a holding company with investments in subsidiaries operating in their own right and holding their own property assets. There is the need to take security from the individual operating companies and the notes of each company show this to be the case.

Were the security to be wholly based on the holding company, any subsidiary could trade out its property assets without repaying the attendant loan, leaving the bank to rely on the shares in the subsidiary company (held by the parent company) that may well not have any remaining asset backing for its balance sheet borrowings.

◆ As operations rely on developing, renting and realising properties, the major assets of each company will be changing and security taken must allow for these events. Neither company specifically states that floating charges have been taken, but it is very likely these have been incorporated, particularly where properties are in course of construction.

◆ Company 'A' holds its money deposits in the holding company whereas Company 'B's' money deposits are spread over its subsidiaries. The security taken should allow for potential claim on these funds. Company 'B' does not specifically state this is the case.

◆ The security shown to support Company 'A's' advances is more comprehensive on first examination because the lender to Company 'B' appears to be relying heavily on the charges taken against properties. The trading position of Company 'B' would also appear to be the more precarious at the date of the balance sheet. There is a prima facie case for the lending bank to review the size of its commitment to Company 'B' and to monitor its future trading more closely.

9.2 Security definitions

A **surety** is a person whose property is charged as direct security or who acts as guarantor for another's financial obligations. In relation to a charge on property, a **chargee** is the person entitled to use the property when there is default in meeting the obligation that the charge was created to secure.

A **fixed legal charge** on property has to be recognised by anyone subsequently acquiring title to the asset or any interest in it. An **equitable fixed legal charge** may be ignored by any subsequent acquirer of a legal title or interest, if acquired in good faith and for value, providing there was no actual or constructive notice of the existence of the equitable interest at the time of acquisition.

A **floating charge** given by a company on a class of its assets confers on the chargee (ie the bank lender) the right to take all the assets of that class owned by the company at the time when the charge crystallises for payment of the secured debt. The chargee is entitled to appropriate the property on a default in meeting the obligation the charge was created to secure and has the power of sale where the charge is given by deed (section 101 of the Law of Property Act 1925). A floating charge has no right to possession of the charged property and it normally crystallises when the chargee appoints a receiver (see later) under the charge contract after the company has failed to pay the secured debt when it becomes due.

A **legal mortgage** on property transfers legal title to the mortgagee (nee chargee) on condition that it will be returned when the obligation is met without recourse to the charged property. An **equitable mortgage** is where there is only an equitable interest in the property and/or there is an enforceable contract to create a legal mortgage. A **debenture** is a document acknowledging a debt and, specifically, is a written contract by which a company gives a charge on its property as security for payment of a debt owed to, say, a bank.

A **guarantee** is a legal promise by the guarantor (who gives the guarantee) to make good any failure by the principal debtor (the borrower) to meet financial obligations owed to the principal creditor (the lender). To be legally enforceable, the guarantor (or agent thereof) must sign a written memorandum of the promise. A **pledge** of goods for a financial obligation gives possession of the goods to the creditor on condition that possession will be returned when the obligation is met. A **lien** arises when the possessor of goods for a service has the right to hold them until payment is made for that service.

Where a company grants a floating charge, provision may be made therein for a **receiver** to be appointed by the chargee to sell (as the company's agent) the charged assets in order to meet the company's obligations to the chargee (ie the bank). If the appointment is created under a floating, or a fixed and floating, charge on substantially the whole of a company's assets, the receiver is an **administrative receiver** under the terms of the Insolvency Act 1986 and the Enterprise Act 2002 (that sets out the statute law on administration).

An **administrator** is appointed by the court in response to a petition brought by the company itself, or its directors, or by a creditor, to try and formulate a plan to deal with the company (debts) without the company being put into liquidation. Where the court orders a company to be wound up, the official receiver attached to the court becomes the company's **liquidator** under the terms of the Insolvency Act 1986 or, if substantial assets are to be administered, an insolvency practitioner is appointed liquidator. If the realisable assets of the company will not meet the expenses of liquidation and the company's affairs do not require further investigation, the official receiver will apply to the registrar of companies for the company to be dissolved.

9.3   What type of security is available?

The question is really in two parts: what security is available now and what is likely to be available in the future? Taking a fixed legal charge over the assets in question will satisfy the former and taking a floating legal charge on all assets of the company/ group can cover the latter. A charge gives a creditor a security interest in property/ assets without the transfer of possession. There are only four principal types of security recognised by English law: the mortgage, the equitable charge, the pledge and the contractual lien. The use of different types of security may be summarised generally as follows:

Assets:	Security available:
Freehold/leasehold property	Fixed and floating charge on registered or unregistered title by a legal or equitable charge ranking as a first or second (etc) charge
Plant/machinery (fixed in place)	Fixed legal or equitable first charge.
Other assets present and future Eg book debts, uncalled capital, goodwill	Fixed equitable first charge held at present or in the future.
Eg fixtures/fittings, equipment, book, debts, stock, intellectual rights, motor vehicles, moveable plant	First floating charge held at present or in the future.
Revenue stream	Prior rights thereto by contract
Contracts	Stand-in performance
Trading risks (overseas)	Insurance policies
Obligations/indebtedness (generally)	Third party guarantees, pledge, lien, company debenture
Independent assets	
Eg quoted investments, life policies	The assets themselves with transfer documents signed, but not dated

Security may also be available outside the ownership of the company, such as with private limited companies where the principal/majority shareholder/owners can be called upon to agree to a first charge (or second charge if a building society or other lender already holds a first charge) on their residence or other properties. This is frequently done where the company rents the premises from the owner. If the business is not a company the bank lender will look to all the assets of the business owner/borrower/shareholder held in his/her name.

9.4   Rights of the chargee

There can be a **legal chargee**, who is given legal title to the property or land and has an immediate right of possession. An **equitable chargee** has no right to possession unless it is in the charge contract, but if in doubt, on application, the court can appoint a receiver to take possession under its jurisdiction pending court authority to sell the property to settle the debt. A legal chargee/mortgagee may take possession simply because of choice and, in so doing, accepts responsibility as a mortgagee in possession, but an equitable mortgagee must show good reason why the court should comply with the equitable mortgagee's request and take possession through its receiver.

The receiver is neutral whose task is to administer property for the benefit of all parties to the proceedings, whereas the chargee wishes the property to be administered solely for its own benefit. This can be done by adding a clause in an equitable charge (such as a floating charge) giving the right for the chargee to appoint a receiver to possess the charged property and sell it for the chargee's benefit.

A chargee who does take possession of the charged property must account to the surety (ie the person providing third party security or an indemnity for performance of the obligation) for all rents and profits the surety would have received, but for the default of the chargee. This also means that the chargee exercising possession of a business will stand in the place of the mortgagor and be accountable to the owner of the equity for all business receipts received or what might have been received.

Where the charged property consists of land that has been leased, the safest way to receive the rent is for the equitable or legal chargee to appoint a receiver of income under the Law of Property Act 1925 providing the chargee can exercise a power of sale. A receiver of income is then deemed to be the agent of the surety.

A contract creating a charge as collateral security for an obligation does not give the right to sue the surety for performance of the obligation. The chargee's right would be against the charged property and not the chargor personally in the absence of contract terms to the contrary. Enforcement of the secured obligation would otherwise be by an ordinary action for recovery of the debt. When the surety's rights are ended (foreclosed) the chargee cannot sue under the charge contract to recover the debt unless the right of possession of the charged property is given up, but if the property had been sold (not foreclosed), the chargee has the right to sue.

9.5 Floating charges

A floating charge confers on the chargee the right to take all the assets of that type that the company owns, at the time when the charge crystallises, for payment of the secured debt. Usually, a floating charge crystallises when the company has failed to pay the secured debt when it becomes due and the chargee appoints a receiver under the charge contract. Prior to crystallisation, the company may fully deal with the assets of the charged class in the normal course of business without reference to the chargee. On crystallisation, a floating charge becomes a fixed equitable charge on the specific assets of the charged class owned by the company at that time.

A floating charge crystallises when a receiver is appointed, or when the company goes into liquidation, or when it ceases business, or when the chargee gives notice within the terms of the charge contract that the charge is converted into a fixed charge, or if the company deals with charged assets otherwise than as carrying on its business or on the occurrence of any other event specified in the charge contract to be an event of crystallisation.

These events may typically include the chargee converting the charge into a fixed charge, a levy of execution or distress is made on the company assets, another chargee appoints a receiver or a creditor petitioning for the company to be wound up by the court. The prime condition to be satisfied is that the debt secured by the charge has not been paid when due. In relation to a bank overdraft that is repayable on demand, the demand must have been made and not met. The Insolvency Act 1986, section 122 defines various grounds as evidence to support a winding up.

- The company fails to comply with a written statutory demand for payment of a debt exceeding £750.
- Execution of a judgement made against the company anywhere in the UK fails wholly or partly.
- If it is proved to the satisfaction of the court that the company is unable to pay its debts as they fall due.
- If it is proved that the company's assets are less than its liabilities, taking into account prospective and contingent liabilities.

There appears to be some doubt whether a second floating charge created by a company that crystallises before a first floating charge will give it priority over subsequent crystallisation of the first charge [see *Griffiths v Yorkshire Bank plc* [1994] and *Re Household Products Co Ltd and Federal Business Development Bank* (Ontario [1981])].

Before a floating charge crystallises, it does confer on the chargee an interest in, and rights over, the assets in the class charged. These include an interest in land and it makes no difference that it is a contingent or future interest. A bank has the right to retain money paid into an overdrawn account where it holds a floating charge on that debt and can obtain an injunction to prevent the company (otherwise than in the normal course of business) from dealing in assets held under a floating charge, or ask the court to appoint a receiver if an event (whether or not in the normal course of business) threatens the security held under the charge.

Under a composite fixed and floating charge the chargee may take the property subject to fixed charges and treat the remainder as subject to the floating charge and therefore available to pay any preferential creditors and liquidation expenses. In the case of *Evans v Rival Granite Quarries Ltd* [1910] CA, a floating charge was determined to be not a charge on an individual asset until the charge crystallises. As Buckley LJ said:

> 'The nature of the security is a mortgage presently affecting all the items expressed to be included in it, but not specifically affecting any item till the happening of the event which causes the security to crystallise as regards all the items.'

Whether a charge is a fixed or a floating charge is a matter of effect. Referring to the case of *Re Yorkshire Woolcombers Association Ltd* (1903) Vaughan Williams LJ reported:

> '*If a contract of charge contemplates that the company will deal with the assets covered by the charge without reference to the chargee, then it is likely to be a floating charge, whereas if the assets can be dealt with only after being released from the charge by the chargee, then it is likely to be a fixed charge*'.

Romer LJ stated (inter alia) in the same case:

> '*...if a charge has three characteristics...it is a floating charge:*
>
> *if it is a charge on a class of assets of a company present and future...*
>
> *if that class is one which, in the ordinary course of the business of the company, would be changing from time to time...*
>
> *if you find that by the charge it is contemplated that, until some future step is taken by or on behalf of those interested in the charge, the company may carry on its business in the ordinary way as far as concerns the particular class of assets being dealt with...*'

The earlier ruling laid down in 1979 by the *Siebe Gorman* case, is that the creation of a so-called 'fixed charge' on a company's book debts avoiding the Insolvency Act 1986 section 40 (but still allowing the company to use the money collected and remain under a floating charge if the chargee did not specifically direct the debts to incur a fixed charge) failed under a subsequent ruling of the Privy Council in *Agnew v Commissioner of Inland Revenue* [2001] (the *Brumark case*), where it was determined that the assignment and collection of book debts are just alternative ways of turning a debt into money, so a charge contract allowing either method of realisation without the chargee's permission must create a floating and not a fixed charge. Specifically, where book debts were paid into a company operating account and freely drawn on, this could only give rise to floating charge security.

A more recent test case was settled by the House of Lords (in *Re Spectrum Plus Ltd (in liquidation)* [2005] in a ruling stating that a charge over present and future book debts, where the chargor was required to collect and place those debts in a designated account with the chargee bank, but the chargor was free to draw on the account for its business purposes provided the overdraft limit was not exceeded, was in law a floating charge even if it was expressed as being a fixed charge. This confirms the *Brumark* decision. *Spectrum* devolved upon the key issues of control and substance. That is, the chargor was left free to use the charged asset and to remove it from security. It was the restrictions on the use that Spectrum could make of the payments made by its debtors that were important.

As a result of these recent decisions banks have had to re-standardise the conditions of their security in respect of floating charges. The Enterprise Act 2002 revised some security rights prior to *Spectrum*: it abolished the right of a holder of a floating charge created post-September 2003 to appoint a receiver and also abolished a major part of the Crown preference to be paid prior to unsecured debtors out of a prescribed part of a company's net property in a liquidation.

The Insolvency Act 1986 sets out the situations when a floating charge can be avoided. An administrator may avoid it if the charge was created at any time within the period of 12 months before the date of presentation of the petition on which the administration order was made or during the period when the petition was pending. The same time period before the commencement of winding up is given to a liquidator and applies to persons not connected with the company. Charges given to persons connected with the company have a period of two years. Connected persons are a director or shadow director of the company, an associate of either of these persons or an associate of the company itself (as defined, but including family relatives, business partners and companies under their control).

Section 245 of the Act is intended to prevent an unsecured creditor of a company obtaining a floating charge to secure the existing debt and thereby gain an advantage over other unsecured creditors. Thus, when a company is being wound up, the property secured by a floating charge that can be avoided under this section of the Act cannot be utilised by, or on behalf of, the chargee to pay anything other than, inter alia, at the time of or after the creation of the charge:

◆ the value of money paid or goods or services supplied to the company;
◆ the value of the discharge or reduction of any debt of the company;
◆ or any interest becoming due on either of the above sums under the terms of the agreement.

The value of goods or services is the amount of money at the time of supply that could reasonably be expected to be obtained in the ordinary course of business on the same terms as were supplied to the company.

Where a bank obtains a floating charge over an insolvent company's property as 'continuing security for all present or future indebtedness to the bank on current account', then each payment out of the account after the charge is given is money paid to the company in consideration for the charge. If the account is overdrawn at the time the charge was given, then payments into the account are presumed to pay off the existing overdraft on a first-in-first-out basis (*Devaynes v Noble, Clayton's Case* [1816]) and the bank is left with debts incurred after the charge was created.

9.6 How easy is it to take security?

It should be mentioned first that the bank must initially ascertain that the company, by its articles and directors' resolution, has sufficient powers to borrow, give security and specifies who may execute charges.

Where the asset available to be charged to secure a loan is situated abroad, this can raise problems relating to legal jurisdiction/procedures and the management of the asset to be realised, the possibility of local taxes liability, exchange controls and currency risks. If the asset is a ship, an aircraft or container/pallet, there will be the problem of tracing and sequestrating the asset. Fortunately, to provide protection where there is no possession, there are, by statute, government administered registers to record non-possessory charges for registered (since 1925) and unregistered (1972) land, ships (1995), trade marks (1994) and designs (1949), patents (1977) and aircraft/hovercraft (1972).

Security on **land** is through registering the encumbrance at the District Land Registry or, if the property is unregistered, through the bank physically holding all the deeds of title in its own safe custody. The bank will hold the registered land certificate with a written undertaking from the company to execute a formal mortgage if ever the bank requires. Alternatively, with the certificate, the bank may prefer to lodge a completed form of mortgage with the company's request not to register the mortgage but to have discretion to do so at any time.

In each case, the charge must be registered with the registrar of companies within 21 days of creation, otherwise the charge is void against a liquidator or other creditors of the company. Immediately prior to registration, the bank should make a search at Companies House to ensure that no prior charge is in existence. Charges requiring registration relate to the issue of debentures, on uncalled share capital of the company, on land and any interest therein, on the company's book debts, a floating charge on the company's property, a charge on calls made, but not paid and a charge created or evidenced by an instrument that, on execution, would require registration as a bill of sale.

Quoted stocks and shares are easy to take as security and will be held by the bank in safe custody, together with a signed, but undated, transfer of title so, should the bank have to realise the investment, it can do so without further referral to the company for authorisation. In case the company is holding the shares as trustee, a fact that might not be known by the bank, a legal mortgage is also best taken on the investments.

Life policies on key directors/owners in force for the period of the bank facility are also easy to take as security and will be lodged with the bank. The life company needs to be notified of the bank's interest should a future claim arise. The bank should have the option to repudiate the loan agreement secured by the policies in the event that the assurance company fails to pay under the policy where the assured has provided material falsehoods as to insurability. There is an insurable interest where a creditor insures the life of the debtor.

Security of **documents of title to goods** will be by way of a pledge and the physical assets will be held through bills of lading and/or trade invoices and/or warehouse receipts giving title of the goods to the bank. The bank should put the goods into its own name and have this acknowledged by the warehouse keeper because a warehouse receipt is not by itself negotiable. The customer will be required to sign a letter of pledge and give authorisation for the warehouse keeper to hold the goods to the bank's order. The bank should also insure the goods.

9.7   How relevant is the asset as security?

It is important for the priority of charges to be evident. If the chargee has a legal charge, there is still recourse to the property if the underlying obligation secured by the charge is not met. If the chargee has an equitable charge then the property remains charged only if the new owner had notice of the charge at the time of acquiring the property. If the first charge is a legal charge then there is recourse to the property in priority to a second charge. Again, if the first charge is a legal charge, there is priority only if, at the time the second charge was created, the second chargee had notice of the first chargee's interest. If there are two equitable charges over the same property, priority is by order of creation.

The type of security available determines its relevancy. A personal guarantee offers no control on the guarantor's assets. Shares in an unquoted company, apart from the difficulty of valuation, may be impossible to sell and there may be restrictive conditions as to a future disposal in the company's articles. A whole life policy may prove valueless if the assured commits suicide. Even a freehold building may have its drawbacks if it has dangerous asbestos in its structure. A leasehold building may have onerous restitution of condition liabilities and restrictive operating clauses; the property will be subject to rent reviews, the lease has a finite period to run and, if the bank takes possession, there is the problem of obtaining a new tenant.

When considering the relevance of an asset as security, one should not forget the statutory limitation periods set by section 20 of the Limitation Act 1980, ie 'no action shall be brought to recover any principal sum of money secured by a mortgage or other charge on property (whether real or personal) after the expiration of 12 years from the date on which the right to receive the money accrued'. For instance, a cause of action which arose from a claim for a debt that had originally been secured on a mortgage was subject to the 12-year limitation period, even if the mortgaged property had been sold by the lender before proceedings had been commenced to recover the outstanding debt (*West Bromwich Building Society v Wilkinson* [2005] HL).

9.8   What is the value of the security?

Real estate may have several valuations raised by qualified (RICS) valuers. The company may have a **going concern** valuation of its assets when it is trading, a **market valuation** on properties and assets suggesting what these assets might attract at a public sale and a **bricks and mortar valuation** of the property as it stands. There may also be an **insurance valuation** in case of loss and rebuild. The bank will wish for a bricks and mortar valuation for conservativeness since, if the security has to be possessed to repay the bank debt, the indicative option left will be to sell the property as rapidly as possible. Note that there is no obligation on the bank to sell at other than the best offer received at the time. A more detailed definition of the types of valuation is given in Chapter Six under the 'property' section.

Land by itself can reduce in value, depending on the purpose it is to be used and possibly subject to changes in the use of surrounding plots. A compulsory purchase order may, or may not, be equivalent to a bricks and mortar valuation. Farmland value will vary according to the grading of the soil and market value for farm properties generally. Buildings on the land can deteriorate and require maintenance. If they have been built or adapted for a specific use, their value will be less than a multi-purpose property. Rental values will be subject to market demand for letting and the perception of what yield investors require before investing.

Quoted stocks and shares will have a present value that can be easily realised, subject to selling charges, but their value will change according to market buying and selling demand by the public and the marketability of the shares. In this latter respect, dealing in the shares of major companies will be much easier than for small companies where the number of shares in issue can be relatively small. Any share valuation must allow for potential falls in market values.

Endowment policies raised on the lives of key directors will have day-to-day guaranteed surrender values. As it may take time for probate to be obtained in the event of death, the bank should allow for the loss of loan interest from the surrender value as a deduction prior to repayment. A whole life policy will only raise a value for security purposes on death. In either case, the bank may have the liability of paying premiums on the policy if the customer refuses to pay to safeguard the security cover.

Director/owner **guarantees** are taken in part to formalise the personal commitment to the company and be a preventative of diminution to the company's net worth in case excessive dividends are declared. In terms of their intrinsic value, this may be substantive or may be of straw. It can prove difficult and costly to claim under a guarantee and they should not be classified as prime security.

Guarantees may be limited as to time and/or amount, or may be open-ended without any constraints . Even so, a guarantee entered into by a guarantor who had agreed to pay sums falling due under an original guarantee where this had subsequently been materially varied and could constitute a replacement of the original agreement, would make the guarantor not liable for sums falling due under the new agreement (*Triodos Bank NV v Dobbs (No 2)* [2005] CA).

Imported **trade goods** will have an invoice value, but this may not be achievable in the event of possession and subsequent physical sale, particularly in the case of perishable goods. The value of exported trade goods will depend on the creditworthiness of the overseas importer or, if title is by irrevocable documentary credit or avalised bill of exchange, the standing of the importer's bank.

9.9 How can the security be perfected?

A bank usually takes a charge on all of a company's assets through a fixed charge on specified fixed assets and a floating charge on the company's whole undertaking and property outside the fixed charge. A receiver appointed under this charge is called an 'administrative receiver' (Insolvency Act 1986) who realises the charged assets for the sole benefit of the named creditor(s) holding the charge. In practice, this means the company's assets are sold to satisfy any preferential debts first, followed by secured debts and then the amounts due to other creditor(s). The alternative for the holder of a floating charge is to have an administrator to be appointed (by the court).

The charge on company assets must be registered with the registrar of companies at Companies House and care should be taken to view the register to ensure that no (previously unknown) prior charges have been lodged to affect the current charge. Great care has to be exercised when taking security to prevent their loss in favour of the rights of a company liquidator or failing to prove that the taking of a guarantee was valid.

Bank charge forms are standardised and reflect the individual wording chosen by each bank. Some clauses will be common to all forms. Typical examples include the following.

- ◆ **Continuing security**, allowing the security to remain after the original borrowing has been repaid.
- ◆ **All moneys**, allowing the bank to demand repayment now and in the future of all amounts outstanding.
- ◆ **Prior charges**, allowing the bank to close a debtor's account and credit future receipts into a new account to retain priority for the original secured debt [see *Re Clayton's Case*].
- ◆ **Additional security**, allowing the bank to add further security or dispose of existing security without impairing the original charge.
- ◆ **Successor**, allowing the bank to transfer security to a third party, such as when debts are being securitised and on-sold.
- ◆ **Conclusive evidence**, specifying the exact amount of debt charged.

9.10 Does the security need monitoring?

The reason for taking security is to have a tangible asset that can be preferably easily and quickly realised in the event that the loan will not be repaid. For the loan to be fully repaid, the security must exceed the principal value of the loan amount outstanding, together with the costs of realising the security and recovery of the interest charge and any fees due as a result of the loan default. The amount of default interest charged should be set in the loan agreement, together with the fact that it is to incur interest on interest at stated compounded dates. Regular monitoring of the security (at least annually for well-maintained accounts and more frequently where the account or the security holds a greater credit risk) is a necessity for the bank to ensure that the required margin of value over the outstanding debt is retained.

Land and buildings have proved to be one of the most reliable means to take security and retain (or improve) its value. Valuation of this type of asset is not an exact science, particularly for commercial properties, and, depending on the type of property, this is why a loan value of between 60% and 80% to bricks and mortar for a first charge is the most usual guideline. A subsequent 'desk valuation' without personal inspection may suffice for monitoring with a formal updating every few years or when the customer requests additional facilities or incurs financial difficulties.

Plant and equipment (including motor vehicles) can have a security value between 10% and 25% of their book figures, depending on whether they are moveable or immoveable and standard or specialist built machines. The bank should review the break-up value of the customer's balance sheet annually and allow for significant changes to the assets owned. **Stocks** can have an overall average value of between 30% and 35% of their book values, with finished or near-finished stock offering a higher percentage than this and raw materials a lower percentage.

Trade book debts may be valued at between 65% and 70% of their pre-VAT invoiced amounts, subject to a lower percentage where the portfolio holds a significant amount of overdue debts.

The monitoring of **quoted stocks and shares** can readily be done by reference to the prices reported in the daily or official press. In this instance, the security agreement should have a clause granting the bank the right to ask for additional collateral in case of need to safeguard against any major fall in share prices. Endowment policies should be monitored for the payment of premiums as the guaranteed surrender values will not reduce, but should rise automatically as more premiums are paid.

9.11   How easily can the security be realised?

A legal chargee has an immediate right of possession of the charged property whether or not the surety has defaulted, unless there is an agreement to the contrary. The surety is the person who has provided the security or indemnity for the performance of the obligation. If no right of sale is granted by the charge contract, the chargee may apply to the court for an order to sell the charged property. A chargee entering into possession becomes the owner of the business and is accountable to the owner(s) for everything received or might be received. Any profit made on selling charged property after the secured obligation is met must be held on trust for the surety. The chargee has a duty to take reasonable care to obtain the true market value of the property, limited to the value actually obtained at the time of sale unless varied in the charge contract.

The Law of Property Act 1925 gives a power of sale only where the surety has failed to comply within three months' notice to repay the secured debt, or interest payable on the secured debt remains unpaid two months after becoming due or there has been a breach of a term of the charge contract other than those relating to the repayment of principal or interest. There is also the power for a chargee to appoint a receiver of income acting as agent of the surety where the property charged is land under deed that has subsequently been leased and accrues rent.

A creditor given security cannot be forced to utilise that security and may decide to commence an ordinary action for repayment of the debt. Where the charge is given as collateral security for another's obligation, the chargee's right is against the charged property and there is no right to sue the surety for performance of the obligation. If a secured obligation is settled without recourse to the security, then the security contract automatically terminates and the security is said to be discharged. A person whose property has been charged always retains an interest in that property and this interest, or 'equity of redemption', ends when either the obligation is met, or the right to redeem is ended by court order, or the chargee exercises the power to sell the charged property or the property is sold by court order.

No action can be taken by a creditor to realise any security until the secured obligation becomes due to be met and the discharge has not materialised. The case of *Williams and Glyn's Bank Ltd v Barnes* (1981) concerned the allegation that the bank had unreasonably refused to continue to finance the company and a demand for repayment of the overdraft would put the company into liquidation. Ralph Gibson J said:

> *'Where money is lent on overdraft by a bank, and there is no agreed date for repayment, and no special terms which require implication of a further term as to the date of repayment, then it is clear to me that the overdraft is repayable on demand.'*

He continued:

> *'...when a bank lends money to a customer there is no reason to suppose that, in the absence of agreement to that effect, the bank must regard the fulfilment of the customer's known purpose as the agreed, or only, source of repayment. Borrowing from a bank may be replaced by borrowing from another bank or moneylender. If the borrowing cannot be replaced, because of the parlous state of the borrower's business, or of the market generally, I know of nothing in the ordinary contract of lending which requires the lender to share the borrower's misfortune.'*

9.12 What security should be asked for?

Having determined that security is required and ascertained what security is to hand, the bank will need to weigh up the advantages and disadvantages of each option in relation to the risk involved and the type of borrowing facility to be agreed. Where the risk is other than short term, a first fixed and floating charge on the assets of the company will provide the best security with the minimum of monitoring. The type of short-term borrowings will indicate what form of security to apply. It may involve one or more of the following representative choices.

- Taking the title of goods where overseas trading is done.
- Relying on a floating charge where the premises are rented and the plant is being purchased on hire purchase.
- Accepting that book debts are ring-fenced with a prior charge to support a factoring or invoice discounting facility.
- Agreeing an account setoff where the company holds money on deposit from time to time as well as utilising borrowings.
- Taking security on the cash flow to arise from a major contract to enable the financing of the contract to be completed.
- Deciding that a particular customer is undoubted and no formal security is needed other than to put in place agreed operating covenants.
- Deciding that the business owner should supply a personal guarantee in addition to security supplied by the company.
- Deciding to accept the existing security of a major borrower on a pari passu basis with the other lenders.

Appendix 4 sets out the typical clauses that a bank loan agreement can cover. Each bank will have its own standard wording and the examples should only be taken as a general guide.

Ten

Forecasting, control procedures and monitoring

10.1 Forecasting future trading

The occupation of commercial trading does not give an automatic right to make a profit. The aim of the trader is to be profitable, but, in order to do so, several factors have to interrelate in the correct way and each of them should be considered when forecasting the future. These points will be discussed in turn. The lending banker should understand the reasoning behind forecasting and how specific forecasts are compiled.

Operating targets:

◆ sales income has to be of sufficient size to exceed expenditure;
◆ expenditure has be controlled sufficiently so as not to exceed sales;
◆ the business has to function efficiently to enable sales to be achieved;
◆ the management has to ensure that as many contributory factors to trading have been allowed for when adopting a future business strategy;
◆ the business overall has to be flexible enough to adjust to future external (and internal) influences on its operations.

10.1.1 Income from sales

The type of product(s) and their markets will determine whether forecasting will be easy or difficult. Each business should recognise its limitations in these respects.

The size of the overall market may be immaterial to the business. An established market with many competitors will require an effective pricing and marketing policy to enter and succeed. Forecasting, therefore, should concentrate on these areas. A niche player, regardless of the size of the market, will find that pricing is less important than service, quality and supply.

Forecasting then will depend more on internal factors of the business to maintain quality supply. A new product will have to create a market and the forecasting emphasis should be placed on performance and in promoting the product and the brand image. Again, in the first instance, pricing is not the most important factor.

Products may have a relatively large intrinsic value, reliant on a high profit margin rather than bulk sales to achieve income. Forecasting should concentrate on the quantities likely to be sold. Low value goods will be reliant on the size of individual orders and their shipment costs. Goods with a high labour content will rely on worker relations, incentives and productivity to attain the best returns. Goods having a high material content will rely more on consistent supply and its costs. The product(s) may have a low shelf or technology life. The former requires replacement forecasting and the latter perhaps research and development costs to maintain competitiveness. Only after all these variables have been correctly assessed can the trader consider forecasting and projecting sales of his or her own business.

10.1.2   Control of expenditure

A business with a poor sales team and poor penetration of a potentially lucrative market may well succeed if the underlying operating costs of the business are sufficiently lower than the sales income being generated. Expenditure should be judged by its necessity.

◆ Premises must be rented if they are not owned.

◆ A workforce, raw materials, light and heat will be needed to produce goods for resale but production may be sub-contracted out at less cost.

◆ An advertising budget is particularly difficult to judge on cost-effective grounds. Are additional sales being raised now and for the future by passive advertising? Would more active (telesales) efforts and direct managerial approaches to potential customers produce more response? Has the business considered the merits of advertising and selling by way of a website? Would this be more cost-effective? Would a simple shop window rejig and a resited interior activate customers for more impulse buying?

◆ Is all business expenditure regularly reviewed for possible pruning? Have these aspects been properly accounted for in the forecasting of expenditure?

10.1.3 An efficiently functioning business

Each principal item of business income and expenditure should be examined as to its efficiency to improve trading returns and whether it can be improved before adopting a forecasting strategy.

◆ The marketing team may be judged on the sales they achieve per capita and their returns from different geographic areas. For the larger businesses, this may extend to the returns from branches.

◆ Production may be judged by the hourly output per worker/machine and the proportion of unproductive hours in each period. The cost of production for the number of units sold will indicate what selling prices may be set for how much profit that can be earned.

◆ The costs of transport may be compared with outsourcing this element of service. The investment in, and earnings from, the business will indicate whether the return achieved is acceptable.

◆ The personal drawings from the smaller business or bonuses/dividends from the larger corporate business will show whether the withdrawals are excessive.

10.1.4 The contribution of the management

The delegatory powers adopted by the management may, on the one hand, stifle incentive and innovation and, on the other hand, allow no interaction between different production areas or plants (where one centre may be underutilised and another fully stretched). Similarly, funds may be invested in business products offering low profitability to the detriment of other, more profitable, product lines. The provision of additional or replacement equipment may or may not have been fully planned ahead and the effect on future trading may not have been calculated insofar as it will affect cash flow and current financial resources.

10.1.5 Flexibility of future operations

Having a financial strategy for 'a rainy day' were events to run adversely for the business is often considered a luxury for those firms that are constantly operating at the extreme limits of their operational capacity, whether it be on the personnel, productive, managerial or financial fronts. This approach becomes even more prevalent during times of high growth and profitable trading, yet these are the times when the greatest care should be taken to maintain this growth and profitability.

Two forecasting scenarios should always be planned for in case of need: that more money may have to be taken from other sources if trading receipts fall, temporarily or otherwise and, secondly, what is the easiest action to take to reduce overheads with the minimum of disruption were the business downturn to last longer than was anticipated. The first remedy could be to have undrawn borrowing facilities at hand in case of need or to build up working capital reserves in the business so that could either resource could be channelled to cover a cash shortfall.

The second remedy could be to invoke a mixture of prevention and rescue: an example of preventive action would be not to employ additional permanent staff until it is proven there is a continuing need to increase the workforce and to have the costly procedure of making some staff redundant. There is much to be said for a business to retain a core of key, experienced personnel, especially younger persons of supervisory potential, to carry the business through a difficult trading period and to sub-contract unskilled labour from local sources. Forecasts of the effects of forced redundancy would greatly assist the management to be prepared should the worst situation occur.

10.1.6   The forecasting template

Individual circumstances will determine how each business prefers to set out the detail of its profit and loss account and any cash flow statement for management purposes, therefore the example shown in Appendix 5 taken from an actual case study is only a guide how a detailed forecasting template may be drawn up. The calculations are computer-related (specifically Microsoft Excel spreadsheet format), although they can be adapted for other computer formats or even hand written use. The computer knowledge required is relatively simple: how to add/deduct/ divide/ multiply/copy and freeze (by using the dollar sign) cells and groups of cells.

A less detailed example typically shows income and expenditure on a monthly basis for forecasting at least 12 months ahead and possibly for the second year as well; thereafter, the calculations may be drawn up quarterly with annual totals. Totals should be added at the end of each accounting year. Thus, a business wishing to compile a forecasting spreadsheet from 1 January, but having a year ending of 31 March, might show its initial monthly income and expenditure from January to March, then for 12 months from April monthly through to the end of March in the following year with an annual total.

10.1.7   The profit and loss account

The starting point for spreadsheet entries will usually be the latest monthly trial balance. As each month is entered in the (computerised) ledgers, the main income and expenditure heads can be transposed into the spreadsheet. It is assumed that the monthly figures will be taken from postings a week or so after the month end and will include recently received invoices relating to the previous month, but will not include adjustments for other accruals (of debtors, creditors and prepayment of expenses) and therefore the net profit shown will only approximate to the finalised (true) profit for the period were all accruals to have been correctly accounted for.

The reason for picking a monthly profile is that many costs are paid monthly and the sales/bought ledgers will be ruled off monthly. It will, therefore, be easier to relate the actual monthly trading figures as they arise to the projections made earlier.

'Monthly' usually means calendar months, but the business may account on a four week/thirteen period year if it wishes. Depreciation can be calculated in advance and then worked out on a monthly basis. For those micro-businesses that do not compile a monthly trial balance, there should be some records denoting what the monthly sales were and amounts for the expenditure heads can be taken from the last set of annual accounts transposed onto a monthly basis.

The greatest difficulty will be to incorporate a figure each month for stock. Examples how this can be estimated are shown later in this chapter, but many businesses not operating with a sophisticated stock control system will carry forward the most recent stock figure until a revised estimate is available from a partial or full stocktake every three or six months.

An example of the typical income and expenditure headings to be met is given in Table A.

Table A

Income	*Month 1*	*Month 2*	*Etc*
Sales total			
Expenditure			
Direct costs:			
Wages			
Materials			
Transport/other			
Sub-total			
Indirect costs:			
Salaries			
Rent and rates			
Light and heat			
Telephones			
Post and stationery			
Insurances			
Motor and travel			
Advertising			
Financial costs			
Sundries			
Sub-total			
Net profit			
Sales analysis:			

Many businesses will incur a seasonal demand for sales. When forecasting ahead, a seasonality benchmark can be built into the projected figures by taking the proportion of sales achieved for each month of the previous year as a percentage of that year's annual total and then assume that, for each month of the following year, an identical seasonality of demand will occur. Should any month in the preceding year have been affected by special circumstances, the ensuing year's forecast should make special allowance to reflect a more 'normal' return. The resulting figures forecast may have to be adjusted should national holidays arise in different months of the year. Table B sets out how the benchmarking calculation will look.

Table B (start of year January)

Sales	January	February	March	April etc	Year to Dec
Last year:	8,000	13,000	16,000	18,000	150,000
Proportion %	5.3	8.6	10.6	12.0	100
This year:					
Projection	9,540	15,480	19,080	21,600	180,000
Actual	8,200	14,000	18,500	23,600	

Note: 5.3% = 8,000/150,000; 9,540 = 5.3% x 180,000, etc.

This method is a reasonable guide for those businesses that rely mostly on cash sales, but further modifications will be required for businesses such as building and construction where the incidence of large contracts can significantly affect turnover month by month. In these cases, any contract of size should be shown separately so that a better monthly comparison of performance can be made. The sales projections for the ensuing year will be the total of sales expected to be received from each major contract (based on monthly certificates) and an estimate of income arising from other jobs. Table C provides an example.

Table C (start of year January)

Sales	January	February	March	April etc	Year to Dec
Last year:					
Contract 1	5,000	5,000	0	1,000	
Contract 2	6,000	0	1,200	0	
Other contracts	4,000	3,000	3,000	3,500	
Total sales	**15,000**	**8,000**	**4,200**	**4,500**	
This year:					
Contract 7	7,000	7,000	3,000	0	
Other contracts	2,000	1,500	3,500	5,900	
Projected sales	**9,000**	**8,500**	**6,500**	**5,900**	
Actual sales	8,200	6,000	4,500	8,600	

Manufacturing businesses can adopt another form of spreadsheet analysis, either as a supplementary sheet or embodied in the final sheet. This can take into account the value of production expected in future months and its conversion into invoiced sales. Table D provides an example and shows the monthly production being invoiced in the following month. If required, cumulative totals of orders and sales may also be included.

Table D (start of year January)

Sales	January	February	March	April etc	Year to Dec
Last year:					
Orders in hand	15,000	16,000	10,000	11,000	
Production value	3,000	4,000	2,000	500	
Total sales	**2,500**	**3,000**	**4,000**	**2,000**	
This year:					
Orders in hand	19,800	16,400	17,200	15,300	
Contract 4	7,000	7,000	3,000	0	
Other contracts	2,000	1,500	3,500	5,900	
Production value	9,000	8,500	6,500	5,900	
Projected sales	**6,600**	**9,000**	**8,500**	**6,500**	
Actual sales	7,200	8,500	8,700	7,100	

These variations in accounting spreadsheets have been highlighted to indicate the different situations that arise with different types of businesses. The detail provided might be too extensive to implement in practice where the sole owner or proprietor manages all financial matters in conjunction with his or her other business tasks. A broader brush approach may be necessary, but should still facilitate easy updating of the projections to take account of actual sales achieved and any other changes in circumstances. A complete example of what is meant is given in Appendix 5.

10.1.8 Expenditure analysis

When projecting business costs, a distinction must be made between costs that are directly dependent on the level of sales (variable costs) and costs that are independent of sales (fixed costs). As the level of sales varies, so will the variable costs associated with producing those sales, either through producing or purchasing more or fewer goods for resale. The fixed costs will be incurred regardless of the level of sales and its associated costs.

Forecasting expenditure should take into account the budget laid down for the business. Many items such as rent (varying only at review times) and rates (varying annually as set by the local authority) can be forecast with good accuracy. Other items may be more difficult, such as motor and travel costs, but a reasonable idea will have been gained from the expenditure incurred in the previous year and how many vehicles are being used for what purpose. Most items will accrue each year with increments attached to allow for cost inflation.

10.1.9 The implication of value added tax

The profit and loss account spreadsheet, of course, will be based on all figures shown net of input and output taxes where the business is registered for VAT. When it is adjusted into a cash flow format, this will change to include VAT on both income and expenditure. In most cases, the rate to add to the profit and loss account figures will be the standard rate, but fuel will have its own reduced rate and there will be zero rated supplies. Where the zero or exempt rated supplies are significant, separate calculations should be done to ensure that an accurate cash flow income and expenditure is raised.

The (monthly or) quarterly VAT net settlement figure to Customs and Excise will be calculated as the result of adding all the VAT due on inputs and outputs and this figure should be taken into account as a separate receipt or payment in the month it is settled. Where partial VAT exemption is applicable, special VAT calculations will be required. This also applies to the new flat rate VAT system for small businesses that is being introduced.

10.1.10 Other expenditure adjustments

Since the profit and loss account includes a provision for **depreciation** rather than a payment, this item has to be added back to reduce expenditure when calculating the cash flow. Equipment or other **fixed assets** acquired for cash during the year will have to be accounted for as expenditure in the cash flow calculation only, but should be shown as a non-operating item after the operating result has been compiled. Estimated calculations of the future **tax** liability on business trading should also be made and these estimates should be included in the cash flow spreadsheet. Additional **equity investment** in the business and **loans** raised (with the repayments as they occur) will also have to be included in the cash flow.

10.1.11 Forecasting cash flow

There are a number of ready-made software programs currently available to convert historic accounting postings into a cash flow basis. It is possible, however, that the business wishes to make cash flow projections for the business internally that can be modified to allow for different operating situations that may arise in the future. As has been mentioned earlier, the spreadsheet examples given show the cash actually received each month from past sales, or that projected to arise from future sales, and will include VAT on all items if the business is VAT registered. This should not be confused with the profit and loss figures compiled from the bookkeeping records which will be accounted for net of VAT and will have a year end debtor or creditor for VAT in the balance sheet.

In many respects, a cash flow forecast is more important than a profit and loss projection because it shows what total net cash is being generated by the business for the management to judge whether the inflow of cash and total available resources are remaining healthy or whether remedial measures to improve the position should be initiated. Many businesses have reported rising sales and profits, but have run out of monetary resources to continue to trade.

It is also important to read a cash flow in conjunction with other operating data of the business gained from the accounting records and sales marketing returns. Consider the hypothetical case of a business with the following trading results:

Incl VAT	Month 1	Month 2	Month 3	Month 4	Month 5
Orders in hand	20,000	24,000	27,000	30,000	34,000
Sales invoiced	8,000	11,000	12,000	12,500	13,000
Cash received	7,000	8,000	10,000	9,000	8,000

Orders are increasing fairly well month by month, but the conversion into confirmed sales is falling. Assuming a two-monthly delay for an order to be produced and delivered, in month 3, the order conversion rate into sales was 60%, whereas by month 5 this had dropped to 48%. The management should be looking to see why orders are being cancelled or completion is being delayed. Assuming also that month 1 invoices should be converted into cash by month 3, in the example provided months 4 and 5 indicate a shortfall in cash expectations. This will have an effect on the working capital available to the business and may be a pointer that debtors are not being chased sufficiently.

10.1.12   Scope of the template

The standard cash flow spreadsheet will commence with the cash brought forward from the earlier period, add the income received, deduct the expenses paid and then show the cash carried forward to the following period. The opening and closing cash will be that held in the business bank account and these entries are usually given at the foot of the spreadsheet. As an example, Table E takes notional trading figures for one month and converts this into a cash flow statement assuming that the standard VAT rate is 17.5%.

Table E

Profit and loss account

(£'000)	Month	Calculation	Notes	**Cash Flow**
Income				
Sales	4,400	4,400 x 1.175 =	1	5,170
Expenditure				
Direct costs:				
Wages	320		2	320
Materials, etc	2,200	2,200 x 1.175 =	1	2,585
Indirect costs:				
Salaries	240		4	240
Rent	300		2	300
Utilities	180	180 x 1.05 =	3	189
Other costs	670	670 x 175	1	787
Depreciation	150		4	0
Net profit	**340**			
Operating cash flow				749
Less Irrecoverable VAT		(5,170 – 4,400 – 2,585 + 2,200 – 189 + 180 – 787 + 670 =) 4		259
Less Equipment purchased			4	400
Less Loan repayments			2	120
Net cash flow				+ 30
Opening cash				230
Closing cash				200

Note 1: assumed all items subject to standard rate VAT.

Note 2: items not subject to VAT.

Note 3: utilities costs assumed charged at 5% VAT rate.

Note 4: adjustments for cash flow purposes.

10.1.13   The balance sheet

It is suggested that the forecast balance sheet is limited to the principal headings met in the annual accounts:

- fixed assets – showing land/buildings and other (less depreciation);
- current assets – showing stocks and trade debtors and any cash;
- current liabilities – showing trade creditors and other creditors;
- borrowings – showing short-term (up to one year) and long-term;
- capital – that is employed in the business.

The first step is to compile an **opening position** of these items, taken from the last available set of audited accounts or possibly from subsequent management accounts if that is preferred. Amendments to the **fixed assets** occurring each year can be added (or sales subtracted) and the **depreciation** figure (calculated either on a straight line basis in equal annual amounts or on a depreciating balance as a percentage of the previous years total) can be worked out on an annual basis.

The **net current assets** position will arise from the assumptions made for the cash flow: if sales and purchases are received and paid respectively two months in arrears and the year end is 31 December, the sales and purchases amounts shown for the previous November and December should be added together (net of VAT) and will comprise the **trade debtors** and **trade creditors** at the year-end.

Similarly, if the assumption in the model has been that stocks are equivalent to two months' purchases (net of VAT), then this will be the **stock** figure at the year end. An addition may be made for **work-in-progress** (excluding any profit element) if it is substantial. **cash in hand or overdrawn** will be the actual amounts given by the bank statements. **Other creditors** will be sums outstanding for VAT/PAYE (three months' VAT if payable and settled quarterly and one month's deductions for PAYE plus the employer's percentage portion) and the tax calculated to be due on the profit made in that year. Other items may be added according to the individual circumstances of the business.

Borrowings will comprise commercial bank and leasing/hire purchase/ factoring debts and possibly loans outstanding from the proprietors. The lenders should have provided a schedule of the monthly/quarterly repayments due with the balance outstanding after each payment; this balance of the capital and interest combined will be the sum still owing. Net off the totals for fixed assets, net current assets and borrowings to arrive at the **capital employed** and retained in the business by the proprietor. A quick, approximate check on this figure is to take the opening position of the capital account and add the profit after tax.

Due to several items in the balance sheet that have been affected by calculations based on preceding months figures, the two figures of employment of capital and capital employed will not be exactly similar and therefore for the balance sheet to balance, the **other creditors** item should be amended by the required amount. A more sophisticated computation will be needed for an exact balance to be achieved and it is suggested that, for broad forecasting purposes, this approximate guide should suffice.

10.2 Forecasting retail sales and profits

It is assumed that the retail outlet sells a large number of separate items, but these can be grouped into three different gross profit margins. A forecast spreadsheet should be raised monthly as follows (only four months are shown for simplicity and VAT has been ignored). Note that the forecast sales should be adjusted to equate with the number of working days in each month that occurred in the previous year.

The analysis based on different margins (the figures in the example are for representative purposes only) will probably make it easier for the retailer to forecast future sales for each trading category rather than having to rely on one 'average margin' that will be less accurate when the profit is estimated. It will also provide a guide, in case it is needed, as to which goods are slow and rapid selling items and can be concentrated on to improve profitability for a given overall turnover. By comparing on a monthly basis the future estimated sales to what actually occurred one year earlier the seasonality of sales would be recognised. A final adjustment to forecast sales could arise if any exceptional circumstances occurred either during a particular month of the previous year or in the coming year, eg shop closure or a stock 'sale'.

10.2.1 Sensitivity (variances) analysis

Once the forecasts have been compiled to the retailer's (or manufacturer's, etc) satisfaction, **sensitivity analysis** (otherwise known as **'trading variances'**) can be introduced to ascertain what effect their changes have on the projected profits; this entails:

- changing the sales forecasts; and
- changing the gross margins; and
- changing expenditure items, including interest rates on borrowings.

Consider the following hypothetical profit and loss forecast by the management (for brevity, the figures are shown quarterly). The management has projected a gradual increase in sales and a steady gross profit percentage. Additional direct labour has been recruited in the third quarter. Other costs have been assumed pegged at their current levels.

(£'000)	Quarter 1	Quarter 2	Quarter 3	Quarter 4	Full Year
Turnover	440	480	520	560	2,000
quarterly increase		*+ 9.0%*	*+ 8.3%*	*+ 7.7%*	
Materials	179	205	212	238	834
Labour	120	121	142	143	526
Cost of sales	299	326	354	381	1,360
Gross profit	141	154	166	179	640
Gross profit %	*32%*	*32%*	*32%*	*32%*	*32%*
Indirect costs	90	90	90	90	360
Finance	20	20	20	20	80
Net pre-tax profit	31	44	56	69	200

The bank believes that certain forecasts are flawed and a sensitivity analysis is required. Turnover is not expected to rise by more than 5% in the second and third quarters and fall by 5% in the fourth quarter as industrial confidence wanes. In addition, the bank economist believes that raw material prices will rise by 10% for the third quarter and a factory floor general wage award of 5% will occur for the fourth quarter. Rates, amounting to one-tenth of indirect costs, are also expected to increase from the second quarter by 8%, an increase that the company had not allowed for since its estimates were raised. The FX dealers read the market as expecting a small, gradual increase in cost of borrowing over the year. How will these changes affect the profit forecast?

Revised (£'000)	Quarter 1	Quarter 2	Quarter 3	Quarter 4	Full Year
Turnover	440	462	485	460	1,847
quarterly increase		*+5.0%*	*+ 5.0%*	*– 5.0%*	
Materials *	179	191	218	215	803
Labour	120	121	142	150	533
Cost of sales	299	312	360	365	1,336
Gross profit	141	150	125	95	511
Gross profit %	*32%*	*32.5%*	*25.8%*	*20.7%*	*27.7%*
Indirect costs	90	91	91	91	363
Finance	20	21	21	21	83
Net pre-tax profit	31	38	13	– 17	65

* Note: materials costs have been adjusted, first for the proportionate change in turnover projected and, secondly, for the increase in prices.

The bank will discuss with the company whether the new assumptions and outlook are valid and, if changes are necessary, a compromise should be reached. The bank will want two decisions to be resolved: what will the company do to avert the sensitivity forecast fall in profits and how will this affect cash flow and the credit advanced to the company? A further example how changes in trading assumptions can affect profit is shown by Table F.

Table F: forecast of sales and profits

(£'000)	Month 1	Month 2	Month 3	Month 4
Actual sales last year at:	<u>70</u>	<u>80</u>	<u>66</u>	<u>72</u>
Margin A (50%)	40	40	36	42
Margin B (60%)	20	30	20	20
Margin C (70%)	<u>10</u>	<u>10</u>	<u>10</u>	<u>10</u>
Total sales	<u>**70**</u>	<u>**80**</u>	<u>**66**</u>	<u>**70**</u>
Gross profit:				
Goods @ margin A	20	20	18	21
Goods @ margin B	12	18	12	12
Goods @ margin C	<u>7</u>	<u>7</u>	<u>7</u>	<u>7</u>
Total gross profit	<u>**39**</u>	<u>**45**</u>	<u>**37**</u>	<u>**31**</u>
Forecast sales this year at:	<u>78</u>	<u>78</u>	<u>70</u>	<u>70</u>
Margin A (50%)	48	48	40	40
Margin B (60%)	20	30	20	20
Margin C (70%)	<u>10</u>	<u>10</u>	<u>10</u>	<u>10</u>
Total sales	<u>**78**</u>	<u>**78**</u>	<u>**70**</u>	<u>**70**</u>
Gross profit:				
Goods @ margin A	24	24	20	20
Goods @ margin B	12	18	12	18
Goods @ margin C	<u>7</u>	<u>7</u>	<u>7</u>	<u>7</u>
Total gross profit	<u>**43**</u>	<u>**49**</u>	<u>**39**</u>	<u>**45**</u>
<u>**Direct costs:**</u>				
Last year	31	35	29	39
as per cent of sales	*44*	*44*	*44*	*56*

Sensitivity analysis:
(examples)

Change margin A to 60%	
Effect on the gross profit	+ 4.88 (ie 60% x 48 = 28.8 – 24 =)
Or Increase sales of goods A by 10	
Effect on gross profit	+ 5.0 (ie 50% x 10 =)
Together with margin A at 60%	+ 5.8 (ie 60% x 58 = 34.8 – 50% x 58)
Total change to gross profit	+ 10.8

10.3   Forecasting manufacturing sales and profits

The forecasting steps that can be adopted by a retailer/wholesaler in principle may be appropriate for a manufacturer. Where a larger turnover is entailed, a more broad calculation to the forecasts may be fitting. Rather than commencing at income projections and deducting expenditure estimates, it may be better to choose a reverse approach.

Table G

Expenditure projections:		**Monthly**
Labour cost (converted to monthly cost)		£4,000
Add Employer's NI (say @ 12.8%)		£512
Employer's pension commitment (say @ 6%)		£240
Expected production of widgets	1,200	£4,752
Cost of materials per widget excluding labour	£6.50	
Materials costs		£7,800
Direct distribution, etc costs (say 2% of production)		£252
Total direct non-labour costs		£8,052
Direct overheads total		**£12,804**
Gross profit (calculated on target average per cent of 60% on sales)		**£19,206**
Less Indirect overheads (as estimated – not shown in detail), say		£3,206
Projected net profit		**£16,000**

Note: direct costs comprise 40% of sales in the example = £12,804;

hence gross profit is 12,804 x 60/40 = £19,206; and

sales will be 19,206 + 12,804 = £32,010.

Some businesses will adopt a different rough calculation by adding a set percentage onto the labour charge and a different percentage onto the materials charge. Often, there will be no 'profit element' built into the indirect costs, but a percentage is added as a final costs contingency total or allow for sales discounts for early payment or valued customer rebates.

10.4   Monitoring and control procedures

Monitoring of lending is a key element of a bank's duties. After the lending bank has given approval for a new or additional credit facility for the company and the documentation and any security has been put in place, it is not a time thereafter for the bank just to say that the lending proposition has been fully investigated and one can now wait for the company to fulfil its commitments. The company may strive very hard to do so, but any trading environment is susceptible to adverse external influences as much as the company may internally choose to adopt poor operating judgements after what has been an exemplary track record.

The management of a business may have a very modest or very sophisticated system in place for **controlling** its performance, usually depending on the size of its operations. The business operating with around a dozen employees will probably have a bookkeeper and two or three marketing personnel, but no specialist management team; this task will be performed by the owner who may, or may not, be conversant with credit control and monitoring procedures. Frequently, the control will consist of a graph of weekly/monthly sales/orders and little else, with a check on sales/profit margins done annually when the accountant visits the premises. This procedure does not fulfil a proper management duty.

The larger company will have a management team, each dedicated to specific responsibilities, who probably meet weekly on an informal basis and formally at least monthly to discuss the past month's trading returns. There is no set proforma management return to cover every type of business, although many characteristics are common to all. There are many factors described in this chapter that should be controlled and monitored by the management and recognised by the lending bank in order to achieve optimum business performance.

The bank should constantly bear in mind what general external commercial and internal influences may occur that have not been recognised at the time of the original assessment of the company and how they are likely to affect the risk of non-repayment of the amount borrowed and its servicing costs. Some of these are listed below.

External influences	Questions to ask
Changes in interest rates	Will the change affect repayment of the facility
Changes in fiscal policy	Will they create an adverse trading climate
Changes in competition	Will this affect turnover and profitability
Local planning news, etc	How will it affect the business
Governmental controls	Will this lead to unexpected higher expenditure
Technological advances	Will the company's present markets diminish
Trading markets	Can any adverse changes be nullified

Internal influences	Questions to ask
Key staff changes	Will the company change its trading policy
New products	Will they be a success or require much research and development
New expansion plans	What will be their net effect on resources
Loss of customers	How important will this be in sales terms
Selling price changes	Will their overall effect be beneficial or not
New marketing policy	What is the assessment of cost to reward

The aim of the bank will be to recognise, as much in advance as possible, if any of these changes will adversely affect the company's business and, if so, enquire from the company whether the changes are relevant enough to affect the borrowing covenants or lead to a request for additional finance. If the difficulties spotted are pronounced, the next step will be to request a meeting with the company to discuss their effect on the bank's financing and the company's proposed remedial measures that are deemed necessary.

This degree of advance monitoring requires a full and up-dated understanding of the company's business. It applies to the larger corporation as much as the smaller business. As an example of the former, a certain public company had loan facilities outstanding to a number of major banks. There was public knowledge of the difficulties being experienced with products that incorporated a particular ingredient. The company drew down all its then undrawn facilities with those banks' agreement without informing those banks of problems in the offing. A short time afterwards, the company disclosed its financial problems to all the banks. Had the bank(s) taken a prior view of the circumstances surrounding the company's market products, depending on the terms of each facility, there would have been the opportunity for the bank(s) to reduce or withdraw the availability of part of their commitments.

10.4.1   Monitoring actual performance against budget

Annual monitoring of a company's performance is not conducive to initiating a rapid response by the bank to influence its trading and cash flow. This is more akin to going through the motion in the absence of anything known to the contrary. The bank relationship, however, should be a two-way procedure and, in practice, it is surprising how much new business can be gained through occasional, but regular, contact with the customer. Contact in this manner does need a financial background beforehand that, in turn, suggests a reading of the most recent accounts supplied by the company (and website), either at the time they are publicly made available or just prior to contact being made with the company.

At the occasion of a monitoring visit, the banker should have a check list of items to be updated, together with a history of the account, its past needs and points of particular interest on that company that should be regularly raised. The check list will be individual to each bank. A suggested example is given below.

◆ Company details/address/management/personnel contacts.
◆ Customer relationships/record of business contacts.
◆ Past and current business record with the bank (margins/profitability).
◆ Follow-up requests and results.
◆ Regional or central office data/credit limits.
◆ Salient most recent financial results (turnover, net profit and outlook).
◆ Information or news arising since the last contact.
◆ Points to raise at the next contact with the company.

Where the monitoring is to check on the ongoing financial well being of the company, the information requested from the management on a regular basis will be specific to the case. The usual monthly figures requested will be a choice from the following: firm orders received, sales achieved, lists of debtors and creditors outstanding, list of deferred payment accounts, ages of trade balances, totals of cash and bank, etc borrowings outstanding (where more than one bank is involved) and intra-group balances (if any). The aim is to be aware of the key components of trading and cash flow.

A further type of monitoring will compare trading results against the budget set by the company. It is not assumed that the business is about to incur financial difficulties or may require assistance to trade out of an adverse financial condition. There are presumed indications, however, that the bank is not prepared to allow the company to monitor itself; perhaps the account is seen regularly near to its agreed credit limit or should be improving its cash flow, but this is not quite happening. For prudence, a monthly comparison of trading against budget projections is requested. In this case, it will be important to query as soon as possible with the company why any significant divergence of any figure has occurred so that remedial measures may be undertaken.

As an example, orders received and/or sales may be lower than budget. This can be due to one or more reasons, such as uncompetitive pricing, greater competition, poor quality control, late deliveries, a reduced level of production or simply generally lower demand for the product(s). There is a choice of remedial action that the company can take: sales prices can be lowered for a period to stimulate demand and internal measures taken to improve quality, deliveries and production. Alternatively, the company may choose to live with lower sales and reduce operating overheads on the assumption that trading will soon recover. Either way, the bank will need to be satisfied that the remedial action adopted to counteract the failure of meeting budget is appropriate.

In one sense, the **control** of lending is more reactive to events compared with a pro-active monitoring of individual customers' accounts. Once an adverse situation has arisen on a customer's account, control action should be initiated to protect the bank from loss. In another sense, control is exercised in a more general way through head office directives to concentrate, or otherwise, on certain types of lending when gaining new business or viewing existing borrowing that comes up for renewal. A classic case of reactive control would be where a significant rise in house prices, coupled with rising interest rates, leads a bank to review the future size of its lending portfolio in property investment for resale.

10.4.2   The purpose of reviewing customers' accounts

The purpose of reviewing customers' accounts is not to assume that they are acting intemperately with the bank's money, although this may well be the case in certain instances, but to ensure that the account is operated within the agreed terms and to give the bank the earliest notification of anything that has occurred which may impinge on this arrangement.

The Proceeds of Crime Act 2002, effective from February 2003, required all businesses to report any suspicion of money laundering of whatever value and the proceeds of crime. The Money Laundering Regulations 2003, effective from 1 March 2004, obligates all eligible organisations, including banks, providing services in relation to the formation, operation or management of a company to appoint a money laundering reporting officer and have appropriate internal reporting procedures:

◆ to introduce procedures properly to identify customers using large amounts of cash;
◆ to copy the identification documents; and
◆ to maintain records relating to the transactions.

This includes reporting suspicious transactions and, if a payment of more than euro 15,000 is involved, satisfactory evidence of *bona fides* must be obtained from the customer, otherwise the transaction must be terminated. The regulations set out the framework, but no guidance on implementation, such as what constitutes 'suspicion' and what precise measures must be taken to gather customer information.

The frequency of reviewing a customer's account must depend on the circumstances of the individual case. Accounts may be reviewed annually where there have been no problems for some time and where the bank can assume, without asking, that any financial difficulty or changing circumstances will be promptly notified by the company. Accounts that have had, or are having, cash flow problems may require monthly trading figures to be sent regularly and promptly to the bank for monitoring. In more extreme cases, the operation of the account may be required to be monitored weekly or daily.

10.4.3   Information sources for review

The immediate sources of information of how the customer's financial affairs are progressing will be the transactions going through the account(s) being maintained.

This will include the transactions of the day, as well as items in immediate transit not yet cleared. Small, private companies may have just a cheque account and perhaps a deposit account, whereas larger companies with subsidiaries will run many accounts in sterling and currencies that are cleared daily to a net balance, requiring central funding or depositing in the overnight money market.

The bank's computer system will highlight for further examination any anomalies arising in the conduct of the customer's account from that agreed. Further reference to this is discussed in Chapter Seven. The bank should have noted when opening the account any internal money management system in use by the company and have judged its working capability. In turn, this will indicate any areas of financial control for the bank to watch and, if necessary, discuss with the customer. For example, the company may rely on financing a branch through an imprest system, by repaying in arrears the previous month's expenses as a float for the following month. If the following month's costs are higher than the float the account will become overdrawn that may, or may not, have been authorised in advance.

The bank should receive each year the trading accounts of the customer's business for comparison with the year earlier, together with any profit and cash flow forecasts that are available. This will provide the financial background for discussion with the customer at the next annual review of the account, when the opportunity should be taken to enquire of the state of current trading of the business and judge whether the bank can be of further service. It may be necessary to visit the company's offices, for example, if a loan is being advanced for the purchase or extension of property or for the acquisition of new capital equipment.

It has been known for a company to request additional overdraft facilities to finance significantly higher raw materials or finished product stocks than in the past, only for the banker to find that the stocks are non-existent and the money has been spent in other ways. By the time the annual accounts had been prepared and issued, it would have been too late for the bank to safeguard its lending position.

Information sources arising from third parties or publicly reported origins should be treated with caution in case they misrepresent the truth. A carefully worded enquiry to the company would show that the bank was taking the welfare of the business to heart and, if the enquiry were couched around the possibility of a review of the credit limit (ie 'is the present facility large enough?'), this may counsel the company to act earlier rather than later and discuss any problem should cash flow be at a crisis.

10.4.4 'Out of order' report

A business account may be shown as being 'out of order' from the terms agreed between the customer and the bank for a number of reasons. Probably the most common reason is when the account has exceeded its authorised credit limit. This may be due to poor cash management or financial circumstances forced on the business. It will be the banker's important task to discover which circumstances apply. Reasons for poor cash management are inadequate cash flow forecasting, overspending, inaccurate estimation when cash will be cleared on the account (particularly in respect of currency receipts from overseas) and lack of attention to the day-to-day cash resources of the business.

Reasons for adverse financial circumstances usually stem from a lower than expected turnover being achieved. This may be compounded by a lack of quick remedial action that might include delaying the payment of creditors to curbing future expenditure. There may be other reasons for the business having a cash shortfall and exceeding its credit limit: examples are the overstocking of raw materials, debtors proving slower to settle their accounts, a large bad debt, capital expenditure being met out of working capital, personal drawings or salaries exceeding the business earnings and occasional, sizeable cost items (eg quarterly rent).

The lending banker should, first, discover the reason for the 'out of order' report. If the cash position can, or will, be remedied within a short time span, then the adverse report may be discounted from further action so long as the customer realises what has happened and agrees on a suitable solution to prevent a re-occurrence. The banker may purely note simple violations and let the account run its course without further action.

Where there is a more serious reason for the violation, that of adverse financial circumstances, an immediate judgement is required from the banker on two counts: what must the customer do to rectify the situation and what immediate action is required from the bank. In both cases, the customer should first be notified (preferably by telephone followed by a confirming letter) of the breach of account terms. It would be welcome if the customer agrees to correct the situation at once, but a further review of the position should be made if more time is requested to do so. Will acceptance of more time prove the right course or will the financial position get worse?

If the customer cannot immediately restore the account to within its agreed terms, a more thorough examination of the creditworthiness of the business is called for as early as possible. This will have two objectives: to safeguard the bank's position and to discern whether the business can trade out of its predicament. Further action decided upon may lead the bank to take a preference over future incoming receipts, create a separate bank account for the future payment of wages or crystallise any floating security that is held. If the business predicament is shown to be that of a more temporary nature, then the bank may be willing to advance more credit, suitably secured and priced, with strict monitoring procedures.

If the customer cannot or will not respond to the banker's enquiries, an unusual situation with larger businesses, then the bank may have no option but to take steps to close the account. Before this is initiated, all other avenues should be explored as to their consequences, eg the crystallisation of security or appointment of an administrator may have ramifications on the facilities from other banks and perhaps adversely affect the rights of the initiating bank of the closure. Care must also be taken for the bank not to get into litigation that its action did in fact create the collapse of the business.

10.4.5 Causes and warning signs of trading difficulties

In general, there are three basic types of warning signs for a business before possible failure arises: the first occurs when the business changes its previously successful operating profile, the second can occur when external events prejudice its trading operations and the third may emerge internally when a management fails to appreciate an adverse significance.

A **change in operating profile** will lead to the acceptance of additional trading risks. This may take place when a company ventures to trade in a new field or location or markets a new product. Unless the project has been thoroughly assessed for its risks, rewards and financing, it may cause an unacceptable financial loss. The bank should be aware of the new business emphasis and make a broad appraisal of its monitoring requirement: whether to make no change or to raise its monitoring profile during an interim period while there is the risk of failure of the project.

The bank should already be aware of the circumstance of possible **adverse changes in external events** of significance to the well being of the company. An example might be where the franchise for a major part of the business is due for renewal in one year's time. What will happen if this franchise is not renewed? What is the company doing about this risk? Are alternative markets and/or products being found? Another example is changes in the public's preferences in retailing in favour of out-of-town hypermarkets rather than small in-town shops. Is the retailing company adapting to this change? How will it affect the bank relationship? If the retailer does nothing, potentially future turnover, earnings and cash flow will suffer – the warning signs are there.

A **failure by the management** to appreciate warning signs applies to the earlier examples, but it can also apply internally when technical, production or general commercial problems have been unforeseen. These are more difficult for the bank to deduce in advance and in many instances, after a drop in sales or profit has been reported, the bank enquiry as to the reason(s) elicits the proper response from the management. This situation should not be confused with just trading at an inadequate level to meet expenditure and the repayment and servicing of debt. With the former, the management has been inadequate to the task of remedying the problem quick enough, but with the latter the management has been additionally found at fault in its financial forecasting. The judgement of the bank in its assessment of the capabilities of the management has been found lacking and, in the latter example, lacking also in its financial monitoring.

231

A common warning sign of financial difficulties ahead can lie **in overdue trading debts before they become irrecoverable**. Before a debt becomes 'bad', one or more of several errors of judgement must have occurred.

- ◆ When credit to the account was initially granted either a poor credit assessment of that customer was made or even no assessment made at all.
- ◆ The level of credit was too generous or, more likely, subsequent extensions to the limit were allowed without suitable re-appraisal of the creditworthiness of the customer.
- ◆ Regulation of the customer's account by the supplying company has proved inadequate: the terms of trade initially agreed between the parties have failed to be kept by the customer, the supplier has failed to chase the customer sufficiently to recover overdue amounts within the agreed time period and the supplier has failed to stop all future credit being taken (and putting the account on a cash-with-order basis) while setting terms for the gradual recovery of existing overdue sums.

Reference should be made to Chapter Four, 'Why businesses fail'.

10.4.6   Default and bank agreements

The bank will have specified all the events of default in the credit agreement agreed with the customer. The events will be a mixture of common clauses and perhaps clauses special to the particular business of the company (see appendix 4). The more common clauses are:

- ◆ failure to make payments of interest or of principal specified in the lending agreement by the due date(s);
- ◆ cross-default by the borrower in making due payments under other lending agreements;
- ◆ breach of any other clause in the lending agreement, to include non-compliance of covenanted undertakings and failure to adhere to representations made in the lending agreement (eg selling assets);
- ◆ material adverse changes in the circumstances (the financial condition) of the company (note: the interpretation of this clause is usually stated to be at the discretion of the bank);
- ◆ statutory defaults, such as insolvency and breaking or non-adherence to the laws of the country under which the agreement is drafted;
- ◆ changes in control of the company.

A breach of any of these clauses will lead to a demand for repayment of the credit facility and no obligation to make further advances if this is specified in the original facility. The clauses may also extend to other companies within the group. To avoid breaches of what may be termed 'clerical errors', such as forgetting to make a payment by the due date, a clause is frequently inserted allowing the company a number of days (say seven working days) of grace before the breach becomes formalised. Where the company has several bank lenders, the terms granted to earlier bank agreements usually become the template for later deals. What may change, however, is the individual cost of money at the time of the agreement when market influence and the borrower's credit rating will act as a guide.

The **cross-default clause** is important to the bank as it ensures that all banks will be treated as one in the event of failure. The cross-default may be invoked without some of the group banks knowing that default has occurred until later in the proceedings, particularly if it relates to a subsidiary overseas. Corporate borrowers may partially overcome this constraint by compartmentalising the lending to its subsidiaries on a country by country basis, offering security only to bank borrowings in those countries. A material adverse change clause applying to the holding company, however, depending on the wording, may still override the freedom offered by the separation of cross-defaults.

The lending agreement may limit the scope of events of default if mutually agreed between the bank and the borrower. For example, debts below a certain value may be excluded or actions by overseas regulators may change the interpretation of the borrowing. In this latter case, it is usual for the loan agreement to be renegotiated (or even repaid) rather than invoke a default. Occasionally, one bank in a syndicate that is in a different category of risk from other group banks may be allowed special consideration and priority over some security, providing all banks agree thereto. Default of this bank's lending terms will not apply to other lenders to the company.

The **change of control** clause safeguards the bank(s) to the company from a takeover by another entity that would change the lending risk basis without the bank(s) being able to rescind their existing loan agreements should they wish to do so. In turn, this may assist the management in resisting a takeover battle and losing control of the company. In practice, the successful company in a takeover will often renegotiate the existing lending terms applicable to the company taken over and/or substitute its own bank(s) in place of those original banks. This usually means that banks being retained will do so at a lower margin than before and with different lending covenants.

10.4.7 Default and the bank's remedies

When a company is in default, the bank should first act within its individual powers to minimise any potential loss. This may include setting off account balances in credit against the borrower's lending facilities in default, providing both accounts are in the same name and held by the same bank and the lending agreement provides the means to the setoff, ie that the loan is now due and payable (see Chapter Six).

Secondly, the bank will look to all external remedies to prevent the loss of any assets controlled by the defaulting company. This will frequently take the form of **pre-**

judgment attachments (Mareva injunctions) effected as an execution judgment by attachment on the assets of the defaulting party (the defendant) agreed by the court in favour of the bank (the plaintiff). Proof is required that there is a real risk of failing to satisfy the claim and making available the assets that are held by the defendant in the country.

Thirdly, the bank will act to recover the funds now in jeopardy of being fully repaid. The court may decide, at its discretion, that if the remedy of claiming damages will be inadequate or if the loan agreement terms offer a more suitable remedy to settle the claim, an order for **specific performance** of the loan agreement may be granted. There may also be the need for a **prohibitory injunction** to prevent the defaulting company from performing acts to breach the agreed lending covenants. The bank has the option to **sue** in court for damages and the recovery of monies owing arising from the breach of covenants, as well as rescinding the loan agreement. In practice, there will be clauses in the loan agreement stating what (compounded) interest rate will apply as damages.

Fourthly, the debtor company may offer terms for an agreed settlement of the outstanding debt in order to remain in business. The threat of legal action often gains a response and it is less costly than the bank resorting to court proceedings for recovery of the loan. The procedure of restructuring the company's debts in total has the aim to eliminate the need to appoint an administrator over the company's assets and thereby enforce liquidation. The choice of letting the company continue to trade and thereby, in time, repay a greater part of the outstanding debt must be weighed against the possibility that the company will eventually fail or will take so long to repay monies due that the bank(s) would have been better off by cutting their losses early for a lower repayment sum and using the proceeds to offer interest-earning loans to other businesses.

Each **restructuring agreement** will be tailored to the individual characteristics of the company in distress. It effectively means that a completely revised business plan and cash flow forecast will have to be drawn up (by the lead bank/s) to be agreed by the debtor company and all participating banks. Invariably, it will include an element of the bank(s) writing off part of their original debt and, perhaps, taking equity shares in exchange. The security taken and lending covenants will be most stringent, as will future monitoring of the bank account and trading against the forecast returns. There will be a period of freezing the lending status quo of all banks prior to negotiating an ongoing lending settlement. This will be managed by the lead bank(s) that will periodically report to all the other banks as to the progress of negotiations, the current trading situation of the company and the choices the banks have in order to raise a settlement agreeable to all parties.

On a restructuring, the banks will take a greater interest in matters of company policy and in the treatment of trade creditors to prevent any action on their part to prejudice the company's future operations. Part of the bank debt (and possibly the debt of some major trade creditors) may be formalised into bonds (see Chapter Eight) with prior repayment rights. The agreement will include measures how the banks will be repaid over time. Some banks may wish to remain as principal banks to the company while others may wish to withdraw their support as early as possible. The former banks may agree to allow early repayment to the latter banks, but at a cost.

10.4.8 Cross-firing

This is the name given where a customer exploits the time taken to clear funds through an account and the bank honours cheques deliberately drawn on the account by the customer before they are cleared, knowing that there would otherwise be insufficient funds in the account to meet their presentation and without having prior approval from the bank for the account to become overdrawn. When the cheques are presented for payment (usually) two days later, the money has been banked elsewhere and the original account becomes overdrawn. The misuse of the bank account must be systematic and accounts may be used at different banks or branches of a bank or even in conjunction with different accomplices. The bank also has to continue to allow sums to be paid away from cheques banked before they are cleared. The cross-firing will fail if either the customer stops replacing the money withdrawn by new cheques or the bank stops paying money away against funds that continually remain uncleared.

Where many banking and cheque transactions are made into and out of an account daily, it may be difficult to ascertain whether cross-firing is being applied. Probably the best check is to monitor the amount and regularity of uncleared effects. If the customer wishes to make a singular fraudulent withdrawal, approximately an identical amount has to be continually replaced and this should be easily spotted. If the customer wishes to increase the deception, then the uncleared amounts will balloon in total and there will be a noticeable increase in turnover through the account as well. As the restitution of uncleared balances has to be done within the presentation time window, the relative incidence of bankings to cheque payments may raise a pattern that can be recognised as cross-firing.

If the account shows round-sum bankings and cheque withdrawals, this may be a sign of trading weakness and/or cross-firing. Trading weakness may arise through the business not being able to settle trade creditors fully on time or poor credit management by failing to collect the full amount of trade debtor balances when due. Cross-firing does not require round sum transactions to be adopted, but this is frequently the case for the customer to keep a more easy record of the amounts involved. Where the payee and the drawer of cheques are identical, this may indicate cross-firing or simply reimbursement of one account of the customer from another that is in credit. The frequency and size of these transactions will offer a clue which explanation is correct.

10.4.9   Over-trading

Over-trading has been defined as expansion of a business without sufficient financial support. Expansion usually results in an increase in sales, although there can be start-up businesses that incur costs and run out of money (ie capital) prior to commencing trading. Over-trading may only occur for a short period or it may prove endemic. An example of the former would be where staffing, production and stocks are increased in anticipation of higher sales, so that when the additional sales eventually materialise the positive cash flow of the business is restored. An example of the latter would be where an anticipated increase in sales does not materialise and the business is over-geared for the size of trading being attained and the available financial resources invested in the business.

It can be difficult to recognise when a business is over-trading before it runs into significant cash flow problems. An approximate test as to whether a manufacturing company is, or is not, over-trading might be as follows.

10.4.9.1   Test A

1. Estimate the present average monthly level of sales.
2. Take the expected average present gross profit per cent on sales.
3. Estimate the annual cost of indirect expenses and convert to a monthly basis.
4. The net profit will be 1 x 2 + 3. Convert to an annual basis.
5. Deduct from the net profit any capital expenditure (less sale proceeds) expected during the year.
6. Deduct also any total of irrecoverable VAT for the year.
7. The result will be the financial resources being generated by the business in a full year.
8. Compare step 7 with the cash resources of the business (ie present cash in hand and available bank facilities not yet drawn). If the resources are inadequate, then the business is over-trading relative to the financial support that is available.

In some cases the present average gross profit percentage is not available and to take an historic figure from the previous year's statutory accounts would be misleading. If so, step 2 may be substituted by the following:

2a Calculate the present monthly direct cost of labour and overheads.
2b Calculate the estimated cost of materials necessary for the forecast level of sales. Then continue with step 3 as before.

Note: the reason for estimating some costs annually and then converting them to a monthly basis is to allow in the calculations for expenses that occur less frequently than monthly. A broad estimate of irrecoverable VAT is to calculate (the current rate of 17.5%) VAT on total sales and deduct from this the VAT on total expenses after ignoring non-VATable expenses (ie wages, salaries, rent and rates, insurance and loan interest).

It will be crucial for a business not to over-trade and raise the spectre of insolvency. It is equally important for the bank to realise in good time whether such a situation is likely to arise and to broach alternative remedies to the company concerned. The test steps shown above, while estimating many figures on a present day basis, still rely on historic expense forecasts. The additional trading may refer to a new project for which no historic returns are available. How can it be seen whether the new project will lead to over-trading? Consider the following test.

10.4.9.2 Test B

1. What current numbers of units are being produced and what is their budgeted cost of production?
2. How many production units are proposed for sale, including the projected expansion, over a measured future period?
3. What will be the revised overheads of production (ie 1 + 2)?
4. What is the forecast level of unit sales over the same period?
5. Are steps 2 and 4 compatible? Assuming this is so ...
6. How much additional financing will step 3 require (including any additional labour and capital equipment) and over what period before receipts from the additional sales are received?
7. Does the business have additional finance readily at hand?
8. If there is a financial shortfall, the company will be over-trading. Will this be for a short period until sales receipts increase or will the shortfall require additional financial support?
9. What will be the position of the bank if a request for additional credit is made?

The bank should already be aware whether the management of the company is capable of trading over a period when it is difficult to match cash flow with outgoings. The individual circumstances of each company will vary, but a typical 'action plan' listing a suggested order of assessment for the company to relieve its financial position brought about by over-trading is as follows.

1. Reduce production to what can be quickly sold.
2. This may lead to putting production staff on short time (if the situation is deemed temporary) or making redundancies.
3. Cancel outstanding capital equipment replacement programmes.
4. If there is a turnover deficiency (where the over-trading has been due to expanding production capacity), try and increase immediate sales without unduly prejudicing existing profit margins or, if the problem is a surfeit of orders, extend the period of supply and, in an extreme case, consider sub-contracting production.

5. Review all expenditure budgets for cuts to improve cash flow.
6. Accelerate recovery of sales debts and pay creditors later.
7. Limit the retention of stocks to a critical minimum and endeavour to order replacement stocks on short time delivery.
8. Upgrade monitoring of cash flow to a daily need (if required).
9. Consider the injection of additional permanent (additional shares) or working (loans from the directors and/or the company's bank) capital AND agree in advance with the bank how the new funds will be used.

Similar tests apply to service companies. For retail businesses, the critical evaluation will be to achieve the correct balance between sales and stocks and not to over-spend in areas that may, or may not, prove to be rewarding such as marketing. Other companies operating in the service sector will have to operate with the correct balance between expensive staffing and the business that is won. In each case, the bank will be forewarned if frequent excess borrowings are seen over the previously agreed credit limit or the customer takes sales receipts in cash to settle bills without paying the funds first into the bank.

The bank has to be aware of any resilience of the management to change past practices and not to take at face value the obvious response that the financial difficulties are temporary and the company will trade itself out of its predicament. This is rarely the case where there are unrecognised fundamental problems and a willingness to change past practices is accepted. Too many companies have been milked of profits through the owners taking out capital in the form of excessive salaries or dividends. When trading returns and cash flow drops, there can be a resistance to reinvest money into the business if it is easier for the bank to meet the shortfall. The bank must look upon each new application for support as a new proposal and judge the situation at the time on its merits.

10.4.10   Temporary difficulties

If the situation of over-trading is not easy to discern, consider the position of a business that is in temporary difficulties. Is the trading difficulty temporary or not? If it is temporary, then the bank should be aware that support now is critical to enable the company to regain profitability and at the same time release the bank from having the company placed in a liquidation procedure when loans may or may not be fully repaid. Equally, for the bank to put new funds at the disposal of the company may exacerbate the loss incurred. How can this dilemma be resolved?

Some general rules of engagement can be laid down.

◆ What was the reason for the difficulties in the first place?
◆ What did the management do about it and was it successful?
◆ Will the difficulties resolve themselves naturally?
◆ Can the difficulties be easily combated by internal measures?
◆ What will be the cost of these measures relative to the reward?

If the difficulties are externally driven, then the question to answer is whether they will dissipate or remain for a period, in which case can the company survive over this period? If the management recognises the problem(s), is it raising pertinent solutions for adoption? If the problems are more far reaching, what is the time scale for their resolution and what is the cost of financing? The bank should initially be sympathetic about assisting the company unless the management has reneged on its agreed commitments. After all, the bank agreed to lend to the company at its initial assessment. There is the celebrated case, not made public, of the clearing bank that changed its mind six times before allowing the public company in question to fall into liquidation. This exudes commitment to the customer but a failure to take a decision.

10.4.11   Unpaid cheques and control action

The short answer for the bank on this conundrum is never to refuse to meet a cheque of acceptable amount presented for payment outside the agreed limit of the company's credit without referral to the customer for an explanation. This assumes that the customer can be contacted that day for an explanation and all previous conduct of the account has been exemplary. If there have been previous problems for the customer in meeting presented cheques and/or problems for the bank in obtaining suitable explanations as to the customer's conduct, then the customer has presumably been forewarned that a credit limit is what it says and cheques over this limit in all likelihood will be peremptorily refused.

The bank should be aware that to refuse a cheque on unclear grounds may lead to the company losing public credit status and possibly be drawn into liquidation that, in turn, may be the prelude to legal action for compensation. In the circumstances, the bank should review the past conduct of the account and make a re-appraisal of the conditions of support. This may lead to taking additional security for increasing the credit limit, providing advice on the future running of the account or limiting the credit to be made available with a programme of redemption of outstanding loan balances. Having to refuse payment of a cheque, unless the reason is clerical, is a major step for the re-appraisal of the customer company as a credit risk.

How does the bank know whether an unpaid cheque or failure to meet a loan repayment is the precursor of worse financial difficulties for the company without enquiring why the situation arose? The bank would fail in its obligations solely to look to its security and not enquire further as to the financial position of the company. The initial requirement is to have an up-to-date financial position of the company to hand as soon as possible. After this, a meeting with the management is essential to provide explanations for the previously supplied financial data. Thereafter, the management should be asked what they intend to do to rectify the situation and what revised forecasts of trading are to hand. If these are acceptable to the bank, they should be regularly monitored thereafter.

10.4.12 Management information

The tests of good management of a business are:

◆ the extent of, and how quick, financial information is supplied;
◆ what the information conveys; and
◆ whether the necessary action is subsequently initiated.

Computer programs off-the-shelf offer ready-made data that frequently is not user-friendly to the company in question. Larger companies have their own systems but have an equal Achilles heel if the information becomes too verbose and levels of control flounder under 'red tape'.

Each business has its own critical measures of monitoring. A so-called 'cash cow' such as a hypermarket chain will be looking to receive an optimum cash return on space utilised and selling at what profit margins. A construction company will be looking to tender at the right margin to make a profit and to curb operating costs where the contract is placed at a fixed price. In an ideal world, each bank loan should be supported by a company budget and trading forecasts that are regularly monitored by the bank so that variances can be quickly picked up and mutually resolved.

Monitoring takes up personnel time, which is costly, even if it is computer generated. Usually, only the companies in difficulty receive regular monitoring and are in receipt of weekly or monthly returns of critical financial information like sales achieved, the orders in hand and the total and ages of trade debtor balances. Larger companies will be constrained by covenants to control the total of borrowings relative to the net (equity) worth of the business. Each facet of information is important for the bank to assess constantly its lending risk and not just rely on loose annual verbal forecasts by the company management of what sales might be achieved in the coming year.

The decisive action for the bank when fully monitoring an account is to get as much up-to-date information as possible on trading in advance of the supply of any historic accounting information or explanations given by the management. This means assessing the general trading environment of the company and benchmarking other similar companies trading in the same field. Ideally, the question should be raised for a peer company to be asked: 'what do you think of company "x"?' This question is the most frequently requested by investors before investing equity in a business. Why should it not apply to a lending bank, subject always to any confidentiality constraints?

10.4.13 Covenants in facility agreements

Covenants are undertakings drawn up by the lender(s), accepted by the borrower, to adhere to certain obligations for the duration of the loan agreement. In principle, they safeguard the lender(s) from acts that the borrower may initiate to reduce the security for the loan. This security may be tangible (ie a debenture) or an operating restriction. Common clauses are:

◆ a negative pledge – restricting the company from granting security over its assets to third parties;

◆ to maintain the assets of the company – by not disposing of them without prior approval and ensuring that they are fully insured against loss;

◆ to maintain the net worth of the company – by limiting its borrowings to a set figure and/or restricting the amount of dividends that may be declared to its shareholders;

◆ to maintain its identity as to the type of business to be conducted and/or the type of companies it may acquire;

◆ to maintain its individuality against a takeover or amalgamation when control may become invested in others;

◆ financial covenants. Some banks prefer a minimum of covenants in favour of regular monitoring.

The drafting of the negative pledge clause will be important, as the company will be wishing to restrict its influence on existing prior charges or future short/medium-term loans having a lien on certain assets (eg hire purchase agreements, import/export arrangements, title retention, account setoffs and sale and leaseback arrangements). Any covenants must be clear whether they are to apply at one regularly recurring date or for each trading day.

The financial covenants set can vary according to the standing of the borrowing company. There are usually clauses restricting the total amount of borrowings (relative to the overall net worth of the business), a minimum level of earnings to interest payable on the outstanding loans and possibly a minimum ratio of current assets to current liabilities. The definition of borrowings is usually extensive, embracing lease and hire purchase obligations, contingent liabilities such as guarantees and indemnities and other deferred indebtedness such as pension obligations.

10.4.14   Settlement risk

There is settlement risk when forward financial commitments are entertained. The risks associated with foreign exchange dealings and interest rate exposures are discussed in Chapter Eight. Other risks abound. Settlement may seem simple enough between one bank situated in the Far East and another in Europe, but if one market closes before another market opens, there is potentially a period of risk that the deal is not covered between banks for changes in pricing.

The situation may also arise internally, where one branch overseas commits itself to large foreign exchange deals or commitments that are not covered elsewhere within the bank. In this case, the branch may instigate a rollover position to cover its unauthorised dealings. Internal audit procedures and authorisations may be inadequate initially to prevent a build up of the now loss-making liability. Bank headquarters are asked for more capital to support the unauthorised operation. Eventually, the adverse settlement position becomes known and the bank concerned incurs large losses in closing the open positions.

It is difficult to account for collusion within a bank to cover unauthorised dealings other than to monitor all outstanding (exchange or loan) positions at the end of each day and to regulate the extent of the size of dealings during each day. Dual responsibility is probably the best initial form of defence and astute monitoring is the second best defence after initiating comprehensive operating control procedures.

10.4.15   Proceeds of crime and money laundering

The Proceeds of Crime Act 2002, effective from 24 February 2003, and the Money Laundering Regulations 2003, effective from 1 March 2004, have given banks and other organisations (as defined) extensive legal obligations to comply with. Failing to report knowledge or suspicion of money laundering is punishable by a jail sentence of up to five years. If assistance has been given in any way to support the offence the jail term may extend to 14 years. It is an offence to disclose information that may prejudice an investigation where there is a suspicion that a report has been made to the National Crime Intelligence Service.

The three main money laundering offences are:

◆ concealment;
◆ making arrangements for using or possessing criminal property;
◆ acquiring criminal property.

Criminal property (ie cash or other tangible or intangible property) covers any benefit from criminal conduct where the alleged offender knows or suspects that it has been obtained by dishonest means. Banks and other financial institutions have been subject to money laundering obligations for some years and the new legislation extends this to non-financial organisations. There is no *de minimis* threshold for reporting suspicions. Any suspicion must be reported to the appointed money laundering reporting officer. It is unclear at present whether one can validly claim that one did not believe that a disclosure would prejudice an investigation.

Many banks have had to up-grade their existing monitoring procedures and ensure that staff have sufficient training and awareness to identify and report any suspicious activity. Essentially, there is a need to know your existing customer sufficiently and to vet adequately all new customers. In practical terms, illegal money may arise in an account either for the use of the recipient or to be transferred away to another haven, for which purpose the bank, by acting as agent of the transferor, will add some credence to the operation. In the first case, the bank has to know its customers well enough to be able to judge whether a particular deal is within the normal trading of that business. In the latter case, the detection relies largely on inspection of the 'strange' or unusual transfer by the bank.

Eleven

Specialist lending

11.1   Factoring and invoice discounting

Perhaps the most important aspect of factoring or invoice discounting is that it ring-fences the lender's debtor balances to the money advanced. Typically up to 80% of a previously approved debt is advanced to the borrower within two or three working days to be used as working capital in the business. All debts have to be approved as suitable for financing by the lender. If the debt has been factored, the lender will have acquired a good title from the borrower and will be collecting the amount outstanding in its own name. If the debt has been invoice discounted, the title remains with the borrower who collects the amount owing.

As the **factor** will be administering the borrower's portfolio of sales ledger debts and collecting the amounts when due directly from the borrower's customers, the customers will know that the transaction is being factored and this may give rise to some doubts as to the borrowers financial worthiness. The portfolio being factored may be the borrower's complete sales ledger or just debts selected by the lender as being creditworthy to finance. If any debt is not paid, according to the agreement between the borrower and lender, the lender may, or may not, have recourse to the borrower for restitution of the amount(s) unpaid by the customer(s).

The risks to the (bank) lender are twofold: that a customer fails to pay and recourse to the borrower is not available and, secondly, that the borrower may not be able to repay on recourse. The lender will be relying on each individual debtor for repayment in the first instance and it will be important to initiate a rapid response to collect overdue debts should there be any delay in settling the amount(s) due.

The lender should also be monitoring the borrower's account for two reasons: the business may have other financial difficulties outside its debtors' ledger that could prevent it from meeting its liabilities under the factoring agreement. Examples could be poor quality controls leading to goods being returned, or production problems leading to lost orders or default in repaying another loan. If customers get knowledge of this there may be added difficulty in collecting debts. Also, the business may suffer a downturn in trading. This will reflect in future in lower sales, fewer debtors and, ultimately, in a reduced cash flow.

Where **invoice discounting** is adopted, the borrower continues to operate the business' sales ledger and notifies the invoice discounter (the lender) when each sale is invoiced. The lender discounts the invoice amount at the agreed percentage of face value of the invoice and remits the money to the borrower. The customer settles directly with the discounter and the role of the discounter is hidden. Any invoices that are overdue for payment are immediately charged back to the business. Recourse may or may not apply, as before. The risk to the lender is that the borrower will not repay the amounts advanced.

The following table provides a summary of the characteristics of each service:

Facility steps	Factor	Invoice discounter
Ownership of the debts	Yes	No
Trader raises invoices to customer	Receives copy invoice	Receives copy invoice
Trader receives percentage of invoice value	Pays the trader	Pays the trader
The customer settles the invoice	Receives money direct	Awaits payment
Trader repays the loan	–	Receives repayment
Balance of the debt	Pays balance to trader	–
If the customer is a late payer	Chases the money due	Trader chases customer
Treatment of bad debts	Liable if no recourse	Recourse to trader
Charges payable by the trader	Interest on the advance Ledger administration fee Turnover management fees Money transmission fees Possibly arrangement fee	Interest on the advance Turnover management fees Money transmission fees Possibly arrangement fee

The lender will be examining the sales ledger of the trader for 'unsuitable' debts to eliminate them from the financing agreement. Elimination may be due to the debts' size (too small), their frequency (occasional rather than regular), their age profile (too old and potentially liable to offer a poor recovery), the type of business of the customer (too risky or too specialist) and the makeup of the sales ledger overall (if a large proportion of outstanding debts relates to just a few large customers, they may only be accepted up to a maximum figure outstanding at any one time).

Once the agreement with the trader has been running successfully for a period, the lender can be asked to increase the percentage of ledger balances being advanced. This is usually done through a top-up loan in its own right, perhaps effectively financing 100% of the debts, that will run coincidentally with the factored or discounted advances.

Although the lender can operate factoring or invoice discounting for any sales ledger size, it is usually the case that where total debts regularly outstanding are below £100,000, the operational costs for the trader of invoice discounting will be prohibitive relative to the usefulness of the facility. A higher figure will apply for factoring but, in mitigation, the trader will not have any operational costs attributable to staffing and maintaining the sales ledger and chasing overdue debts.

Factors and invoice discounters operate in a highly competitive market. They frequently charge a variable interest rate rivalling the margins over base on overdrafts quoted for the best corporate clients. The size and quality of the sales ledger of the trader will determine how fine the turnover percentage fee will be charged, ranging from about 0.2% pa up to 1%, and several percentage points higher for smaller debt portfolios. Sometimes the arrangement fee may be waived. The factor's management fee will be regularly reviewed and calculated according to the lending bank's work involved. There will be a regular review by the lender of the conduct of the account and the other fees being levied.

The usefulness of this type of lending service may be apparent where a business is expanding rapidly and effectively outgrows its available capital employed. The balance sheet may have only limited equity capital and asset backing as security on which to base a more conventional loan and the bank perhaps may not be willing to see the overdraft facility continue to increase beyond a certain size. A rapid injection of additional cash could be needed to finance the business's continued and profitable growth.

Subject to an agreed overall credit exposure, an invoice discounting facility expands automatically to meet further increase in sales and debtor balances. This will take the pressure off the overdraft facility limit and enable the business to finance several times its net worth. As profits catch up with the burgeoning cash flow, the business should, in time, be able to refinance itself on more conventional and less expensive credit lines. Note that the converse applies: the facility is reduced if the value of the portfolio of debts being factored or discounted falls. The business should be aware that reliance must not be placed on maintaining the size of the facility in this situation.

Consider a notional example of a discounting facility in operation:

(£'000)	Mth 1	Mth 2	Mth 3	Mth 4	Mth 5	Mth 6
Value of debts	200	300	400	300	200	200
70% discounted	140	210	280	210	140	140
30% not discounted	0	0	60	90	120	90
Total cash received	140	210	340	300	260	230
Compared with: no discounting	0	0	200	300	400	300
Difference	+ 140	+ 210	+ 140	0	- 140	- 70
Difference (cumulative)	*+ 140*	*+ 350*	*+ 490*	*+ 490*	*+ 350*	*+ 280*

It has been assumed in the example that all debts would normally be collected two months after invoicing. Were the table to extend to months 7 and 8, each would have shown a negative cash flow of 140, so that by the end of month 8 the cumulative difference in cash flow would equate to zero. In practice, of course, sales would continue after month 7. The average value of debts outstanding per month in the example was 200 and the average difference cumulatively was 280, not a bad increase in working capital over the period relative to the value of the debtors ledger. Note that the converse applies in that the facility reduces should the value of the portfolio of debts being factored or discounted fall. The business should be aware that reliance must not be placed on maintaining the size of the facility in this instance.

Debts cannot be factored where they are subject to a fixed charge in favour of another party that is not the factor involved. Debts being collected and factored usually have a floating charge placed on them and where a fixed and floating charge is held by other lender(s), there should be an agreement in place to determine the rights of the various lending parties on the assets of the business. Factoring can be beneficial to companies based overseas who are exporting into the UK and collecting UK debts, as well as for UK exporters collecting currency debts from overseas where the exchange risk can be minimised to a few days rather than weeks or months for the UK company to collect its receivables.

11.2 Asset finance

There are a number of different ways to finance the acquisition of individual assets, each tailored to offer specific services within the basic lending format. The options are:

◆ hire purchase;
◆ lease purchase;
◆ contract purchase;

- contract hire;
- operating lease;
- finance lease;
- general asset-based lending.

Hire purchase finance is a rental agreement allowing the hirer to purchase the asset for a nominal sum at the end of the rental period. Depending on the extent of the indebtedness, if the rental payments are not met the lender can repossess the asset or sue for the balance due by the company under the agreement (the Consumer Credit Act 1974). A percentage down payment is required and this may be supplemented by any allowance given for a traded-in asset. The hire purchase interest is then added and the balance owing is repaid in equal instalments over the agreed term. The purchaser has the benefit of tax allowances from day one and can charge the interest cost against profits. VAT is payable at outset by the purchaser, but can only be recovered on a subsequent disposal, in the case of motor cars, if there is no private use.

The lender will be accepting the credit risk of the purchaser, therefore, all the usual credit checks should be done. As there will be a front-end deposit paid, initially the size of the debt will probably be covered by the resale value of the asset. The type of asset will determine the period of the hire purchase agreement; computers and vehicles are likely to have a three-year maximum period and assets holding their value better will be on a longer period. Care is needed on specialised plant that has to be built to order and may therefore hold little residual value to other parties.

Lease purchase gives the lessee (the user) possession and use of the asset for a period of time through paying rentals, but it does not give title to the asset, although there can be an option at the end of the lease period to acquire the asset for a nominal sum or to re-lease at a nominal cost over additional years. The lessor (providing and financing the asset) retains title over the leasing period(s) and claims tax relief as the asset's owner. The lessee charges the rental amounts against its corporate tax liability.

The lease agreement will stipulate the penalties the lessee has to pay for incomplete performance and the lessor can repossess the asset for non-compliance of the terms after the due notice period has expired. The bank lessor will usually have several companies with different year ends to own the asset(s) to obtain the earliest tax allowances. Banks will probably prefer a leasing deal to a hire purchase commitment due to the greater flexibility it offers for repossession of the asset in the event of default. It is also beneficial to offset the profits earned from other banking activities against the tax allowances claimed on the cost of the asset that is leased.

Contract purchase is similar to lease purchase but the company is contracted to acquire the asset at the end of the lease period. The asset is not shown in the balance sheet of the prospective purchaser, but a 'note to the accounts' will indicate the contract liability to be paid. Ownership is achieved at the end of the lease period. The lessor gains tax relief as the asset's owner. The lessee cannot reclaim

VAT on a subsequent sale. The bank lessor may appreciate the fact that the asset will definitely be taken over by the lessee, but this agreement option really favours the lessee if the asset is likely to be used for quite a number of years.

Contract hire, unlike contract purchase, potentially favours the lessor in that at the end of the lease period, the lessor will have the task to sell the asset. This could result in a favourable resale price and profit for the lessor if the residual value has been correctly judged (or if the asset has been fully depreciated in the contract terms so that any residual value amounts to a profit). There is the danger, however, that technological advances can cause the asset (eg computers) to be obsolete long before the end of the hire period, so that the calculated residual value no longer exists, resulting in a end-term loss for the lessor. The bank lessor would be wise to write off the asset's full value by the end of the original lease.

Finance leases give the lessee substantially all the risks and rewards (ie the risks of maintenance and insurance and the rewards of usage) associated with ownership of the asset and, as such, the asset should be capitalised in the balance sheet of the lessee. Legal title of the asset, however, remains with the lessor. The definition accepted for 'substantially all the risks and rewards' is taken as 90% or more of the present value (calculated using the interest rate specified in the lease agreement) of all lease payments (including any initial payment) of the fair value of the leased asset. The lessee pays the lessor rental for the cost of the asset and its accompanying finance charges. The lessee does not (directly) take over ownership of the lease at the end of the lease period and usually the asset is replaced (if required) through a new lease.

Operating leases give the lessor ownership of the asset with all the standard tax allowance advantages. The lessee pays a rental and does not capitalise the asset in its balance sheet as the period of the lease is deemed substantially less than the useful economic life of the asset. The lessee does not (directly) take over ownership of the asset at the end of the lease period and an ancillary lease can be agreed at nominal rental cost. The bank lessor acts as owner and financier to the finance or operating lease agreement and the asset usually reverts to the supplier of the asset on expiry of the lease period(s) for disposal. As financier, the bank is ambivalent whether the deal is a finance lease or an operating lease, as the risks involved are identical.

General **asset-based lending** is often part of a larger financing package where an overdraft facility provides the business with working capital, a term loan finances assets of permanence to be used in the business (eg property), bills of exchange may finance imports/exports, invoice discounting will be used to assist with the rapid collection of debts and leasing will finance the acquisition of assets having a more limited life such as motor vehicles or plant and machinery where specific tax or cash flow advantages are required rather than through a short/medium-term loan. The 'pool' of assets provides the security, supported by the credit standing of the company. No specific reliance is placed on trading prospects and cash flow, although the capacity to repay the instalments over the period of the contract will be important.

Hire purchase reduces the immediate need for cash and provides the user with some security of retention of the asset under the Consumer Credit Act 1974, providing sufficient payments have been paid. Lease purchase is similar, but offers additional flexibility in its terms. Contract purchase enables the asset to be 'off balance sheet' until the contract period expires, although VAT cannot be reclaimed. Contract hire does not offer ownership, but the payments can be deducted in full from taxable profits.

Where the company enters into a lease which entails taking substantially all the risks and rewards of ownership of an asset, the lease is treated as a finance lease; the asset is recorded in the balance sheet as a tangible fixed asset and is depreciated over its estimated useful life or the term of the lease, whichever is shorter. Rentals payable are apportioned between the finance element and are charged to the profit and loss account and the capital element reduces the outstanding obligation for future instalments. All other leases are accounted as operating leases with the rental costs charged to the profit and loss account on a straight line (ie equal annual) basis over the life of the lease.

It is possible to offload the lending risk of default by the borrower(s). This is to enter into a finance contract with specialised financial institutions that are willing to underwrite the risk. An alternative option for the lender is to securitise the debt portfolio and sell the package to other banks or interested parties. This option applies to most types of fixed asset, including property-backed loans.

The table hereafter summarises the more usual aspects of each form of asset finance, although care should be taken not to be too strict on demarcation as individual contracts may have their own options as choices. All the options offer the trading business a cash flow advantage compared with outright purchase and the different taxation characteristics are an important part of the package.

Trader's position:	Hire purchase	Lease purchase	Contract purchase	Contract hire	Operating lease	Finance lease	Asset lending
Ownership	At end of agreement	Optional at end	At end of agreement	No	No	No, option to re-lease	Yes at start
Capitalised	Yes	No	No	No	No	Yes	Yes
Maintenance	No	Yes	Yes	Yes	Optional	Optional	No
Tax offset Allowed	On interest	On interest	On interest	On instalments	On instalments	On instalments	On interest
VAT payable	At outset	At outset	At outset	On each instalment	On each instalment	On each instalment	
VAT recovery	On asset cost	On asset cost	No	On payments	On payments	On payments	On asset cost
Lender's position:							
During the agreement	Owns the asset	Owns the asset	Owns the asset	Owns the asset	Owns the asset	Owns the asset	May be secured
Interest rate	Fixed	Fixed or variable	Fixed	Fixed	Fixed	Fixed or variable	Fixed or variable
Repayments	Fixed	Flexible	Flexible	Fixed	Flexible	Flexible	Flexible
Payments cover	n/a	n/a	n/a	Cost plus interest	Cost less end value	Cost plus interest	Cost of loan
On end sale	Trader owns	To third party	Trader owns	To third party	To third party	To third party	Trader owns
Security	The asset	The asset	The asset	The asset	The asset	The asset	The asset

11.3 International trade finance

Small businesses with occasional sales to customers abroad will probably invoice in sterling and ask for payment in advance through the post, by credit card or funds cleared through their bank. Electronic banking provides two main types of services: balance and transaction reporting (BTR) and electronic funds transfer (EFT). In the UK, information is limited to cleared or closing balances of the previous day and a forecast for the end of the current day that includes low value UK automatic settlements through the Bankers Automated Clearing System (BACS), but excludes corporate transfers through the Clearing House Automated Payments System (CHAPS).

Overseas transfer settlements may be done by telegraphic transfer (TT), the banks' Society for Worldwide Inter-bank Financial Telecommunications (SWIFT) clearing system, or through other systems such as Western Union Quick Pay clearing, the Trans-European Automated Real-time Gross Settlement (Target) for euro payments, or the Clearing House Inter-bank Payment System (Chips) for US dollars. The choice reverts to rapidity and cost: credit cards are relatively slow and expensive for large transfers, whereas SWIFT is quick but costly for small sums.

As the transactions build up in amount and quantity, it may be pertinent to set up a currency bank account abroad for collections and payments. Depending on which overseas country is involved, it is usually beneficial to choose an international home bank with branches in that country rather than a local bank having no direct connections to the home bank. The reason for this is that the local bank will probably clear any cheques through its local clearing bank for subsequent clearance through its international branch, creating additional bank charges en-route and a time lag of up to two weeks before good value is received at home.

There are three principal payment methods for multiple trading overseas: by open account, documentary collection and documentary credits. **Open account** is easy to operate and may be conducted in sterling or currencies. It is risky, in that there is no control over the goods or security of the goods and no guarantee of payment. It involves the trading parties dealing with each other on credit terms and completing deals by agreed settlement dates. Failure to do so leaves the injured party the right to sue for the debt and/or restitution of the goods. This payment method is usually chosen where both parties are well known to each other and willing to accept the risk.

Documentary collection is where settlement is effected through a bill of exchange (or similar draft) either for immediate payment (on sight) or at some stated future date (a term draft). A bill of exchange is defined [the words outside these brackets] in section 3 of the Bills of Exchange Act 1882 as:

> 'An unconditional order in writing, addressed by one person [the drawer] to another, signed by the person giving it, requiring the person to whom it is addressed [the drawee] to pay on demand or at a fixed or future determinable time, a sum certain in money, to or to the order of, a specified person [the payee] or to bearer.'

The advantage of this method of payment is that the bill can be discounted for cash earlier than its maturity if accepted to do so by the bank. Where the bank signs the bill it is guaranteeing payment thereof and the (now 'avalised') bill may be discounted in the market at a more fine (cheaper) interest rate. To avoid misunderstandings, there are Uniform Rules for Collections for banks to abide by when collecting settlements.

Documentary credits are letters of credit (L/C) where an issuing bank conditionally or unconditionally guarantees the terms of payment of its customer's (the applicant's) debt to a named third party (the beneficiary) on the presentation of stated documents evidencing the shipment of title of specified goods to the applicant. This may be done in two ways: the issuing bank may undertake to pay the sum due to the beneficiary, or accept bills drawn by the beneficiary, providing the terms of the L/C are complied with or the issuing bank may instruct a confirming bank of its choosing (usually situated in the country of the beneficiary) to raise the conditional payment undertaking with an advising bank appointed by the beneficiary. The undertaking may be specified revocable or irrevocable.

There is a Uniform Customs and Practice for Documentary Credits updated every few years to account for changes in banking practices, giving internationally accepted rules and definitions governing the liabilities and duties of all parties to such credits. Part of this agreement is embodied in the Uniform Rules for Bank-to-Bank Reimbursements (URBBR) relating to documentary credits. The steps of a typical transaction would be where:

1. an overseas importer asks its own bank to guarantee payment (by issuing an irrevocable L/C pertaining to the goods);
2. requests the confirming bank to contact the UK exporter as its advising bank to ensure that the sales contract terms and details are in order so that they can confirm the credit;
3. the exporter will check the documentary details of the transaction, return them to its advising bank and ship the goods to the importer;
4. the advising bank then sends the documents stating the amount due to the overseas confirming bank, which sends them to the importer;
5. when the goods are delivered the exporter tenders the documents for release of the goods.

The transaction does not necessarily require a bill of exchange if the overseas issuing bank guarantees payment, in which case it is called a 'deferred payment credit'.

The UK exporter has to take account of the potential risks when trading with the buyer of the goods, the country risk where the goods are being shipped to and the period of transit of the goods. It will be important to know the credit status of the buyer and the country in question and any regulatory controls that may prevent payment (the exporter's bank may assist in this respect). Export credit and transit insurance may be available. VAT is raised in the country of shipment and the rules are complex, but, broadly speaking, if the invoice shows the required details of the transaction, it will be eligible to be classed as an input (a purchase) or an output (a sale or supply) for the respective parties.

Where a credit insurance policy supports the transaction, the bank may finance up to 95% of the value of the deal. Exports of small value may be accommodated under the bank's own block policy cover, usually with recourse if the terms of the policy are not adhered to. Alternatively, the credit standing of the borrower may be sufficiently high to obtain a blanket line of credit, part of which may be used to support its overseas trading. The Export Credit Guarantee Department (ECGD) used to cover short-term export risks, but this is now done by NCM Limited.

An **acceptance credit** is where a bank has discounted a trade bill of exchange to raise immediate funds for the customer. That is, the exporter draws a bill of exchange supporting the trade on its own bank which the bank endorses and accepts liability thereof. The bill then becomes a 'bank bill' that can be discounted in the money market at a fine rate for immediate cash. Most bills are of three to six months duration and for individual sums representing the value of the underlying transaction, usually in excess of £50,000.

A summary of the situations met when dealing in trade finance is given by the following table.

Situation	Problems	Results	Action
Exporting in £	Currency appreciates	Increased profit	Repatriate or hold overseas
	Currency depreciates	Lower profit	Cover forward
Importing and paying in currency	Currency appreciates	Lower profit	Buy forward
	Currency depreciates	Increased profit	Buy spot
Borrowing in £ to buy currency	Currency appreciates	Higher cost	Buy forward or forward option
	Currency depreciates	Lower cost	Ignore option
Borrowing in currency	Currency appreciates	Higher repayment liability	Raise currency income
	Currency depreciates	Lower repayment Liability	Try to match with currency assets

Trader	Situation	Exchange result	Action
Importer	Currency purchased	Currency appreciates	Take up option
Importer	Currency purchased	Currency depreciates	Abandon option
Exporter	Currency being sold	Currency appreciates	Abandon option
Exporter	Currency being sold	Currency depreciates	Take up option

11.4 Forfaiting

It has been mentioned that a trade bill of exchange (ie a bill of exchange supporting a trade) can be accepted and guaranteed (ie avalised) by a bank for payment of a (customer's) debt. If there is an extended credit period, typically spanning from six months or one year up to seven years, the importer gains from having several years to settle the debt and the exporter obtains immediate payment of the full debt and passes on all the risks and responsibility for its collection to a **forfaiting** financier. The administration and collection costs and the fixed discounting interest rate that is charged may be for the account of either party, as mutually agreed.

In essence, the buyer (the forfaiter) foregoes the legal right to claim upon any previous owner of the debt; the bill is non-recourse. Most forms of debt (eg trade receivables and promissory notes, not only trade bills) can be forfaited. A promissory note is defined in section 83 of the Bills of Exchange Act 1882 as:

> *'... an unconditional promise in writing made by one person to another, signed by the maker, engaging to pay, on demand or at a fixed or determinable future time, a sum certain in money, to, or to the order of, a specified person or to bearer'.*

Unless the importer is of undoubted standing, the forfaiter will be relying on the unconditional guarantee (ie the aval) of the bank accepting the bill for eventual payment. As the aval is written 'per aval' in the case of a promissory note or 'per aval for {the drawee}' for bills of exchange directly on the bill or note and signed by the avaling party, it is preferable to a formal guarantee being separately raised. The creditworthiness of the underlying bank will have to be acceptable to the forfaiter. The fixed cost of the discounting is set in advance over the life of the credit. This form of credit is prevalent in assisting the exporter finance the sale of capital goods.

11.5 Trade barter

Where it is difficult to export hard currency for the payment of goods due to exchange control regulations or for other reasons, it is sometimes useful to consider trade barter of goods to finance the deal. Machinery parts, for example, may be swapped for a like value of steel or coal. The risks are high unless the two parties each have an acceptable credit rating and/or are known to each other. The risks include a loss in value of one part of the deal, or unexpected excise duties may have to be paid to release the goods or the goods may be susceptible to deterioration in the case of perishables.

11.6 Small firms loans guarantee scheme

The SFLGS (for short) is backed by the government to assist small businesses with a workable business proposal, but lacking security, to borrow money from approved (mostly bank) lenders. The scheme has been running for a number of years and subsequent amendments have been brought in periodically, the most recent being to widen the eligibility of businesses. Not all banks and other financial lenders offer SFLGS and it has been alleged that many banks prefer to provide their own products rather than offer the scheme. It has been alleged that the scheme has suffered a very high ratio of bad debts from time to time.

The **lenders** that do supply SFLGS-backed loans take all the commercial decisions as to the credit risk of the potential borrower and the viability of the loan proposition, as well as stipulating the terms of any loan (ie the interest rate cost to the borrower, any security required and any arrangement fee). The government agency will then approve (or otherwise) and guarantee the loan. This guarantee amounts to 75% of the amount outstanding and due at the time the borrower defaulted on the loan repayments (prior to 1 April 2003 some loans were issued with an 85% guarantee). For supplying the guarantee, the government agency receives from the borrower a 2% annual premium calculated on the loan amount outstanding each year. The premium may be consolidated into the loan subject to the maximum advance criterion.

The **potential borrower** should expect to be asked to supply a business plan, financial forecasts, an estimate of the finance required, a risk evaluation of the business and proof of personal commitment to the project. There will also be regular monitoring of the business until the loan has been fully repaid. It will be important for the potential borrower to accept that, should a default arise, the liability will be for the full amount outstanding, not just the 25% outside the SFLGS guarantee.

The **aim** is to aid business development; this may include research and development work, financing a project, starting up a new business, expanding an existing business or generally to improve efficiency. Specific uses not allowed are buying a company's shares or a partnership, replacement of an existing loan or overdraft, the financing of interest payments, repayment of another loan, or direct aid for exporting. Other exclusions are loans for agriculture and horticulture, self-employed artists, financial services and insurance, postal and medical services, gambling, intermediary and ticket agencies, formal education, fisheries, forestry, real estate, sporting organisations, publicly-owned bodies, tied public houses and transport.

The SLFGS is **governed** under the European Community rules on state aid. This restricts the maximum amount that one organisation can borrow over any consecutive three-year period. The government checks each applicant's eligibility in case earlier state aid restricts the maximum loan that may be granted. The maximum loan is £250,000 where no other state aid is involved and the minimum loan is £5,000. This top limit is restricted to £100,000 for successful businesses having traded for less than two years. So-called 'connected borrowers' have to be included when calculating the maximum loan, such as associated companies being companies with common directorships and shareholders owning 20% or more of the company.

The **commercial terms** available allow loans supported by the scheme to have a maturity of from two to ten years. Some lenders allow small borrowings up to £30,000 to incorporate capital repayment holidays within the life of the debt of up to a maximum two years at one time, whereas other lenders require the repayment holiday to be taken in periods of no more than three months.

11.7 Debt securities

Banks may provide loans to commercial quoted companies through acting as corporate finance managers for the issue of marketable securities that will be purchased by large-scale individual portfolio investors, financial organisations having cash flow to invest (eg pension and life assurance companies), other commercial businesses holding surplus cash and other banks either with surplus cash or wishing to trade in these securities for a profit. The managing bank(s) will earn placement and underwriting fees for the issue to be fully subscribed and will usually take for its own account some of the security to be issued, partly for investment purposes and partly to ensure that an orderly trading market will ensue.

After discussion with the company wishing to raise finance, the bank will promote the type(s) of instrument to be used. If the company is not an internationally recognised name, a selling run may be needed to introduce the borrower to prospective lenders. The bank's skills will be to choose the cost of the debt instrument as being a balance between the maximum return for the lenders and the minimum cost for the borrower. As part of the assessment procedure, the bank will speak to credit reference agencies to obtain their valuation of the borrower's corporate risk and this will be compared with the cost of similar debt issues previously raised in the market by similarly valued companies. The characteristics of various forms of security used to raise funds are described briefly hereafter.

Debt raised by a commercial entity may be in bearer or registered form. If the debt is payable to bearer, it is usually a negotiable instrument traded over a clearing system such as Euroclear, where good title can be transferred by delivery and the document is usually kept for safe keeping by a custodian. A registered debt, on the other hand, is not a document of title and the register of holders confers ownership. The security can raise short, medium or long-term money. Maturities up to one year are usually in bearer form for ease of negotiability and called **commercial paper**; longer than one year, the security is called a **bond** or a **note**.

11.7.1 Commercial paper

Public companies of good credit standing will issue short-term commercial paper, typically between one and three months maturity, to gain direct access to funds that might otherwise be more expensive to raise conventionally by a formal overdraft or bank loan. There will be an investment house or bank(s) through which an issue programme will be managed. Where the issue is made in the euro-market (defined as the market constituting the European financial centres that deal in negotiable corporate loans of the currency of a country outside that country), the issue will be of **euro-commercial paper** (ECP) and is, in most cases, issued at a discount to its face value rather than offering an interest rate coupon. Trading in this paper is directly between buyer and seller and not through a central exchange.

11.7.2   Bonds and notes

Commercial companies wishing to borrow over long periods will raise the money through bond issues. The credit standing of the (publicly quoted) company will be sufficient for investors to see that placing their money with the company will provide them with a regular fixed return over the investment period. The investors will require certain covenants to assure them that they can claim repayment or take security in the event that the company falls on adverse times.

A **bond** is an interest in a negotiable loan. Bonds issued in registered form in the UK are called **loan stock** or **debenture stock** (debentures for short). A **eurobond**, as partially explained earlier, is usually a bearer bond issued as a marketable loan that has a nominal value expressed in the currency of one country, but issued outside that country. A **note** is synonymous with a bond, but is usually used in the context to describe a repayment period less than five years from issue (see Chapter Seven, 7.4.10).

11.7.3   Debentures

A **debenture** is a document acknowledging a debt and is a negotiable loan issued by a company that charges some or all its assets as security for the payment of interest and the repayment of principal. A **mortgage debenture** is where there is a significant fixed charge over the asset(s). An **unsecured debenture** is where no asset is charged and this is usually called **unsecured loan stock**. For a company to have access to the public debt market in the UK and issue debentures, it must be a public limited company.

11.7.4   General issue characteristics

A company wishing to raise a loan of significant size, of a set amount, with a medium or long-term maturity, will do so through a domestic or eurobond issue. This is usually syndicated at outset to a number of managing banks, for negotiated fees, that will then market the bonds in smaller packages to other bank and investment house participants. In the UK, the issue will be offered on a private basis to prospective buyers, otherwise, if it is offered to the public, the issue will have to be done through a formal prospectus. Where the issue is substantial and therefore offers good marketability, it may be listed on one or more European Stock Exchanges.

Debt securities may offer a zero, fixed or a floating interest rate. Some securities may be convertible into (equity) shares. The advantage of a **convertible** security is that the borrowing company can issue the debt at a lower fixed interest cost through offering at outset added value in the form of a set conversion rate into equity shares to apply at a stated future date(s). The debt security may be **subordinated** to other debt issues, in which case the interest rate coupon will be higher than those debt issues that offer greater security to the holder in the event of a default. The debt may have a 'bullet' (ie repayment in full at maturity), a 'balloon' (repayment of principal with an incremental value added) maturity profile or be issued at a 'discount' for repayment at face value.

Security debt may be issued on a **high yield** basis where the company has no positive cash flow due to it being a start up business or where it is in a development phase offering investors in the equity a potentially highly successful investment but the equity will raise insufficient funds without an element of debt input. High yield debt is usually subordinated to bank debt. The advantage of high yield debt to the issuing company is that the operating covenants offered will be less onerous than for a bank loan but the disadvantage is that it will be more costly than a conventional borrowing. That is, the covenants will be reactive: if something occurs it will trigger a reaction (eg default) but if the company trades within the agreed guidelines (eg operating ratios), the company may do what it likes, for as long as it likes, within the life of the debt.

Senior debt is issued by a group subsidiary company that holds significant assets of the group and thereby offers the greatest balance sheet security for the issue. **Mezzanine debt** is the generic term for debt that is subordinated to bank and secured loans, but ranks above the equity in the company in the event of default.

Documentation of debt securities is mostly standardised and the clauses will be similar to bank loan agreements covering the legal requirements of issue, representations and warranties (to the underwriters, etc), indemnities (against any breach of representations and warranties), covenants (such as a negative pledge that prevents the raising of security for future specified, debt), tax grossing-up procedures (so that the issuer has responsibility for any overseas withholding taxes) and events of default (particularly the non-payment of interest or principal, cross-defaults, and breach of the issue terms). Issues with maturities of less than one year will waive most of these clauses.

11.8 Equity finance

Equity finance may be defined as capital invested in a business having some permanence that holds the right to any surplus of the company's assets on a winding up or on the annual distribution of profit after accounting for all third party liabilities. This capital will be reflected in, but not necessarily shown by, the company's balance sheet as, for instance, where the book value of assets is stated at historical cost rather than their current market value. Investment may be for the medium term, as with venture capital where these investors wish for an exit from their investment by a certain period, or long term, to enable the company to continue to trade on an ongoing basis.

A public or private issue of shares can be the cheapest form of raising finance. For the company, the size of future profit distributions in the form of dividends each year, if increasing, will be at a lower cost than servicing the fixed interest due on an equivalent amount of debt. For the lending bank, the greater the proportionate element of equity capital in issue relative to its borrowings, then the lower the credit risk to the bank. Most banks have specialised subsidiaries or divisions set up to invest in a modest amount of the equity of its customers usually in conjunction with loan finance if the customer's need is for high risk **venture capital.**

There may be several types of equity capital in issue: **deferred** shares bear a restriction on a profit distribution unless other classes of shares are paid dividends of specified amounts, **ordinary** shares will have the right to any amount of annual dividends to be declared and will have the right to any surplus assets after all other classes of liability have been repaid unless this right is given to any deferred shares in existence, **participating preference** shares carry the right to receive all or part of the declared ordinary dividend, but will stand prior to ordinary shares if the company is would up and **preference** shares are entitled to the subsequent payment of earlier years' dividends that had accrued but not been paid due to insufficient distributable profits being available (and are usually called 'cumulative preference shares'), but non-cumulative preference shares do not. A company's articles of association describe the rights of each class of share issued.

There may be sub-classes of shares issued for specific purposes, each having its own rights and obligations. For example, ordinary shares may have full voting rights but 'A' ordinary shares none. The latter form is not now recommended for public company shares, but it has been evident in the past where a few minority shareholders have wished to retain control over the company. Preference shares have also become less popular in favour of holding loan stock offering a higher income yield, but they are still issued when venture capital is being raised and the venture capital investor(s) want part of their investment held in slightly greater security. Preference shares may also have the right to be redeemable or convertible into ordinary shares based on a formula set out at the time of their issue to apply at a specified date(s) in the future. The formula will take into account subsequent changes to the number of ordinary shares in issue, eg if the company has a one-for-one scrip issue, the formula will halve the conversion factor to retain the status quo.

Public companies that wish to have their (ordinary shares and/or preference shares and/or debt securities) publicly quoted must obtain an official listing in the UK and adhere to the minimum standards set out under the Financial Services and Markets Act 2000 (Part VI). Up to 30 April 2000, the London Stock Exchange was the nominated UK listing authority, but since then this role has been taken over by the Financial Services Authority (FSA). The form of issue may be a **public offer for subscription**, a (more selective) **placement of shares** frequently managed by a bank, that might result where an asset or company is purchased and new shares are issued as vendor consideration, an **intermediaries offer** via brokers to a wider market than with a placing or a **rights issue** or an **open offer** to shareholders, the difference being that the number of shares offered in the former is in proportion to existing shares held, whereas the latter has no restriction.

Equity finance is used partially or wholly as part of the consideration to acquire another private or public company. Some shareholders may prefer to continue to hold an equity interest in the acquiring company for their own tax or investment reasons, rather than taking the consideration tendered wholly in cash and/or loan stock. The Companies Act 1985 gave companies the right to purchase their own shares (via a special resolution) and, as from 1 December 2003, shares of listed companies may be held in treasury for subsequent disposal, cancellation or re-issue. While held in treasury, no dividends can accrue on these shares.

A **rights issue** of shares will have as its prime aim to re-capitalise the company. The value of the company pre-rights will have the same overall value post-rights. That is, the number of shares in issue multiplied by their pre-rights price, plus the number of rights shares at their rights price, will be added together and divided by the number of post-rights shares in issue to give the shares a post-rights initial value. The rights issue may or may not be underwritten by the managing bank(s). If it is not underwritten, to ensure that all the shares on offer are taken up, the issue is most likely to be at a **deep discount** to its pre-rights market price. This will have the advantage of saving on underwriting fees, but the disadvantage of not obtaining as large a sum from the issue. A deep discount is aimed to encourage existing shareholders to take up the rights issue.

A **public offer** for shares may be fixed at outset of the offer or may be part of a **book-building** exercise by the advising banks. In the latter case, the managing banks will underwrite the issue, but leave open the size and/or the offer price, which would be set after soundings had been received from potential investors approached, collated and agreed as acceptable to the issuing company. As can be seen, the options of the funding vehicle for the company are many and the banks involved in managing the deal and/or lending to the company require specialist expertise to judge the best method to adopt for their customer, as well as limiting their own risk when acting as underwriter or lender.

11.9   Term lending

11.9.1   Introduction

A term lending facility used to be characterised as having a fixed period longer than one year, with a fixed or variable interest rate charged on the amount borrowed and repayable in the interim only if the borrower was allowed to make early settlement by its terms or otherwise broke some covenants specified in the conditions of the agreement. Draw down of the loan could be divisible into smaller maturities within its overall term.

Standard short-term lending, on the other hand, would have been by way of a bank overdraft, usually on a 12-month renewal basis, charged at a variable interest rate and repayable on demand, but otherwise offering a facility up to a predetermined amount that may be re-drawn day by day by the borrower until its renewal date. Alternatively, short-term loans may be made available commonly of a fixed one, three, six or 12 months' duration before repayment is due in full. Repayment may be effected through the request for a further loan amount by the borrower.

Whereas short-term lending would often be unsecured, depending on the status of the borrower as decided by the lender, term loans would usually be made available providing some security was taken by the lender to guard against possible non-repayment. This security was to reflect the period of risk involved in recognising that unforeseen events might occur since the loan was first taken out that could adversely affect the borrower's financial standing and ability to repay the indebtedness.

Some of these views have undergone changes as competition to lend has become more pronounced and as the financial requirements of borrowers have become more sophisticated. A bank overdraft is now not always 'repayable on demand' (but is still subject to default clauses) and the facility can still be re-drawn as required by the borrower during its period of validity.

11.9.2   The types of facility on offer

Term lending is any credit offered that is not an overdraft that, by definition, is repayable on demand. Facilities classified as **short term** are usually for three or six months' (but can be one, two or twelve months') duration and based on LIBOR (the London inter-bank offered rate, being the rate of interest at which top creditworthy banks in London (at 11.00 am on working days) offer to lend each other money in a particular currency for a particular period). Similarly LIBID is the London inter-bank bid rate. **Medium-term** facilities are greater than one year and can go up to five or possibly seven years. Facilities that are deemed **long term** have a life greater than five years and typically have a maturity above ten years.

11.9.3   Short-term facilities

LIBOR-based facilities are market driven. The interest rate on LIBOR-based loans is fixed until maturity and paid at maturity and is an accurate reflection of the average going rate for money in the inter-bank market at the time it is set. On the other hand, money drawn by way of overdraft borrowed on current account usually has its rate of interest calculated on a day-by-day basis by reference to the base rate set by the Bank of England from time to time in response to overall economic policy guidelines laid down by the Treasury. It is usually set in this manner but some banks charge overdrafts instead by reference to a preset, fixed borrowing rate. In this respect, the preset rate may be more or less profitable to the bank concerned depending on the volatility of base rate and whether the preset rate accurately mirrors these changes.

The borrower will pay the set LIBOR rate at each maturity date plus the bank's lending margin agreed between the two parties plus any 'mandatory liquid assets' (MLA) costs of the bank over the borrowing period. The MLA costs vary from bank to bank and reflect what it has cost the bank to adhere to the reserves ratios set by the Bank of England. The facility can be drawn in currencies and the principal can be rolled over into a similar or different maturity period according to the terms laid down in the lending agreement.

11.9.4 Lending for the short term

A company having the option to borrow on overdraft or by short-term LIBOR will choose the former if it believes that interest rates will fall to gain advantage of the prospective drop in interest rates, and vice versa. Note, however, that the LIBOR market may be presuming the same thing and may be mirroring the fall already when quoting its LIBOR rate for the next (lending) period. If there is an option to borrow by discounting a bill of exchange, this will be another way to set in advance the borrowing cost although, in this case, the cost of borrowing will be paid at outset of the discounting period.

The prospective borrower has a further choice to make when requiring a short-term facility: unlike an overdraft, if the requirement unexpectedly dematerialises part way through the borrowing period, there is no possibility of repaying the fixed term loan early and thereby saving on the interest cost. The company could mitigate the cost through placing the surplus funds on deposit. A clear indication of need throughout the borrowing period, therefore, is a prerequisite when activating term borrowing. Short-term borrowing is best adopted principally for ongoing working capital purposes or to meet occasional cash flow shortages.

11.9.5 Medium-term options

A so-called **'evergreen'** facility will typically be a credit line for three years that is automatically rolled over after two years for a further year and this is then repeated at each subsequent anniversary. In this manner, the company will be drawing on a facility that will have at any one point in time between two to three years to run to expiry. There will be a caveat in the agreement that the facility can be refused future rollovers if a default occurs by the borrower or, perhaps, if the lender at its sole discretion considers that repayment of the facility is in jeopardy.

Considering the position of the bank as lender, by granting an evergreen facility, the bank will not be earning a lending margin that it might normally expect to achieve from a medium-term loan as the margin will be built up through a number of shorter-term rollovers with no repayment of principal unless the borrower decides not to renew the full amount. Conversely, were the borrowing to be drawn as a medium-term loan, the bank could expect to receive regular repayments of capital as well as interest. On the other hand, if the company is a good credit risk, the bank might well prefer to have the facility constantly fully drawn.

A medium-term loan often incorporates terms specifying that the lending margin will be x% during the first three years, say, and x+1% during the final two years to recognise that the commitment and the lending risk over five years is potentially more risky than over three years. This may be correct in theory, but, in practice, it lends itself to the company repaying the facility early after three years to be replaced by a cheaper two-year credit. If the company is deemed an above average risk, the bank, if it lends medium term at all, would be prudent to offer a **programmed loan** facility that regularly reduces the debt at each payment date and charges a fixed interest margin to reflect the higher risk.

The availability of medium-term loans should be regarded principally to finance capital assets that have a limited life where their purchase would otherwise reduce the day-to-day working capital of the business to the detriment of trading. The running cost and repayment liabilities should be able to be met comfortably out of retained profits and the use of the money should give the company additional earnings that exceed the overall cost of the facility over its life. Whether or not the bank takes security for the loan should be judged, similar to short-term credit, on a case-by-case basis. For sizeable corporations, the facility agreement will set out conditions of default and operating ratios the company must adhere to. Smaller companies may be asked, in addition, for some form of formal security.

11.9.6   Long-term facilities

In one sense, the request for long-term funds from a bank that principally accepts short-term deposits is an anachronism. If long-term financing is required, it should be provided through money from sources that accept the long-term investment risk, such as equity capital or specialist finance units that can better match these assets with long-term liabilities. Apart from property lending (when loans can have a maturity of up to 25 years or more), banks tend to limit their advances to 15 to 25 years unless they can partially or wholly offload the lending risk to other parties.

Borrowing short to lend long for a clearing bank is fraught with risks, because if short-term deposits are withdrawn or increase in cost, they may not be easily replaced and, if they are, their cost may exceed the income arising from the long-term loans. Having said that, non-speculative property purchases financed by short-term deposits has been one of the safest areas to lend in recent times. The reason has been that, on a long-term view and speaking generally, property values have risen during the life of the debt sufficient to repay the borrowing without difficulty when realising the asset.

When lending long term, the bank should take particular care that the borrower will be able to :

- ◆ service the loan and effect repayment (which may be out of future cash flow or realisation of the asset being offered as security);
- ◆ ensure there is good legal title to the property (and/or whatever is being taken as security);
- ◆ make sure the value of the security will not deteriorate over the life of the loan (and monitoring of its value will not be onerous);
- ◆ make sure realisation of the security will be relatively straightforward, whatever event may occur in the future to take this step;
- ◆ confirm that the costs of setting up the facility will be borne by the borrower, including legal and valuation fees;
- ◆ ascertain that adequate and appropriate security is, in fact, being taken.

Where the **security** taken is not a first charge on asset(s), its valuation is much diminished. Precise valuation criteria will vary from bank to bank, but a typical valuation model already described is repeated here for clarity:

Stage One:

Property asset:	Open market valuation (OMV)
(or the asset's cost if this is lower)	
Value for the first charge:	70% of OMV

Stage Two:

Property asset:	OMV or cost if lower
Deduct	Value of the prior (first, etc) charge
	= Net value of the asset
Value for the second charge:	**45% of the net value of the asset**

The above example is quite conservative in its valuation and another calculation would be to group both charges together and then compare this total to the value of the asset.

	Base
Property value (OMV or FSV, as appropriate)	<u>100</u>
Proportion of the property value:	
Loan having a first charge, say	70
Loan having a second charge, say	<u>20</u>
	<u>90</u>
Second charge cover:	$((100 - 70)/20=)$ 1.5 times

It is assumed that the second loan will wish to have some security cover to allow for realisation expenses and variation in the value of the asset.

In the first case the property value was deemed to be (45% of 30 =) 13.5 and the second charge cover was therefore (13.5/20=) 0.67 times

A third and quite common method of valuation is as follows:

		Base
Property value (OMV)		<u>100</u>
Proportion of property value as security:	70%	70
Loan having a first charge, say		<u>70</u>
Value remaining for any second charge		<u>nil</u>

Note: were the OMV to be 120; 70% value would be 84 less 70 attributable to the first charge, leaving the full value of 14 to cover the second charge. That is, the loan with the second charge would be deemed secure to a value of 14.

In practice, as mentioned earlier, there are a number of ways to value the cover for a loan holding a second charge.

There is greater scope to 'match' day-to-day borrowings by a business with any surplus funds held on current account, thereby improving the financial flexibility for those businesses susceptible to seasonal fluctuations in their cash flows. Thus, the business will only pay interest on the net amount outstanding daily. The bank will be looking to see how the net balance on the account changes from month to month: any regular ('hard core') borrowing may be open to transfer on to a loan account with a programmed repayment basis where the credit granted to the borrower has a maximum limit set.

The market for some types of term business loans, while still relying principally on the perceived status of the borrower, will be widened under the new Basel 2 Accord proposals (see Chapter Two) through banks being able to accept greater internal control in assessing their credit risk and, thereby, their capital adequacy ratios. Specifically, the risk associated with residential property lending has been recognised through having a lower risk weighting in a bank's loans portfolio. Other influences on term lending strategy that have arisen are explained in the following paragraphs.

11.9.7 The swaps market

There is now easy availability of offsetting parties in the swaps market, where variable interest rate loans may be converted into fixed rate commitments, or vice versa. A bank may not wish to take on a long term loan at a fixed interest rate and will therefore wish to 'swap' it for a variable rate with a counterparty. However, this can prove a little difficult and/or expensive if the maturity is for an unusual period.

11.9.8 Debt securitisation

Debt securitisation options, where a bank's portfolio of loans may be bundled together and sold off to third parties privately or by tender. The selling bank eliminates these assets from its balance sheet and can now entertain new loan business, ideally at greater profit margins including arrangement fees. The party(ies) acquiring the portfolio needs to have an appetite for this form of investment and its inherent risks and to accept that the portfolio may not be subsequently marketable. There will be a greater incentive for banks to sell loans outstanding to borrowers in distress to reduce their portfolio carrying costs.

11.9.9 Debt offsetting insurance

Other loan risk-sharing possibilities include acceptance of offsetting partial or complete risk cover through premiums payable under specialised commercial insurance contracts, while the bank still retains ownership of the underlying loans. A substantial insurance group of very good credit risk standing will add its name as effective underwriter to the loan(s) to cover an event of default. This is not to say that the bank(s) concerned have an inferior credit rating, but rather they wish to limit their exposure in this area and rely more on front-end fees for income.

One caveat should be highlighted in respect of future front-end fees payable: under the proposed International Financial Reporting Standards (IFRS) changes, commission fees and attendant costs will have to be spread over the life of the underlying agreement to which it relates.

11.9.10 Programmed term loans

There has been a steady increase in the availability of programmed loans. These offer preset conditions of repayment (the 'programme') usually based on a fixed interest rate agreed at outset. Some agreements allow a variable interest rate, with the difference between the outset interest rate and the sum of the actual interest rates (calculated at an agreed margin over the Bank of England base rate) becoming payable at the end of the loan agreement. In this case, the agreement is really offered at a variable interest rate, with the interest variances settled at maturity.

Programme loans are offered to individuals and small/medium-sized businesses. They are easy to set up and control, incorporate an arrangement fee and require no other monitoring providing the borrower maintains the repayment terms. They should not take the place of reviewing the business account on a regular basis, otherwise changes in the financial needs of the borrower will go undetected and, like all other types of loan, there is still the risk of default and loss for the bank. The table set out in Appendix 6 shows three types of programmed term loan taken for a notional period of ten years and their relative profitability in gross earnings capability for a lending bank. The results are summarised below.

Loan to base 100	**Present value**
1. Equal annual instalments of interest and principal	39.09
2. Interest only payments with principal repaid at end	38.50
3. Equal instalments of principal annually plus interest	39.17
Add to each example, say, a front-end arrangement fee of	2.00
Compare this with a continuous loan, but	
4. Interest and a renewal fee paid annually	43.88

It may be that the bank considers the borrower to be undoubted and the loan can afford to be continuously outstanding in full, in which case example 4 may be the best earnings option, but assume that the loan becomes irrecoverable after five years. Each example will show the following position:

(Profit includes front fee earned)	Profit 'turn' earned to date	Maximum loan write off
Loan example 1	23.43	57.23
Loan example 2	21.75	100.00
Loan example 3	23.73	50.00
Loan example 4	25.14	100.00

In terms of repayment risk, example 3 would appear on the facts presented to be the most effective method of lending for the bank.

Two important variables not accounted for in the examples are changes in profitability arising from any changes in variable interest rates and the assumption that use of the released capital will be invested in a further loan immediately at a similar interest margin. In practice, the bank should be able to control these potential changes to maintain its profitability. What it may not be able to control is the risk of default with the repayment, other than through the conditions set out in the loan documentation and the borrower's action to repay the loan early.

11.9.11   The risk of default

The bank exercises control over a borrower accepting a term loan by:

First: correctly assessing the lending risk of the borrower.
Secondly: setting up adequate terms and conditions of lending.
Thirdly: monitoring the account regularly to ensure compliance.
Fourthly: if default is likely, examining a rescheduling of the loan.
Fifthly: if default occurs, activating steps to recover the debt.

Assessing the bank's risk when lending to the borrower will take into account the usual tests to determine creditworthiness except, in this case, the long-term nature of the debt outstanding will require a longer forecasting period and appraisal of the influences that may be expected to affect the trading of the borrower. The lending terms may build in a greater margin of comfort for the bank in respect of the debt outstanding compared with the realisation value of the security taken. The bank should also list all incidences that may occur in future to affect the borrowing and negate the effect of any adverse situations through imposing special conditions of lending at the outset of the loan.

The following are some examples of special conditions that may be set for the borrower to meet without asking the bank for special permission to change these terms:

◆ stating a minimum sum of equity to be retained in the business;
◆ setting a total limit on all future borrowings outstanding to a set value or as a percentage of the equity retained in the business;
◆ ensuring that all fixed assets over a certain value are to remain within the ownership of the company;
◆ if the business is not a company, limiting the amount of annual drawings the proprietors may take out of the business;
◆ requesting the borrower to supply the bank monthly with totals of turnover achieved, orders in hand, the total of trade debtors outstanding and all debts over a certain age.

Where a business has a liquidity problem, the frequent remedy is to reschedule the borrowing(s) to enable the business to trade out of its 'temporary' predicament. The test will be whether a repayment holiday will prove sufficient to resolve the problem or whether the provision of additional credit will prove to be exacerbating the situation and causing a greater loss subsequently for the bank.

The bank will have to judge whether the difficulty will be temporary or not. An example can be cited where a manufacturer could not finish its product because the major parts supplier was involved in a strike. The bank allowed the manufacturer to increase its borrowing on condition that, when the products were completed, the proceeds would be used to repay the additional indebtedness. In the event, the manufacturer used this money instead for other purposes and the subsequent liquidity shortfall proved its downfall.

The remedial options open to the bank are to offer one or more of the following:

◆ accept a repayment holiday, while still charging the business interest on the amount outstanding;

◆ extend the maturity date of the borrowing to reduce the monthly repayments to the bank;

◆ repay the original amount borrowed early and replace it with more appropriate credit, perhaps by a short-term overdraft to allow the bank a greater degree of freedom for future action;

◆ allow the business an increase in the facility originally granted on strict terms as to how the additional money is to be used. This may be offered in conjunction with the request for additional security and an increase in the interest margin on the loan.

Where a condition of default has occurred under the terms of the loan the directors of the company will become personally liable if they continue to trade while the business is insolvent. If a company is, or is likely to become, insolvent the procedure is for the company to go into administration under the Insolvency Act 1986, as amended by the Enterprise Act 2002. The administrator may decide to rescue the company as a going concern or realise its assets to the creditors. The creditor bank will look to perfect its own security for repayment and this may entail addressing the court for an administration order as a holder of a floating charge over the company's property if the company directors or other creditors have not already done so.

11.9.12   When is it appropriate to offer a term loan?

The general guideline is that a term loan should be granted when a business wishes to incur expenditure on an asset(s) that is expected to have an effective business life at least matching the maturity of the loan. In this way, the business will not continue to have a debt to repay after the asset has ceased its useful life, at which time a replacement asset will be required that in itself may require financing. In practice, the bank will wish to see that there is a suitable time margin in hand from the date the debt is repaid to the sale or scrapping and replacement of the asset. Certain intangible assets may be included in this reasoning eg patents.

If the asset being financed is sold or disposed of early, in theory the attaching term loan should be repaid, but if the proceeds are used to acquire a replacement asset, then the debt is usually left to run its course to maturity. A term loan may be agreed by a bank not relating to any specific asset expenditure, but merely to spread the company's borrowings over a time period so that when each loan comes up for renewal, the amount to be refinanced will be more manageable in size and undue reliance will not be placed on one interest rate applicable that would be the case if all the borrowing has the same maturity date. In this situation, the covenant (ie standing or creditworthiness) of the borrower should be strong and acceptable to the bank.

11.9.13   The rollover of term loans

Where the borrower's creditworthiness is good, the bank will allow the term loan at its maturity to be renewed for a further period. This may be automatic where the conditions of the original loan have not been breached and the trading outlook for the borrower continues to be satisfactory. In other cases, the bank will have to assess the rollover under its usual lending criteria and possibly change some of the terms of the facility. The bank should guard against the circumstances where a term loan matures requiring a balloon (ie full) repayment at maturity and the business is not in a position of being able to comply, thereby effectively claiming a loan renewal in lieu of default. This scenario can be eliminated through the bank offering a programmed loan or where there are period payments of principal (and interest) over its effective life.

11.9.14   Changes in covenants

What term lending covenants have been modified? One example is lending to housing associations, when an association purchases a portfolio of tenanted housing stock, usually occupied by deprived or poor families, at rents that are (at least initially) set at sub-market levels. The purchase price will reflect the condition of the housing stock (that may require immediate or planned refurbishment) and rents will be part subsidised by the government.

The lending banker will be faced with immediate negative equity in capital terms and possibly an element of interest rollup in the initial years before rents are sufficient to service and repay the loan. In this case the strength of the borrowing covenant becomes paramount: the housing association will have previously obtained capital subsidy from the government agency, the Housing Corporation, on the value of the tenanted properties and the housing association will have recourse to request additional future rent increases and permission to sell a certain number of properties to improve operating cash flow. Similar public finance initiatives are now operating in other business sectors as joint ventures between the government and commercial enterprises.

11.10   Franchising

Franchising may be defined as the exclusive right given to a number of operatives [the franchisees] in a certain area to exploit a business idea or trade or service that is given by the owner (the franchisor) of that idea, trade or service in return for payment. An increasing number of start-up businesses, or established concerns having insufficient working capital to exploit a new product or idea are resorting to franchising their operations to gain a rapid, large scale exposure in the market at minimal cost and own effort. The franchisor will set the ground rules of the franchise and thereby hold a great deal of control, including the appointment and location of each franchisee.

The franchisee will be paying an up-front (and possibly an annual refresher) fee to the franchisor in return for exclusive area rights to operate the franchise and probably receive prior training, the benefit of national advertising and ongoing central advice. The right of exclusivity, however, only applies to the area specified by the original appointment and does not apply where a franchisee subsequently, independently, encroaches on another franchise area.

Bank lending to franchisees is considered a lower risk than if the franchisee were operating independently. The reasons are that the franchisee has been previously vetted as suitable for trading in this manner (and possibly will have conducted a successful 'pilot' exercise), there will be central assistance at hand from the franchisor in case of need, the business being franchised out will have had a successful track record in other areas and the franchisee failure rate will have already been established unless the franchise operation is completely new.

Twelve

Case studies

Case Study 1 – HR Trailers Ltd

The following case study illustrates the use of SWOT analysis. It concerns an established and successful business that runs into difficulties, presenting the relationship banker with a series of decisions to make.

Introduction

In June 2004, HR Trailers Ltd (HRT) has asked the bank for an overdraft facility of £300,000. Your task is to review the information about HRT provided below and then, using business risk assessment techniques, assess the viability of the company to assist in making a decision about HRT's request.

Information available about HR Trailers Ltd (HRT) as at June 2004

General information

HRT sells high-specification agricultural machinery to the agricultural industry. Although these trailers look like any other, they are more advanced and have a much greater capacity.

HRT has the exclusive rights to sell and distribute the specialist 'Visions' trailer which is manufactured by SORA Trailers (Far East) Inc. The 'Visions' trailer is a minor product among SORA's trailer product range but the market niche it fits does require specialist knowledge and commitment to service. The main requirements of HRT's customers are for a high-powered trailer with a high capacity.

HRT's machines are priced between £6,000 and £10,000 each, ignoring any customisation requests. Terms are net 30 days for the basic machines to major establishments and commercial firms. Substantial deposits are taken on those orders for customised machines. The delivery period for a customised machine is about six weeks, which includes the time taken to configure the trailer to the customer's requirements, while standard machines, if in stock, are dispatched within 48 hours after satisfactory credit enquiries. Customers are told, on placing their customised order and paying their deposit, that delivery will be in six to eight weeks. If the delivery is later than this, customers can invoke certain conditions on the sale contract. They can start to claim discounts on their final invoice and, in some circumstances, cancel their order and receive their deposit back.

The company operates from a distribution unit, with offices above, in Sunderland. Storage capacity is fully utilised at these premises and will not support further expansion. The technical support and customisation department is particularly cramped for space. There is an extensive range of new and second-hand specialist equipment in the factory that is slowly being incorporated into a formal production line.

Management

The management team is young and consists of five people. The company was formed in 1999 by Fred Young and Sally White who are joint managing directors and the major shareholders. The company's bankers have been B Bank from its very beginning and there has never been a problem with the conduct of the account. Fred Young and Sally White have been responsible for all aspects of the company's growth and for building up the present management team. They are supported by three senior people responsible for sales, technical support and distribution. Previously, they both held senior positions at SORA UK Ltd. Fred Young worked for SORA UK Ltd for seven years rising to board level. He left because he saw no possibility of a meaningful equity participation. The company employs 19 people in total.

Fred Young identified in the very beginning the niche market for specialised machines and left SORA UK Ltd, which is a shareholder in HRT, with its blessing and an agreement to be its sole distributor in the UK to this specialised market. Despite the close association between the two companies and SORA UK's investment in HRT (see overleaf), SORA UK Ltd has adopted a distinctly hands-off approach to the way in which HRT is operated. It is happy to see HRT push itself aggressively to the forefront of the market, making a name for itself and SORA's products.

Sally White is qualified in business studies and worked at SORA UK Ltd for eight years as a marketing executive. Her role at SORA UK Ltd included advising on new products, market research and responsibility for a promotional budget of £2 million. Fred is the communicator and driver of the business with ambition and energy to build the company. Sally is equally ambitious but she acts as a foil to Fred, bringing a practical and steadying influence to the company.

Market

The company's customers range across a broad spectrum. The order book is currently healthy with orders at capacity for the next four months. Throughout this niche market, HRT has earned an excellent reputation by recommending and providing the right machine for each specific use. It offers a complete range of models and 'customisations' based on the 'Visions' trailer. With HRT's advantages of a skilled and knowledgeable sales force and full customisation service, HRT is approaching the quality of service and product sophistication normally associated with main suppliers.

Competitive position

The company feels it has an added advantage over its competitors by providing a customisation service. This integration of distribution and customer service, from a local base within the UK, gives it added flexibility in fulfilling customers' orders. The company believes that its strong link with a major trailer manufacturer provides an effective barrier to new entrants to the market. The company aims to ensure that levels of stock of the basic machines are customer led.

Employment

Many of the workforce in the factory are school leavers trained from scratch by a core of HRT's skilled workers. The high turnover of workers in the factory has now reduced and stabilised. Labour relations appear to be good.

Expanding the business

Early in 2004, HRT used its own resources to buy out the shareholders in Scottish Trailers, its principal competitor. Following this acquisition, HRT has become the market leader in the UK and the pressure on work space is increasing. The company expects sales to grow by over 100% across the board, as a result of the purchase of Scottish Trailers, and has approached SORA UK Ltd concerning an equity investment in HRT.

After discussions SORA UK Ltd earmarked a £1.4 million financial package to support continued expansion and growth of the company, on the understanding that HRT aims to seek a full stock market listing within the next two to three years. The SORA financial package is made up as follows.

	£
Share premium	308,400
Preference shares	691,600
Total cash injected into HRT	1,000,000
(*Subordinated loan not yet drawn)	400,000
Total investment by SORA UK Ltd	**1,400,000**

* *The subordinated loan has been made available for a maximum period of five years of trading. It is earmarked for specific purposes relating to the expansion of the business.*

The SORA UK Ltd investment is subject to various terms and conditions linked to a stock market flotation. The terms set out a timetable for the issue of shares and look for one-third of the shares to be issued within 12 months. In addition, sales are expected to achieve an annual growth rate of 7% above that resulting from the acquisition of Scottish Trailers. The shareholders, as at Jan 2004, are Fred Young (43%), Sally White (43%), and SORA UK Ltd (14%).

Share options in the future may be made available to other senior members of the management team. The directors hope that the company will achieve a stock market floatation within the next 12 months. Extensive work has been carried out by a major firm of accountants and these accountants are now retained by SORA UK Ltd to carry out 'due diligence work'. Up until June 2004, the company has operated with strong credit balances. Even taking into account the new money invested by SORA UK Ltd, however, HRT has experienced a drain on its resources. This has partly been caused by buying out Scottish Trailers and partly by the increased working capital requirements resulting from the booming sales.

Financial position

As at 31 March 2004, the company has retained profits of £686,000, net assets of £836,000 and credit balances with the bank of £729,000. The financial report confirmed the first three months' cash flow forecast figures.

HRT has approached the bank for an overdraft facility of £300,000 to fund its increased working capital requirement resulting from continuing sales growth and the research and development expenditure on its new trailer system. The company expresses its key trading advantages as:

◆ its technical knowledge and back-up;

- the close relationship with its main supplier, SORA Trailers (Far East) Inc;
- the support and financial commitment of SORA UK Ltd to the company through its minority share holding and investment;
- the company culture fostered by the management team.

The company believes for the following reasons that it has a very strong competitive edge. In order to reduce costs, many firms are prepared to invest in more advanced machines to cut down on manpower costs. The format of the business is well suited to the existing market conditions and is cushioned from the worst effects of the economic downturn because of its acknowledged position of service in this niche market. There is a potential to increase prices as a result of HRT's domination of this market. The integrated customisation and selling operation provides low costs and flexibility.

The management team possesses a balance of skills and is highly motivated. The company has an enthusiastic and highly knowledgeable workforce.

Financial information

The following financial information has been presented at the same time as the overdraft request. HRT's financial year ends 31 March.

Summarised profit and loss account for 2002, 2003 and 2004

	12 months to 31.3.02	12 months to 31.3.03	12 months to 31.3.04	Forecast to 31.3.05
	£000s	£000s	£000s	£000s
Sales	259	1,945	4,659	9,164
Gross profit	148	1,127	2,988	5,699
Profit before tax	69	202	810	1,165
Retained profit	65	140	686	463
Net assets	68	458	836	2,299

Forecast profit and loss account for 12 months to 31 March 2005

	£000s
Sales	9,164
Material costs	(3,465)
Gross profit	5,699
Labour	(1,013)
Consultancy fees	(673)
Advertising	(661)
Other overheads	(2,187)
Profit before tax	1,165
Taxation	(408)
Dividend	(116)
Profit carried down	463

This is the first balance sheet showing the inclusion of Scottish Trailers.

Consolidated balance sheet as at 31 March 2004

	£000s	£000s
Fixed assets		806
Current assets		
Stocks	1,265	
Debtors and prepayments	834	
Bank	729	
	2,828	
Current liabilities		
Trade creditors	(1,529)	
Other creditors	(634)	
Corporation tax	(281)	
Hire purchase	(51)	
VAT	(150)	
	(2,645)	
Net current assets	183	183
Creditors> 1year		
Hire purchase	(153)	(153)
Net assets		836
Financed by:		
Share capital		150
Retained profits		686
		836

Forecast balance sheet as at 31 March 2005

	£000s)	£000s
Fixed assets		1,793
Current assets		
Stocks	1,745	
Debtors and prepayments	1,825	
Bank		23
	3,593	
Current liabilities		
Trade creditors	(1,750)	
Other creditors	(435)	
Corporation tax	(395)	
Hire purchase	(50)	
VAT	(217)	
	(2,847)	
Net current assets	**746**	**746**
Creditors> 1 year		
Hire purchase	(204)	
Deferred tax	(36)	
	(240)	(240)
Net assets		**2,299**
Financed by:		
Share capital	1,150	
Retained profits	1,149	
		2,299

Assessment using CAMPARI

Character

Information gained – the management is young and consists of five people, some of whom have worked together before at SORA UK Ltd. They appear to form a good, enthusiastic and motivated team whose skills complement each other well. The company has always been loyal to the bank and has conducted its account satisfactorily. The workforce is young but has been trained by the company and appears now to be operating well. The company appears to be aggressively sales led but may well be weak in terms of financial control.

Information required – there is very little information on the personal backgrounds of any of the management team. More information is required about their personal commitments, domestic circumstances and assets. There is some information about their business backgrounds but again this area could be explored further. From the information available, it is difficult to gain a feel for the business or the major people involved.

Ability

Information gained – the management team seem to be well qualified and experienced in their own spheres of operation. Although young, it appears to be a competent, as well as very ambitious, team. The company has captured a niche market not only by aggressive salesmanship but also by providing the right product at the right price. It has built up a solid reputation. Fred Young, in particular, seems to have had the ability to see the opportunity and to seize it. As a result of these factors, the growth of the company has been impressive but financial management and planning appear to be weak.

Information required – the management team has been able to cope well so far but how well will it react when problems occur? The ability of the management to cope with more difficult circumstances needs to be explored. There does not appear to be any very coherent plan for growth apart from acquisition. The following should be examined:

- ◆ what was the basis of the decision to purchase Scottish Trailers?
- ◆ what was the profitability of Scottish Trailers?
- ◆ was Scottish Trailers borrowing and if so was this taken into account?
- ◆ to what extent was the viability of Scottish Trailers examined?
- ◆ what will be the impact on customer service to both existing HRT and new Scottish Trailers customers?
- ◆ how well organised is the business to cope with such growth?

Lack of planning seems to be indicated by the fact that the purchase of Scottish Trailers has driven the business towards an overdraft situation which is only now being addressed. Further to this, the business was already short of space before the takeover; the situation can only be worse now. How will this affect the performance of the company?

Margin

Information gained – the company has not been in the position of borrowing funds before so no margin has been set to date.

Information required – in considering what margin to apply and other fees, it will be important to examine the extent of any other borrowings. It will also be important to explore what the duration of the overdraft is expected to be, the availability of security, the nature of the advance and its usage.

Purpose

Information gained – the overdraft is for working capital purposes in order to fund rapidly expanding sales and to fund research and development. This sales growth is mainly as a result of the purchase of Scottish Trailers. This has itself caused a considerable drain on resources and precipitated the requirement for an overdraft facility.

Information required – there is no very clearly defined purpose for the overdraft. To some extent it seems retrospective in terms of replacing funds drained out to purchase Scottish Trailers. If the overdraft is truly to be used to fund working capital requirements as a result of increased sales, evidence of market research to indicate the real potential for such growth over and above that which would be expected as a result of the takeover of Scottish Trailers, should be examined. What is the state of the order book? What is the debtor position – are sales being converted into cash quickly enough? The situation appears to demand a visit to the company to look into these questions in some depth.

Amount

Information gained – the request is for a £300,000 overdraft facility. Gearing is satisfactory in relation to the overdraft.

Information required – there is very little information about how the figure is assessed except that the cash flow forecast indicates a maximum cash shortfall of £151,000. If this is a realistic figure, there appears to be plenty of room for contingencies. It is important to find out and test the assumptions behind the amount requested and to conduct variance analysis to explore 'what if' questions. There is no indication as to whether finance charges have been included. What other factors affecting costs have been taken into account? For example, with the absorption of Scottish Trailers and continued rapid growth, what is expected to happen to wage costs? What provision has been made for corporation tax? What plans have been made to alleviate the lack of space? It is vital to find out about all these assumptions and to test them thoroughly.

Repayment

Information gained – repayment is ultimately to come from net cash flow surpluses as a result of sales growth.

Information required – if funds are to be provided, is an overdraft the most appropriate means of doing so? If repayment is to come from net cash flow surpluses, we need to question in detail the assumptions of the cash flow forecast. For example: how efficiently are funds collected? How have terms of trade changed following the purchase of Scottish Trailers?

Insurance

Information gained – the request for funds appears to have been made without the overt offer of any security. From the balance sheet, however, there is adequate cover under fixed and current assets.

Information required – before contemplating offering the facility, the issue of security will have to be looked at very carefully to establish exactly what is available from the business and in the form of personal assets. It may be an idea to get the directors to make a personal financial commitment to the business to heighten their sense of responsibility and we would want to take a debenture.

Assessment using SWOT

Internal attributes

◆ **Money**
  Strengths: strong cash flow at the present time; strong level of retained profits providing a good base of financial support.
  Weaknesses: the rate of growth is a drain on resources; dependence on SORA UK Ltd and the unknown strength of SORA UK Ltd; is the proposed flotation a sign of weakness?
  Why was cash paid for Scottish Trailers?

◆ **Management**
  Strengths: young; enthusiastic; involved; well qualified and well matched.
  Weaknesses: unknown and doubtful financial skills; untried in adversity; possibly overenthusiastic and lacking in caution; doubtful understanding of the dangers of rapid growth; small team with ill-defined responsibilities; there is insufficient information about the involvement of SORA UK Ltd.

◆ **Labour**
  Strengths: a small but trained workforce now committed to the company.
  Weaknesses: in the past, a high turnover; low initial level of skill.

◆ **Plant**
  Strengths: new and second-hand equipment in use.
  Weaknesses: no apparent planned replacement policy.

◆ **Premises**
Strengths: one site.
Weaknesses: following the purchase of Scottish Trailers, space is cramped and there is no room for expansion.

◆ **Stock**
Strengths: aims to be customer led; delivery of standard machines in 48 hours.
Weaknesses: lack of storage space; possibility of retention clauses; is the company overstocked? Stock makes up a large proportion of working assets. How is stock valued?

◆ **Products**
Strengths: good reputation; good quality service; customisation; wide customer range; strong demand.
Weaknesses: reliant on one supplier and one basic product line.

◆ **Marketing**
Strengths: market leader and strong marketing orientation.
Weaknesses: reliance on SORA UK Ltd; lack of effective competition to keep company sharp.

◆ **Financial systems**
Strengths: no evidence.
Weaknesses: financial control appears to run second place to sales push; financial systems are not sophisticated enough; there is a need for an experienced finance director.

External attributes

◆ **Competition**
Opportunities: very little competition and backed by strong supplier.
Threats: attractive market for new competitor, especially from outside the UK.

◆ **Technology**
Opportunities: well-qualified team able to adapt technology to customer requirements.
Threats: vulnerable to new technology that can rapidly change the market; these are the most significant areas with regard to a SWOT analysis.

Case study 2: Clothing Imports Ltd and Light Engineering Ltd

The banking facilities available from XYZ Bank for two companies trading from very modest industrial premises in the North of England as at the end of 2003 were as follows.

Light Engineering Ltd

	£	
Overdraft	60,000	Security:
Loan	18,000	
	78,000	1st charge company premises:
		Freehold value £55,000
		Debenture

Clothing Imports Ltd

	£	
Overdraft and/or irrevocable documentary credits	200,000	Security: 1st charge company premises:
		Freehold value £60,000
	200,000	Debenture

The following comprises extracts from the financial accounts of these two typical, private limited company customers. As the names suggest, Light Engineering Ltd is engaged in the manufacture of light machinery mainly against firm orders. Clothing Imports Ltd is a merchant engaged in the import and subsequent wholesale of ready made-up fashion clothing from the Far East.

Profit and loss accounts

	Light Engineering Ltd			Clothing Imports Ltd		
	2001	**2002**	**2003**	**2001**	**2002**	**2003**
	£	**£**	**£**	**£**	**£**	**£**
Sales	200,000	220,000	210,000	900,000	1,050,000	1,300,000
Materials consumed	55,000	66,000	59,000	810,000	956,000	1,209,000
Direct labour	75,000	81,000	80,000	-	-	-
Cost of goods sold	130,000	147,000	139,000	810,000	956,000	1,209,000
Gross profit	70,000	73,000	71,000	90,000	94,000	91,000
Admin & distribution expenses	(59,000)	(60,500)	(59,500)	(57,000)	(59,500)	(78,000)
Operating profit	11,000	12,500	11,500	33,000	34,500	13,000
Interest paid	(5,000)	(5,500)	(6,500)	(8,000)	(8,500)	(11,000)
Profit before tax	6,000	7,000	5,000	25,000	26,000	2,000
Tax	(2,000)	(2,200)	(1,000)	(8,000)	(10,000)	(–)
Attributable profit after tax	4,000	4,800	4,000	17,000	16,000	2,000

Balance sheets

	Light Engineering Ltd			Clothing Imports Ltd		
	2001	**2002**	**2003**	**2001**	**2002**	**2003**
	£	**£**	**£**	**£**	**£**	**£**
Current assets						
Cash	1,000	1,000	-	-	-	-
Debtors	44,000	51,000	46,000	150,000	170,000	230,000
Quick assets	45,000	52,000	46,000	150,000	170,000	230,000
Stock	10,000	15,000	15,000	135,000	190,000	257,000
Work in progress	25,000	29,000	25,000	-	-	-
Total current assets	**80,000**	**96,000**	**86,000**	**285,000**	**360,000**	**487,000**
Current liabilities						
Creditors	9,000	13,000	11,000	140,000	180,000	280,000
Hire purchase	1,000	1,000	1,000	2,000	2,000	2,000
Bank	38,000	47,000	43,000	90,000	105,000	138,000
Tax	1,500	1,700	500	8,000	10,000	5,000
Directors' loans	4,500	6,500	5,000	10,000	10,000	10,000
Total current liabilities	54,000	69,200	60,500	250,000	307,000	435,000
Net current assets	26,000	26,800	25,500	35,000	53,000	52,000
Fixed assets						
Property at cost*	35,000	35,000	35,000	36,000	36,000	36,000
Plant and machinery	47,000	45,000	55,000	5,000	4,000	3,000
Fixtures and fittings	2,500	3,000	2,200	2,000	2,000	4,000
Motor vehicles	8,000	7,000	5,000	8,000	6,000	10,000
Total fixed assets	92,500	90,000	97,200	51,000	48,000	53,000

	Light Engineering Ltd			Clothing Imports Ltd		
	2001	**2002**	**2003**	**2001**	**2002**	**2003**
	£	£	£	£	£	£
Deferred liabilities:						
Bank loans	20,000	19,000	18,000	-	-	-
Long-term HP	13,500	8,000	10,900	6,000	5,000	7,000
Total long-term liabilities	33,500	27,000	28,900	6,000	5,000	7,000
Net tangible assets	85,000	89,800	93,800	80,000	96,000	98,000
Share capital	40,000	40,000	40,000	20,000	20,000	20,000
P & L account	45,000	49,800	53,800	60,000	76,000	78,000
Shareholders' funds	85,000	89,800	93,800	80,000	96,000	98,000
*Net current value	45,000	50,000	55,000	60,000	60,000	60,000

Cash flow statement (FRS1)

Although SI 2004/16 permits exemption from cash flow statement production (for a qualifying business), the value of analysing such a document remains high. Adjustments are made for non-cash items, such as revaluation of assets (if specifically written into the annual accounts) and depreciation. Neither of these relate to movement of real funds/cash.

Also note the following, which is provided in the notes to the accounts:

	Light Engineering Ltd	*Clothing Imports Ltd*
Depreciation for 2002:	£ 8,000	£2,000
Depreciation for 2003:	£10,000	£2,000

In this case we have:

Cash Flow Statement (FRS 1)

		Light Engineering Ltd		Clothing Imports Ltd	
		2002	**2003**	**2002**	**2003**
	Net profit before interest & tax	12,500	11,500	34,500	13,000
	Non-cash movements	8,000	10,000	2,000	2,000
A	**Gross funds from operations**	**20,500**	**21,500**	**36,500**	**15,000**
	Interest paid	(5,500)	(6,500)	(8,500)	(11,000)
	Interest received				
	Dividends paid				
B	**Net cash flow from returns on investments & servicing of finance**	**(5,500)**	**(6,500)**	**(8,500)**	**(11,000)**
C	**(Taxation)**	(1,800)	(2,200)	(8,000)	(5,000)
D	**Net operating funds (A+B+C)**	13,200	12,800	20,000	**(1,000)**
	(Increase)/decrease in stock	(9,000)	4,000	(55,000)	(67,000)
	(Increase)/decrease in debtors	(7,000)	5,000	(20,000)	(60,000)
	Increase/(decrease) in creditors	6,000	(3,500)	40,000	100,000
E	**Net working capital movement**	**(10,000)**	**5,500**	**(35,000)**	**(27,000)**
F	**Operational cash flow (D+E)**	**3,200**	**18,300**	**(15,000)**	**(28,000)**
	Receipts from sale/(payments to acquire) intangible fixed assets				
	Receipts from sale/(payments to acquire) tangible fixed assets	(5,700)	(17,200)	1,000	(7,000)
	(Purchase) sale of investments				
	Other				
	Extraordinary items				
G	**Net cash flow from investing activities**	**(5,700)**	**(17,200)**	**1,000**	**(7,000)**
H	**Net cash flow before financing (F+G)**	**(2,500)**	**1,100**	**(14,000)**	**(35,000)**
	Increase/(decrease) in ordinary share capital				
	Increase/(decrease) in long-term borrowing	(6,500)	1,900	(1,000)	2,000
	Increase/(decrease) in short-term borrowing	9,000	(4,000)	15,000	33,000
J	**Net cash flow from financing**	**2,500**	**(2,100)**		
K	**Movements in cash and cash equivalents**		**1,000**		
L	**Total net cash flow from financing (J+K)=H (opp sign)**	**2,500**	**(1,100)**	**14,000**	**35,000**

Note: How to work out 'Tax Paid'

Last year's balance sheet figure + amount due on this year's profit – this year's balance sheet figure

See also Chapter Eight.

I Capital gearing

The most common ratio extracted by bankers is the capital gearing ratio. To simplify comparison of trends we will calculate this as a percentage. It is defined as:

$$\frac{\text{actual borrowed money}}{\text{net worth}} = \frac{\text{actual usage of lines of credit}}{\text{shareholders' funds}} \times 100$$

ie borrowed money expressed as a % of net worth

	2001	**2002**	**2003**
	£	**£**	**£**
Light Engineering Ltd			
Actual borrowed money:			
Bank overdraft	38,000	47,000	43,000
Bank loan	20,000	19,000	18,000
Current and deferred HP	14,500	9,000	11,900
Directors' loans	4,500	6,500	5,000
	77,000	81,500	77,900
Net worth	85,000	89,800	93,800
Capital gearing ratio	**91 %**	**91 %**	**83%**
Clothing Imports Ltd			
Actual borrowed money:			
Bank overdraft	90,000	105,000	138,000
Current and deferred HP	8,000	7,000	9,000
Directors' loans	10,000	10,000	10,000
	108,000	122,000	157,000
Net worth	80,000	96,000	98,000
Capital gearing ratio	**135%**	**127%**	**160%**

Having arrived at these capital gearing ratios it is now necessary to consider qualifying our calculations.

Capital gearing adjusted for directors' loans

The above calculations include directors' loans as actual borrowed money in the numerator of the ratio. Such loans may or may not be interest-bearing. If they are not interest-bearing, it could be argued that they are a form of shareholders' funds, in which case they could be subtracted from the borrowed money side of the ratio, and added on to the shareholders' funds or net worth side of the ratio.

Light Engineering Ltd

	2001	2002	2003
	£	£	£
Actual borrowed money (as above)	77,000	81,500	77,900
Less: directors' loans	4,500	6,500	5,000
Revised actual borrowed money	72,500	75,000	72,900
Net worth (as above)	85,000	89,800	93,800
Add: directors' loans	4,500	6,500	5,000
Revised net worth	89,500	96,300	98,800
Revised capital gearing	**81%**	**78%**	**74%**
Clothing Imports Ltd			
Actual borrowed money (as above)	108,000	122,000	157,000
Less: directors' loans	10,000	10,000	10,000
Revised actual borrowed money	98,000	112,000	147,000
Net worth as above	80,000	96,000	98,000
Add: directors' loans	10,000	10,000	10,000
Revised net worth	90,000	106,000	108,000
Revised capital gearing	**109%**	**106%**	**136%**

As can be seen, this amendment has had the effect of reducing the capital gearing ratio.

There is no straight answer as to whether directors' loans (or indeed other forms of quasi-capital, such as family loans which often occur in private companies) should be put on one side of the ratio or the other. It is down to a banker's judgement. That judgement, however, should be influenced by the stability of the loans. In the case of Clothing Imports Ltd, where the loan has been stable for three years, it would seem appropriate to regard the loan as supplementing shareholders' funds and, as such, including it in the net worth side of the equation.

Capital gearing adjusted for 'hidden reserves'

In calculating the capital gearing ratio we have taken the book value of the balance sheet assets. These, for balance sheet purposes, are valued on a going-concern basis. Break-up valuations are considered later in this book, but we shall consider at this point assets that we know have a different 'market' value.

In the case of companies where the bank has a first charge over the company's properties, the banker will have specific knowledge of the current value of these properties. For each of the two above companies, it is shown that the current value of the properties significantly exceeds the book value and, therefore, you could adjust the net worth side of the ratio properly to reflect these 'hidden balance sheet reserves'.

Light Engineering Ltd

	2001	2002	2003
	£	£	£
Revised actual borrowed money			
(as (a) above)	72,500	75,000	72,900
Revised net worth (as (a) above)	89,500	96,300	98,800
Add: current value less book value of property	10,000	15,000	20,000
Revised net worth	99,500	111,300	118,800
Revised capital gearing ratio	**73%**	**67%**	**61%**

Clothing Imports Ltd

Revised actual borrowed money			
(as (a) above)	98,000	112,000	147,000
Revised net worth (as (a) above)	90,000	106,000	108,000
Add: current value less book value of property	24,000	24,000	24,000
Revised net worth	114,000	130,000	132,000
Revised capital gearing ratio	**86%**	**86%**	**111%**

If current valuation is less than book value then the difference should be deducted from net worth, which would increase the capital gearing ratio.

Hidden reserves may also occur in stock and work in progress but caution should be used in these circumstances, because such items are generally more difficult for a banker to value than freehold property.

Capital gearing adjusted for contingent liabilities

The capital gearing ratio definition referred on the one side to actual borrowed money or actual usage of lines of credit. The two may not be identical. Actual borrowed money as revealed in a company's balance sheet will not include any contingent liability facilities that the company may have. Such contingent liabilities may include documentary credits, indemnities, negotiated bills, forward exchange contracts, etc.

Whether these contingent liabilities should be included in the gearing ratio is open to question. On the one hand it can be argued that only interest-bearing liabilities should be included, in which case contingents can be ignored. On the other hand, before marking a contingent liability facility, a banker will certainly want to justify it against balance sheet strength, in which case it would seem appropriate to include contingents in the gearing ratio.

Many bankers adopt a sort of compromise. While they include them as a liability in the ratio, they regard contingents as 'soft' liability and will often be prepared to countenance higher gearing levels if the make-up of the ratio is substantially comprised of 'soft' liabilities.

By way of illustration let us assume that Light Engineering Ltd had no contingent liabilities outstanding, but that Clothing Imports Ltd had the following outstanding at its year ends.

	2001	2002	2003
	£	£	£
Irrevocable documentary credits	40,000	50,000	60,000

Clothing Imports Ltd's capital gearing ratio could therefore be further adjusted as follows.

	2001	2002	2003
	£	£	£
Revised actual borrowed money as (a) above)	98,000	112,000	147,000
Add: IDCs	40,000	50,000	60,000
Revised net worth (as (b) above)	114,000	130,000	132,000
Revised capital gearing ratio	121%	125%	151%

Potential capital gearing

So far we have been calculating actual gearing. A banker will also need to consider the gearing position assuming full utilisation of whatever lines of credit are available, ie full *potential gearing*, in order to assess the full exposure to net worth.

The information given at the very beginning of the case study shows that total facilities marked by XYZ Bank as at end 2003 for the two companies are:

Light Engineering Ltd	£78,000
Clothing Imports Ltd	£200,000

To this must be added hire purchase commitments (it is assumed there are no undrawn hire purchase credit lines) at 2003 balance sheet date, ie:

Light Engineering Ltd	£78,000 + £11,900 = £89,900
Clothing Imports Ltd	£200,000 + £9,000 = £209,000

Revised net worth 2003 (as (b) above)

Light Engineering Ltd	£118,800
Clothing Imports Ltd	£132,000

Potential gearing is thus:

Light Engineering Ltd

$$\frac{89,900}{118,800} \times 100 = \textbf{76\%}$$

Clothing Imports Ltd

$$\frac{209,000}{132,000} \times 100 = \textbf{158\%}$$

Caution: it has been assumed that XYZ Bank are the sole bankers to both companies here. In considering potential gearing a banker must make himself fully aware of any additional lines of credit that may be marked by other institutions, as such lines (even if undrawn) will have an impact on potential capital gearing. Even small companies can have contingent liability lines, such as IDCs, with banks other than their main bankers.

Capital gearing ratio summary

	2001 %	2002 %	2003 %
Light Engineering Ltd			
Actual capital gearing	91	91	83
Adjusted for directors' loans (a)	81	78	74
Further adjusted for 'hidden property reserve' (b)	73	67	61
(Contingent liabilities (c))	Not applicable		
Potential capital gearing (d)	Not available		76

Clothing Imports Ltd

Actual capital gearing	135	127	160
Adjusted for directors' loans (a)	109	106	136
Further adjusted for 'hidden property reserve' (b)	86	86	111
Yet further adjusted for contingent liabilities (c)	121	125	157
Potential capital gearing (d)	Not available		158

The next ratio is an extension of the capital gearing ratio.

2   Total liabilities/net worth ratio (leverage)

Before going on to comment on the interpretation of the trends seen so far, we need to consider a second ratio, defined as:

$$\frac{\text{total liabilities (current + deferred)}}{\text{net worth}} \times 100$$

For both companies we will use the net worth adjusted for directors' loans and hidden property reserves. The contingent liabilities outstanding for Clothing Imports Ltd will be included.

	2001 £	2002 £	2003 £
Light Engineering Ltd			
Current liabilities	54,000	69,200	60,500
Less: directors' loans	(4,500)	(6,500)	(5,000)
	49,500	62,700	55,500
Add: deferred liability	33,500	27,000	28,900
Total liabilities	83,000	89,700	84,400
Net worth (as (b) above)	99,500	111,300	118,800
Leverage	**83%**	**81%**	**71%**

Clothing Imports Ltd

Current liabilities	250,000	307,000	435,000
Less: directors' loans	(10,000)	(10,000)	(10,000)
	240,000	297,000	425,000
Add: deferred liability	6,000	5,000	7,000
	246,000	302,000	432,000
Contingent liabilities (as (c) above)	40,000	50,000	60,000
Total liabilities	286,000	352,000	492,000
Net worth (as (b) above)	114,000	130,000	132,000
Leverage	**251%**	**271%**	**373%**

3   Interpretation of the capital gearing and leverage ratios

We have calculated different measures of capital gearing and in addition the leverage ratio (total liabilities to net worth). We must now consider what these ratios reveal. We have demonstrated that gearing ratios can be calculated in several different ways and that the results can vary considerably. Before considering whether a ratio points to problems, the banker must be fully aware of what is (or is not) included in each side of the ratios.

Ultimately the capacity of a company to service its debt from cash flow is a truer test than any capital gearing ratio. The higher the level of gearing based on balance sheet calculations, the less, proportionately, is the cushion of net worth before the lender's money is placed at risk.

The first thing to notice is the trend. Light Engineering Ltd's gearing ratios reveal a falling trend, suggesting that it is increasingly able to finance its operations. This is also revealed by the leverage ratio. In contrast, Clothing Imports Ltd shows a rising capital gearing trend, particularly in 2003, implying greater reliance on borrowed funds to finance its increasing level of operations. Even more revealing is the huge rise in the leverage ratio. This latter ratio is really an extension of capital gearing. It can, and in this case does, reveal that, apart from borrowed money, the company is relying heavily on its creditors to finance its turnover. A steeply rising trend in this ratio can indicate that a company is undercapitalised and could be vulnerable if external liabilities are reduced due to factors beyond its control (eg creditors reducing terms of trade).

As mentioned earlier there is no simple mathematical formula to give a satisfactory gearing level; it is a matter of judgement. The banker will find it useful to bear the following points in mind.

(a) Any judgement will be assisted by further ratio analysis and a banker will generally feel happier with a highly-geared situation if the customer has a long and profitable track record than if it is a new business or an established one with a poor recent history of profit performance.

(b) Whether or not the banker's lending is secured and what that security comprises are two important questions. Generally, the higher the gearing ratio, the more crucial becomes the quantity and quality of the security.

(c) What the gearing ratio comprises will be significant. If much of the borrowed money side of the ratio includes 'soft' contingent liabilities, high gearing levels are likely to be acceptable. Similarly with net worth – what is the asset structure? If the bulk of net worth is dependent upon stock or plant and machinery, the banker may feel less happy than if it comprised readily saleable freehold property. Also, is net worth heavily dependent on directors' loans that could easily be withdrawn? Overall, the banker must judge just how strong a buffer is that net worth before the bank's own money is placed at risk.

(d) The type of business – this is crucial when assessing gearing levels. Generally speaking a wholesaler with a quicker cash flow profile (such as Clothing Imports Ltd) can be expected to maintain and manage higher gearing levels than a manufacturer with a slow working capital process, such as Light Engineering Ltd. Because of this a banker will often be more generous in lending (in gearing terms) to a wholesaler than to a manufacturer.

(e) The structure of the business – the banker may feel more comfortable in lending to a sole trader or partnership where there will be the addition of personal covenant, as opposed to a limited liability company.

Light Engineering Ltd is quite highly geared for a manufacturer. Clothing Imports Ltd is certainly highly geared and the adverse trends are of concern. Although the security position suggests no immediate risk to the bank we will need to look at other ratios carefully to build up a more complete picture.

4 Interest cover

Interest cover can be measured on a historic profit basis by the ratio:

$$\frac{\text{profit before interest and tax (PBIT)}}{\text{interest paid}}$$

	2001 £	2002 £	2003 £
Light Engineering Ltd			
PBIT	11,000	12,500	11,500
Interest paid	5,000	5,500	6,500
Interest cover (historic profit basis)	2.2:1	2.3:1	1.8:1
Clothing Imports Ltd			
PBIT	33,000	34,500	13,000
Interest paid	8,000	8,500	11,000
Interest cover (historic profit basis)	4.1:1	4:1	1.2:1

The interest cover ratio tells us how many times interest paid is covered by profits before interest and tax. Obviously the higher the ratio the better. A ratio of 2:1 or less is considered low and can make a business vulnerable to fluctuations in interest rates. Also low cover has implications concerning the ability of a company to finance other areas of its business from retained profits and its ability to provide repayment of its debt from profits.

The interest cover ratios for Light Engineering Ltd look fairly tight for 2001 and 2002 and tight for 2003. During 2003 operating profits fell, while at the same time the company incurred higher interest charges.

As regards Clothing Imports Ltd, the interest cover ratio looked quite healthy up to and including 2002. The decline in 2003 gives cause for concern, however, and if the trend were to continue the company would be unable to cover the interest on its debt for 2004, let alone provide any repayment. Clearly the company has borrowed heavily in 2003 to finance its increased turnover, but has failed to maintain its former profitability and former cash generation.

5   Control ratios

Debtor recovery rate

This is defined as:

$$\frac{debtors}{sales} \times 365$$

This ratio calculates the number of days taken to collect debts (debtor turnover).

	2001	2002	2003
	£	£	£
Light Engineering Ltd			
Debtor	44,000 x 365	51,000 x 365	46,000 x 365
Sales	200,000	220,000	210,000
Debtor recovery rate	80 days	85 days	80 days
Clothing Imports Ltd			
Debtors	150,000 x 365	170,000 x 365	230,000 x 365
Sales	900,000	1,050,000	1,300,000
Debtor recovery rate	60 days	59 days	65 days

Interpretation

This ratio provides an approximate indication of the efficiency of a company's credit control procedures. The length in days of the debtor recovery rate needs to be considered in the light of the company's terms of trade and those common for the sector in which the company operates. Obviously the debtor recovery rate should bear some resemblance to agreed terms of trade. The quicker the debt recovery rate the better, in so far as this will have a beneficial cash impact. Debtors are generally financed by bank overdraft and so minimising debtors by improving the debtor recovery rate will save interest charges and thus improve profits.

Perhaps more important than the absolute values of this ratio is the trend that is revealed. A falling debtor recovery rate, ie a lengthening of credit given, could indicate:

◆ lax control by the invoicing department of the company;
◆ market competition that has forced a company to extend its terms of trade in order to maintain its sales outlets;
◆ slow paying and potential bad debts that may be included in the company's debtor book.

The above comments may imply that a trend that reveals a more rapid debtor recovery rate, ie a shortening of credit given, is always a good thing. Although a rapid recovery rate will have a beneficial effect on cash flow, it may have been caused by the company having to put pressure on its debtors because of cash flow problems. Too much pressure could result in a loss of future sales.

Enquiry of the directors will reveal just what is causing a particular trend in the debtor recovery rate. Obtaining a full age analysis of debtors is also worthwhile to give the full spread of debts. This will be examined in more detail later.

As regards these two companies, in both cases the trends do not indicate any extreme variations.

Stock turnover rate

This is defined as

$$\frac{stock}{cost\ of\ goods\ sold} \times 365$$

This ratio indicates the number of days that stock is held. (For simplicity's sake, in the following calculations, stock has been taken to include work in progress. It is often advisable, however, to break the stock figure down into raw materials, finished goods and work in progress, and to obtain separate ratios for each element in order to ascertain the stock component that underlies any particular trend.)

	2001 £	2002 £	2003 £
Light Engineering Ltd			
Stock and WIP	35,000 x 365	44,000 x 365	40,000 x 365
Cost of goods sold	130,000	147,000	139,000
Stock turnover rate	98	109	105
Clothing Imports Ltd			
Stock	135,000 x 365	190,000 x 365	257,000 x 365
Cost of goods sold	810,000	956,000	1,209,000
Stock turnover rate	61	72	77

Interpretation

A rapid turnover is beneficial in that cash is tied up in stock for a shorter period. The optimum period of stock turnover will depend on the nature of that stock and the type of business concerned.

Again, trends are the thing to watch. A lengthening of the stock turnover rate may indicate obsolete items or damaged stocks that may ultimately be unsaleable. It is also important to remember that stockholdings may be seasonal.

For Light Engineering Ltd, the ratio is reasonably static. A stock turnover of 100 days, ie over three months, should be considered, bearing in mind the greater proportion of stock lies in work in progress as opposed to 'items on the shelf'. As with all manufacturing companies, work in progress will depend on the length of time it takes to make an end product. This will vary depending on the type of product being manufactured.

The stock turnover for Clothing Imports Ltd is in many ways easier to comprehend, because all stock held will be finished goods awaiting a buyer or awaiting call-off from a firm order. A definite trend is being revealed here, and enquiry of the directors as to what is causing the trend is warranted. It may be that the stock includes unsaleable items due to changes in fashion or stock that is out of season, or it may merely represent the fact that the company is carrying more lines as a deliberate policy to back up increased sales.

Creditor repayment rate

This is defined as $\dfrac{\text{creditors}}{\text{cost of goods sold}} \times 365$

This ratio indicates the number of days taken to pay creditors.

Some banks use: $\dfrac{\text{creditors}}{\text{purchases}}$

	2001 £	2002 £	2003 £
Light Engineering Ltd			
Creditors	9,000 × 365	13,000 × 365	11,000 × 365
Cost of good sold	130,000	147,000	139,000
Creditor repayment rate	25 days	32 days	29 days
Clothing Imports Ltd			
Creditors	140,000 × 365	180,000 × 365	280,000 × 365
Cost of goods sold	810,000	956,000	1,209,000
Creditor repayment rate	63 days	69 days	84 days

Interpretation

As with debtor recovery rate, this ratio should be considered in the light of the terms of trade enjoyed by a business from its suppliers.

Again, it is the trends that need to be analysed. While lengthening this ratio will have a beneficial impact on cash flow, an escalating trend will usually imply problems – a company may be delaying payment to creditors because of cash flow problems. On the other hand, a shortening of this ratio may indicate concern on the part of creditors or a change in terms of trade from suppliers.

As regards Light Engineering Ltd, credit taken does not particularly indicate anything. Turning to Clothing Imports Ltd, the rising trend, particularly from 2002 to 2003, can be seen. Enquiry of the directors is appropriate here, to be supported by an age analysis of creditors. It appears the company has financed its expanding sales in part by taking longer credit. The bank facility of overdraft £138K + IDC usage £60K, against the agreed composite facility of £200K, may well mean that to maintain the overdraft usage within the agreed limit, the company has had no alternative but to delay paying creditors. By obtaining an age analysis of creditors the bank will be able to assess the problem more fully.

As a final comment under this ratio, care should be taken to establish just what the creditor figure comprises. Only trade creditors are relative to cost of goods sold. If possible, expense creditors (ie rates, power, PAYE and other sundry and tax creditors) should not be included in this ratio.

6   Liquidity ratios

Current ratio and quick asset ratio

The current ratio is defined as $\dfrac{\text{current assets}}{\text{current liabilities}}$

The quick asset ratio is defined as $\dfrac{\text{quick assets } (= \text{ current assets less stock})}{\text{current liabilities}}$

By their nature these two ratios can be looked at together.

◆ The current ratio provides a measure of the ability of a business to meet its short-term liabilities from funds generated by current assets.
◆ The quick asset ratio, by excluding stock from the comparison between current assets and current liabilities, expresses the cover for current liabilities in terms of cash or near cash (ie debtors). To that extent the quick asset ratio provides the more immediate measure of short-term liquidity.

	2001	**2002**	**2003**
	£	**£**	**£**
Light Engineering Ltd			
Current assets	80,000	96,000	86,000
Current liabilities	54,000	69,200	60,500
Current ratio	**1.48:1**	**1.39:1**	**1.42:1**
Quick assets	45,000	52,000	46,000
Current liabilities	54,000	69,200	60,500
Quick asset ratio	0.83:1	0.75:1	0.76:1

Clothing Imports Ltd

Current assets	285,000	360,000	487,000
Current liabilities	250,000	307,000	435,000
Current ratio	**1.14:1**	**1.17:1**	**1.12:1**
Quick assets	150,000	170,000	230,000
Current liabilities	250,000	307,000	435,000
Quick asset ratio	0.6:1	0.55:1	0.53:1

Interpretation

Again the trend of the ratios needs to be examined. A falling trend in the current ratio, besides indicating a reducing ability to meet payments for current liabilities from current assets, may indicate reducing profit margins or losses. Also a reducing current ratio may arise from investment of liquid funds in fixed assets or alternatively borrowing on overdraft to finance fixed asset purchases.

Generally, the current and quick asset ratio should move in line. A static or increasing current ratio together with a falling quick ratio would indicate an increasing amount of money tied up in stockholding. A surplus of current assets over current liabilities is usually a sign of good business liquidity.

Turning to the example case study, the ratios for Light Engineering Ltd have held up well. The quick asset ratio is less than 1:1 and so the company would be reliant on quickly translating work in progress into finished goods, and then its debtors into cash, in order to meet all its current liabilities.

While the current ratio for Clothing Imports Ltd shows little movement, the quick asset ratio is revealing a declining trend. It should be recalled that both the stock turnover ratio and creditor repayment ratio were showing adverse trends – and the effect of this is borne out in the falling quick asset ratio. A picture is emerging of declining liquidity when measured by the quick asset ratio and the lengthening of the creditor repayment and stock turnover ratios. In monetary values the gap is now considerable:

quick assets	£230,000
current liabilities	£435,000

7 Working capital turnover

This is defined as $\dfrac{\text{sales}}{\text{net current assets (working capital)}}$

This ratio determines the relationship between sales and working capital.

	2001	2002	2003
	£	£	£
Light Engineering Ltd			
Sales	200,000	220,000	210,000
Net current assets	26,000	26,800	25,500
Working capital turnover	**7.69:1**	**8.21:1**	**8.24:1**
Clothing Imports Ltd			
Sales	900,000	1,050,000	1,300,000
Net current assets	35,000	53,000	52,000
Working capital turnover	25.71:1	19.81:1	25.00:1

Interpretation

Again it is the trend that is important. A rising trend may indicate possible overtrading, whereby sales are increasing without the necessary additional working capital. Although a degree of overtrading can often be managed in the short term by good control over debtors, stock and creditors, over a period there will be increasing pressure on liquidity and the bank overdraft. Because the ratio provides an indication of the working capital needed to finance a given level of sales, it can be used to calculate approximately the additional level of working capital required to finance a projected increase in sales.

The ratios for Light Engineering Ltd show a modest rising trend but nothing significant.

Turning to Clothing Imports Ltd – the company increased its sales by 17% from 2001 to 2002. It can be seen that the ratio fell across this period. This has been possible by investing the retained profit into working capital to finance the sales expansion. From 2002 to 2003 sales expanded more rapidly, by 24%. This time the ratio has fallen back to its former level of 25:1. The nominal profit retention has not enabled the company to match its increased turnover.

This clearly has a bearing on liquidity, particularly if sales are projected to increase still further in 2004. The company has already extended its credit taken, and unless stock turnover or credit given can be shortened, increased sales will necessitate still further reliance on creditors (which may not be possible) or increased bank borrowing (which may not be agreed).

By way of example, let us project forward on a further increase of 24%. The following ratios for 2003 were applicable for Clothing Imports Ltd:

Debtor recovery rate   65 days

Stock turnover rate   77 days

Creditor repayment rate   84 days

Sales   £1,300,000 x 24% = £312,000 = increased sales

Total sales for 2004   £1,612,000

- If we further assume that the gross profit margin (see next section) for 2004 will remain at 7%, gross profit = £113,000. Therefore cost of goods sold = £1,499,000.
- So applying a debtor recovery rate of 65 days to sales, projected debtors at 2004 balance sheet date = (1,612,000/365) x 65 = £287,000.
- Applying a stock turnover rate of 77 days to cost of goods sold, projected stock = (1,499,000/365) x 77 = £316,000.
- Total projected current assets = £603,000.

How can this be financed?

- Applying a creditor repayment rate of 84 days, projected creditors = (1,499,000 x 84/365 = 344,000.
- Assume other current liabilities, ie hire-purchase, tax and directors' loans, remain the same: total £17,000.
- Applying the 2003 working capital turnover ratio to the projected sales level:

$$\frac{£1,612,000}{\text{net current assets}} = 25$$

Net current assets: $\dfrac{£1,612,000}{25} = £64,000$

- Therefore projected bank overdraft at 2004 year end is:

	£
Total projected current assets	603,000
Less: projected creditors	344,000
Less: other creditors	17,000
242,000	
Less: projected net current assets	64,000
Projected bank overdraft	178,000

With this type of approximated calculation, the bank overdraft then represents the 'balancing item' and this means a sizeable increased borrowing requirement that the bank may not be prepared to finance.

Second method

This time we take out the bank balance from the working capital cycle and calculate

        debtors + stock – trade creditors

	2001	2002	2003
	£	£	£
Debtors	150,000	170,000	230,000
Stock	135,000	190,000	257,000
	285,000	360,000	487,000
Trade creditors	140,000	180,000	280,000
Net balance	145,000	180,000	207,000
Sales	900,000	1,050,000	1,300,000
Net balance/sales	16%	17%	16%

This alternative capital measurement therefore equates to approximately 16% of sales. The 2004 sales are projected to increase by £312,000.

Therefore, the projected extra capital required is: £312,000 x 16% = £49,920

Although a gradual rise in profits will improve liquidity, this will not suffice and the bank will be needed as the 'balancing' item to fund the increased sales turnover.

7   Profitability ratios

Gross profit margin

This is defined as $\dfrac{\text{gross profit}}{\text{sales}}$ x 100

This ratio is calculated to show gross profit as a percentage of sales.

	2001	2002	2003
	£	£	£
Light Engineering Ltd			
Gross profit	70,000 x 100	73,000 x 100	71,000 x 100
Sales	200,000	220,000	210,000
Gross profit margin	**35%**	**33%**	**34%**
Clothing Imports Ltd			
Gross profit	90,000 x 100	94,000 x 100	91,000 x 100
Sales	900,000	1,050,000	1,300,000
Gross profit margin	10%	8.95%	7.0%

Interpretation

This ratio will vary from business to business, eg a manufacturer with a high fixed cost structure will have a higher gross profit margin than a merchanting-type business (high volume – fine margin).

Trends in the gross profit margin should be noted carefully and the underlying reasons ascertained. A declining trend could indicate one or a combination of the following:

- ◆ the business is becoming less profitable due to competition in the marketplace forcing it to reduce its pricing policy;
- ◆ similarly, it could be due to an increase in costs of one or more of the components of cost of goods sold, which the business cannot, due to competition, pass on to its customers;
- ◆ a deliberate policy by the business proprietors to reduce prices in order to increase sales volume.

Looking at Light Engineering Ltd, the gross profit margin fell from 35% to 33% from 2001 to 2002. Further analysis of the components of the cost of goods sold figures will show why.

	2001	**2002**
	£	**£**
Materials consumed	55,000 x 100	66,000 x 100
Sales	200,000	220,000
Margin	27.5%	30%
Direct labour	75,000 x 100	81,000 x 100
Sales	200,000	220,000
Margin	37.5%	36.8%

Direct labour expressed as a percentage of sales actually fell, which in itself would boost the gross profit margin. It can be seen that this has been more than offset by an increase in materials consumed as a percentage of sales. An increase in materials costs then, relative to sales, has been the cause of the decline in the gross profit margin from 2001 to 2002.

During 2003 the margin pulled back to 34%, reversing the trend: how was this achieved? A similar exercise to the above will enable the reader to demonstrate that, comparing 2003 with 2002, direct labour costs increased as a percentage of sales. This was, however, more than compensated for by a reduction in materials consumed as a percentage of sales.

Turning to Clothing Imports Ltd, a reducing trend can be seen, which is cause for concern. If this trend were to continue, and the gross profit margin fell by a further 1% in 2004, on the same level of sales the following gross profit would be achieved:

sales £1,300,000 x 6% = £78,000 gross profit

Assuming similar fixed costs, ie administration and distribution costs of £78,000, the company would only break even. After interest charges a loss would be incurred.

It may be that the directors of Clothing Imports Ltd deliberately reduced gross margins to boost sales. Enquiries of the directors will need to be made to ascertain the reason behind the falling trend in gross margins.

Gross profit margin (% of sales) is all about pricing and costing. By comparison with non-financial analysis a greater understanding of the risk can be seen as well as the right questions for the customer. How does an increased or reduced price impact on the level of sales? Will a reduced price actually bring about increased sales volume? Will an increased price cause a loss in sales volume? This is a business decision regarding risk in each case, and estimates will be required in order to undertake some form of sensitivity analysis.

The other element in gross profit margin relates to COGS (if opening and closing stock are ignored, then this is essentially 'purchases'). What price is paid for raw materials? Consider the scope for increasing prices (for both the businesses' suppliers and buyers) referring back to Porter's Five Competitive Forces (Chapter Three). What scope is there for sales price increases? Consider both marketing mix and strategy: all full non-financial analysis should have already provided an indication to these issues.

8   Operating profit margin

This is defined as $\dfrac{\text{operating profit (PBIT)}}{\text{sales}} \times 100$

This ratio reveals the net operating margin before finance charges and tax.

	2001 £	2002 £	2003 £
Light Engineering Ltd			
Operating profit	11,000 × 100	12,500 × 100	11,500 × 100
Sales	200,000	220,000	210,000
Net margin	5.5%	5.7%	5.5%
Clothing Imports Ltd			
Operating profit	33,000 × 100	34,500 × 100	13,000 × 100
Sales	900,000	1,050,000	1,300,000
Net margin	3.6%	3.3%	1.0%

Interpretation

This ratio represents the premium gained by a business for its output over its production costs. Profit before interest and tax is used to isolate interest and tax charges from other costs of production. In interpreting this net margin it is important to observe any trend. The absolute value of the ratio will vary considerably from industry to industry, with low margins allied to high volume and vice versa. Variations in net margins from one year to another will be determined by variations in the gross profit and the overhead expenses. Having isolated the gross profit margin in the previous section, it is variation in the proportional expenses of overheads in relation to sales that will be revealed by an analysis of this ratio.

Looking at Light Engineering Ltd, it can be seen that the net operating margin is fairly steady.

Now turning to Clothing Imports Ltd, it can be seen that the net operating margin has fallen significantly during 2003. This company has also sustained a steadily reducing gross profit margin. It is worthwhile ascertaining whether the two margins are reducing at the same rate. This is simply identified by the ratio

$$\frac{\text{net operating margin}}{\text{gross profit margin}} \times 100$$

2001

$$\frac{3.6}{10} \times 100 = 36\%$$

2002

$$\frac{3.3}{8.95} \times 100 = 36.87\%$$

2003

$$\frac{1.0}{7.0} \times 100 = 14.28\%$$

The two margins are not moving in line. We shall concentrate on the greatest variation, ie 2002 to 2003, where net margin as a percentage of gross profit margin fell substantially. This must mean that there was a proportionate increase in overhead costs from 2002 to 2003. This can be ascertained by the following ratio

$$\frac{\text{overheads}}{\text{sales}} \times 100$$

2002

$$\frac{59,500}{1,050,000} \times 100 = 5.67\%$$

2003

$$\frac{78,000}{1,300,000} \times 100 = 6.0\%$$

As well as a decline in gross margins, the fall in net profit margin in 2003 was exacerbated by increased overhead costs. Overall, the decline in gross profit margins, coupled with the decline in net profit margins for Clothing Imports Ltd, is cause for concern.

9   Cash flow statement (FRSI)

Business failure usually occurs because of a cash crisis. It is important to appreciate that a cash crisis can occur even though a business is turning in profits. Such cash crises may be preceded by a series of funds flow deficits revealed in the cash flow statement.

Look again at the statements shown for the two companies in question:

◆ net funds generated (absorbed)] – to what extent have the companies covered their tax payments and purchase of fixed assets from their own funds generated by operations?
◆ working capital change – if positive, can this be maintained? Increasing sales usually results in a need to increase working capital. Is working capital change 'swallowing up' all net funds generated by operations, as in 2002 for both Light Engineering Ltd and Clothing Imports Ltd? Alternatively, is an increasing working capital requirement exacerbating an already deficit net funds generated position, as in 2002 for Clothing Imports Ltd?
◆ cash funds deficit – how long will the business be able to continue to fund this from increased bank borrowing? Sooner or later a business may reach the limit of its creditworthiness.

The application of cash and where it comes from is essential for the survival of any business.

The cashflow statement is a valuable tool as it examines the flow of money in and out of the business, that is, where the money comes from and how it is used. Many profitable businesses have failed because they have not generated sufficient cash to continue trading.

In many cases a cashflow statement will not be produced (nor required under SI 16) and so an understanding of how it is structured will enable you to consider the key elements without one. This could be derived from profit & loss and balance sheet information.

Using the format laid down in this chapter, consider what the business has actually done over that accounting period. Be aware of what generates and what uses up 'cash':

Sources of cash	Uses of cash
Profits	Losses
New debt	Repay debt
New capital	Dividends
Reduce stock	Increase stock
Reduce debtors	Increase debtors
Increase creditors	Reduce creditors

Sources of cash	**Uses of cash** *(continued)*
Sell assets	Capex
Grants	Interest costs
Interest income	Tax

There is a need to account for non-cash items such as depreciation, revaluation reserves or interest capitalisation. Details of these figures are found in the accompanying notes to customers' accounts.

Cash is the lifeblood of a business and it is essential to understand how it is being used so that risks can be highlighted and appropriate measures taken. A profitable business can still fail by poor cash management. Reasons for this could include:

◆ too many debtors or stock;
◆ debtors not collected in good time;
◆ losses;
◆ too much capital expenditure.

Despite being profitable on paper, without receipt of funds into a bank account, cheques and payments may be refused causing loss of business credit, unpaid invoices/wages/salaries and loss of confidence.

11 Summary on ratios

What the ratios revealed and the interpretation of the trends seen forms a guide to the financial health of the business being analysed. In assessing a business in this way it is important to appreciate that we are looking at historical information, but this assessment will enable the bank to have a firm basis upon which to consider future borrowing requirements. Before the assessment can be completed, the bank will need to review the future corporate plan and forward projections of a business: what did we glean from our ratio analysis?

Light Engineering Ltd

This company is maintaining its profitability on a static sales turnover. Its gearing position is improving, in part from retained profits, but also from increasing hidden balance sheet property reserves. Liquidity and control ratios do not reveal anything untoward. The company's working capital position is not under any duress.

Overall, you may not be too concerned with present bank exposure. The company's future plans will need to be discussed. Will they be able to generate sufficient sales in 2004 to maintain their position? Their 'bottom line' retained profits have been modest. There is little leeway if sales levels cannot be maintained. On the 'flat' sales turnover performance it is fortunate that they have been able to hold overhead costs at £60,000. A 10% rise in overheads on the same turnover would eliminate profits. Clearly much will depend on forecasts.

Clothing Imports Ltd

This company looks much more interesting: it has expanded its sales rapidly but only generated profit before tax of £2,000. The increased sales turnover has been accomplished only by reducing profit margins, and overall profitability has shown a marked decline. The effect of the above has been to escalate capital gearing levels, particularly the wider measure of total liabilities/net worth. Gearing is high and so the bank's margin of safety rests very heavily on the security cover. Interest cover has declined. Liquidity has declined – with the company having to extend its credit taken to finance its increased sales levels. Working capital requirements are under some strain. The company will not be able to expand sales at the same rates as in these three years without increasing its bank borrowing and/or credit taken.

Overall, the directors' strategy for 2003 needs questioning, together with their forward plans and budgets for 2004. Do they recognise the cash flow implications of another year of growth similar to that seen in 2003?

Case study 3: Handmade Tables Ltd
– building the budgets

Introduction and background

The date is February 2004.

This firm of handmade table manufacturers has been established for only three years, but during that time has made its presence felt in what is a fairly limited and specialised market. The operation has just moved from cramped garage-type accommodation to a modern 4,000 square-foot warehouse on an industrial estate, in order to cope adequately with an increased order book. Capital expenditure in the new premises has totalled £15,000 so far, most of which has been financed by hire purchase (short-term industrial finance).

The business produces a range of nine handmade tables, three in each type of wood, ie oak, teak and mahogany.

The tables have a long lifespan, depending on the use to which they are put. With the growth in turnover, the principal director has found himself under increasing pressure in the day-to-day running of the company.

You have just succeeded in convincing the director of the merits of budgeting and cash flow forecasting, which should enable him to plan and control the future operation of the business in a more positive manner. He appears hesitant about how he should proceed and you have volunteered to offer general advice on the preparation of forecasts for the next six months.

Information available

There is a seasonal pattern to sales, with a marked increase in March and April following the annual Furniture Exhibition held in London in February, and increased sales during the summer months.

The following sales information has been supplied by the director.

1. The average selling price of each type of table is as follows.
   a) Oak   £200
   b) Teak   £160
   c) Mahogany   £140

2. Sales of the oak tables run at 35 per normal month. The teak version sells the same number in a normal month, while in a normal month 70 are sold of the mahogany model.
   In the two months following the February exhibition a sales increase of 50% is seen on a normal month, while May, June and July show a 30% increase on a normal month. January and February are normal months. Due to the holiday shutdown, August can be regarded as normal.

3. Half of total production is exported.
4. UK sales are on a cash-on-delivery basis, while the average time of settlement for exports is two months.
5. Close control is maintained over materials used, which comprise 40% of the selling price. Levels are held as low as possible and lead times are not a problem (except for oak at 20% of selling price).

   The receipt of purchase invoices coincides with the month in which the materials are used, and purchases are paid for two months after delivery.
6. The anticipated changes in the levels of stock during the six months are as follows.

Stock at 28 February 2004 =	£15,000
March	+£1,010
April	+£1,010
May	– £528
June	+£472
July	– £2,020
August	– £2,944
Stock at 31 August 2004 =	£12,000

   Purchases during January and February 2004 were £12,000 and £13,000 respectively.

   Assume that the stock purchases figure is the materials used in a month, adjusted for stock levels held at the month end.
7. The company employs ten men on the production line (five of whom are self-employed and all of whom are part-time). They are paid £80 per week each gross.

   The company's National Insurance contributions for employees are 13.5% of wages. A wage review is due on 1 August, when a 15% increase will be payable.

   May and July will be 'five-week months'. PAYE is paid up to date and is always paid during the same month as the wages.
8. Turning to the company's overhead costs, the following points apply.
   a) Rent of £7,000 per annum is payable quarterly in January, April, etc, and no rent review is due during 2004/05.
   b) Rates in 2004 amounted to £1,200. Although the local authority has made no prediction for 2005, the indications are that the overall increase for 2004/05 fiscal year (ie commencing 5 April 2004) will be 20%. They are payable half-yearly, in May and November.
   c) The company is now employing a secretary/bookkeeper at £40 per week plus National Insurance contributions. She will also receive the August increase of 15%.
   d) Telephone usage fluctuates little during the year, the annual bill being £640, with payments made in March, June, September and December.
   e) Hire purchase (short-term industrial finance) commitments are paid by a monthly standing order for £542 (capital and interest). Annual HP interest charges total £2,700.

f) Bank charges are passed quarterly and based on the following figures:
- I Loan of £1,650 taken up at the end of February. Monthly capital repayments are £84, first payment made in March. The annual interest is £248;
- I bank commission charges – £500 per annum.

g) Light and power are not appreciably affected by seasonal influences, as a constant level of heat is required to enable the materials used in manufacture to set properly.

   Payments are made in February, May, August and October, and total £4,000 for the year.

h) The fixed assets of £18,000, at cost, are being depreciated on a straight-line method over five years.

i) Directors' salaries are £15,600 per annum inclusive of National Insurance contributions.

j) Ignore Corporation Tax for the purpose of this exercise.

k) It can be assumed that the remaining overhead costs detailed below are spread evenly throughout the period.

Insurance	£800 per annum
Motor expenses and travelling	£3,000 per annum
Repairs and renewals	£500 per annum
Printing and stationery	£200 per annum
Advertising	£2,000 per annum
Accountancy	£300 per annum
Sundries	£2,000 per annum

   The accountant's bill is usually paid in two equal parts in October and November each year.

l) Opening bank balance to be £2,500 overdrawn.

m) Ignore inflation.

Additional notes

- ◆ VAT on tables is at 15%, **but export orders are exempt.**
- ◆ All purchases of materials bear VAT at 15%.
- ◆ VAT recoverable on other outgoings has been ignored for the purpose of this exercise.
- ◆ The VAT period covers the quarters ending March, June etc with payments to be made by the 20th of the following month.

Material purchases

A profit budget includes materials consumed (*ie used in month*) for profit purposes, but the VAT calculation will be based on the *purchases* in the month. A cash flow forecast includes purchases + VAT (where appropriate) with a timing allowance for terms of trade.

Let us now consider the preparation of:

◆ an operating budget for a six-month period commencing on 1 March 1998 – (this will incorporate an overheads budget for the period stating in the space provided the assumptions under which various items have been included);
◆ a cash flow forecast for the same period.

Sales budget

We need to prepare a sales budget from the information available. In due course we will need to have regard for the VAT implications and the timing differences, as regards the inflows included in the cash flow forecast, but initially we should consider only the assumptions upon which the sales forecast has been based and these may include the following:

◆ is the company dependent on one product or customer?
◆ does the sales forecast allow for discounts given?
◆ what assumptions have been made re growth of new markets?
◆ are there any technological developments in the pipeline that might affect sales?
◆ what length of credit taken by debtors has been assumed in calculating inflows?
◆ are there any exchange rate risks?
◆ has allowance for seasonality of sales been made?
◆ are sales dependent on delivery of new plant and machinery?
◆ has an allowance for bad debts been made when forecasting receipts from sales?

Once satisfied that these areas have been considered we can proceed to prepare a sales budget.

We know from our discussions that sales increase by 50% in the two months following the furniture show and that May, June and July have sales 30% above a normal month. We can now prepare a sales forecast for the six-month period incorporating this information.

Handmade Tables Ltd – sales budget for a six-month period to 31 August 2004

						£s				
Sales	Price	Volume per month	March	April	May	June	July	August	Totals
Oak	£200	35	7,000	7,000	7,000	7,000	7,000	7,000	
Teak	£160	35	5,600	5,600	5,600	5,600	5,600	5,600	
Mahogany	£140	70	9,800	9,800	9,800	9,800	9,800	9,800	
Sub-total			22,400	22,400	22,400	22,400	22,400	22,400	134,400
+50%			11,200	11,200					22,400
+30%				6,720	6,720	6,720			20,160
Totals			33,600	33,600	29,120	29,120	29,120	22,400	176,960

The monthly sales figures can be carried forward into the budget document.

Material content in sales

When assessing the materials content in sales we again need to question the assumptions that have been used in arriving at the figures. Such questions may include the following:

◆ how are costs of materials assessed?
◆ what materials are needed and when?
◆ are raw materials readily available?
◆ what are deliveries like?
◆ what minimum and maximum stock levels have been set?
◆ has due allowance for discounts on bulk orders been made?
◆ is the company pursuing a stocking or de-stocking policy?
◆ is the company dependent on sub-contractors?
◆ what period of credit allowed has been assumed?
◆ materials are imported – has the exchange risk been covered?

We are told that materials consumed comprise 40% of the selling price. We can therefore calculate the materials figure for inclusion in the budget.

£s				**Net of VAT**			
	March	April	May	June	July	August	Totals
Sales	33,600	33,600	29,120	29,120	29,120	22,400	176,960
Materials	13,440	13,440	11,648	11,648	11,648	8,960	70,784

Wages

Before calculating the anticipated level of wages for the budget period we must consider the wider aspects of the business' wages policy including any likely increase to the wages total.

We must take into consideration:

◆ whether the business has allowed for anticipated wage increases during the budget period?
◆ has due allowance for recruitment, retention and training of employees been made?
◆ what assumptions regarding availability of skilled labour have been made?
◆ have all labour costs been included, ie employer's share of National Health contributions, pensions, bonuses, etc?
◆ has the cost of overtime/shift work been incorporated in the plan?

There are several ways of entering wages in the budget, any of which are acceptable.

They are set down here in descending order of preference.

a) Total wages for six months = 12.837% of sales.
Each month should therefore bear an equivalent percentage of that month's sales as wages costs.

eg	March	April	May	June	July	August	Total
£	4,313	4,313	3,738	3,738	3,738	2,876	22,716

This method directly relates the wages cost to sales income.
Care: in the cash flow forecast the total would have to be reapportioned as in (c) below.

b) Total wages for six months = £22,716 therefore each month should bear:

$$\frac{£22,716}{6} = £3,786$$

This method treats wages as a fixed cost running on at a constant level despite fluctuations in the sales pattern
Care: in the cash flow forecast the total would have to be reapportioned as in (c) below.

c) *4-week 'months'* – 10 men @ £80 x 4 weeks   =   £3,200
+ National Insurance for 5 men @ 13.5%   =   £ 216
Total   £3,416
5-week 'months' – 10 men @ £80 x 5 weeks   =   £4,000
+ National Insurance for 5 men @ 13.5%   =   £ 270
Total   £4,270

This method relates more closely to cash flow than to the operating budget. If sales income were split down into weekly figures it would be more relevant to the latter.

So we will use method (a) and transfer the monthly totals into our budget form.

In this example the workforce is paid weekly on a Thursday, and five of them are self-employed. Directors' salaries are not included in the direct wages.

Overhead costs

In this case study many assumptions are given but the relative calculations are as follows.

Area	Amount in cash flow	
Admin salaries		
22 weeks @ £40 per week =	£880	
4 weeks @ £46 per week =	£184	
	£1,064	
x 13.5% National Insurance	£144	
Total admin salaries	£1,208	Payable monthly
Rent:		
Agreed rental £7,000 pa	£1,750	Payable quarterly, Jan/April/July/Oct
No rent review due		
Rates		
1 month @ £1,200 pa (ie = 1/12)	£100	
5 months @ £1,200 pa + 20% =	£600	
Total	£700	Payable half yearly May/November
Telephone		
£640 pa	£320	Payable March and quarterly
Insurances		
Premiums of £800 pa	£400	Spread evenly throughout the period
Light and heat		
Total £4,000 pa	£2,000	Payable March and quarterly
Motor and travelling expenses		
Estimated at £3,000 pa	£1,500	Spread evenly throughout the period
Repairs and renewals		
Estimated at £500 pa	£250	Spread evenly throughout the period

Area	**Amount in cash flow** *(continued)*

Printing/stationery

Estimated at £200 pa £100 Spread evenly throughout the period

Advertising

Estimated at £2,000 pa £1,000 Spread evenly throughout the period

Accountancy

Estimated at £300 £150 Spread evenly throughout the period
Paid in two equal parts in October and
November each year

Sundries

Estimated at £2,000 pa £1,000 Spread evenly throughout the period

HP interest

Annual HP interest charge £1,350 Monthly payments
£2,700 pa Remember that in the cash flow we
have to include the capital element of
the debt as well as the interest

Bank charges

Bank loan interest £84 Monthly payments

Bank charges £145 Quarterly amount payable in March

£190 Quarterly amount payable in June

Depreciation

Fixed assets at a cost of
£18,000

To be depreciated on a
straight-line basis over five
years.

£18,000 ÷ 5 = £3,600 pa £1,800 A charge against profitability but not a
cash flow item

Directors' salaries

£15,600 pa to include
National Insurance

Finally check that all
expenses have been
included

The total figure from the overheads budget is divided equally over the six-month period; this avoids false hopes in good months when little overheads are paid.

We can summarise our calculations in the following manner, taking 1/6 of the total as the monthly figure for inclusion in our budget.

Overheads budget for the six-month period ending on 31 August 2004

Area	Amount	Assumptions
Admin salaries	1,208	£40 pw + 13.5% NI
Rent	3,500	Agreement
Rates and water	700	+20% from April
Telephone	320	Usage
Insurance	400	Premiums
Light and heat	2,000	Assessed
Motor and travelling	1,500	Estimated
Repairs/renewals	250	Nominal
Printing/stationery	100	Assessed
Advertising	1,000	Directors' budget
Accountancy	150	As last year
Sundries	1,000	Estimated
HP interest	1,350	Current contracts
Bank charges	374	Interest and commission
Depreciation	1,800	Assessed
Directors' salaries	7,800	6 x £1,300
Total	**23,452**	**ie £3,908 per month**

We are now in a position to finalise our operating budget.

Operating budget for a six-month period to 31 August 2004

£s							Totals
Sales	33,600	33,600	29,120	29,120	29,120	22,400	176,960
Less Cost of sales							
Materials consumed	13,440	13,440	11,648	11,648	11,648	8,960	70,784
Direct wages +NI	4,313	4,313	3,738	3,738	3,738	2,876	22,716
Total cost of							
Sales	17,753	17,753	15,386	15,386	15,386	11,836	93,500
Gross profit	15,847	15,847	13,734	13,734	13,734	10,564	83,460
Less overheads (from overheads budget)	3,908	3,908	3,908	3,908	3,908	3,908	23,452
Net profit/ (loss)(pre-tax)	11,939	11,939	9,826	9,826	9,826	6,656	60,000

We are forecasting that the business will make a profit of £60,000 over the six-month period to 31 August 2004.

Profit budgets checklist

- ◆ Are sales realistic?
- ◆ Check the projected gross margin against past performance.
- ◆ Ensure that all overheads are included.
- ◆ Check realism of depreciation.
- ◆ Ensure that figures exclude VAT.
- ◆ Ensure that finance charges are included.
- ◆ Check arithmetic.
- ◆ Apply common sense to figures: do they make sense?

Value added tax

Now that we have completed the operating budget we are in a position to consider the VAT implications of our sales and purchases.

◆ As previously indicated VAT has been ignored on the overhead costs although in practice many of the costs would attract VAT.

◆ We are told that VAT on tables sales is calculated at 15%, but that export orders are exempt.

◆ Half the sales thus bear VAT at 15%.

◆ All purchases of materials bear VAT at 15%.

◆ We are told that receipt of purchase invoices coincides with the month in which the materials are used and that purchases are paid for two months after delivery.

◆ We need to allow for the stock changes to arrive at the purchases figure for VAT purposes.

◆ The purchases in January and February are shown to be £12,000 and £13,000 respectively.

The **purchases** for the remainder of the period are calculated as follows.

	£s					
Month	**March**	**April**	**May**	**June**	**July**	**August**
Materials consumed (40% of sales)	13,440	13,440	11,648	11,648	11,648	8,960
Stock change	+1,010	+1,010	-528	+ 472	-2,020	-2,944
Purchases	**14,450**	**14,450**	**11,120**	**12,120**	**9,628**	**6,016**

15% VAT is then calculated on the purchases figures and added to the purchases figure for outflows in the cash flow forecast.

Value added tax - 2004 in £s

Month	Jan	Feb	Mar	April	May	June	July	Aug
Total sales	18,900	18,900	33,600	33,600	29,120	29,120	29,120	22,400
½ sales on two months' credit								
Sales (VAT exempt)	9,450	9,450	16,800	16,800	14,560	14,560	14,560	11,200
½ sales in cash								
VATable sales	9,450	9,450	16,800	16,800	14,560	14,560	14,560	11,200
VAT on sales	1,418	1,418	2,520	2,520	2,184	2,184	2,184	1,680
Total purchases	12,000	13,000	14,450	14,450	11,120	12,120	9,628	6,016
VAT on purchases	1,800	1,950	2,167	2,167	1,668	1,818	1,444	902
Net amount	**(382)**	**(532)**	**353**	**353**	**516**	**366**	**740**	**778**
Total payable						1,235		
Total receivable			561					

Having completed our template we can see that we have VAT liabilities as follows for the first three months of the year: January £382 due to the business, February £532 due to the business, March £353 payable. The net payment due from Customs and Excise will be £561 payable by the 20th of the following month. As we complete the second quarter's VAT calculation we see:

◆ April £353 payable;
◆ May £516 payable;
◆ June £366 payable.

In July the business will send a cheque to Customs and Excise for the total sum due of £1,235. We will need to include the net payment and net receipt in our cash flow forecast.

We are now in a position to turn the operating budget into a cash flow forecast. We clearly need to have regard for the timing differences involved in the inflows and outflows of cash.

We are aware that one half of the sales are for cash plus VAT and that payment is received in the month that the sale is effected.

The other half of the sales is the export orders and although free from VAT the business does not receive this inflow of cash until the period of credit given (of two months) is observed.

We must begin by preparing a summary of the likely inflows from the information that we have.

Sales – inflows for the six months ending 31 August 2004 in £s

Sales	Jan	Feb	March	April	May	June	July	Aug
In month	18,900	18,900	33,600	33,600	29,120	29,120	29,120	22,400
Half sales on two months credit sales (VAT exempt)		9,450	9,450	16,800	16,800	14,560	14,560	
VATable sales	9,450	9,450	16,800	16,800	14,560	14,560	14,560	11,200
VAT	1,417	1,417	2,520	2,520	2,184	2,184	2,184	1,680
Inflows in month	**10,867**	**10,867**	**28,770**	**28,770**	**33,544**	**33,544**	**31,304**	**27,440**

With two months' credit terms involved, one half of January's sales become March's cash inflows; similarly one half of February's sales are the cash inflows in April.

Thus:

◆ cash sales for March £16,800, plus VAT @ 15% = £19,320;
◆ debtor monies in March relate to January sales of £9,450.

We can then continue to complete the analysis for the remaining months on a similar basis.

The cash sales in each month, being one half of the sales totals plus VAT are also included.

The totals calculated are ready for inclusion in the cash flow forecast.

Payments to creditors

We are told that payments to creditors are made two months after purchase, therefore purchases made in January will be paid for in March. Having already calculated the purchases totals we can complete a template, setting down when the payments will be made.

Creditors' payments analysis   £s

Month	Jan	Feb	March	Apr	May	June	July	Aug
Materials consumed (40% of sales)		13,440	13,440	11,648	11,648	11,648	8,960	
Stock change		+1,010	+1,010	−528	+472	−2,020	−2,944	
Total purchases	12,000	13,000	14,450	14,450	11,120	12,120	9,628	6,016
Add VAT	1,800	1,950	2,167	2,167	1,668	1,818	1,444	902
Total paid	13,800	14,950	16,617	16,617	12,788	13,938	11,072	6,918
Amount paid on two months' credit		13,800	14,950	16,617	16,617	12,788	13,938	

We are now able to complete the cash flow forecast as regards both inflows from sales and outflow payments in respect of purchases.

We can also transfer into the cash flow forecast the overheads costs, allowing for the timings of payments as scheduled.

Cash flow forecast for six months ending 31 August 2004 in £s

Receipts	Mar	April	May	June	July	Aug
Cash sales	19,320	19,320	16,744	16,744	16,744	12,880
Debtors (two months)	9,450	9,450	16,880	16,880	14,560	14,560
VAT refund	–	561	–	–	–	–
Sub-total	28,770	29,331	33,544	33,544	31,304	27,440

Payments	March	April	May	June	July	August
Creditors (two months)	13,800	14,950	16,617	16,617	12,788	13,938
Wages + NI	4,313	4,313	3,738	3,738	3,738	2,876
Rent, rates and water	–	1,750	720	–	1,750	–
Heat, light and telephone	160	–	1,000	160	–	1,000
Admin salaries	182	182	227	182	227	208
HP	542	542	542	542	542	542
Bank loan	84	84	84	84	84	84
Bank charges	145	–	–	190	–	–
General overheads	708	708	708	708	709	709
Directors' salaries	1,300	1,300	1,300	1,300	1,300	1,300
VAT payable	–	–	–	–	1,235	–
Sub-total	21,234	23,829	24,936	22,103	22,373	20,657
Net cash flow/(outflow)	7,536	5,502	8,608	11,441	8,931	6,783
Opening balance	(2,500)	5,036	10,538	19,146	30,587	39,518
Closing balance	5,036	10,538	19,146	30,587	39,518	**46,301**

As we can see there is no borrowing requirement identified, indeed good credit balances are likely to be generated. This will very much depend on the accuracy of the forecasts.

Case Study 4   Boffin Ltd

A new company has been formed with an initial capital of £25,000. Part of this will be used to purchase machinery (£18,000 plus VAT) and stock (£3,000 plus VAT) in the first month. The VAT rate is 17.5%. The directors have found a factory and although they consider the rent to be somewhat high, no premium has been charged. They estimate that fixtures and fittings will cost £2,400 plus VAT and will be bought in the first month. The directors have prepared a budget and their forecast figures are deemed realistic. Their own income will be paid as wages. They are known personally and considered to be honest and hard working.

The request is for an overdraft facility of £20,000 for working capital purposes covering the next twelve months. This will be used partly to purchase additional stock costing £7,000 plus VAT to increase the overall stock value up to £10,000. As security there is the offer of personal guarantees supported by second charges on the directors' homes (total values £120,000 less mortgages outstanding of £70,000). Their wives are going to work as a secretary and a bookkeeper in the business.

To support their request a profit budget and cash flow forecast for the next 12 months have been prepared. The directors have confirmed that their calculations show that there will be useful credit balances available at the end of the first year of trading. Indeed, they suggest that the requested overdraft facility will be only lightly used. As their banker, you are not convinced that this will be the case and arrange a meeting with the directors with a view to obtaining a better 'feel' for the business, and to have a look at the operation of the proposed business. A list of questions to ask the directors has been compiled for the meeting, including:

Questions to resolve
   ◆ How many product lines will there be?
   ◆ What would be the effect of changes in the product mix?
   ◆ Do all products yield the same profit contribution?
   ◆ What is the state of the market the business will be trading in?
   ◆ What market research on trading prospects has been undertaken?
   ◆ What contact has been made with potential customers?
   ◆ Are there any firm orders to date?
   ◆ Will the business be dependent significantly on any one customer or product?
   ◆ What technological developments may be in the pipeline?
   ◆ What are the normal terms of trade to be adopted?
   ◆ Will any goods be exported?
   ◆ Are there any seasonal factors to affect sales demand?
   ◆ Who are the competitors and how do their products compare?
   ◆ Is the plant and the labour force ready to start production?
   ◆ What is the production period? Significant sales are forecast for the first month;

◆ What allowance has been assumed for bad debts?
◆ Is there to be a discount policy for sales?

If the forecasts are to be realistic the management should have considered all possible factors likely to limit trading and accounted for these in its business plan and budget. These will include the following:

Factors to allow for

◆ Are sufficient funds on hand to finance the forecast trading?
◆ Is the space available for production sufficient?
◆ Are the trading forecasts robust enough to allow for changes in demand?
◆ Does the work force have the right skills for the job?
◆ Are the abilities of the proposed management adequate for the tasks?
◆ Will the capacity of the production machines meet the sales demand?
◆ Has the availability of production materials been sourced and costed?

Only by recognising such constraints at an early stage and appreciating the future results of proposed present actions can the company hope to avoid major unforeseen pitfalls. After close questioning the directors state that their forecasts are based on the following assumptions:

Forecast assumptions

1. Credit given on sales is expected to be two months (ie inflows from sales in month 1 will be received in month 3).
2. Credit taken on materials purchased is expected to be three months (ie purchases in month 1 will be paid for in month 4).
3. Materials will be used in the month in which they are bought.
4. Fixtures, fittings and machinery have to be paid for in month 1.
5. Rent is payable quarterly from month 1 (£7,200 per year).
6. Rates are payable half-yearly from month 1 (£1,800 per year).
7. Wages (not salaries) are paid weekly (total £600 per week gross). There are five week trading periods s in months 4, 7, 9 and 11.
8. All other costs are payable in the same month as they occur.
9. Finance costs are budgeted at £750 per quarter payable in months 3, 6, 9 & 12.
10. Depreciation on machinery is calculated at 10% per annum, straight-line basis.
11. Depreciation on fixtures & fittings is calculated at 20% per annum straight-line.
12. VAT is paid for the first quarter in month 4; the second quarter in month 7 etc

13. Both wages and salaries in the budget are gross figures including PAYE and employer's NI. It is assumed that total deductions will amount to 25% of the gross totals each month and will be paid over to the Revenue in the month following the wages/salaries payment.

As banker you are concerned at the suggestion that the terms of trade can be so favourable to the company and decide to undertake some sensitivity analysis of the directors' proposals. This will include amending the terms of trade so that credit given will be three months (ie inflows from sales in month 1 will be received in month 4) and credit taken will be two months (ie purchases in month 1 will be paid for in month 3).

Your revised cash flow forecast (not shown for this example) based on these amended terms of trade indicates that the requested overdraft facility of £20,000 is not going to be sufficient to meet the company's needs. Indeed, within three months the company is likely to be considerably in excess of the proposed limit with a likely borrowing requirement of almost £30,000, together with substantial excesses over the remainder of the year. The annual sum for administrative wages, rent and rates, and finance costs alone totals £40,800 for a full year, not £27,480.

Further questions then arise.

◆ How likely is it that sales will total £10,000 in month 1?
◆ What is the effect on profitability if annual sales were 10% below forecast?
◆ What if sales were 20% below forecast?

The sales projection in the profit budget is £168,000. The gross profit is £44,400, giving a gross profit percentage of 26.4%. The overhead costs are forecast to total £27,480. This has been disproved but, for the moment, the total is retained for sensitivity analysis until all figures can be discussed with the directors. A reduction is sales would have the following effects on company trading performance.

£	Directors' forecast 100%	Forecast 1 −10%	Forecast 2 −20%
Turnover	168,000	151,200	134,400
(Direct) operating variable costs	123,600	111,284	98,919
Gross profit	44,400	39,916	35,481
Gross profit %	26.4%	26.4%	26.4%
(Indirect) overhead fixed costs	27,480	27,480	27,480
Projected net profit	**16,920**	**12,436**	**8,001**
Variance from budget	–	−26.5%	−52.7%

If the decrease in sales were coupled to a 20% increase in overhead costs (to £32,976) over budgeted figures, the profit for the year would under Forecast 2 reduce to £2,505.

Break-even analysis

How much turnover does the business have to achieve to avoid making a loss on trading? This fundamental question can be answered by calculating the break-even turnover point for the business. That is the point at which the total (ie fixed and variable) costs are equal to turnover. Fixed costs do not vary with changes in turnover, whereas variable costs do. For example, materials consumed and the labour force necessary to manufacture products are variable dependent on the level of production sold. Administrative wages are incurred independent of production levels and where a business grows sufficiently to require additional administrative employees, the requirement is not directly related to any given level of sales.

Taking the example of the directors' forecasts for Boffin Ltd,

Net profit = Sales less Direct costs less Indirect costs. ie
£16,920 = £168,000 - £123,600 (73.57% of sales) − £27,480

For break-even point, the net profit must equate to zero. Thus

£0 = 26.43% (ie 100% less 73.57%) of break-even sales − £27,480

If 26.43% of break-even sales = £27,480 then full break-even will be when sales are 100%, or £27,480 x 100/26.43 = £103,973.

This calculation may be alternatively computed by solving the following fraction

Indirect fixed costs / gross profit % = Break-even sales ie
£27,480 x 100 / 26.43 = £103,973

If the sales forecast proves to be accurate, and the projected gross profit margin is achieved, the break-even point will be passed in the ninth month of the trading year. Any profits will thus be earned in the latter part of the year. Before accepting the budget figures we need to ensure that we have considered all aspects affecting the budget and cash flow forecasts. These will include:

Sales

What are the trends? Are sales increasing or decreasing in line with reasonable expectations? Are sales rising in line with inflation or is genuine progress being made? What will be the sales mix? Are the expectations of anticipated sales reasonably achievable? What would be the effect if sales were lower than forecast? What would be the effect of sales higher than forecast?

Cost of sales

Changes in materials and wages costs will affect the gross profit. Are the materials costs realistic? What would be the effect of, say, a 10% increase in materials?

Gross profit

This can be affected by increases or decreases in the cost of materials; higher or lower selling prices; pilferage; stock valuation; increases in wages costs where they are a part of the cost of sales. What are the trends? Is the gross profit percentage realistic and achievable? What would be the effect on profitability if the gross profit percentage obtained was (say 10%) lower?

Overhead costs

Have all the fixed overhead indirect costs been included? We conclude not. Examine individual amounts where they would make a significant difference to profit. Have likely or expected increases in overhead costs been allowed for?

Interest

Compare the interest charge to the amount of borrowed funds. Is the amount of interest cover by the forecast profit acceptable?

Profit

Is the projected profit likely to be achieved? How does it compare with past performance?

Cash flow forecast

Are the quoted terms of trade realistic and being observed? What would be the effect on cash requirements of changes to the terms of trade? Are the timings of the payments of overhead expenses realistic? The estimates are likely to be based on a month-by-month basis of actual cash received and paid. Is the opening cash book balance correct? Has VAT been allowed for, if appropriate, and correctly calculated as to timing? Has the cash flow been correctly compiled from the budget? Has depreciation been excluded from the cash flow calculations? Is the cost and repayment of any borrowing requirement correctly projected?

Varying the cost of various expenditure items and changes to the assumed gross profit margin can now be made by way of further sensitivity tests to compare various break-even scenarios. The most common change necessary that is frequently met in practice is optimism regarding the sales forecast.

Conclusion

The directors' estimates are far too woolly to be taken at their face value and there are grounds to suppose that the business will not be viable as the trading months progress if it is relying on the shareholders' capital and proposed borrowings. The directors should be faced with the calculation of the possible break-even position (once all profit and loss account items have been assessed as acceptable forecasts) and cash flow shortfall. The lending proposition as it stands cannot be accepted.

Case study 5 – M Group Ltd

The group is involved in cash-and-carry wines and spirits, with three warehouses and six retail shops. The business commenced in 1980 and has grown rapidly in recent years. The board of four directors includes the proprietor and his wife, a sales director and a chartered accountant acting as finance director. Recent debenture figures have not been obtainable due to the company transferring its records onto computer. There has been pressure of late on the bank account with some excess positions arising that have been reported to the bank's control department. The company directors have told you that the bank account problem is only temporary, caused principally because of the cost of moving premises. Draft accounts have just been produced for the company's most recent financial year ending on 31 March. A comparison with earlier years discloses the following:

(£m)	Audited accounts			Draft accounts
	2001	**2002**	**2003**	**2004**
Sales	9.3	19.0	30.4	36.1
Gross profit	0.59	0.91	1.30	1.20
Gross profit %	6.2%	4.8%	4.2%	3.4%
Overheads	0.48	0.69	1.10	1.70
Profit/(Loss)	0.10	0.22	0.15	(0.48)

The group results indicate the rapid growth of the business in the last four years, with sales going from £9.3 million to £36.1 million coupled with a deteriorating gross profit margin nearly halving to 3.4 % on sales. The draft accounts also reveals significantly increased overheads, resulting in a trading loss of £484,000. The premises and computer upheaval have meant that no management accounts have been prepared during the latter part of the past year and the draft loss came as a shock to the board of directors. This led to the appointment of investigating accountants with the

332

brief to ascertain the current trading position and the company's future cash flow requirement. Their report has now been received and also confirmed the serious divergence between the growing volume of sales achieved coincident with reducing gross profit margins being earned and the profit necessary to meet ballooning overhead costs. The accounting records were judged to be most inadequate and were a contributory cause of this state of affairs.

The following figures were provided to illustrate the bank's position:

Balance Sheets	At 31.3.04		At 20.5.04	
	draft	break-up	forecast	break-up
Assets subject to fixed charge:				
Freehold deeds	283	175	283	175
Leasehold	9	–	9	–
Goodwill	70	–	70	–
Trade debtors	1,318	1,197	1,102	956
Realisable value (A)	1,680	1,372	1,464	1,131
Assets subject to floating charge:				
Fixtures and equipment	420	50	420	50
Motor vehicles	60	30	60	30
Stock	5,568	4,202	4,150	3,058
	6,048	4,282	4,630	3,138
Less: preferential creditors:				
PAYE/NIC *	(28)	(28)	(58)	(58)
VAT	(299)	(299)	(799)	(799)
Wages and holiday pay	(10)	(23)	(10)	(23)
Other preferential debts	(3)	(3)	(66)	(66)
	(340)	(353)	(933)	(946)
Realisable value (B)	5,708	3,929	3,697	2,192
Realisable assets (A+ B)	7,388	5,301	5,161	3,323
Bank indebtedness	2,510	2,510	2,743	2,743
Surplus on bank's charge	4,878	2,791	2,418	580
Unsecured creditors	4,459	3,759	1,999	1,399
Net assets/(liabilities)	19	(968)	419	(819)

* *Note*: By concession, these debts are now no longer classified as preferential.

The accountants also made the following report:

> 'The group business has such a high turnover of stocks, with very short periods of credit given and taken, that the balance sheet can change dramatically in short periods of time. This is highlighted by the reduction of surplus on the bank's charge on a going-concern basis between 31 March and 20 May from £4.8 million to £2.4 million. [See also break-up surplus for the bank's charge: changing from £2.8 million to £580,000]. In our view the bank's position is not satisfactory ... the bank can never be sure as to what the position is. ... losses are highly likely to be continuing.'

A few weeks later a receiver was appointed.

Case study 6   Sparks Ltd

Sparks Ltd have been a customer of your bank for over 20 years and trade as wholesalers and suppliers of a range of electrical components to industrial businesses. The directors, Richard Lee (aged 49) and Charles Proctor (aged 52) each own 50% of the company and draw remuneration in the same proportions. Lee is responsible for sales and Proctor is in charge of finance and administration. The company currently has overdraft facilities of £300,000 secured by a debenture. The overdraft was renewed for 12 months a short while ago, at which time the company supplied a profit and loss forecast for the year to 30 September 2005.

Richard Lee calls to see you. He tells you that Proctor has recently suffered a mild heart attack and is seriously considering giving up work. He wants Lee to buy him out of the business and has put a value of £400,000 on his shares. Lee wishes to go ahead and buy the shares at this figure, and his initial thoughts are as follows.

1. He can raise £100,000 himself: £50,000 from savings and £50,000 by increasing the mortgage on his house (value £300,000 with an existing mortgage of £40,000).
2. The suggestion is that the company buys back sufficient shares to cover the remaining £300,000. He sees this being financed by a ten-year loan of £200,000 and utilising the existing overdraft facility to provide the balance of £100,000.
3. A book-keeper will be employed to replace Proctor at a salary of £25,000 pa.

You are required to set out, with reasons, your response to this request.

Profit and Loss summary

Years to 30 September £'000 rounded	Actual 2002	Actual 2003	Draft 2004	Forecast 2005
Sales	1,732	1,909	2,024	2,250
Gross profit	626	612	649	720
Directors' remuneration	136	172	173	180
Interest paid	21	24	21	23
Profit before tax	87	30	21	113
Retained profit	78	18	10	—

Balance Sheet summary

As at 30 September £'000 rounded	Actual 2002	Actual 2003	Draft 2004
Fixed assets			
Leasehold property	14	12	11
Fixtures and fittings	24	24	18
Motor vehicles	97	104	116
Total fixed assets	135	140	145
Current assets			
Cash	7	7	7
Debtors	423	475	483
Stock	386	360	367
Total current assets	816	842	857
Current liabilities			
Creditors	(255)	(240)	(310)
Bank	(151)	(167)	(109)
Hire purchase	(39)	(48)	(46)
Taxation	(9)	(12)	(12)
Total current liabilities	(454)	(467)	(477)
Net current assets	362	375	380
Employment of capital	**497**	**515**	**525**
Financed by:			
Ordinary shares	2	2	2
Profit and loss account	495	513	523
Capital employed	**497**	**515**	**525**

Selected accounting ratios

As at 30 September £'000 rounded	Actual 2002	Actual 2003	Draft 2004	Forecast 2005
Net gearing (%)	36.8	40.4	28.2	–
Current ratio	1.80	1.80	1.80	
Quick ratio (acid test)	0.95	1.03	1.04	
Credit given (days)	89	91	87	–
Credit taken (days)	84	67	82	–
Stock turnover (days)	127	101	96	–
Gross margin (%)	36.2	32.0	32.1	32.0
Net margin (%)	5.0	1.6	1.1	5.0
Interest cover (times)	5.1	2.3	2.0	6.0

Operation of bank account (£ 000):

High	202 *Dr*	225 *Dr*	180 *Dr to date*
Low	5 *Cr*	30 *Dr*	60 *Cr to date*
Average	145 *Dr*	172 *Dr*	139 *Dr to date*

Bank account interest margin: 3% over base rate.

Comment

Share buybacks are allowed under s 162 of the Companies Act 1985 but the action must be authorised by its Articles of Association and the shares can only be purchased if they are fully paid (ie held by existing members). The shares of unquoted companies once repurchased must be cancelled and the money used for the repurchase must come from distributable profits or the proceeds of a new share issue. However, a private company may make a payment out of capital if its Articles allow. If a company goes into liquidation and is insolvent within one year after making a payment out of capital the member from whom the shares were purchased and the directors who made the statutory declaration of solvency are liable to repay the amount paid out of capital insofar as this is necessary to pay the company's debts (s 76 of the Insolvency Act 1986). Sparks Ltd has sufficient undistributable profits to buy back its shares.

The existing proprietors, Lee and Proctor, have built up a good business and they must have been competent managers to do so. Who will replace Proctor when he is gone? If the management become stretched, will Lee be able to devote the same amount of time as before to his marketing role, particularly as the company's projections require sales to increase by over 11%? Weakening the management team, at the same time as putting the business under greater financial pressure by reducing the capital it has available, is not an ideal situation.

Suggested answer

The first issue to be considered is the price being paid for the shares. On a net asset basis, £400k looks a high price for 50% of £525k of net assets; on a P/E basis the price is too high, with the price earnings ratio being 81 times based on the historic 2004 figures, The price can only be justified based on the 2005 forecast as adjusted for a reduction in costs as a result of the reduced directors' remuneration.

Looking at the historical financial performance it can be seen that the current balance sheet structure is strong with low gearing. The business is liquid with both current and acid test ratios showing a healthy position, which is also reflected in the good credit given and credit taken figures and low overdraft usage. Profitability has been disappointing, however, particularly at the net level. The last time the business made a decent net profit was two years ago when the gross margin was 36.2% rather than the 32% it is now.

It does not look as though the business could carry a lot more debt, but it has to be recognised that the directors have been able to pay themselves high remuneration in the past and this could be regarded as 'quasi profit' if the remuneration level drops. If the trading projections for 2005 look optimistic, their achievement will require much tighter control of overheads than has been the case in the past. Although the sales targets look ambitious, the company has a good track record of achieving good sales increases to date.

In respect of the proposition itself: given his income and despite his age, Lee should be able to raise the extra mortgage he suggests, so the main issue is whether the company can carry the extra debt burden. There is headroom within the overdraft facility to accommodate £100k but this will almost certainly create a future hard core and it will be better to fund this element by way of a loan. The deal will require cash outflow in terms of interest and loan repayments of circa £50k, against which can be set the director's salary saving of £60k, made up as a remuneration share of £85k (for last year) less a book-keeper's salary of £25k. Repayment does therefore look theoretically possible.

The company gearing would rise significantly to almost 200% viz 2004 net debt of £148k plus new debt of £300k = £448k as a proportion of shareholders' funds £525k less the buy-back of £300k = £225k. £448k divided by £225k = 199%. The new capital structure will be uncomfortable at this level. Security as shown by the revised balance sheet is poor, with debtor cover available of only one times and less than two times current asset cover. Moreover, as a wholesaler, the business is at high risk of reservation of title in relation to the stock. Given the level of gearing and the thin security cover, Lee's guarantee looks necessary, supported by the equity in the value of his house amounting to £210k after a re-mortgage. As Lee will be the sole management figure some form of key-man insurance is suggested to safeguard the bank's interest.

This is a marginal lending proposition that could be argued either way. Repayment looks feasible but gearing and security are uncomfortable and this tends to suggest that the price being paid by Lee is rather too high. He should be advised to go away and renegotiate the price. If an absolute reduction is not achievable then some of the consideration could be deferred on an 'earn-out' basis. This would seem sensible, where part of the consideration would only become payable if future profits achieved certain targets (in effect allowing the business to pay more consideration at times when it could afford to do so). An alternative might be for Proctor to leave a tranche of the consideration in the business as working capital earning interest at a rate lower than the company could borrow funds in return for a debenture ranking after the bank in priority.

Whatever the decision, a detailed business plan and advice on the share buy-back structure are required, probably with the assistance of outside accountants. The bank should also test the trading forecasts through some sensitivity analysis.

Case study 7   Lendal Holdings Ltd

The company breeds pigs from a breeding unit at Cliffe; runs a pig fattening unit at Cleckheaton and manufactures portable, environmentally controlled, containerised pig units from a factory situated at a Leeds industrial site. In addition the company has set up a newly established manufacturing business in America and a further pig breeding unit in Canada. The prices of the pig units ranges from £5,050 to £27,000 ex VAT and offers the farmer through its controlled environment the capacity to produce a higher number of weaners per sow annually together with a better food conversion ratio. The products have proved popular and demand has increased over the years.

In December 2004 the bank manager to the group notified the bank's head office credit analyst with the following information on the operation of the account in 2004 (all debit balances):

(£'000)	Highest	Lowest	Avge balance	Limit	Turnover
2002		38		385	
2003		56		695	
2004					
Jan	92	48	67	171	67
Feb	94	35	59	171	50
Mch	82	38	60	171	56
Apr	106	77	92	171	43
May	125	88	109	171	44
June	148	126	138	171	36
July	179	135	155	171	76
Aug	197	173	186	171	33
Sept	255	201	227	171	82
Oct	230	186	211	171	66
Nov	261	212	230	171	63
Dec	264	216	241	171	62

The credit analyst agreed that the deteriorating position was unsatisfactory and pointed out that the overdraft limit had formally expired the previous August. The overnight position of the account was £264,000 in debit. It was difficult to match the directors' statement that the business was trading profitably, albeit having a temporary cash flow problem, according to the run of bank balances on the account. The financial controls appeared lax to say the least; there was no up-to-date information on current debtors (bad debts?) or creditors (pressure to settle?); and the pig industry trading outlook was not known with certainty. After subsequent discussion with the directors an investigating agricultural accountant was appointed.

The accountant reported that six operating areas had been specifically examined:

1. The management accounts produced at 31 August 2004 with projections to 28 February 2005;
2. The quality of management and the controls exercised;
3. The value of assets if there was to be a forced sale situation;
4. The company's products and the outlook for the pig industry generally;
5. The current state of the debtor and creditor balances;
6. The situation of the North American investments.

The financial accounts had a year end on 31 October and the most recent audited figures were compiled to 31 October 2003. A summary of recent results showed:

(£'000)	2002	2003
Turnover	524	1,095
Trading profit	19	57
Profit as % of Turnover	3.7%	5.2%
Capital employed	96	148

The accountants stated that company had performed a stocktake at 31 August 2004 together with management accounts raised on the basis of a Statement of Affairs, culminating in a 'balancing figure' of £114,000 that was taken to reserves. Romalpa (reservation of title) terms applied to an unknown quantity of stocks within a total value of £145,000. The North American operations accounted for £75,000 debtors and an unknown sum in creditors. A provision for bad debts was necessary of £27,000. Preferential creditors amounted to around £30,000.

Although the pig industry at the moment was quite depressed, there was still a reasonable order book for units, together with repeat orders for the replacement of old pig housing units. As regards management, David Ball was away in America and there was no opportunity to meet him, so most discussions at the occasion of my visit were with Ron Naylor whom I think could be best described as a general manager. He is technically competent and certainly close to the technical production of the different pig units. The following data was obtained from the management returns:

Lendal Holdings Ltd and subsidiary companies: Management consolidated balance sheets

(£'000)	Draft at 31 Aug 2004		Projected at 28 Feb 2005	
Fixed assets		436		447
Stocks	209		210	
Debtors	272		312 *	
Current assets	481		522	
Bank overdraft	243		330	
Creditors	452		405	
Current liabilities		695		735
Net current liabilities		(214)		(213)
Deferred liabilities:				
Tax etc	(72)		(72)	
Loans	(35)	(107)	(23)	(95)
Employment of capital		**115**		**139**
Ordinary shares	1			1
Profit & Loss account	114			138
Capital employed		**115**		**139**

* *Note*: includes USA 100 and Canada 142.

Further analysis of stocks and fixed assets at 31 August 2004 revealed the following:

Stocks and work-in-progress at 31 August 2004 (in £'000s) consisted of Agricultural items 76; Engineering 73; Pigs 56 and Construction 4, making a total of 209. Within this figure work-in-progress amounted to 63.

Fixed assets were also analysed at 31 August 2004 to be:

	wdv b/f	additions	sales	depreciation	wdv c/f
Land	49	3	0	0	52
Buildings	132	89	0	0	221
Plant	96	32	0	19	109
Vehicles	36	30	4	13	49
Fixtures	5	0	0	1	4
Leased fittings	9	0	9	0	0
Totals	**327**	**154**	**13**	**33**	**435**

Retained earnings

Turnover to 31 October had been estimated at £1,330,000 on a group basis. This level of activity is up on the previous year's turnover of just over £1m. As mentioned, no monthly or quarterly profit and loss accounts were at hand and the only basis for a profit projection, therefore, would be an estimate on a historic return of 5% net, giving a projected profit of £66,000, but this is, of course, only feasible if the level of overheads has been contained, and this must be questionable bearing in mind the American and Canadian ventures.

The aim was to project the company's profit and the resulting reserves balance at 28 February 2005 based on the turnover calculation and the assumed net profit percentage. Without a full analysis of overheads, including the North American subsidiaries, it is impossible to conclude that the company would have achieved a net profit percentage of around 5%, which would, on a £1.3m turnover projection, give the required level of profit to increase the reserves to the management figure quoted of £138,000.

The balancing figures on the balance sheet are creditors of £405,000 and the bank overdraft of £330,000. An increased bank facility therefore may be required in part to make a reduction in the creditor balances. The details of the group's retained earnings calculation were as follows:

Agricultural interests	£21k per week x 26 weeks =	546,000
Engineering	£4k per week x 26 weeks =	104,000
Turnover forecast (£)		650,000
Net profit assuming 5% return =		32,500
Less loss on pigs @ 80 x £4k x 26 weeks =		8,300
Net retained earnings		24,200

Debtors

Amount as originally indicated (£)	318,000
Less North American investment balances	125,000
	193,000
Less amount set aside for Provisions	27,000
Debtors total	166,000

Creditors

The total excludes any accruals and PAYE that is estimated to amount to about £30,000. Two writs had recently been issued while Naylor was away in America but these had now been settled.

The North American interests

This business was set up in America in 2004 and currently operates from a factory of 10,000 sq ft in Guttenberg in the State of Iowa. The factory employs 16 people, and they are currently manufacturing two pig units per week. According to Naylor there is great demand for pig housing in America, particularly in Iowa due to the extremes in climatic conditions – the average number of weaners sold per sow per annum is only 14 compared with in excess of 20 weaners per sow per annum being obtained at the demonstration unit at Cliffe. Capital of $177,000 was introduced by Lendal UK and additional capital of $105,000 provided by Double L, an American businessman. At that time, a line of credit of $70,000 was negotiated with the Security State Bank of Iowa, supported by David Ball. It is understood that Ball purchased a small townhouse in Guttenberg for $85,000 on which there is a mortgage of approximately 50%. This house is also held as supporting security by the American bank.

Significant changes have occurred since that date with Double L proving to be unreliable, forcing the company to pay back his capital of $105,000 plus $15,000 for stock, giving a total pay out of USD120,000. This in turn led to an increased line of credit being obtained from the Security State Bank of $130,000, and Naylor stated that this is the maximum that the Security State Bank could lend to a corporate client. Capital employed, shown at $151,000 at the then conversion rate of USD1.42 to the £, gives a net worth figure of £106,000.

The injection of capital into the North American operations, plus the funds needed to buy out Double L, has meant that Naylor is preparing a business plan for when he intends to revisit America in mid to end February, to make a presentation to the Iowa Development Credit Corporation and the Norwest Bank in an endeavour to raise additional monies principally to fund the manufacturing operation in that country.

He hopes to be able to return some capital back to the UK from the funding, but this is unlikely as no bank will be keen to lend additional money for expropriation on this basis.

Management figures have been produced for the North American ventures as at 31 October 2004 as follows:

Canada

Two trial units are located at Calgary to explore the feasibility of marketing sow and early weaning units in Canada. No formation financial statement is yet available for Lendal Agricultural (Canadian) Ltd operation but it is believed that the initial capital will be invested as follows:

David Ball	CAND 25,000 already invested by way of the production units
Pierre Moreau	CAND 10,000
Alan Toles	CAND 10,000

On the basis of a CAND 10,000 investment each, David Ball should have CAND 15,000 to be available to repatriate back to the UK. At a current dollar conversion rate of 1.78, this equates to over £8,000. At this stage there is no intention to manufacture in Canada.

United States of America

A management balance sheet has been produced for the American interests as at 31 October 2004:

Lendal Holdings USA Ltd: Balance Sheet at 31 October 2004

	$000
Sources of capital employed	
Capital provided by Lendal UK	177
Capital provided by Double L	105
	282
Less Setting-up costs	(131)
	151

Application of capital employed

Fixed assets

Leasehold building improvements	36
Plant and equipment	22
Office, fixtures, fittings and furnishings	17
	75

Current assets

Credit on bank current account	6
Stock (ten-week purchases)	172
Debtors (accounts receivable: five-week sales)	85
	264

Current liabilities

Creditors (seven-week purchases)	(118)
Bank loan	(70)
	(188)
Net current assets	**76**
Company net worth	**151**

Accountants conclusion

'It is my opinion that the group's cash resources have been strained to the maximum, with the resulting adverse effect on the bank account balance and creditor position. To summarise, during 2004 the company has expanded their head office; developed the fattening unit at Cleckheaton; developed the demonstration unit at Cliffe; and commenced a manufacturing situation in America with a proposed demonstration unit in Canada.'

Asset 'forced-sale' valuations

Estimates of current day valuations would be as follows.

(£'000)	Book value	Forced sale
Factory unit 40,000 sq ft @ £1 psf approx valued at rental over seven years	<u>280</u>	140
House, 4½ acres of land, and pig accommodation for 176 sows to 11 weeks at £1,000 per sow place	<u>176</u>	<u>50</u>
		190
Debtors as at 31/12/04	318	
Less USA/Canadian	(125)	
Less Provision	<u>(27)</u>	<u>(152)</u>
NET	<u>166</u>	80
Stock	209	
Less Work in progress	<u>(64)</u>	
(Less Romalpa)**	<u>145</u>	<u>50</u>
		320
Less preferential creditors estimated		<u>(30)</u>
(excluding realisation costs)		**290**

* *Note*: fixed assets, plant & machinery and motor vehicles discounted.

** Reservation of title by suppliers – additionally, there is Ball's unlimited guarantee.

Bank Recommendations

Audited accounts to 31 October 2004 are to be produced as a matter of urgency.

Quarterly profit and loss figures, together with a stock take, should be carried out at 31 January 2005 to give an indication of progress for the first three months of the current trading year.

There has been no monitoring of liquidity figures, and this must be set up. An urgent meeting with Ball is recommended to discuss the future of his business connection vis-à-vis the cash flow requirements.

A short-term cash flow forecast must be produced as a matter of urgency to pinpoint the way ahead, as regards cash requirements, bearing in mind the American and UK manufacturing set-ups.

If the company and their advisers are unable to come up with the information that is required, an independent firm of accountants should assist in preparing the information which is desperately needed before it is too late to implement a rescue plan.

The group is highly geared, cash flow is under extreme pressure and expansion must be slowed down, to give the companies time to generate profits and a positive cashflow that should be retained within the business to give it an opportunity to survive.

Case study postscript

The warning signs should have been seen much earlier as the bank account trend showed. Quick remedial action was needed but the cash flow problems, unfortunately, were too severe and too advanced to rescue the company and a few weeks later the borrower went into liquidation.

In retrospect, the bank manager had been lax in keeping up to date with the operations of the group. External financial commitments outside the UK company had not been taken on board. Little apparent monitoring of the group had been done until the UK bank account had shown what is now known as insurmountable difficulties. The profitability of the group and its liquidity position had taken second place to the need to expand sales. The bank had not kept track of its security situation very well.

Case study 8 Ashton Baker Marketing Ltd

Ashton Baker Marketing Ltd was established three years ago by an ex-public company marketing executive, Edward Ashton (41), and Colin Baker (42) who had previously worked for a major advertising agency. The company provides marketing consultancy and research services. The two directors each own 50% of the company. The business got off to a slower start than the directors expected and has only just started to make a profit. They have acquired some top-class clients and 38% of their revenue comes from work undertaken for the British subsidiary of the world's largest soft drinks company. A further 18% comes from a major European food company. At present, they have 15 clients on their books

The company's relationship with the bank has not been an easy one since it was formed. Originally, an overdraft facility of £20,000 was agreed but this had to be increased to £40,000 in 2001 to cover cash flow shortages. A hard core developed, and further pressure on the limit resulted in the bank later switching £20,000 on to a five-year loan, while retaining a £40,000 overdraft limit in return for a full security package of a debenture plus guarantees of £60,000 from each director (supported by second charges over their houses, which have equity elements of £80,000 and £120,000). Since then, the company has honoured the new arrangement, but a further hard core has developed and there is again pressure on the overdraft limit.

The directors call to see you. They are under pressure from creditors to bring payments up to date, and the Inland Revenue in particular is insisting that PAYE dues are kept current. They estimate that they need to add an extra £20,000 on the overdraft limit. They believe the business has turned the corner now because, although their accounts for the year to 30 September 2004 showed only a small profit, performance for the second half of the year was much better:

Six months to 30 September 2004

Turnover	£222,512
Gross profit	£166,875
Net profit	£29,700
Gross profit return on turnover	75%
Net profit return on turnover	13.3%

The directors expect October to be their best month ever because the work-in-progress figure at the end of September was the highest it has ever been at £31,000. This should produce a profit of £6,500 when invoiced. They give you a copy of their 2005 budget that they believe is conservative and ask you to lend the additional £20,000 they need.

As banker, you are asked to analyse the company's financial position and set out, with reasons, the response you would make to the request.

Accounting ratios

As at 30 September	Audited 2002	Audited 2003	Audited 2004	Budget 2005
Net gearing (%)	78%	629%	1,493%	
(Directors' loans taken as capital)				
Current ratio	0.83	0.40	0.65	
Acid test	0.71	0.23	0.42	
Credit given (days)	92	53	66	
Credit taken (days)	242	243	219	
Gross margin (%)	81.5%	75.9%	72.0%	75.5%
Net margin (%)	(15.5%)	(20.7%)	0.4%	15.0%

Profit and loss accounts

Years to 30 September (£'000)	Audited 2002	Audited 2003	Audited 2004	Budget 2005
Turnover	128	208	316	450
Market research costs	24	50	89	110
Gross profit	104	158	227	340
Other overheads	43	45	142	150
Interest paid	6	13	12	4
Depreciation	6	10	17	18
Directors' remuneration	29	47	55	100
Indirect overheads	84	115	226	272
Net profit	20	43	1	68

Balance sheets

As at 30 September (£'000)	Audited 2002	Audited 2003	Audited 2004	Budget 2005
Fixed assets				
Leasehold improvements	19	18	16	
Fixtures and fittings	24	25	23	
Motor vehicles	18	54	41	
Trademarks	–	<u>6</u>	<u>6</u>	
Total written down value	<u>61</u>	<u>103</u>	<u>86</u>	
Work in progress	6	21	31	
Debtors	32	30	57	
Cash	<u>2</u>	-	-	
Current assets	<u>40</u>	<u>51</u>	<u>88</u>	
Creditors	(16)	(33)	(53)	
Bank	(17)	(40)	(41)	
Hire purchase		(5)	(15)	(13)
Directors' loans	(7)	(19)	(1)	
VAT and PAYE	<u>(3)</u>	<u>(22)</u>	<u>(28)</u>	
Current liabilities	**<u>(48)</u>**	**<u>(129)</u>**	**<u>(136)</u>**	
Net current liabilities	**(8)**	**(78)**	**(48)**	
Bank loan	–	–	(17)	
Hire purchase		<u>(15)</u>	<u>(30)</u>	<u>(17)</u>
Term liabilities	**<u>(15)</u>**	**<u>(30)</u>**	**<u>(34)</u>**	
Employment of capital	**<u>38</u>**	**<u>(5)</u>**	**<u>4</u>**	
Share capital	58	58	67	
Profit and loss account	<u>(20)</u>	<u>(63)</u>	<u>(62)</u>	
Capital employed	**<u>38</u>**	**<u>(5)</u>**	**<u>5</u>**	

Suggested answer

This question concerned an under capitalised new venture that had hit problems.

The bank has seen the business through its difficult early stages and if possible will want to maintain the relationship into better times if indeed they are reached. The directors have good experience of marketing and ought to complement each other well, but they had little previous experience of running their own business.

The fact that they have been able to recruit some very high-profile top-name customers is a good indication of the professional quality of their work, but having so much of their turnover in the hands of a very few customers is a significant risk. There could also be a temptation to under price work for such high-profile customers.

The directors do not appear to have been good predictors of their performance in the past and the relationship has already been fraught with difficulty for the bank as past arrangements have scarcely been honoured. The directors' problems with the Inland Revenue could be serious and certainly will be if a satisfactory payment arrangement is not established and adhered to.

The current capital structure of the business is poor with an almost total reliance on borrowed funds to provide finance. Despite the previous injection of capital and the profit made in 2004, the shareholders' investment is reduced because of the withdrawal of their loans and sizeable annual remuneration drawings rather than leaving money in the business. The directors' loan withdrawal, in fact, seems to equate to the cash shortfall in the business so the directors have been putting themselves before the needs of the business.

Liquidity is also poor, although it has shown an improvement in 2004 with both the current ratio and acid test getting better. The underlying problem is that there are more current assets to finance as turnover expands; so that with the bank facility fixed, the strain has been taken by the creditors who are clearly getting restless.

Profitability at the net level is extremely thin and is heavily dependent on the directors' valuation of work-in-progress. With so much of the total cost base fixed, the gross margin is extremely healthy and suggests that if the business can indeed increase sales significantly and permanently then there should be good profits flowing through to the bottom line. This assumes that the overheads are indeed fixed, which may be debatable in this type of business.

The sales target does not look unreasonable given recent performance although the directors should be limiting their remuneration allotment until the business becomes more stable and liquidity improves.

The bank needs to see detailed figures to verify that the proposed additional £20,000 facility is going to be sufficient to ensure that the business can survive its present cash shortfall crisis. This information should include aged analysis of debtors and creditors together with a detailed cash flow forecast. Given the directors' lack of financial sophistication, outside accountants ought to be involved and there is a case for a really detailed investigation.

Increased personal guarantees are required from the directors' (if they are not open-ended) with updated valuations of their homes. It is difficult to value the debenture: the debtors are of good standing but there could be counter claims for breach of contract given the small number of customers involved that would have a major impact on profitability. The policy of the major customers should be ascertained: is it their strategy to change marketing firms regularly and frequently?

The request to the bank is clearly unwelcome at the current time but the bank is effectively locked in. Provided an independent investigation is agreed and verifies the forecasts, the bank will probably be willing to stay involved given the extent of the equity in the directors' homes. The business is basically under-capitalised and it would be best for all concerned if the directors found a new equity partner to ease the pressures.

The alternative is for the directors themselves to raise further permanent capital by re-mortgaging their properties. What other suitable assets do they hold to re-finance the business? Perhaps a 50:50 injection of money equally from the directors and the bank could be arranged. A meeting with the directors showing them an analysis where the cash has gone and suggesting how the cash shortfall might be met other than wholly from the bank could be a positive step.

Case study 9   Western Trading Company Ltd

The Western Trading Company Ltd designs and sells men's fashion clothing mainly to leading retailers who operate through a number of High Street outlets. The garments are manufactured by sub-contractors, held in stock by them, and delivered direct to the stores. The directors have become disenchanted with their present bankers and have called to ask whether you would be prepared to take over the company's account and grant an overdraft facility of £100,000 to meet an expanding order book. The company commenced trading on 1 March 2003 and the directors have provided you with audited accounts for their first year along with draft figures for the following six months. The company does not produce management accounts.

All invoices are factored and the factoring company advances up to 55% of the company's outstanding debtors. This relatively low percentage takes into account a number of small customers that have been rejected by the factoring company for an advance. It has a charge on book debts. In conversation with the directors, you establish that the factoring company has refused to increase its lending percentage and that the overdraft is needed to meet future expansion needs. Its present bank has refused to grant an overdraft above £10,000 due to the factoring commitment. The directors are willing to give you a debenture (ranking behind the factoring company facility) and their personal guarantees for £100,000 to support the proposed facility.

Accounting ratios	28 February 2004	31 August 2004
Net gearing % *	–	313%
Current ratio	1.01	1.07
Acid test	0.73	0.73
Credit given (days)	107	71
Credit taken (days)	198	65
Stock turnover (days)	65	42
Gross margin %	21.6%	22.7%
Net margin %	2.6%	4.4%
Interest cover (times)	3.7	7.1

Balance sheets

as at (£'000)	28 February 2004 **Actual**	31 August 2004 **Draft**
Fixed assets		
Leasehold improvements	2	2
Motor vehicles	10	13
Fixtures and fittings	7	16
Book written down value	**19**	**31**
Stock	106	203
Debtors	223	438
Cash	58	1
Current assets	**387**	**642**
Factoring advances	(40)	(232)
Creditors	(325)	(312)
VAT	(8)	(37)
Directors' loans *	(5)	(5)
Overdraft	–	(9)
Tax	(6)	(6)
Current liabilities	**(384)**	**(601)**
Net current assets	3	41
Employment of capital	22	72
Financed by:		
Share capital	5	5
Profit and loss account	17	67
Capital employed	**22**	**72**

* *Note*: Directors' loans are treated as capital

Profit and loss accounts	28 February 2004	31 August 2004
(£'000)	Actual – year	Draft – 6 months
Sales	763	1,129
Purchases	(598)	(873)
Gross profit	165	256
Expenses include:		
Directors' remuneration	(26)	(17)
Interest paid	(7)	(8)
Profit before tax	20	50

Required

Analyse the business and state with reasons your response to the borrowing request.

Suggested solution

This business is being offered to the bank 'off the street' so caution is needed. This is particularly important since the company has been trading for only a very short time. During this period the achievement of the directors in building up sales is not inconsiderable: they must have flair and/or marketing skills and/or original connections. The fact that they have obtained a factoring facility for a 'rag trade' business – a type of business that factors do not like – says something about their persuasiveness. It also reflects a reasonable degree of financial sophistication because the company would not have been able to obtain finance to the extent it has in any other way. The fashion clothing business is a high-risk industry with many failures, so the lack of a formal plan and projections/management accounts for the future is a concern.

Looking at the historic accounts, it needs to be appreciated that this is a seasonal business with spring and autumn peaks that could affect ratio comparison, although in this instance the dates are probably at similar points for their relative seasons. The business at that time was very liquid, partly as a result of the high gearing. In fact, the business would probably collapse if the factoring facility were to be withdrawn. The gearing and liquidity position worsens over the following six months as the business expands.

At the end of February 2004, in effect, creditors and VAT due were funding outstanding debtors and the stock held. By August there was a big discrepancy with this position. All the indications are that the borrowing requirement will increase steadily with further expansion and this now needs to be controlled urgently. The factoring facility has already virtually reached its maximum limit. Any further sales increase will have to be funded 45% from other sources of finance.

The gross profit margin has held up well given the rapid expansion, and the improvement reported in the net profit margin suggests a good control of overheads. The interest cover has also improved significantly, but if the company borrows a further £100,000 this is likely to drop back to near its February 2004 level. Directors' remuneration drawn has been modest and suggests a willingness to curb pay while the company is suffering a liquidity problem.

The security offered to the bank is unlikely to be adequate. Lending against a second charge on debtors behind a factoring company is highly unattractive. If 55% lending is safe for the factors (who have first hand information on the potential debtors' risk) points against the bank increasing the company's borrowing exposure at this time. Effectively the bank will be lending against the fashion stock, that in all likelihood will have to be heavily discounted in a receivership. There is no clue what the directors' guarantees are worth and background information on their track record is sketchy. Neither of these assets will be attractive security unless supported by a formal charge on readily realisable security.

The business overall holds potential to succeed but its expansion is out of control and the bank should be in no hurry to become a lender. Any further working capital need ought to be financed by the factoring company or the directors themselves. It might be worth having our own bank's factoring company examine the debtors ledger to see if a higher percentage advance is possible. A further alternative might be to reconsider the proposition under the terms of the Government's Small Firms Loan Guarantee Scheme. The company would be eligible for an advance as it is not acting primarily as an intermediary agency between sellers and buyers but is owning the stocks for resale and providing added-value to its service.

Case study 10   James the Grocer Ltd

James the Grocer wishes to expand his retail supermarket business by acquiring the premises next door. The cost of the new premises will be £75,000 and he is requesting a loan of £45,000. It is anticipated that extra costs including legal fees, building renovations and shop fittings will amount to £11,000. You are asked to consider whether the company can afford to borrow £56,000 given that the interest rate on the loan will be 10% pa. This is a modest loan proposal of a type that is met quite frequently. Recent accounts of the business disclose the following:

Balance sheets

(£'000) audited figures	Two years ago	Last year	This year
Goodwill at cost	20	20	20
Leasehold improvements at cost	2	2	2
Shop fitting at wdv *	17	14	13
Motor van at wdv *	<u>4</u>	<u>3</u>	<u>2</u>
Fixed assets	<u>**43**</u>	<u>**39**</u>	<u>**37**</u>
Current assets			
Stock	22	25	34
Debtors	12	15	18
Cash and bank	<u>7</u>	<u>15</u>	<u>22</u>
	<u>**41**</u>	<u>**55**</u>	<u>**74**</u>
Current liabilities			
Creditors	50	55	66
Accrued expenses	5	7	6
Corporation tax	<u>2</u>	<u>2</u>	<u>3</u>
	<u>**57**</u>	<u>**64**</u>	<u>**75**</u>
Net current liabilities	<u>**16**</u>	<u>**9**</u>	<u>**1**</u>
Employment of capital	<u>**27**</u>	<u>**30**</u>	<u>**36**</u>
Financed by:			
Share capital	15	15	15
Retained profits	<u>12</u>	<u>16</u>	<u>21</u>
Capital employed	<u>**27**</u>	<u>**31**</u>	<u>**36**</u>

* The written down value of assets is shown after deducting depreciation. In this example no depreciation of goodwill or improvements to the leasehold premises have been made.

Profit and loss accounts

(£'000) audited figures	Two years ago	Last year	This year
Sales	451	511	593
Cost of goods sold	384	439	515
Gross profit	67	72	79
Gross profit margin	*14.8%*	*14.1%*	*13.3%*
Rent	17	17	17
Wages and National Insurance	20	21	24
Sundry other costs	14	14	15
Directors' remuneration	9	11	12
Depreciation	3	3	3
Indirect costs	63	66	71
Net profit before tax	4	6	8
Corporation tax	2	2	3
Retained profit for the year	2	4	5
Retained profits brought forward	10	12	16
Retained profits carried forward	12	16	21

Suggested solution

The project is to take the opportunity of acquiring the premises next door in order to expand the retail supermarket business. At first glance, the balance sheets show an adverse liquidity position (current assets minus current liabilities). This can be typical of many retail supermarkets where the stock is being turned over quicker than the payment terms to suppliers. Also, there is a healthy and accumulating cash balance. Net worth is improving through profit retentions and the business has no bank debt.

Turning to trading; although sales have been increasing there has been a small deterioration in the gross profit margin, possibly due to more sales occurring at lower margins or a more competitive pricing strategy. The resultant profits are low and may not be sufficient to meet the projected annual loan costs of £5,600 before repayments are charged. If the loan principal is to be repaid over 15 years, this cost would add a further £3,700 to the finance charge. The requested loan is nearly double the projected profit retention and the resulting increase in sales to meet this cost would be considerable without allowing for the risk of fluctuations in sales due to any future drop in custom and takings.

On the other hand James has been a long-standing customer and upon enquiry he explains that the present business advertising of £4,000 pa will not recur (will this lead to a fall in sales?) and he is, of course, expecting extra sales from the expanded unit space. Restating the profit and adding back depreciation will generate sufficient cash flow to service the loan.

It should be suggested to James that his accountant provide a forecast of trading assuming that the acquisition proceeds. This will include projecting sales growth due to use of the increased shop area and making any allowance for increased overheads on the new premises eg rates. Acquisition of the premises next door will provide the security of a freehold asset that can be taken as security for the loan advance. Providing the trading projections are conservatively based and there are no external factors likely to affect future business (eg competition), and if the additional loan interest and repayment amount is suitably covered by cash flow (ie projected retained earnings plus depreciation), the request should be viewed sympathetically.

Case study 11   Tubular Glass Ltd

Tubular Glass Ltd has banked with you for over 25 years. It manufactures and sells specialist glassware products, which are used to measure liquids to a high degree of accuracy. The main customers are scientific laboratories, universities, schools etc. Over recent years, the company has suffered increased competition from plastic products which, although less accurate in detail, are much cheaper to make and distribute. Packaging is a major cost for the company. Losses have been made but, notwithstanding this, the company has stayed comfortably within its overdraft limit of £350,000. A hard core of £200,000 has now developed, however, and is increasing in size.

The original founder of the company, John Tumbler, is 75. He remains a director, but following his resignation as chairman in March 2003, he no longer takes an active part in its management. The current chairman and managing director is John's son, Michael Tumbler, aged 50. John is steadily transferring his shares in the company to Michael, who now owns 60% to John's 40%.

Although Michael has worked in the company all his working life, he feels that he has not been allowed by his father to fulfil his potential. He believes the company has stagnated recently and needs to change. He is introducing a new packaging system that is cheaper to implement and his aim is to improve gross margins in the 2005 financial year. He has also been talking to the public company that owns Tubular's biggest UK competitor for glass products. It is willing to sell this business to Tubular. The new business will be integrated within Tubular's existing leasehold premises, where there is surplus capacity. Michael Tumbler believes the costs of integration will be as follows:

Additional costs post acquisition

(£'000)		Purchase cost
Goodwill		15
Plant and machinery purchased		31
Patents taken over at valuation		8
Stock purchased		85
Legal and professional costs re acquisition		10
Working capital requirement:		
Debtors 72 less Creditors 12 =	60	
Initial operating one-off expenses	n/a	60
Total finance required		**209**
Proposed funding: increase in bank overdraft		**200**

Additional sales and profits should be produced over the next two years following the integration of the acquisition over and above those forecast in the company's 2005 budget. To support the requested increase in the overdraft limit from £350,000 to £550,000 the bank will be relying on a debenture over the company's assets together with an unlimited guarantee and second charge on Michael Tumbler's residence that has an estimated equity value of £75,000.

Additional sales and profits forecast post-acquisition

Profit and loss accounts

(£'000)	Year 1		Year 2	
Sales	**463**		**400**	
Direct cost of sales		300		240
Gross profit	**163**		**160**	
Gross margin %	35.2		40.0	
Indirect overheads		129		79
Profit before tax	**34**		**81**	
Net profit margin %		7.3		20.3

The company has a year end on 31 March and recent results and forecasts together with various accounting ratios were as follows:

Profit and loss accounts

(£'000)	2002	2003	2004	2005
	Audited	Audited	Audited	Budget
Sales	**2,158**	**1,811**	**2,074**	**2,181**
Cost of sales	1,421	1,261	1,375	1,321
Gross profit	**737**	**550**	**699**	**860**
Indirect overheads	591	621	573	571
Interest paid	22	12	15	17
Directors' remuneration	163	178	181	185
Net profit/(loss) pre-tax	**(39)**	**(261)**	**(70)**	**84**

Accounting ratios	2002	2003	2004	2005
	Audited	Audited	Audited	Budget
Net gearing (%)	24	44	42	
Current ratio	2.85	2.08	2.22	
Acid test	1.08	0.88	1.10	
Credit given (days)	80	105	97	
Credit taken (days)	151	162	179	
Stock turnover (days)	200	203	149	
Gross margin (%)	34.1	30.4	33.7	39.5
Net margin (%)	(1.8)	(14.4)	(3.4)	3.8
Interest cover (times)	–	–	–	5.8

Balance sheets	**2002**	**2003**	**2004**	**2005**
(£'000)	31 March	31 March	31 March	31 March
Fixed assets				
Plant and machinery	**212**	**193**	**228**	
Debtors	474	520	554	
Stock	780	702	563	
Current assets	**1,254**	**1,222**	**1,117**	
Creditors	153	185	196	
Hire purchase	43	31	36	
Bank	173	310	192	
Tax	71	62	80	
Current liabilities	**440**	**588**	**504**	
Net current assets	**814**	**634**	**613**	
Hire purchase	22	11	83	
Deferred taxation	12	10	–	
Long-term liabilities	**34**	**21**	**83**	
Employment of capital	**992**	**806**	**758**	
Financed by:				
Share capital	100	100	100	
Profit and loss account	892	706	658	
Capital employed	**992**	**806**	**758**	

Required

Set out your analysis of the company and its plans. Give, with reasons, the response you would make to the request for an increased overdraft.

Suggested solution

Managing succession in a family business can be difficult and this question also had to contend with the problems of an under-performing family business. The bank would want to be positive about a long-standing customer but the business has clearly been suffering for a number of years.

The son has blamed his father for the deterioration in the company's fortunes but he must shoulder part of the responsibility for past losses, as he has been involved in the company's management for some years. It is positive that he is prepared to implement change and some of the benefit has already been seen with the reduced loss reported for 2004. The effect of the new packaging system has yet to be seen, however, and his acquisition proposal will, among other things, put a strain on resources. The strategy of the proposal and its trading advantages need to be examined further. Is acquiring a bigger share of a shrinking market the answer? Might not diversification be a better strategy?

Despite the company's decline in fortunes, the balance sheet remains quite strong. Gearing is only 42% with a significant element of borrowing being term debt. The proposed acquisition would reduce the capital base more through the intangible asset (goodwill) and acquisition expenses involved, while extra borrowing would adversely hit gearing (although a best estimate places this at around 77% (debt 585 v net worth 758), which is acceptable in the short term).

Liquidity shown by the current ratio and the acid test is good, but the evidence is that the cash position will continue to erode. The hard core borrowing and credit taken may be expected to increase. Some management improvements undertaken by the son, such as the better stock turnover trend in 2004, auger well for the future but there remain many questions unanswered and unproven. If future sales post acquisition rise by £400,000+ the projections do not indicate an improved gross profit percentage return. Can the additional profit earned before tax achieve a 20% return on sales by year two?

While profitability remains poor, the 2004 sales performance and improved gross margin are encouraging signs in a difficult marketplace. Further sales increases intrinsic to the budget may be tough to achieve and cost savings inherent to the packaging change will be crucial in achieving profitability. Can more be done to reduce overheads? The directors' remuneration looks generous, particularly now that the father makes little contribution to the business, but perhaps the son requires sufficient drawings to purchase more shares from his father.

Examining the acquisition, the price (as represented by the goodwill and net assets acquired) is attractive to Tubular Glass if the long-term profit forecasts are realistic. The financial accounts for the business to be acquired must be viewed and enquiry made whether some due diligence will be performed prior to the purchase. Tubular Glass itself is forecasting a very minor sales growth for the current year. Why is this? Will these factors (eg lack of external demand) be suffered also by the business offered for sale? If synergies can be achieved and profit as forecast is added to the existing business, the deal will be beneficial.

The bank should revalue its security cover on the assumption that the proposed acquisition proceeds. No forced break-up valuations have been calculated. The debenture cover may be broadly calculated as follows:

Break-up projections	Prop'n of book value	Book value 2004 + acq'n	Forced sale values
(£'000)			
Stocks	33.3%	650	217
Debtors	66.6%	650	433
Plant & machinery	20%	260	<u>52</u>
Assets			702
Less current liabilities excluding bank			<u>392</u>
Net assets excluding bank			310
Bank exposure: 350 + 200 =			<u>550</u>
Forced sale company valuation deficit (projected)			<u>240</u> *

* Before deducting the equity (75) in the house and any guarantee proceeds.

The proposition is marginal based on all the available financial information that has been supplied. Before a positive response is considered the bank should obtain answers to the many questions that have been raised; in particular this includes receiving full information on the proposed acquisition and verification of all the trading projections put forward to support the loan request. The potential lack of adequate security is a worry, but if this is believed to be temporary (as profit improves) the trading outlook should take precedence in this case (refer to the next paragraph).

A factoring/invoice discounting facility should be considered for a large portion of the requirement if the debtor book is acceptable. For example, a debtor book of £433,000 that can be discounted to raise 70% (say £300,000) would allow the overdraft to be renegotiated down to £250,000 secured on forced-sale values (s above) of stocks and plant amounting to £269,000. The hard core borrowing should only be considered after the acquisition has had time to be implemented and the financial projections proven.

Finally, there is the family succession situation. Will the father continue to support his son in the major developments that are arising? Some guidance is required that this will be so. What other future strategies has the son for the business? What is the outlook for glassware rather than plastics? Will the son be trying to improve the gross profit margins on the traditional Tubular Glass products? What will be the son's strategy for sales? Does he realise the effects on liquidity of over-trading?

Case study 12   Zhin Nursing Home Project

The following case study features the development of a 72-bedroomed nursing home. Study the project carefully. How would you respond to this request?

Background

Mr Zhin is known to you as a property investor who banks with a competitor. He is said to own properties totalling around £1m. Details of his outstanding commitments are not known. Zhin calls to see you to advise that he has acquired a property, just outside the city, for £400,000. The site is substantial and he has obtained planning permission to demolish and rebuild a 72-bedroom nursing home on the land. With the help of his business consultant, he has prepared a projected profit and loss; projected balance sheet; various notes to the balance sheet and assumptions behind the projections.

The project costs, including a six-month roll up of interest, total £1,680,000. Mr Zhin has £324,000 that he can invest. He requests a loan of £1,356,000 repayable over 20 years together with a temporary overdraft of £60,000 for the first twelve months.

Profit and loss accounts – project forecasts

Years ending 30 June	2005	2006
(£'000)	Forecast	Forecast
Fee income	**782**	**955**
Less: Salaries and National Insurance	318	343
Food and medical supplies (adjusted for stock)	57	47
Advertising	14	6
Other overheads (itemised)	36	61
Bank interest & charges	6	2
Depreciation	29	29
Net profit before loan interest	322	467
Less Loan interest	108	103
Retained profit for the year before tax	**214**	**364**

Balance sheets – project forecasts

As at 30 June	**2005**			**2006**	
(£'000)	Forecast			Forecast	
Fixed assets	cost	cost			
Land & buildings	1,480			1,480	
Interest capitalised	56	1,536		56	1,536
Fixtures & fittings	144			144	
Depreciation	29	115		57	87
Net book value		1,651			1,623
Stock (medicines & food)	2	2			
Cash at bank	176			501	
Current assets	178			503	
Less expense accruals	2	176		2	501
Employment of capital		**1,827**			**2,124**
Financed by:					
Long-term loan		1,289			1,222
Capital account		538			902 *
Capital employed	**1,827**			**2,124**	

* *Notes:* Cash introduced 324 + profit 214 = 538 + profit 364 = 902
Loan advanced 1,356 less repaid 67 = 1,289 less repaid 67 = 1,222

Profit projections

The major assumptions underlying the profit projections for the two years 2005 and 2006 are:

1. Fee income: each resident pays £250 per week in cash and the number of residents will be 25 month 1; 40 month 2; 50 month 3; 60 month 4; and 68 for months thereafter out of a maximum 72 beds available (94% occupancy).
2. Food and medicine has been assumed at £15 per resident per week and the business will pay cash and not incur creditors for any purchases made.
3. Salaries and wages have been included based upon the size of the home and current levels of pay in the industry, with PAYE and National Insurance paid during the same month as the salaries from which they have been deducted.
4. The nursing home has been classified as exempt from business rates.
5. Loan repayments have been calculated over 20 years on a straight line basis, with interest due on the outstanding balance at the commencement of each year at 8% APR.

6. Drawings have been excluded as the proprietor has means of support from his other business interests.
7. It has been assumed that the business will not incur any significant maintenance costs during the first two years following the initial conversion of the property to a nursing home.

Suggested discussion points

Who is Mr Zhin? Why has he approached us and not his own bank? Is he really worth £1 million? What are his current loan commitments? What is his track record? What experience does he have in running a nursing home? Why can he only afford to invest £324,000 in the project?

As to the project itself: the initial debt looks very high, although payback from cash flow is rapid. The payback is, of course, very dependent on the take up of residents, which is stated at 68 residents after only four months. It all looks just too good with a cash positive position of £501,000 at the end of the second year.

The points to enquire about are:

- The occupancy rate peaks in a short period of time at 94%. Has research been done to substantiate this demand? The total of staff salaries charged do not appear to have matched this expansion. Has Mr Zhin obtained formal authority to cater for 72 residents?
- At the start of the project the borrowings will comprise 84% (1,416 v 1,680) of total costs. The usual borrowing multiple based on property assets is around two-thirds of cost ie £1 million. Will there be an uplift to the value of the property to £2.12 million when built so that two-thirds of this revaluation meets the cash requirement of £1.416 million?
- Is any part of the income arising from residents contracted with Local Authorities to give some support to the forward projection of receipts? Why has no allowance been given to late paying residents? One can hardly throw a resident out on the street. What form of contract has been raised with the close relations to settle any outstanding debts?
- The proper management of the nursing home will be crucial to its success and retention of its operating certificate. Will suitably qualified staff be easily recruited and has their expense been fully covered in the cost projections?
- If the bank is satisfied that its interest charges and loan repayments can be accommodated out of trading income, and a loan advance of two-thirds the property value is acceptable, Mr Zhin will be required to invest around £700,000 to meet all the project costs. Is he willing to meet this liability?
- The need for a 20 year loan appears ill-founded if the cash flow is as positive as forecast after just the second year's trading. A monthly cash flow forecast is necessary to discover the maximum borrowing requirement before the project reaches cash break-even point.

If the suggested high profitability of the nursing home can be confirmed to the bank's satisfaction and sufficient security can be offered at outset, perhaps from Mr Zhin's other commercial enterprises, the granting of a short-term overdraft may be possible. Much will depend on the answers to the many questions that have been posed.

Case study 13   Block Builders Ltd

David Block and his sister, Sally, are aged 36 and 34 respectively and have been customers at your branch for many years. They are both university graduates. David qualified as a building engineer and worked for major house builders for eight years, planning and supervising site work. Sally qualified as an architect and worked in private practice for six years. Five years ago, David and Sally decided to form their own building business, Block Builders Limited.

The business has gone well and the directors have proved that they can handle the practical problems involved in running a small building company. The work they have done has included both contracting (house extensions, alterations, office refurbishment, etc) and new house building (mostly under contract for private customers and small developers). In the last year they have acquired a plot of land, obtained planning permission and built four small, detached, houses as a speculative development. The development is now nearly complete, with two of the houses contracted for sale at £160,000 each and considerable interest being shown in the remaining two at the same price.

The market for this type of house in the area is buoyant. The Blocks are aware that a small school near to their existing development has closed and is being sold by the local authority. There is land attached to the school on which they could build four further houses similar to the ones just completed. The local authority has indicated that it would look favourably on granting planning permission for building on the land.

On the basis of this information, the Blocks have decided they must act quickly to buy the school and attached land and have exchanged contracts at a price of £300,000, paying a 10% deposit with completion in one month's time. They call to see you early in 2005 and request a £200,000 increase to their overdraft limit to £275,000.

£	Costs	Income
Purchase of school and land (10% paid)	270,000	
Building cost/sale of four new houses	400,000	720,000
		£260,000
Site Services requirement	55,000	
Conversion of the school into a house	75,000	200,000
	800,000	**920,000**

The current limit on the account is £75,000 and is fully drawn. It is secured by a debenture and unlimited directors' guarantees. The 10% deposits paid on the two houses contracted for sale from the first development have already been credited to the account and completion is scheduled for three weeks' time.

Required:

To consider the Blocks' request and give, with reasons, your response.

Balance sheet

(£'000) as at 31 Dec	2002		2003		2004	
Plant and machinery		32		54		56
Vehicles		10		18		19
Fixed assets		**42**		**72**		**75**
Work in progress	145		143		193	
Land held for development		–		–		36
Debtors	115		106		113	
Current assets		**260**		**249**		**342**
Creditors	90		73		91	
Tax	9		24		25	
Hire purchase	6		14		9	
Bank	62		36		75	
Current liabilities		**167**		**147**		**200**
Net assets		93		102		142
Employment of capital		**135**		**174**		**217**
Financed by:						
Share capital		2		2		2
Retained profits		132		173		216
Capital employed		**134**		**175**		**218**

Profit and loss

(£'000) years ended 31 December	**2002**		**2003**		**2004**	
Turnover	620		834		780	
Operating costs	<u>587</u>		<u>771</u>		<u>711</u>	
Profit before tax		**33**		**63**		**69**
Accounting ratios						
Gearing *	51%		29%		39%	
Pre-tax profit margin on turnover		5.3		7.5		8.8

* Gearing calculated as total borrowings divided by capital employed (net worth).

The Blocks have been good customers whom we would wish to help. Unusually for the building business, they are very well qualified theoretically as well as practically. They have been rather impetuous in contracting to buy the school before talking to the bank and from the bank's point of view this is a 'fait accompli', putting them in an uncomfortable financial position if the bank is unwilling to agree to provide development finance.

There are some positive signs to the project(s): the proposed development is very similar to one the Blocks have just carried out and handled successfully. The market place is buoyant for this type of house and the company's own recent sales are evidence of this. In financial terms the business has performed well to report growing profits and achieving a capital base of £218,000 in five years. A gearing of around 40% is modest for a building company, suggesting competent management in the past.

The overdraft increase requested does not fit the summary cash flow calculation. Providing the sales of the two houses for £320,000 go ahead, this money will be received within three weeks and the balance of £270,000 due on the purchase of the school is scheduled for completion within four weeks. An increase in the overdraft limit of at least £425,000 would appear more appropriate (refer table following). The bank can then make it conditional for the increase in the overdraft to be repaid out of the sale proceeds from the two remaining houses built under project one and the converted school. This would also have the benefit, from the bank's view, of deferring costs on the speculative building of new houses under project two until the earlier proceeds were received.

Estimated cash flow schedule

(£'000)	**Actual**	**Projected**
Present overdrawn balance (historically)	(75)	(75)
Project One: Sale of two houses	320	320
Sale of remaining two houses		320
Project Two: Purchase/refurbish of school	(345)	(345)
Proceeds from sale		200
Building four houses/services	(400)	(400)
Proceeds from sale		720
Cash net (outflow)/inflow	**(500)**	**740**
Current overdraft limit	(75)	
Excess borrowing requirement (refer text)	**(425)**	

If the Blocks intend to continue with their existing contracting business following the first and second projects, their future working capital needs will need to be taken into account when setting a new overdraft limit. This will require a more detailed monthly cash flow projection with suitable operating assumptions as to income and expenditure. Assuming both projects are completed and sold, the net worth of the business will have changed to the following:

Net Worth as at 31 December 2004:	**£ 000**	
Capital employed per balance sheet	218	
Add Profits from project one (320 + 320 =)	640	
Add Profits from project two (720 + 200 – 345 – 400 =)	175	
Book net worth (excludes profits earned since 31 December)	1,033	
Less reduction on forced sale; Plant (80% x 75)	60	
Debtors (67% x 113)	75	
Work-in-progress (say 90%)	175	310
Projected break-up value	**723**	
Borrowing limit: (as requested)		**275**

The security position for the bank based on the above figures shows a gearing of 38% (275/723), although this would increase temporarily to 69% (500/723) based on all the income and cost projections being achieved. A very low realisation value has been taken for work-in-progress on the assumption that a new owner post a liquidation sale of the company may have to incur significant costs in completing the building work. These costs would include re-employing new sub-contractors and obtaining new supplies of materials and perhaps lodging new plans requiring drawings and planning approval.

Most of the company's work has a relatively short life to completion except for financing land for future development. It is assumed that Block Builders will not be tendering for more risky fixed price contracts in future and that the types of work undertaken will continue to offer a similar gross profit margin. The bank should discuss with the company its policy of operating through an employed work force rather than using sub-contractors that can be laid off if continuing work is not at hand.

As the company is now going into speculative development, it is time to tighten up the bank's monitoring procedures: lending should be on separate loan accounts for each project with drawdowns for approved work in progress made following site visits. There will probably be a need also for some sort of overdraft for the continuing contract business.

The request for additional credit is acceptable in principal, but there are a number of aspects that the bank should first enquire on and a meeting should be initiated with the directors to agree to a more suitable borrowing limit together with the better restructuring of the company's facilities in future.

Case study 14   Milner Construction Ltd

Milner Construction Ltd is a firm of contracting builders. The company was established in 1987 and has banked with you since its formation. The founders of the company, Michael Milner and Patrick Greenwood, own all the shares. They are both now in their 40s. They were originally bricklayers and, at first, the company supplied bricklaying services to house builders. As the business grew, the company undertook a wider range of activities: supplying materials, scaffolding, etc as well as labour. Although, at one stage, the company had 120 employees, most workers are now subcontracted on a self-employed basis, leaving just ten full-time employees. The company is now mainly a sub-contractor for large building companies on major construction contracts such as office blocks and shopping centres. Milner's normal minimum contract size is £300,000.

The company currently has an overdraft facility of £500,000 and a separate bond/guarantee limit with the bank of £300,000. As security, the bank holds a debenture that includes a first charge over the company's freehold office building, which was valued at £250,000 three years ago. There are also directors' unlimited guarantees, supported by the equity in their residences totaling £260,000. Six years ago, the company decided to expand into Europe and established a subsidiary in France. This venture was not a success and earlier this year the company closed the subsidiary down and wrote off its investment.

The 2004 audited accounts are now available. The directors call to see you to discuss their requirements for the next 12 months. The company has never produced management accounts or formal forecasts, although its 'back of the envelope' assessments have, in the past, been reasonably accurate. The company currently has underway, or has won, contracts to the value of £1.6m that the directors believe will produce a net profit of £250,000 in the current financial year. In addition, they have a good chance of winning a contract worth £1m in the next 12 months as a subcontractor to one of the UK's largest building developers. This contract will require a performance bond of 15% of the contract value.

The company is fully utilising the current £300,000 bonding facility and is also making full use of the overdraft facility. The directors ask the bank to increase the overdraft limit to £600,000 and the bonds/guarantees limit to £450,000. (The company to date has never had a claim under any performance bond issued on its behalf.)

Required

The current position of the company should be analysed and reasons given as to the response you would make to the borrowing request.

Profit and loss accounts

(£'000) years to 31 July	2002	2003	2004
Turnover	**2,103**	**2,213**	**3,638**
Direct operating costs	1,735	1,806	2,880
Gross profit	**368**	**407**	**758**
Depreciation	27	38	47
Directors' remuneration	96	130	222
Interest paid	51	64	79
Profit before tax	**130**	**120**	**292**
Extraordinary item:			
write off of investment in subsidiary	–	–	359
Taxation	36	50	162
Retained profit/(loss)	**94**	**70**	**(230)**

Accounting ratios

Gross profit margin on turnover		17.5%	18.4%	20.8%
Profit before tax margin on turnover		6.2%	5.4%	8.0%
Interest cover on pre-interest profit (times) 3.5		2.9	4.7	
Gearing on capital employed		92%	122%	312%
Current ratio		0.85	0.95	1.06
Acid test ratio		0.61	0.71	0.70
Credit given (days)		59	93	80
Credit taken (days)		48	47	58
Work-in-progress turnover (days)		28	38	52

Balance sheets

(£'000) as at 31 July	2002	2003	2004
Land and buildings	135	135	133
Plant and machinery	135	110	131
Investment in subsidiary	290	329	0
Fixed assets	**560**	**575**	**264**
Work in progress	132	189	412
Debtors	341	562	796
Cash	0	1	1
Current assets	**473**	**752**	**1,209**
Creditors	227	232	457
Hire purchase	22	18	25
Bank overdraft	226	445	540
Current taxation	83	101	118
Current liabilities	**558**	**796**	**1,140**
Net current assets/(liabilities)	**(85)**	**(44)**	**69**
Term liability:			
Hire purchase	**(100)**	**(83)**	**(115)**
Employment of capital	**375**	**448**	**218**
Financed by:			
Share capital	0.1	0.1	0.1
Profit and loss account	375	448	218
Capital employed	**375**	**448**	**218**

Suggested answer

The company is a long-standing customer that the bank will want to help if possible. The management are experienced in the business but they do not have an unblemished track record. The French venture has been a disaster. Despite this the core business has performed well recently. The steady increase in turnover suggests the directors can successfully tender for new business from major builders, so their reputation must be good. The absence of any claim under the bond facility indicates a high degree of technical competence.

The directors do not appear to be financially proficient as indicated by the lack of management accounts and forecasts ands their decision to embark on the disastrous French venture, but they have proved that they can take hard decisions as shown by the decision to write off this investment that cannot have been very palatable. Not least because of the French subsidiary write-off, the capital structure of the business has weakened significantly. When assessing its capital needs it must be appreciated that the company has been operating without the benefit of the capital invested in the French venture for some time. The current liquidity pressure has arisen more due to a rapid expansion in turnover at home.

One of the problems for the business is that the directors have withdrawn too much cash recently. They do need to be questioned about whether some of the cash previously taken out can be reinvested. If not, there is a hidden reserve in the property to raise finance if the old valuation still holds good. Given the nature of the debtors, large builders, the company may not have a great deal of control over the credit given. There is also likely to be a significant element of 'retentions' in the debtor figure that will increase the locked-up cash as turnover expands. The bank needs to see a detailed breakdown of debtors, with retentions shown separately.

There is probably some scope to squeeze creditors, who are mainly the company's own subcontractors, but it also needs to be recognised that they cannot be coerced too far because their own liquidity is likely to be tight. Fundamentally, in this business there is limited scope to improve liquidity if a desired level of turnover is the objective without a fresh injection of capital. The company should produce a detailed cash flow forecast together with a detailed schedule of bond movements and timings. (Note: these will include tender; performance; advance payment; progress or retention; warranty; and stand-by credit bonds).

Underlying profitability is good as shown by the increasing trend in the gross profit margin and the improved level of retained profit if excess directors' remuneration is added back and the extraordinary write-off is discounted. Basically this is a very attractive business that has made one serious error by investing in France.

Looking at the security available, the historic book values of the properties amount to £510,000 freehold to support credit lines of £800,000 at present or £1,050,000 if the proposed increase in limits is granted. The freeholds need revaluing. The debenture covering other company assets will have some value but this is a business engaged in large contracts and the plant, debtors and work in progress would realise low amounts in a receivership compared with their book values. At best, a sum around £300,000 net of hire purchase liabilities might be realised on a liquidation and this would need to cover the costs of the bank's receiver continuing to trade to complete existing contracts.

Two final comments: the tender for a contract worth £1 million to produce an estimated gross profit return of 25%, if won, will greatly enhance the value of the company. One supposes that sufficient backing of resources (labour, management, etc) has already been estimated and any additional credit need has been included in the request to raise the overdraft limit by £100,000. Secondly, the directors have not provided a summary to support the requirement for the full credit increase of £250,000. The bank must confirm that this sum is applicable to circumstances.

The decision is finely balanced with the fundamental strength of the business being matched against the thin security. The directors have already committed all their personal assets, although they should reinvest any cash that is available from their large drawings. A detailed financial plan is needed and a good financial monitoring system put in place. This might be a situation where the bank would want to use a firm of accountants to complete the forecasts and design an appropriate ongoing monitoring package. Provided this is done and is satisfactory, the previous good track record of the UK business and its lack of call on the bond commitments make the decision to agree an increase in the facilities, on balance, the right one.

Case study 15   Mr Lewis Willis

Lewis Willis is a successful property developer who, jointly with his brother, owns a group of private property companies that have an estimated net worth of around £25 million. Willis is 52 years old and has been a customer of your bank for 30 years in both a personal and business capacity. He calls to see you and wants to undertake a property development on his own by setting up a new company for the purpose. A site has been identified that has planning permission for 60,000 square feet of offices. Three substantive companies have expressed keen interest in taking all the office space when built. He has also had discussions with a number of institutions (pension funds and insurance companies) that would be interested in buying the building from him, once let.

Willis has produced a detailed feasibility study for the project for you to study. He asks if you would be prepared to recommend that your bank lend him the £6.5m needed to complete the development with repayment when the property is sold. Construction will take 12 months and full occupation occurs on completion. No allowance has been made for letting and legal fees, marketing costs or additional interest costs in case the prospective tenants do not materialise. New property of this type is currently being sold on the open market at a 9% pa gross yield. Stamp Duty Land Tax (currently payable at 4% on the consideration) should be ignored.

Required

Consider the proposition, give details of the risks involved and indicate your response to the request.

Project appraisal (feasibility study)	**Value**
	(£'000)
Rental income: Net useable space 60,000 sq ft @ £12.50	750
Capital sale value @ 9% pa income	**8,333**

Bank interest costs rolled up during the first year:	
Agreement charges at 1% flat on facility of £4.5m	45
Assumed 8% pa on average drawings during construction at £2m =	160
Total bank costs rolled up during first year	**205**

Site development: total building cost at £80 per sq ft	4,800
Access roads and site clearance, etc	800
Professional fees at 12% on £.6m	672
Contingency element at 5% on £5.6m	280
rolled-up bank costs during first year	205
Total development costs after one year	**6,757**
Development projected profit before tax (8,333 – 4,384)	**1,576**

Returns and sensitivity calculations:

Project return on development costs	23.3%
Rent yield on cost	11.1%
Running cost per month if the building is not let (£)	45,000
Proceeds lost if the market (sale) yield increases by 1% pa (£)	833,000
Reduction in value if the rent achieved falls by £1 per sq ft	60,000
Loss of sale value if the rent falls by £1 per sq ft	667,000

Suggested response

Willis is a good customer and, if possible, the bank would wish to help him. He has an excellent track record in the business (but then so have other experienced property developers whose companies have become insolvent). This is a business where past track record is not necessarily a guide to future success if the market place fundamentals relating to property turn sour.

Despite all the indications about future tenants, the development is not yet pre-let or sold, so it is open-ended and therefore speculative. Willis has deliberately avoided putting the project through one of his existing companies. Whatever the reason for this, it reduces the risk of loss to him and increases the risk to the bank. This is because the bank cannot look to assets outside the project if things go wrong. Moreover, Willis is investing no money in the venture and the bank will be lending 100%, including rolling up interest for at least the first year. Although there is an apparent 23.3% profit margin on the project, this is unlikely to be sufficient if things go significantly wrong.

There is the risk that it might not be possible to let the building at all if the market becomes depressed or, if it could be let, it might have to be to tenants who are not attractive to an institution wishing to purchase the property. There is a further risk in that a rent of £12.50 per sq ft may not be attainable, particularly if multi-tenancies have to be accepted rather than just one tenant.

It is not known whether the building contract is at a fixed price or is subject to cost escalation. If it is the former, there could be cost overruns. Is the builder financially strong and able to complete the development without any performance problems arising? Cost will be significantly higher if the original builder has to be replaced. There is a 5% contingency built into the development costs; is this adequate in the circumstances. Will structural engineers be necessary; there is no mention of this in the feasibility study.

Are the proposed Institutions who will be acquiring the property in one year's time firmly contracted to do so? Will they still be interested if the development or the rental phases suffer unexpected delays? Is the purchase price agreed at outset? Will the Institutions be willing to become a part of a joint venture with Willis and fund part of the development costs? If the property was not sold and instead had to be let, would the rent yield on cost (after allowing for any rent void periods) be able to pay the bank's interest arrears, service future running costs and repay the borrowing?

In assessing the security value of the site, an independent valuation will be needed and a professional independent view of its ultimate value. A charge over the site is needed and also a floating charge to enable the bank to obtain priority over a Receiver, should one be appointed by another creditor. Any lending for construction would have to be released against architects' certificates.

This proposition is simply too speculative for a bank. Some re-engineering might be possible but this would have to include a significant customer stake in the venture. The bank could then look at the proposition if it were substantially pre-let. Ideally the bank would also expect the property to have been pre-sold and essentially only be required to finance a closed bridging loan.

Case study 16   Grundy Farms (J Grundy and Sons)

Jack Grundy is a farmer who has banked with you for over 20 years. He farms in partnership with his two sons who live in cottages on the farm. Jack Grundy owns all the farm property in his sole name. Grundy is in his 70s and the sons are in their 40s; they have all been farmers throughout their lives. The farm consists of 497 acres that are owned freehold by Grundy. It is an arable enterprise growing a mixture of wheat, oilseed rape and beans. You regard the Grundys as good, practical, farmers but lacking in financial skills.

Over the years, the partnership borrowing has increased steadily. You have tolerated the situation partly because the bank has a charge over the farm and buildings (professionally valued at £850,000 two years ago) and partly because Grundy was involved in prolonged negotiations with a local builder to sell ten acres of land for £250,000. This sale was completed a month ago and the overdraft now stands at £265,000.

Grundy has asked for an overdraft limit of £350,000 (an increase of £100,000) to see him through the next 12 months. In company with your bank's specialist farming manager for the area, you have recently visited the farm and have established that the enterprise's current financial position is as follows.

Growing crops and net assets	value £
Work done ploughing 280 acres at £12 per acre	3,360
Oilseed rape 88 acres at £42 per acre including seeding	3,696
Stocks of fertiliser, seed, etc	6,900
Debtor: VAT refund	2,000
Plant and machinery at book values	54,550
Farmland and buildings (Grundy's estimate)	<u>750,000</u>
Total book assets	**820,506**
Trade creditors	9,897
Tax creditor: PAYE/National Insurance (estimated)	4,500
Hire purchase debt	<u>10,777</u>
Total liabilities	**25,174**

The cropping plan for the current year after the land sale is as follows:

Forecast	Acres	Turnover	Margin *
Winter wheat	236	62,205	42,489
Winter oilseed rape	88	12,100	4,444
Winter beans	44	10,560	8,140
Set aside	52	4,427	4,427
Grassland/rough/buildings	77	–	–
Other subsidies and income		48,768	48,768
Totals	**497**	**138,060**	**108,268**

* Bank farming manager estimate of gross profit before direct/indirect fixed costs.

Required

Analyse the business and indicate the response you would give to Grundy's request.

Profit and loss accounts

£'000 year ended 31 March	2002	2003	2004
Turnover	**125,094**	**122,369**	**154,472**
Direct costs	63,366	51,343	69,142
Gross profit	**61,728**	**71,026**	**85,330**
Overheads	103,428	135,927	155,319
(including interest paid	39,441	59,543	77,169)
Net Loss	**41,700**	**64,901**	**69,989**

Accounting ratios	2002	2003	2004	2005
	Actual	**Actual**	**Actual**	**Forecast**
Current ratio	0.24	0.19	0.16	
Acid test	0.02	0.01	0.01	
Gross profit margin	49.3%	58.0%	55.2%	78.4%
Net Loss margin	(33.3%)	(53.0%)	(45.3%)	

Balance sheets

£ as at 31 March	2002		2003		2004	
Fixed assets						
Plant and machinery		29,783		54,735		47,014
Stock	69,993		77,050		85,546	
Debtors	6,002		2,747		2,533	
Current assets	75,995		79,797		88,079	
Creditors	46,589		24,457		36,976	
Hire purchase	–		16,898		6,064	
Bank overdraft					491,557	
	259,742		381,237		#	
Current liabilities	306,331		422,592		534,597	
Net current liabilities		230,336		342,795		446,518
Employment of capital	(200,553)		(288,060)		(399,504)	
Financed by:						
Opening capital – debit balance	(139,278)	(200,553)	(288,060)			
Profit and loss account – loss		(41,700)		(64,901)		(69,989)
Drawings	(19,575)	(22,606)	(41,455)			
Capital employed	**(200,553)**	**(288,060)**	**(399,504)**			

\# Before the receipt of £250,000 from the sale of land.

Suggested response

The farmer is a long-standing customer who the bank, rightly or wrongly, has persevered with and apparently not been able to persuade to accept proper financial advice. As a result, in spite of the farming prowess of the family, there has been a complete lack of financial management of the farm and it appears incapable of making a profit. But for the sale of land recently for £250,000 to reduce the overdraft and the asset backing of the farm freehold charged to the bank, there would probably have been no alternative but to call in its lending. Given his age, Grundy is unlikely to change his way of farming. The requested overdraft limit may be insufficient. The bank urgently needs a detailed budget and cash flow forecast.

The absence of the farm freehold from the partnership balance sheet makes a number of the standard accounting ratios not very helpful. Even so, the ratios show that the business is highly illiquid, although the reduction in borrowing has improved the position since the year end. The bank has collected sufficient information verbally at the date of the meeting with Grundy to draw up a 'current day balance sheet' as follows:

Position at inspection	Liabilities			Assets
Trade creditors	9,897	Debtor: VAT		2,000
Tax	4,500	Growing crops		7,056
Bank debt	265,411	Stocks		6,900
Hire purchase	10,777	Farm & land etc		750,000
Capital	529,921	Plant and machinery		54,550
	820,506			**820,506**

A new professional valuation is needed to confirm the farm value, the last one being two years ago, but Grundy's figure may not be unrealistic and so the prospective gearing is reasonable at 50%, based on borrowing at around £347,000 (491 + additional 100 + 6 – 250 land sale) against the capital base of £700,000 (850 freehold –400 capital employed + 250 land sale). The main issue, therefore, is whether the borrowing can be serviced. If the forecast growth in profit is right (and it is an independent estimate) the business is unlikely to be profitable. Viz

Turnover (as calculated)	**£138,060**	
Direct costs (say turnover 138,060 - margin 108,268)	29,792	a
Overhead (indirect) costs (say as last year 155,319 – 77,169)	78,150	
Interest charges (say revised 350/last year 500 x 77k) excl repayments	53,900	b
Total costs projected	**£161,842**	

Note:

(a) Assumed to include all direct costs.
(b) Assumes approval of revised overdraft limit.

No account of drawings has been included that represents the labour costs of the family running the farm. So unless overheads can be significantly reduced or turnover significantly improved the borrowing will steadily increase.

It looks highly unlikely that Grundy will be able to service the proposed level of borrowing. Provided the security valuation stands up, the borrowing will be safe in the short term unless there is any form of extended agricultural tenancy on any part of the farm buildings that would pose a problem on a possible disposal. Grundy will have to be pressed to sell more land if the borrowing is to be cut to acceptable levels, although this is likely to reduce the farm income, as the sale it will most probably come from cultivated land rather than grassland. A further alternative is to diversify through converting any redundant farm buildings into tourism lettings or office accommodation, the benefit being that this cost would be eligible for grant support apart from generating additional income for the farm.

While it should be possible to agree an increased facility as a short-term measure, it can only be done on the basis that Grundy re-appraises the future strategy for the farm and accepts professional advice on future planning and disposals.

Case study 17   John Tooth

John Tooth has had an account at your branch since he started his training course at the dental school of a major university ten years ago. Since he graduated five years ago he has worked as a full-time associate for a practice in your area. He currently earns around £36,000 per annum. The present balances on his accounts are current account £1,000 credit; savings account £3,000 credit and car loan account £1,800 debit, repayable at £200 per month.

Tooth requests a meeting with you and explains that Alan Molar, the principal of another local practice, died suddenly in July. The practice was operated by Molar and two part-time associates who were paid 45% of their gross fees. For the past three months, the associates have continued to operate the practice but Mr Molar's widow wishes to sell it as soon as possible.

Molar's practice uses an annexe of his home with a separate entry. It is large enough to live in and could be used as temporary accommodation until Tooth can afford to purchase another residence. Tooth has had the annexe valued at a figure of £106,000. He has been negotiating with the executors of Molar's estate and they have agreed to sell the practice on the following basis: House annex £100,000; Equipment £30,000 and Goodwill £30,000, in all totalling £160,000.

Tooth has examined the equipment; it is in good order and in his opinion worth £40,000. He is keen to purchase the practice. It is situated only two miles from where he works at present and he expects some of his existing patients to follow him. He hopes to be able to increase the income of Molar's practice by at least £20,000 per annum from this source.

Tooth explains that he bought his own terraced starter-home house five years ago with the help of a building society endowment mortgage of £50,000. The house was valued last week at £90,000 and he has a number of potential buyers interested. He has £12,000 saved in a building society account, although this has to settle a tax demand of £6,000 payable on 1 January next. A copy of Molar's accounts are produced which he gives to you. He asks you to help him to fund the purchase of the practice.

Required

Set out, with reasons, the response you would make to Tooth's request.

Alan Molar, dental surgeon

Income and expenditure account

£'000 year ending 31 March	2002	2003	2004
Fees	<u>133</u>	<u>144</u>	<u>153</u>
Materials, drugs etc	14	16	17
Salaries: associates	28	30	33
staff	20	22	25
Premises expenses	25	16	18
Travel and sundries	7	7	8
Finance costs	4	4	4
Depreciation	<u>1</u>	<u>10</u>	<u>9</u>
Total expenses	<u>**99**</u>	<u>**105**</u>	<u>**114**</u>
Net income	<u>**34**</u>	<u>**39**</u>	<u>**39**</u>

Accounting ratios

	2002	2003	2004
Current ratio	0.31	0.57	0.41
Acid test	0.27	0.52	0.36
Gearing	183%	137%	111%
Interest cover (times)	9.5	11.8	10.3
Credit given (days)	33	57	33
Credit taken (days)	106	111	120
Net income margin *	25.3%	27.0%	25.6%

* Note: the margin calculated before deducting drawings.

Balance sheet

£'000 as at 31 March	2002	2003	2004
Equipment	41	37	35
Motor vehicles	12	9	17
Fixed assets	**53**	**46**	**52**
Stock	1	2	2
Debtors	12	23	14
Current assets	**13**	**25**	**16**
Creditors	4	5	6
Bank	12	14	5
Hire purchase	8	4	8
Loan (from father)	20	20	20
Current liabilities	**44**	**43**	**39**
Net current liabilities	**31**	**18**	**23**
Employment of capital	**22**	**28**	**29**
Financed by:			
Capital b/f	19	22	28
Net income	34	39	39
Less Drawings	(31)	(33)	(38)
Capital employed	**22**	**28**	**29**

Suggested answer:

This question concerned the purchase of a professional practice for a dentist. Mr Tooth is a good, long-standing customer. There is background evidence in the balances of his accounts of an ability to save with both the bank and the building society. He has never run a business before and, although it is natural that he should wish to have his own practice, the proposition needs to be approached with caution. Given Tooth's lack of business experience, ideally he should use an accountant to produce a business plan both for himself and the bank.

The proposition falls into two parts: the house annexe purchase and the purchase of the practice. Taking the annexe purchase first, the figures are shown hereafter. There should be no problem in agreeing a mortgage of say £65,000 (to include expenses) at 65% loan to value and given Tooth's expected drawings. The legals should be drawn up carefully in view of the proximity of the annex to the residence.

Annex purchase price		£100,000	
Sale of existing house	90,000		
Less mortgage thereon	50,000	40,000	
Finance requirement		60,000	+ expenses

There could be pressure for a bridging loan so that the purchase can be completed quickly. In all the circumstances, it would probably be unwise for Tooth to enter into an open-ended bridging loan for two reasons: first, if there was any difficulty in selling his own house he would be starting up in business on his own with additional interest charges that he could well do without when trying to find his feet in the new venture. Secondly, the annex as such should be cleared for a mortgage in principle as it is may not be considered as a standard lending proposition by lenders. Given mortgage approval, a bridging loan on a closed basis should not pose any problem.

Turning to the purchase of the practice, the amount required is as follows:

Equipment	£30,000
Goodwill	£30,000
	£60,000

Is the asking price reasonable? Tooth ought to be competent in assessing the value of the equipment but, if there is doubt, an independent valuation should be undertaken. The value of goodwill is more problematic. Essentially, this is what the business is worth to a purchaser because it assures him/her of a future income from day one. It is the equivalent of payment for the privilege of earning money from an existing client base. The figures show that the business has been steadily profitable and could be attractively priced at a goodwill figure of £30,000, being less than one year's profit before drawings. A frequent 'rule of thumb' is to value a business at around three times net profit after proprietor's salary (ie drawings). In this case Molar is taking a reasonable sum out of the business but it amounts to virtually all the annual profits, suggesting the business is not as profitable as it should be.

Tooth has savings available of £9,000, but some of this may be needed to meet legal expenses and renovate the new premises. The 2004 balance sheet figures show current assets of £16,000, of which creditors are financing only £6,000. It would appear that there is a need for a working capital overdraft facility of around £10,000 to cover this gap, perhaps even more, and a further £8,000 to repay the hire purchase debt if that is the choice.

This is where a business plan would be useful and, in particular, a detailed cash flow forecast. In any event, a budget is going to be needed to establish on reasonable assumptions that Tooth can afford the repayments on a practice loan of, say, £60,000, plus his mortgage of £65,000. A summary of the estimated financing requirement would be as follows:

Financing requirement (£'000)	**Cash in**	**Cash out**
Net proceeds from house sale	40	
Purchase of practice and annexe		160
Own savings	9	
New mortgage on annex	65	
Working capital requirement		18
Totals	114	178
Bank funding requirement	**64**	

The next test is to ensure that Tooth can service the debts:

Business income (£'000)		**Annual**
Tooth's practice		36
Molar's practice	39	
Add Forecast of increased earnings	20	
Add back finance costs	4	59
Total income projected		95
Less Finance costs (say): on mortgage	4	
on bank advance	5	9
Net income available		**86**

Security available to the bank will exclude a first charge on the annex (unless the bank decides for security reasons to advance this mortgage as well in return for a first charge). A personal guarantee from Tooth will be necessary even if the bank advances the full £129,000, since the valuation of the property only comes to £106,000. All the indications are that the cash flows to meet the loan repayments will be strong with plenty of margin for error. A detailed analysis of the existing balance sheet is not necessary given that Tooth is only acquiring the assets and not the business as a whole. This means the accounting ratios will change depending on Tooth's own financial position.

One issue that ought to be considered is whether Tooth will indeed be able to bring in an additional £20,000 worth of business because his existing employer is not going to like this and he may have a contract which restrains him from poaching customers within a certain geographical area. Another is that some of Molar's clients may have a personal link to him and could go elsewhere. An idea of the loyalty of the customer base would be helpful. A third factor to resolve is the standing of Molar's existing staff: will they be willing to remain and be employed as before? If so, Tooth may not be able to make cost savings and it will be left for him to increase client charges to improve Molar's past practice profits. In turn, will this cause clients to move to other dentists? If Molar's practice is National Health registered the regular income will be advantageous but treatment charges will be fixed.

On balance, the financing of professional practices is to be welcomed and the earnings to be generated from the acquisition will significantly exceed the proposed financing costs, including loan repayments. Subject to satisfactory answers to the questions raised, the request should be approved.

Case study 18   Wagstaff

Ken and Mary Wagstaff have maintained a satisfactory joint account at your branch for a number of years. Mr Wagstaff is 41 years old and has been the manager of a newsagent's shop in your local shopping centre for five years. Mr Wagstaff calls to see you. The company he works for is a national retail chain. It has decided to dispose of a number of its shops and he has the opportunity to buy the unit he manages. He tells you the following:

He believes that he will have to offer £67,000 to purchase the business. The shop is leasehold and a 20-year lease was granted in December 1999 at a rent of £10,000 pa subject to reviews every five years. The landlord is a national insurance company. A purchase price has been calculated by Wagstaff as Fixtures and fittings £15,000 and Goodwill £52,000, totalling £67,000 plus Stock to be acquired at an agreed valuation. The current stock figure is around £30,000. Separate profit and loss accounts are not made up for the shop unit but Wagstaff has extracted the following figures from the returns he submits to head office.

Profit and loss accounts

Years ending 30 June (£'000)	2002 Actual	2003 Actual	2004 Actual	2005 Budget
Sales	**415**	**450**	**487**	**584**
Direct costs	341	367	395	474
Gross profit	**74**	**83**	**92**	**110**
Gross profit %	*17.7%*	*18.3%*	*18.9%*	*18.8%*
Salaries (incl. manager)	32	35	37	38
Rent	10	10	10	16
Other expenses	15	17	18	20
Indirect overheads	**57**	**62**	**65**	**74**
Net profit	**17**	**21**	**27**	**36**
Net Profit %	*4.0%*	*4.7%*	*5.5%*	*6.2%*
Credit taken (days)	36	41	35	35
Stock turnover (days)	22	20	21	21

Mr and Mrs Wagstaff have £30,000 in building society accounts that they inherited from Mrs Wagstaff's mother, who died last year. The Wagstaffs jointly own their house which they believe is worth £75,000 (subject to a £30,000 endowment mortgage). They also own a two-year-old van. Mr Wagstaff's current salary from the shop is £18,000 pa. His wife, who has not worked recently, would assist him in the shop and this would enable him to save wages of £8,000 pa currently paid to other staff. Wagstaff asks for your assistance to purchase the business.

Required

Set out your analysis of the business and its requirements, and indicate how you would respond to the request.

Suggested answer

This question was a very small scale management buy-out of a newsagency and retail tores owned by a large chain. The Wagstaffs have been good customers of the bank and can provide a substantial capital stake from their own resources. Mr Wagstaff has a good knowledge of the business having run it for five years and under his stewardship it has apparently been successful. All the indications therefore are that management will be good, but it is still necessary to question why the national chain has decided to sell and what the competition is and how it might develop. Newsagents are having to face increasing competition from supermarkets.

A particularly important issue will be the price being paid. No value is being put on the lease, which is probably sensible, but there may be a dilapidation liability to consider and a view needs to be taken as to whether the fixtures and fittings are in good condition and are indeed worth £15,000. The bigger issue is the value of goodwill. At just under two times last year's net profit it does not seem unreasonable and an alternative assessment would be on the basis of average sales: the goodwill amounts to five-and-a-half week's sales, which again does not look unreasonable.

The amount Wagstaff needs to borrow is basically £67,000 plus the value of stock, say £30,000, less the £30,000 he and his wife have invested in the building society ie £67,000. Legal expenses etc need to be added and, more importantly, a view has to be taken as to what sort of working capital facility is needed to finance ongoing trading. £30,000 or thereabouts will have to be paid for the stock immediately but the business ought to negotiate to finance some of this on credit as replacement items are bought. The purchase price may be open for payment by instalments in return for Wagstaff continuing to buy goods from his former employer.

Comparing the historical credit taken and stock turnover figures suggest that in the long term it may be possible to finance virtually all the stock on credit. It has to be recognised that the current credit terms are for a national chain and may not be available to a small shop. The issue has to be pursued with Wagstaff and a simple cash flow forecast drawn up in the light of whatever credit terms he could obtain. It does look as though an overdraft limit of £10,000/£15,000 should be adequate.

A term loan of say £40,000 over five to ten years should be well within the business's capacity to repay given the strong historical track record and net profits being earned. Repayments on a loan over five years will be around £10,000 against last year's net profit of £27,000. Some caution is needed because both the historical and budgeted profits are for the current owners and may not reflect the new situation. Also the rent is budgeted to jump by £12,000 in a full year, although wage costs will be £8,000 lower. A forecast 20% increase in sales appears on the face of it quite a high task. On what was this based? Wagstaff needs to produce a proper budget with forecasts reflecting how he views the situation.

A charge over the lease is required as security and a second charge over the Wagstaffs' house would also be appropriate. This may cause some heart-searching by the couple and care will be needed to cover the legal situation of joint ownership of the residence so that the property can be fully vacated if need be.

Overall the request is straightforward and is capable of agreement subject to a satisfactory budget and cash flow forecast.

Appendix 1

Bank of England Industry Sectors Analysis

Industry Sectors: Analysis

Sectors at 17 May 2005 comprising	Financials	Non-financials	Cyclical services	Cyclical consumer gds	Non-cyclical Services	Non-cyclical Consumer gds	General Industrials	IT	Basic Industries	Resources	Utilities
TOTALS	Financials	Non-financials	gen'l retailers, leisure, media, transport	auto-mobiles, house-hold gds, textiles	food retail, drug retail, telecoms	food & drinks, pharma-ceuticals, household prods, tobacco	electronics, engineering, aerospace	hard-ware, soft-ware	paper, steel, chemicals, construct'n	mining, oil, gas	electricity, other

Number of quoted companies:

	Financials	Non-financials	Cyclical services	Cyclical consumer gds	Non-cyclical Services	Non-cyclical Consumer gds	General Industrials	IT	Basic Industries	Resources	Utilities
FTSE Actuaries all share market	221	475	203	16	19	54	46	42	48	31	16
Alternative Investment Market (AIM)	120	599	191	29	13	61	58	97	29	120	1
AIM shares not declaring a dividend	88	461	131	21	12	48	38	75	20	115	1
percentage of shares not declaring	73	77	69	72	92	79	66	77	69	96	100
Average dividend yield % pa	3.88	2.87	2.81	3.78	2.36	2.87	3.15	1.29	3.08	2.92	4.11
Dividend cover (times)	1.89	2.18	1.90	2.23	2.53	1.89	1.75	2.20	3.39	2.65	1.38
Price/Earnings ratio	13.63	15.96	18.75	11.88	16.70	18.42	18.18	35.38	9.57	12.96	17.63

Suggested interpretation of data:

	Financials	Non-financials	Cyclical services	Cyclical consumer gds	Non-cyclical Services	Non-cyclical Consumer gds	General Industrials	IT	Basic Industries	Resources	Utilities
High growth expectation								X			
Reliability of earnings											X
View of cyclical outlook			X	X	X						
View of non-cyclical outlook						X					
Cyclical industries and earnings							X				
Mature industries having limited growth prospects									X		
Mature industries of a cyclical nature										X	

A view of the Financial Risk (in relative and broad terms**)**

	Financials	Non-financials	Cyclical services	Cyclical consumer gds	Non-cyclical Services	Non-cyclical Consumer gds	General Industrials	IT	Basic Industries	Resources	Utilities
Low					X	X		X	X	X	X
Medium		X	X	X	X	X	X		X	X	

Industry Sectors: Lending

(Note: approximate analysis only)

Sectors comprising	UK resident	Financials	Non-financials	Cyclical Services (gen'l retailers, leisure, media, transport)	Cyclical consumer gds (automobiles, household gds, textiles)	Non-cyclical services (food retail, drug retail, telecomms)	Non-cyclical consumer gds (food & drinks, pharmaceuticals, household prods, tobacco)	General industrials (electronics, engineering, aerospace)	IT (hardware, software)	Basic industries (paper, steel, chemicals, construct'n)	Resources (mining, oil, gas)	Utilities (electricity, other)
at 31 March 2005	713,735	545,529	168,206	42,211	11,651	23,384	24,068	15,276	9,184	34,692	77	40
at 31 March 2004	657,503	494,122	163,381	39,543	10,871	20,882	24,226	15,717	10,537	32,851	87	54
change per cent	8.6	10.4	3.0	6.7	7.2	12.0	-0.7	-2.8	-12.8	5.6	-11	.6

Detailed analysis: (excludes Financials) (selected items only) as at 31 March

Manufacturing:

	Total	Food & beverages	Textiles	Paper & publishing	Chemicals, rubber, plastics	Metals etc	Machinery, transport	Electrical equipment	Other manufacturing
2005	40,902	8,597	1,762	5,788	4,328	5,151	6,138	3,801	5,337
2004	42,866	9,275	1,781	5,413	5,098	5,582	6,555	3,822	5,340
change per cent	-4.6	-7.3	-1.1	6.9	-15.1	-7.7	-6.4	-0.6	-0.1

Wholesale, Retail:

	Total	Motor vehicles	Other wholesale	Other retail	Transport & communication	Hotels & restaurants	Agriculture	Mining	Utilities
2005	82,020	9,889	12,711	15,471	20,565	23,384	8,563	2,832	4,908
2004	76,193	9,090	11,076	14,951	20,194	20,882	8,286	2,874	5,880
change per cent	7.6	8.8	14.8	3.5	1.8	12.0	3.3	-1.5	-16.5

Other sectors:

	Total	Real estate	Construction	Rent of equipment	Professional activities	Computer activities	Leisure activities	Personal (secured)	Personal (unsecured)	Public sector
2005	900,654	123860	19425	6043	25372	3141	8935	527336	139922	30317
2004	839,594	104504	16758	7580	22084	2957	8273	505357	126176	28865
change per cent	7.3	18.5	15.9	-20.3	14.9	6.2	8.0	4.4	10.9	5.0

Appendix 2

Term lending: case study

The case study has its financial figures summarised in a format changed from that necessary to meet the requirements of the Companies Acts in order to emphasise the points on which the lending banker will judge the company for the offer of a term loan. The salient information available for the year in question is as follows.

◆ The group is a commercial clothing supplier.
◆ Approximately one-eighth of turnover arises outside the UK and virtually all production is sourced from overseas.
◆ Committed bank facilities as yet undrawn at the year-end and expiring within one year amounted to £13.7mn.
◆ Bank loans repayable in the second year totalled £5.5mn and due thereafter totalled £2.7mn.
◆ Sterling borrowings comprised £13.0mn of the £14.4mn outstanding, all at floating rates including overdrafts, revolving acceptance credits and LIBOR-based facilities.
◆ Forward currency hedging contracts (£3.5mn) and an interest rate cap (£1.5mn) mature within one year.

How should the lending bank view the group's future term borrowing?

Financial summary

Balance Sheet			**2004**
As at 31 January			(£m)
Tangible assets:	Land and buildings *	6.2	
	Plant, equipment, etc	<u>5.2</u>	11.4
Net current assets:			
Stocks:	Work-in-progress	7.8	
	Finished goods	<u>20.5</u>	
		28.3	
Trade debtors less creditors		5.9	
Less other creditors, provisions, etc (net)		<u>1.5</u>	<u>32.7</u>
Employment of capital			**<u>44.1</u>**
Borrowings:	Due within one year	6.2	
	Due after one year	<u>8.2</u>	14.4
Shareholders funds			<u>29.7</u>
Capital employed			**<u>44.1</u>**

* The freehold was revalued at the year end.

Profit and loss account		**<u>2004</u>**
Year ended 31 January		(£m)
Turnover		**<u>70.4</u>**
Operating profit before depreciation	6.8	
Less Depreciation	<u>1.4</u>	5.4
Less Interest on borrowings		<u>1.0</u>
Profit before tax		4.4
Tax (£1.4) and distributed profits (£1.7)		<u>3.1</u>
Retained earnings		**<u>1.3</u>**

Cash flow statement		**2004**
as at 31 January		(£m)
Operating cash flow (retained profit + depreciation)		2.7
Add Sale proceeds of asset sales	1.5	
Borrowings raised	0.0	
Increase in creditors less debtors	<u>1.8</u>	<u>3.3</u>
Total cash inflow		6.0
Less Capital expenditure on fixed assets	0.6	
Repayment of borrowings	<u>8.0</u>	<u>8.6</u>
Net cash reduction		**<u>2.6</u>**

There are a number of initial points to note from the analysis:

Positive aspects

- Interest charged on present borrowings is easily covered by the historic operating profit.
- Operating margins in 2004 increased slightly from 7.2% to 7.5% as a result of a drop in marketing and administrative costs.
- The group is not highly geared at 50% of shareholders funds.
- The book values of tangible assets amount to three-quarters of the sum of long-term borrowings.
- Long-term assets exceed the value of long-term debt.
- One factory was sold during 2004 and the company hopes to sell the other factory in due course and relocate to leased premises.
- Trade debtors exceed the total of trade creditors.
- There were negligible capital commitments contracted at the date of the balance sheet.
- The company has stated that the current year has started well with a strong order book (not shown in the financial summary).

Negative aspects

- The value of finished stocks is relatively high, perhaps suggesting a potential risk factor were the goods difficult to sell at their present profit margins.
- Sizeable borrowings are due to be repaid or renewed in the coming year after a sizeable debt repayment made in the past year.
- The hedging strategy is sound, but it is short term and covers only one-third of borrowings;
- The overall gross trading margin fell in 2004 from 39.2% to 38.8%;
- The dividend pay out ratio is high (57%) compared with retained earnings;

♦ The business is not generating a positive cash flow;

♦ The company's track record over the past five years shows static turnover and after-tax profit earned, except for one year (2002) when profit halved (why?);

♦ The freehold revaluation indicates no 'hidden' asset open market valuation;

♦ If the factory is relocated, there may be a temporary loss of production and attendant costs to bear;

♦ The company had a net pension liability of £6.7mn at the balance sheet date (not shown in the financial summary).

Should the company continue to rely on its undrawn short maturity facility to maintain a suitable level of working capital in future or should it put in place a greater proportion of term debt?

Comment: it would have been interesting to discover whether the finished stocks held overseas were of sufficient value to be used to raise finance locally more cheaply than through a sterling facility whether or not hedged for any currency risk. The financial statements state that 90% of borrowings are sterling-based, £5mn (one-third) of which has been 'capped' at an interest rate of 4.5% pa for two years and for eight years thereafter has been 'swapped' into a fixed interest rate of 4.97% pa.

It is not stated at what margin the overdraft is being charged, but the cap/swap does go some way to offset any future increase in market interest rates. The pension shortfall, of course, does not affect cash flow until the liability crystallises. The quality of financial management will be a key factor in judging whether the risk of lending over the long term is acceptable.

It should be noted that all the above financial figures and comments have been based on historic, publicly available data without the benefit of confidential information that would normally be given to the company's bankers, including current year trading forecasts.

In the event, the financial statements disclosed some of the future financial strategy pertaining to the company:

♦ The directors are asking the shareholders for permission to purchase up to 10% of the company's shares in issue. This will reduce the burden on cash flow of the cost of the annual dividend.

♦ At the year end, a new bank loan of £3.75mn was raised, repayable in instalments up to 2013, at an interest cost of LIBOR plus 1.25% pa. For security, a series of cross-guarantees were put in place between various group companies.

♦ At the year end, the uncommitted bank facilities remained in place and, after a restructuring of facilities, total borrowings amounted to £14.4mn, representing gearing of 48% on net shareholders funds.

♦ The directors expect the shown level of debt to reduce over the next few years based on no strategic acquisitions or ventures being entered into and the 'core' (ie on-going) borrowing for the group is stated as £5mn.

The following year. For the year ended 31 January 2005, most trading returns were nearly identical to 2004: turnover £70.7mn, operating profit £5.6mn, gross margin 39.3%, pretax profit £4.7mn, but net borrowings fell by c.£3mn to £11.5mn, largely due to stock and debtor reductions. In April 2005, however, it was announced that an acquisition was made for cash costing £4mn, funded out of undrawn facilities. After eliminating existing debt balances and acquiring cash held by the new acquisition the net cost to the group will reduce to £1.9mn. The deal is expected to be earnings enhancing in the first year. Goodwill of £1.6mn arising through the acquisition will no longer have to be amortised against profits under the new International Financial Reporting Standard (IFRS).

Comment: the company has appeared to adopt a more progressive operating strategy through acquiring a small competitor business. It is concentrating more on growth in turnover, presumably as the scope to improve earnings through cost savings reduces. Substantive borrowings remain to be repaid in 2005 and a further extension of the average maturity period of debt via term loans would be welcomed, together with greater hedging of interest and currency risks.

Appendix 3

Simple derivative examples

In practice financial calculators will be used with built-in programmes, but it might be useful for descriptive purposes to go back to basics without going into higher mathematics and formulae:

Example 1: Simple interest

A deposit of £100 is made at 4% pa interest for 91 days.

The proceeds after 91 days will be £100 plus interest:

$100 + [100 \times (4/100) \times (91/365)] = £100.99$

Example 2: Compound interest

A deposit of £100 is made at 4% pa interest for 365 days and reinvested for a further 365 days until maturity in two years time.

The proceeds in two years will be:

After year one: $100 + [100 \times (1 + 4/100)] = £104.00$
After year two: $104 \times (1 + 4/100)] = £108.16$

Example 3: Daily compounding

A deposit of £100 earns interest at 4% pa for 365 days compounded daily.

The effective interest rate is:

$100 \times \{[1 + (4/100)/365]$ to the power of $365\} - 1 = 4.08\%$

Example 4: Future value to present value

A deposit earns interest for 91 days at 4% pa and has a future value of £100.

Its present value is:

$100/[(1 + (4/100) \times 91/365] = £99.01$

Check: £99.01 invested for 91 days at 4% pa will earn interest of £ 0.99
added to the initial deposit of £99.01 = £100 after 91 days.

Example 5: Internal rate of return

The internal rate of return ('IRR') is used to calculate the internal (ie the company's) value of a set of future investment or project cash flows and is the single discounted overall annual percentage rate that, when applied to each individual cash flow, will give a present day value of zero. The present day (ie the first) figure in the cash flow will be negative as it represents the original investment cost. Subsequent cash flow figures will be positive, representing the future income returns, or negative if there is additional expenditure. The IRR return is then compared with the target return set by the company to decide whether the investment is to proceed.

Start of year	Initial investment	Cash flow annually	Net flow	Discounting factor	Present value
1	2,000		− 2,000	1.000	− 2,000
2	0	500	+ 500	0.9091	+ 455
3	0	500	+ 500	0.8264	+ 413
4	0	600	+ 600	0.7513	+ 451
5	0	600	+ 600	0.6830	+ 410
6		440	+ 437	0.6209	+ 271

In this example, the discounting factor (the IRR) is 10% pa. Thus the present day value of 600 at the beginning of year 4 (ie end of year 3) discounts back to a present value of 451. The sum of the present day values, after allowing for the initial investment, is zero. The calculation principle is that given by Example 4.

Example 6: Annuities

An annuity calculates the value (ie the yield) of a series of cash flows that can be purchased by an initial investment. The yield is the IRR. Example 5 provides an example and answers the question: what is the present value of the cash flows in years two through to six using an interest rate yield of 10% pa? The answer is the sum of each year's present value, ie £2,000.

Example 7: Trading strategies and risk

A bank will quote for a deal by offering two prices: a **bid**, at which level it is prepared to buy, and an **offer**, at which level it is prepared to sell. The higher rate is the dealing rate offered to the customer to buy, and the lower rate is the dealing rate the customer would get by selling to the bank. As described earlier, a **call** is to buy in a deal and a **put** is to sell. This applies throughout market dealing, even though a call on an FRA is equivalent to a put on an interest rate futures contract.

A company holds currency A and wishes to hedge against currency B. Its options are:

1. do nothing and assume that currency A will appreciate against currency B, taking the risk of an adverse movement between the currencies (that currency A will depreciate against currency B);
2. sell currency A forward to lock in the present cross exchange rates (and lose the opportunity of currency A appreciating against currency B);
3. buy a put option in currency A, taking the view that currency A will appreciate without the risk of being wrong.

The company has also borrowed funds that will require rolling over for another term. There are three similar choices open to the company:

- to wait until the rollover date and take the interest rate ruling at that time on the borrowing;
- to buy an FRA to fix in advance the cost of the borrowing;
- to buy an agreed amount of an FRA, in a stated currency, at an agreed interest rate, for an agreed maturity, on an agreed delivery date. This is called an **interest rate guarantee** and fixes the maximum cost of the future borrowing (or, if selling, fixes the minimum return on a future deposit).

Example 8: Forward-forward

The company has a 'gap' in its cash flow in three months time but will reinstate its positive cash flow in six months time. Borrowing is required from month three to month six. The opportunity is taken to take advantage of borrowing interest rates currently available in the market. The borrower:

- pays LIBOR + 1% (say) to the lending bank;
- receives LIBOR (say) under the FRA;
- pays the fixed FRA rate under the FRA agreement.

The net cost to the company will be the 1% LIBOR differential plus the cost of the FRA that will be known at outset. The company has hedged its interest cost exposure through an FRA. There is no exchange of principal.

Example 9: Interest rate swap

The company in Example 8 might also have hedged its exposure through taking up an interest rate swap. In this case, the interest flows (not the principal) are exchanged and, in practice, the flows are netted out where they coincide at an exchange date. The fixed and floating rate exchanges may be at different payment intervals. For example, the company will:

◆ borrow funds and pay interest (say) every three months at a cost based on three months LIBOR plus the lending margin;
◆ receive from the counter-party interest on the borrowing at an agreed fixed interest rate throughout the term of the borrowing;
◆ pay the counter-party the agreed fixed swap rate on the deal.

In Example 8, the settlement was at the beginning of the deal and quoted on a discount basis. For a swap, the settlement is done at the end of each relevant payment period.

Example 10: Currency swap

Similar to an interest rate swap, a currency swap exchanges cash flows in two different currencies, usually with the added exchange of the principal amounts of the currencies at a pre-agreed rate set at inception of the deal that is reversed at maturity. This exchange of principal, however, can be notional between the parties. The value of each currency at commencement of the exchange must be identical. In this example the company has borrowed in currency A at a fixed interest rate and wishes to swap this into currency B at a floating rate. The steps are:

◆ the exchange rate between currencies A and B is set at outset between the parties and the notional or actual exchange of principal is made;
◆ the interest rate payments relating to each currency principal are swapped and paid over, each in their chosen currencies, between the parties at their pre-arranged interest dates;
◆ at maturity, the reverse notional (or actual) exchange of principal is made at the currency rates set at inception.

Note that the appropriate value of each different cash flow is its net present value (calculated on a discounted cash flow basis) converted at the spot exchange rate.

Appendix 4

Security clauses

Examples of security clauses of a loan agreement

Each loan agreement will have its particular clauses to meet the circumstances of the customer and the bank. An example is shown below and reflects how earlier descriptions given in Chapter Eight on security aspects can be embodied in a formal facility letter. The brackets [ ] would have details relating to the particular security included therein.

Legal charge over freehold property

Amounts outstanding under the facility will be secured at all times by a [first] legal mortgage over [ ] properties acceptable to the bank. The bank shall require a valuation of [ ] properties in a form to the bank's satisfaction and undertaken by a valuer that meets the bank's approval, showing the aggregate *[type of value required]* value to be not less than [ ].

The bank reserves the right, at any time during the period of the facility, to have a *[further]* valuation of the properties undertaken at the company's expense by valuers nominated by the bank and to ask the company to substitute *[alternative/additional]* properties in order to maintain the aforesaid value of the bank's security margin.

The aggregate amount of drawings by the company under the facility from time to time outstanding shall not exceed *[70]* % of the aggregate value of the properties at such time charged to the bank which value shall be determined by the bank.

In the event that such percentage shall be exceeded for any reason, the company shall, at the bank's request, either forthwith deposit with the bank by way of security for such drawings such cash and/or additional security that the bank may require or reduce the drawings outstanding so as to ensure that such percentage shall not exceed the satisfactory required percentage. Should the company fail to provide such security or reduction, the bank is irrevocably authorised to realise, without the company's prior agreement, all or any of the properties to ensure that such excess is eliminated.

Mortgage debenture

Amounts outstanding under the facility are to be secured by a [first] legal charge in a form to the bank's satisfaction over the company's assets and undertaking.

Deed of postponement

The bank shall require the execution in a form to the bank's satisfaction of a deed of postponement under which the charge created by a debenture dated [ ] in favour of [ ] shall rank in priority to the charge referred to in paragraph [ ] up to the principal sum of [ ] together with interest thereon.

Charge over shares

The company will complete to the bank's satisfaction lien and share transfer forms in blank and deliver to the bank the share certificates in respect of the company's holdings of the following shares [ ].

Charge over lease/rental agreements

Amounts outstanding under the facility are to be secured at all times by a first legal charge over leasing and rental agreements current from time to time which must be acceptable to the bank and have outstanding rentals discounted at [ ] % pa of not less than [ ] % of such amounts.

The bank reserves the right at any time to require the lessees and hirers under their respective leasing and rental agreements charged to the bank to make payments direct to the bank to an account that will be designated and controlled by us. The company shall have the right at any time to substitute any leasing or rental agreements that are charged to the bank with new leasing or rental agreements.

Guarantees

[The company][and subsidiary companies] 'the guarantors' are to enter into a joint and several guarantee of their obligations to the bank under the terms of this facility letter in a form to the bank's satisfaction. Each guarantor is forthwith to agree with the bank that they will perform and observe all the obligations and liabilities to be undertaken in the facility letter.

The said guarantors represent and warrant to the bank by signing the duplicate copy of this letter that the giving of the guarantee to the bank pursuant to the provisions of this paragraph will be within their corporate powers and that all relevant corporate action has been taken or will be taken by each guarantor to enable it legally to execute the said guarantee and that the said guarantee when executed will constitute valid and legally binding obligations on each of them in accordance with its terms.

Setoff clauses

The bank shall open a blocked account in the company's name. The company agrees to maintain at all times in this account a sum not less than the outstanding balance of the loan. [No]/interest will be payable on the account. The company will not be entitled to payment of the whole or any part of the amounts standing at any time to the credit of the account unless and until the bank shall have received payments of the principal and interest on the loan and then only to the extent of such payments.

The company undertakes that at all times the account will be maintained by the company free of any charge, lien or encumbrance and the company will not assign or otherwise dispose of any legal or equitable interest therein. The company irrevocably authorises the bank to apply all monies from time to time standing to the credit of the account towards satisfaction of any liability that may at any time be outstanding under the company's loan facility or to debit the account with the amount of principal or of accrued interest on the loan then due and payable and such amount shall be deemed to have been paid to the bank on account of the principal or interest aforesaid.

In addition to any right of setoff or any similar right to which the bank may be entitled at law or in equity, the bank may at any time without notice combine and consolidate all or any of the company's accounts with the bank anywhere and setoff any monies whatsoever and whether on current deposit or any other account and in whatever currency or currencies against any of the company's liabilities whatsoever in whatever currency that may be owing or incurred by the company to the bank whether alone or jointly with any other person or persons, company or companies and whether or not any period of any deposit or by reference to which interest thereon is calculated has expired.

Representations and warranties

The company's acceptance of the loan facility and the company's acceptance of the proceeds of each drawing made hereunder shall constitute the company's continuing representation and warranty that:

- the company has full power, authority and legal right to borrow hereunder and to observe the terms and conditions of this facility and that there is no provision in any corporate document, mortgage, indenture, trust deed or agreement binding on the company [and the company's subsidiaries] or affecting the company's property that would conflict with or prevent the company from accepting the facility on the terms and conditions stated herein or would prevent the company's performance or observation of any of the terms hereof;
- there are no law suits or other legal proceedings pending or, so far as the company's directors know, threatened before any court, tribunal or administrative agency which in the opinion of the directors will adversely affect in any material respect the consolidated financial condition or operations of the company [and its subsidiaries];
- The company [and its subsidiaries] is not in any breach of any other agreement for borrowed money;
- There has been no material change in the assets and undertaking of the company [and its subsidiaries] since the date of the company's last published annual audited [consolidated] accounts that adversely affects the financial position as therein disclosed.

Undertakings

By the company's acceptance of the facility the company undertakes that during its continuance and until all the company's obligations hereunder have been fully met.

- The company [and its subsidiaries] will not without the bank's prior written consent create any pledge, mortgage or other charge over any of the company's assets [including uncalled capital] and/or undertaking, property or revenues present and future or permit any lien to arise and that should any such incumbrance be created by operation of law or otherwise, the same shall forthwith be discharged.
- The company will not without the bank's prior written consent dispose of the company's interest in [property]/[shares]. In the event of any default the bank may at any time require the company to [...].
- Drawings under the facility will only be made in respect of goods invoiced by the company that are subject to firm orders covering at least [ ] % of invoiced value [excluding any taxes charged thereon]. The goods financed by a drawing hereunder will be stored in a separate reserved space of [the company's warehouse]/[a warehouse acceptable to the bank] that the company will allow

the bank access to at all reasonable times. The bank at any time for any reason shall request the company to facilitate title to the goods to be put in the name of the bank and the company shall not [unreasonably] withhold permission to do so.

◆ The company will provide the bank with the following financial information within [a reasonable period to be agreed with the bank]:
   – a copy of the company's annual audited *[consolidated]* accounts;
   – quarterly management reports;
   – monthly list of trade debtors analysed by age;
   – such other information as the bank may from time to time reasonably request in a form to be agreed by the bank.

Net tangible assets

◆ The company will maintain its [consolidated] net tangible assets [as defined] at all times at a minimum of [£] or [%] of the net tangible assets as shown in the company's latest published annual audited accounts, whichever is the higher.

Total borrowings

◆ The company's total borrowings [as defined] will not at any time exceed [%] of the company's net tangible assets [and if lesser] or the aggregate of [%] of the [defined] value of the company's freehold properties and [%] of the company's trade debtors not more than [90] days old and [%] of the company's book values of stocks and work in progress.

Interest cover

◆ The company's [consolidated] profit before interest charges, taxation and dividends for each annual accounting period will not be less than [ ] times the company's [consolidated] interest charge for the period.

Dividend restriction

◆ The company will not make any payments in respect of dividends [or management charges] in excess of [%] of the company's net profit after tax in respect of each of the company's annual accounting periods.

Working capital ratio

◆ The company's [consolidated] current assets [as defined] will at all times [exceed]/[not be less than % of] the company's [consolidated] current Liabilities [as defined].

Conditions precedent

Before the facility is made available to the company the bank shall have received in a form to the bank's satisfaction:

◆ copy of a resolution of the company's board of directors duly certified as a true copy by the company secretary, accepting the facility on the terms and conditions of this letter, approving the execution and delivery of the agreement constituted by this letter and appointing *[persons]* to sign *[drawdown requests, etc]*;

◆ the duly executed *[charge/deed of postponement, etc]*;

◆ a certified up-to-date copy of the company's memorandum and articles of association;

◆ specimen signatures of the persons authorised to sign as above;

◆ payment of *[any]* arrangement or commitment fee.

Events of default

The typical events of default for a loan agreement may be summarised.

◆ Failing to make any payment on the due date.

◆ If any representations or warranties or documentation provided shall be incorrect in a material respect.

◆ If there is default in the performance of any other term or condition of the facility or any other event occurs in the bank's opinion to place the facility in jeopardy.

◆ If a petition is presented or an administration order is made.

◆ If an order is made or resolution passed to wind up the company other than for purposes of reconstruction or amalgamation on terms previously approved by the bank while the company is solvent.

◆ If a meeting is convened or proposal made to enter into any arrangements or composition for the benefit of creditors.

◆ If an encumbrancer, receiver, administrative receiver, manager or similar officer is appointed over the whole or part of the company's undertaking and assets.

◆ If any mortgage or charge becomes enforceable, whether or not the chargee/ mortgagee thereof takes any steps to enforce the same.

◆ If any indebtedness or obligation for the repayment of any borrowed monies becomes due and payable prior to the specified maturity date due to any default or is otherwise not paid when due.

◆ If the company suspends or threatens to suspend its business or a substantial part thereof or suspends payment of debts within the meaning of the Insolvency Act 1986 section 123 or re-enactment thereof.

◆ If there is a *[material]* change in ownership of the company that has not previously been approved by the bank.

- If the company ceases to be a {*wholly owned*} subsidiary of [ ] or if the company ceases wholly to own [ ] subsidiaries.
- The company will immediately notify the bank in writing *[address]* of the occurrence of any event of default and at any time after the occurrence thereof the bank, whether or not notified by the company, may by notice in writing *[address]* declare that all amounts due under the facility are immediately due and payable and such declaration shall be effective from the date of such occurrence or such other date as the bank may specify in the said notice.

Note that many of the above clauses will incorporate wording to include guarantors of the company's obligations.

Other clauses

The loan agreement will include wording as to:

- the definition of terms;
- treatment of costs in the event of default;
- calculation of mandatory reserve assets liabilities;
- changes in (taxation etc) circumstances;
- loan repayment and prepayment and cancellation terms;
- arrangement fees and commitment commission;
- minimum utilisation terms;
- interest margins;
- drawdown options;
- currency options;
- facility availability; and
- general conditions as to legal jurisdiction, etc.

Appendix 5

Detailed forecast example of future trading

Sheet 1: General guidelines to the compilation

Sheet 2: Actual results of the previous year.

Actual trading results are shown for each month of the year 2003. It has been assumed the quantities of items produced were sold at 1.65 during the first half of the year and a price increase to 1.73 was adopted thereafter when new plant came on stream and produced a slightly modified item selling for 1.50. This enabled a higher production to be achieved by five less workers. Turnover for the year nearly reached £2.5 million and a profit before tax of £449,176 was earned. Cash held at the beginning of January was £25,000.

When calculating the cash flow, a one month time lag for invoicing sales at the month end and a further one month credit has been allowed before the cash was received (*Note 1*). VAT at 17.5% has been added to the profit and loss account sales (*Note 2*) and for simplicity it has been assumed that 80% of non-labour costs have also been subject to VAT at the standard rate (*Note 5*).

Labour costs have been paid out in the month they have occurred (*Note 3*) but two months' credit has been taken before paying other costs and materials costs have been assumed ordered in advance and paid in the month of production (*Note 4*). January and February other costs are calculated from the spreadsheet since they relate to the last two months of the previous year. The VAT payable is settled quarterly and is the net sum of outputs and inputs for the previous three months (*Note 6*).

The new equipment purchased is shown as paid in July (*Note 7*) and the business has had to repay the principal of a bank loan at the fixed rate of £8,000 per month (*Note*

413

8) with the interest (not shown) included in other costs. Taxation paid in September relates to corporation tax due on the previous year's profits at the rate of 20% *(Note 9)*. A dividend has been declared out of the previous year's profits and paid in March after the audit *(Note 10)*. The business shows a healthy position at the end of 2003 with £111,212 held in the bank.

Sheet 3: Projected results for 2001

With the new equipment installed, the management has decided that production can be increased to 1.8 million units from 1.47 million units achieved in 2003 *(Note 12)*. The quantity of items produced each month in 2004 has been assumed as the same percentage produced in 2003 *(Note 11)* as adjusted up to the higher annual output budgeted for the year. With the new plant output having been established, it has been possible to market all production at a standardised selling price of 1.75 per unit *(Note 13)*. The labour costs are shown for either four or five weekly payments per month depending on when the payment days fall in each month *(Note 14)* and the average cost from January onwards is based on the wage bill brought forward and adjusted for a wage increase of 3% pa *(Note 16)*. The number of production employees is projected to remain steady at 60 throughout the year *(Note 15)*.

The variable cost of materials has been estimated by multiplying the production output by the cost taken per item *(Note 17)*. Fixed labour costs have also assumed a pay increase of 3% pa and been allocated evenly each month over the ensuing year *(Note 18)*. Other fixed costs have been separately calculated for each item (not shown) and shown for each month when they are expected to occur *(Note 19)*. Depreciation will be calculated on the bases laid down for each asset (ie worked on a straight line or reducing balance) and adjusted as each item of new equipment is purchased. When items are acquired part way through the year, depending on the method adopted for calculating depreciation, either one-twelfth of the annual charge for the new item is added to the depreciation sum, or the depreciation charge for the whole year can be apportioned and charged against the remaining months of the year. The cash flow calculation is on the same basis as for the year 2003 example *(Note 20)*.

Sheet 4: Actual results for 2004

As each month's trading results are known, the actual figures are substituted for the estimated figures. In the example given, the fall off in sales led, first, to a reduction in selling price from June and, when this did not stem the dropping sales, the number of production (and some fixed cost) employees were made redundant in December. The business also had to suffer an increase in material costs from August. As a result, it was seen that the forecast cash flow of the business could not afford to pay off the loan early and meet the corporation tax bill due in September. The loan was therefore continued and serviced on its original repayment schedule.

A BUSINESS

Appendix 5   Sheet 1

A manufacturing concern that, for simplification, has one staple product and requires a projection of cash flow to determine whether further new equipment can be purchased in 2001.

General Guidelines:

Sheet 1 provides the underlying assumptions of the model.

Sheet 2 displays on a monthly basis the results for the previous year 2003.

Sheet 3 displays the trading projections for the ensuing year 2004 based on the monthly seasonality indicated by Sheet 1.

Sheet 4 displays the actual results for the year 2004 (it is assumed that the present time is January 2005).

Sheet 5 displays the Balance Sheets of the business monthly from the beginning to the end of year 2004.

NOTES TO SHEET 2: PROFIT AND LOSS ACCOUNT and CASH FLOW. Actual result for 2003.

1   Sales are those invoiced two months earlier based on the principle that January invoicing will be done in February and the cash received in March (credit allowed being at least 30 days after the month end).

2   VAT on sales relates to sales invoiced in the month.

3   Labour costs are the wages of the month in question.

4   Other costs from March 2000 comprise materials costs of the month in question with no supplier credit and Fixed Other Costs of two months earlier (assumed when the bills were paid).

5   VAT has been assumed as averaging 80% of standard rate on the costs of that month (refer note 4).

6   The Net VAT payable is the amount irrecoverable from sales for the preceding three months (on Outputs less Inputs) and paid one month after each quarter's end.

7   The capital expenditure figure for new plant has been assumed. Note that the VAT payment in October 2000 has accounted for the VAT incurred in July on the equipment.

8   The loan repayments comprise a total of interest and principal each month.

9   The Corporation tax liability has been assumed as stated and paid in the months shown.

10   The profit distribution (dividend) figure has been assumed as stated.

NOTES TO SHEET 3: PROFIT AND LOSS ACCOUNT. Projected result for 2004.

11   Seasonal variations in monthly sales (and thus production) have been allowed by allocating the projected total annual production monthly in proportion to that achieved from the old plant in the previous year.

12   The unit output per month is the projected annual total from both the old and new plant required by the sales budget multiplied by the monthly percentage production.

13   A new price has been set for the year 2001 and, for simplicity, has been taken at the same value per unit for items produced by both the old and new plants.

14   The variable labour cost is calculated by multiplying estimated employee numbers by their average annual cost to the business (including Employer's NI and pension) and spread monthly in 4 or 5 weekly periods.

15   The number of employees includes additional labour to work the new plant.

16   Employee costs include a 3% wage rise at the beginning of the year based on the wage bill for December 2000.

17   Materials costs have been calculated by multiplying the forecast quantity of output by the expected average cost per item of components per unit produced.

18   Fixed labour costs have also allowed for the number of weeks in each month that wages will be paid.

19   Other fixed costs have been assumed and in practice will be separately estimated for each cost centre.

20   For cash flow assumptions refer to Notes 1 through to 10 above.

NOTES TO SHEET 4: PROFIT AND LOSS ACCOUNT and CASH FLOW. Actual result 2004.

21   The example has assumed that sales did not materialise as well as expected from April 2004 and the business accordingly cut its selling prices and started to reduce output from June 2004.

When sales did not recover to the original levels expected the business did not start to lay off workers until December.

The variable materials average cost per item has changed according to the (assumed) ruling market prices.

Because of the projected strong cash flow the business had scheduled to repay the loan early in August 2001. When the cash position started to deteriorate the early repayment idea was abandoned.

The business found it possible to reduce slightly its fixed labour costs but underestimated its other fixed overheads.

Note the differences between the monthly Operating Results and Net Cash In/Outflows. For the year as a whole the Pre-tax Profit was double the Net Cash Inflow.

415

A BUSINESS

PROFIT AND LOSS ACCOUNT

Year 2003 — Appendix 5, Sheet 2

		Actual January	Actual February	Actual March	Actual April	Actual May	Actual June	Actual July	Actual August	Actual September	Actual October	Actual November	Actual December	Actual YEAR
OUTPUT	(quantity)	114,985	113,031	98,640	87,120	109,890	99,000	107,250	125,400	125,400	125,400	125,400	125,400	1,356,916
PRICE	(per item)	1.65	1.65	1.65	1.65	1.65	1.65	1.73	1.73	1.73	1.73	1.73	1.73	1.69
New Plant Output	(quantity)	0	0	0	0	0	0	9,200	14,600	19,300	24,600	24,600	24,600	116,900
Price	(per item)	0	0	0	0	0	0	1.50	1.50	1.50	1.50	1.50	1.50	1.50
Total TURNOVER	(£)	**189,725**	**186,501**	**162,756**	**143,748**	**181,319**	**163,350**	**199,611**	**239,156**	**246,206**	**254,156**	**254,156**	**254,156**	**2,474,837**
COSTS	(£)													
Variable Labour		57,810	61,880	63,427	54,177	55,532	56,920	61,844	65,782	67,426	69,112	70,840	72,611	757,361
	number employed	50	50	50	50	50	50	53	55	60	60	60	60	54
	average cost per capita	13,874	14,851	15,222	13,002	13,328	13,661	14,002	14,352	13,485	13,822	14,168	14,522	14,025
Materials etc		59,680	48,940	46,880	47,574	49,708	50,499	56,527	63,246	69,761	76,951	76,647	76,311	722,725
	average per item produced	0.52	0.43	0.48	0.55	0.45	0.51	0.49	0.48	0.48	0.51	0.51	0.51	0.49
Total		**117,490**	**110,820**	**110,307**	**101,751**	**105,240**	**107,419**	**118,371**	**129,028**	**137,187**	**146,063**	**147,487**	**148,922**	**1,480,086**
Fixed Labour		5,920	5,920	5,920	5,920	5,920	5,920	5,920	5,920	5,920	5,920	5,920	5,920	71,040
Other		36,240	35,670	36,562	30,000	30,750	31,519	32,307	33,114	33,942	34,791	35,661	36,552	407,107
Depreciation		5,354	5,354	5,354	5,354	5,354	5,354	5,884	5,884	5,884	5,884	5,884	5,884	67,428
Total		**47,514**	**46,944**	**47,836**	**41,274**	**42,024**	**42,793**	**44,111**	**44,918**	**45,746**	**46,595**	**47,465**	**48,356**	**545,575**
Combined Total costs		165,004	157,764	158,143	143,025	147,264	150,212	162,482	173,947	182,933	192,658	194,951	197,278	2,025,661
OPERATING RESULT before tax		**24,721**	**28,737**	**4,613**	**723**	**34,055**	**13,138**	**37,129**	**65,209**	**63,272**	**61,497**	**59,204**	**56,877**	**449,176**

CASH FLOW

	Notes	Actual January	Actual February	Actual March	Actual April	Actual May	Actual June	Actual July	Actual August	Actual September	Actual October	Actual November	Actual December	Actual YEAR
SALES (Outputs)	1	180,000	180,000	189,725	186,501	162,756	143,748	181,319	163,350	199,611	239,156	246,206	254,156	2,326,526
VAT @ 17.5%	2	33,202	32,638	33,202	32,638	28,482	25,156	31,731	28,586	34,932	41,852	43,086	44,477	465,305
TURNOVER INFLOW		213,202	212,638	222,927	219,139	191,238	168,904	213,049	191,936	234,542	281,008	289,291	298,633	2,791,831
COSTS: Labour	3	63,730	67,800	69,347	60,097	61,452	62,840	67,764	71,702	73,346	75,032	76,760	78,531	828,401
Other	4	95,680	83,940	83,120	83,244	86,270	80,499	87,277	94,765	102,068	110,066	110,589	111,102	1,128,619
Add VAT @ 17.5% on costs	5	15,540	15,484	13,638	13,198	13,444	12,899	13,142	14,305	15,591	16,844	18,218	18,284	180,588
net VAT payable	6	0	0	0	50,644	0	0	45,590	0	0	63,054	0	0	159,288
EXPENDITURE OUTFLOW		174,950	167,224	166,105	207,183	161,166	156,238	213,773	180,772	191,005	264,996	205,567	207,917	2,296,896
GROSS OPERATING INFLOW		38,252	45,414	56,822	11,956	30,073	12,666	-724	11,164	43,538	16,012	83,724	90,716	439,612
CAPITAL EXPENDITURE (incl VAT)	7	0	0	0	0	0	0	57,400	0	0	0	0	0	57,400
LOAN repayments	8	8,000	8,000	8,000	8,000	8,000	8,000	8,000	8,000	8,000	8,000	8,000	8,000	96,000
TAXATION payable	9	0	0	0	0	0	0	0	0	80,000	0	0	0	80,000
DISTRIBUTION of profit	10	0	0	120,000	0	0	0	0	0	0	0	0	0	120,000
NET CASH INFLOW		30,252	37,414	-71,178	3,956	22,073	4,666	-66,124	3,164	-44,462	8,012	75,724	82,716	86,212
CASH in hand brought forward		25,000	55,252	92,666	21,488	25,443	47,516	52,182	-13,942	-10,777	-55,240	-47,228	28,496	28,496
CASH in hand carried forward		55,252	92,666	21,488	25,443	47,516	52,182	-13,942	-10,777	-55,240	-47,228	28,496	111,212	111,212

A BUSINESS — PROFIT AND LOSS ACCOUNT — Year 2004

Appendix 5 — Sheet 3

All monthly columns headed "Projected".

	Notes	January	February	March	April	May	June	July	August	September	October	November	December	YEAR
percent of production	11	8.47	8.33	7.27	6.42	8.10	7.30	7.90	9.24	9.24	9.24	9.24	9.24	100.00
OUTPUT (quantity)	12	152,532	149,940	130,850	115,568	145,773	131,327	142,271	166,348	166,348	166,348	166,348	166,348	1,800,000
PRICE (per item)	13	1.75	1.75	1.75	1.75	1.75	1.75	1.75	1.75	1.75	1.75	1.75	1.75	1.75
Total TURNOVER (£)		**266,931**	**262,395**	**228,987**	**202,244**	**255,103**	**229,823**	**248,975**	**291,109**	**291,109**	**291,109**	**291,109**	**291,109**	**3,150,000**
Wages weeks in month		5	4	4	5	4	4	5	4	4	5	4	4	
COSTS														
Variable Labour — number employed	14	60	60	60	60	60	60	60	60	60	60	60	60	60
average cost per capita	15	14,958	14,958	14,958	14,958	14,958	14,958	14,958	14,958	14,958	14,958	14,958	14,958	14,958
Labour		86,295	69,036	69,036	86,295	69,036	69,036	86,295	69,036	69,036	86,295	69,036	69,036	897,472
Materials etc	16	83,893	82,467	71,967	63,562	80,175	72,230	78,249	91,491	91,491	91,491	91,491	91,491	990,000
average cost per item	17	0.55	0.55	0.55	0.55	0.55	0.55	0.55	0.55	0.55	0.55	0.55	0.55	0.55
Total		**170,188**	**151,503**	**141,004**	**149,858**	**149,212**	**141,266**	**164,545**	**160,528**	**160,528**	**177,787**	**160,528**	**160,528**	**1,887,472**
Fixed Labour	18	6,098	6,098	6,098	6,098	6,098	6,098	6,098	6,098	6,098	6,098	6,098	6,098	73,176
Other – per Budget		42,000	37,000	40,000	39,000	41,000	38,000	39,000	35,000	39,000	40,000	37,000	35,000	462,000
Depreciation	19	5,884	5,884	5,884	5,884	5,884	5,884	5,884	5,884	5,884	5,884	5,884	5,884	70,608
Total		**53,982**	**48,982**	**51,982**	**50,982**	**52,982**	**49,982**	**50,982**	**46,982**	**50,982**	**51,982**	**48,982**	**46,982**	**605,784**
Combined Total costs		224,170	200,485	192,986	200,840	202,194	191,248	215,527	207,510	211,510	229,769	209,510	207,510	2,493,256
OPERATING RESULT before tax		**42,761**	**61,910**	**36,001**	**1,404**	**52,910**	**38,574**	**33,448**	**83,599**	**79,599**	**61,340**	**81,599**	**83,599**	**656,744**

CASH FLOW

	Notes	January	February	March	April	May	June	July	August	September	October	November	December	YEAR
SALES (Outputs)	20	254,156	254,156	266,931	262,395	228,987	202,244	255,103	229,823	248,975	291,109	291,109	291,109	3,076,094
VAT @ 17.5%		44,477	44,477	46,713	45,919	40,073	35,393	44,643	40,219	43,571	50,944	50,944	50,944	615,219
TURNOVER INFLOW		**298,633**	**298,633**	**313,644**	**308,314**	**269,060**	**237,637**	**299,746**	**270,042**	**292,545**	**342,053**	**342,053**	**342,053**	**3,691,312**
COSTS: Labour		92,393	75,134	75,134	92,393	75,134	75,134	92,393	75,134	75,134	92,393	75,134	75,134	970,648
Other		119,553	119,019	113,967	100,562	120,175	111,230	119,249	129,491	130,491	126,491	130,491	131,491	1,452,213
Add VAT @ 17.5% on costs		18,347	19,798	20,312	17,774	16,723	19,491	18,380	19,014	21,471	20,911	21,471	21,611	235,303
net VAT payable		76,938	0	0	72,938	0	0	64,610	0	0	82,558	0	0	297,044
EXPENDITURE OUTFLOW		**307,231**	**213,952**	**209,413**	**283,668**	**212,033**	**205,855**	**294,633**	**223,639**	**227,097**	**322,354**	**227,097**	**228,237**	**2,955,208**
GROSS OPERATING INFLOW		**-8,599**	**84,681**	**104,230**	**24,646**	**57,027**	**31,782**	**5,113**	**46,402**	**65,448**	**19,699**	**114,956**	**113,816**	**659,202**
CAPITAL EXPENDITURE (incl VAT)		0	0	0	0	0	0	0	0	0	0	0	0	0
LOAN repayments		8,000	8,000	8,000	8,000	8,000	8,000	8,000	0	0	0	0	0	56,000
TAXATION payable		0	0	0	0	0	0	0	96,000	89,835	0	0	0	185,835
DISTRIBUTION of profit		0	0	180,000	0	0	0	0	0	0	0	0	0	180,000
NET CASH INFLOW		**-16,599**	**76,681**	**-83,770**	**16,646**	**49,027**	**23,782**	**-2,887**	**-49,598**	**-24,387**	**19,699**	**114,956**	**113,816**	**237,367**
CASH in hand brought forward		111,212	94,613	171,294	87,524	104,170	153,197	176,978	174,092	124,494	100,108	119,807	234,763	111,212
CASH in hand carried forward		94,613	171,294	87,524	104,170	153,197	176,978	174,092	124,494	100,108	119,807	234,763	348,579	348,579

Appendix 5

Sheet 4

A BUSINESS — PROFIT AND LOSS ACCOUNT — Year 2004

		Notes	Actual January	Actual February	Actual March	Actual April	Actual May	Actual June	Actual July	Actual August	Actual September	Actual October	Actual November	Actual December	Actual YEAR
BUDGETED SALES	(£)	21	266,931	262,395	228,987	202,244	255,103	229,823	248,975	291,109	291,109	291,109	291,109	291,109	3,150,000
PRICE	(per item)		1.75	1.75	1.75	1.75	1.75	1.65	1.65	1.65	1.65	1.65	1.65	1.65	1.69
Units sold	(number)		122,857	125,714	114,286	102,857	114,286	115,152	133,333	127,273	133,333	139,394	127,273	124,242	1,480,000
OUTPUT	(quantity)		150,000	150,000	150,000	150,000	150,000	140,000	140,000	130,000	120,000	100,000	100,000	90,000	1,570,000
ACTUAL SALES	(£)		**215,000**	**220,000**	**200,000**	**180,000**	**200,000**	**190,000**	**220,000**	**210,000**	**220,000**	**230,000**	**210,000**	**205,000**	**2,500,000**
COSTS															
Variable Labour			74,789	74,789	74,789	74,789	74,789	74,789	74,789	74,789	74,789	74,789	74,789	62,324	**885,007**
number employed			60	60	60	60	60	60	60	60	60	60	60	50	59
average cost per capita			14,958	14,958	14,958	14,958	14,958	14,958	14,958	14,958	14,958	14,958	14,958	14,958	15,450
Materials etc			82,500	82,500	84,000	84,000	84,000	77,000	75,600	78,000	72,000	60,000	60,000	54,000	**893,600**
average cost per item			0.55	0.55	0.56	0.56	0.56	0.55	0.54	0.60	0.60	0.60	0.60	0.60	0.57
Total			**157,289**	**157,289**	**158,789**	**158,789**	**158,789**	**151,789**	**150,389**	**152,789**	**146,789**	**134,789**	**134,789**	**116,324**	**1,778,607**
Fixed Labour			7,036	5,628	5,628	7,036	5,628	5,628	6,267	5,013	5,013	6,267	5,013	5,013	69,170
Other - per Budget			42,000	37,000	40,000	39,000	41,000	38,000	42,000	39,000	41,000	40,000	38,000	38,000	475,000
Depreciation			5,884	5,884	5,884	5,884	5,884	5,884	5,884	5,884	5,884	5,884	5,884	5,884	70,608
Total			**54,920**	**48,512**	**51,512**	**51,920**	**52,512**	**49,512**	**54,151**	**49,897**	**51,897**	**52,151**	**48,897**	**48,897**	**614,778**
Combined Total costs			212,209	205,801	210,301	210,709	211,301	201,301	204,540	202,686	198,686	186,940	183,686	165,221	2,393,385
OPERATING RESULT before tax			**2,791**	**14,199**	**-10,301**	**-30,709**	**-11,301**	**-11,301**	**15,460**	**7,314**	**21,314**	**43,060**	**26,314**	**39,779**	**106,615**

CASH FLOW — Year 2004

	Actual January	Actual February	Actual March	Actual April	Actual May	Actual June	Actual July	Actual August	Actual September	Actual October	Actual November	Actual December	Actual YEAR
SALES (Outputs)	291,109	291,109	215,000	220,000	200,000	180,000	200,000	190,000	220,000	210,000	220,000	230,000	2,667,217
VAT @ 17.5%	50,944	50,944	37,625	38,500	35,000	31,500	35,000	33,250	38,500	36,750	38,500	40,250	533,443
TURNOVER INFLOW	**342,053**	**342,053**	**252,625**	**258,500**	**235,000**	**211,500**	**235,000**	**223,250**	**258,500**	**246,750**	**258,500**	**270,250**	**3,200,661**
COSTS: Labour	81,825	80,417	80,417	81,825	80,417	80,417	81,056	79,802	79,802	81,056	79,802	67,337	954,177
Other	128,491	117,500	124,500	121,000	124,000	123,000	118,000	113,600	120,000	111,000	101,000	100,000	1,402,091
Add VAT @ 17.5% on costs	21,191	19,338	20,318	19,880	20,300	20,160	19,215	18,550	19,530	18,060	16,240	16,100	228,881
net VAT payable	87,894			49,490			39,025			55,755			232,164
EXPENDITURE OUTFLOW	**319,402**	**217,255**	**225,235**	**272,195**	**224,717**	**223,577**	**257,296**	**211,952**	**219,332**	**265,871**	**197,042**	**183,437**	**2,817,313**
GROSS OPERATING INFLOW	**22,651**	**124,798**	**27,390**	**-13,695**	**10,283**	**-12,077**	**-22,296**	**11,298**	**39,168**	**-19,121**	**61,458**	**86,813**	**316,667**
CAPITAL EXPENDITURE (incl VAT)	0	0	0	0	0	0	0	0	0	0	0	0	0
LOAN repayments	8,000	8,000	8,000	8,000	8,000	8,000	8,000	8,000	8,000	8,000	8,000	8,000	96,000
TAXATION payable	0	0	0	0	0	0	0	0	89,835	0	0	0	89,835
DISTRIBUTION of profit	0	0	80,000	0	0	0	0	0	0	0	0	0	80,000
NET CASH INFLOW	**14,651**	**116,798**	**-60,610**	**-21,695**	**2,283**	**-20,077**	**-30,296**	**3,298**	**-58,667**	**-27,121**	**53,458**	**78,813**	**50,832**
CASH in hand brought forward	111,212	125,863	242,661	182,051	160,356	162,638	142,561	112,265	115,562	56,895	29,774	83,231	111,212
CASH in hand carried forward	125,863	242,661	182,051	160,356	162,638	142,561	112,265	115,562	56,895	29,774	83,231	162,044	162,044

A BUSINESS
BALANCE SHEETS

Year 2004	Opening Position	Actual January	Actual February	Actual March	Actual April	Actual May	Actual June	Actual July	Actual August	Actual September	Actual October	Actual November	Actual December	Notes:
FIXED ASSETS	150,000	150,000	150,000	150,000	150,000	150,000	150,000	150,000	150,000	150,000	150,000	150,000	150,000	1
Less Depreciation	50,000	55,884	61,768	67,652	73,536	79,420	85,304	91,188	97,072	102,956	108,840	114,724	120,608	
Net book value	100,000	94,116	88,232	82,348	76,464	70,580	64,696	58,812	52,928	47,044	41,160	35,276	29,392	
NET CURRENT ASSETS														
Stocks	100,483	91,491	82,500	82,500	84,000	84,000	84,000	77,000	75,600	78,000	72,000	60,000	60,000	2
Trade Debtors (2 mths)	582,217	506,109	435,000	420,000	380,000	380,000	390,000	410,000	430,000	430,000	450,000	440,000	415,000	3
Cash at bank	111,212	125,863	242,661	182,051	160,356	162,638	142,561	112,265	115,562	56,895	29,774	83,231	162,044	4
	793,912	723,463	760,161	684,551	624,356	626,638	616,561	599,265	621,162	564,895	551,774	583,231	637,044	
Less:														
Trade Creditors (1 mth)	91,491	82,500	82,500	84,000	84,000	84,000	77,000	75,600	78,000	72,000	60,000	60,000	54,000	5
Other Creditors	152,000	160,454	166,187	88,195	98,974	100,115	97,330	87,724	84,384	86,029	75,569	61,899	64,275	6
VAT Creditor	89,836	17,308	36,190	49,490	11,340	25,900	39,025	19,390	37,030	55,755	24,150	45,080	64,855	7
Tax Creditor	87,894	90,393	93,233	91,173	85,031	82,770	80,510	83,602	85,065	-507	8,105	13,367	21,323	8
Bank Loan	152,000	144,000	136,000	128,000	120,000	112,000	104,000	96,000	88,000	80,000	72,000	64,000	56,000	9
Net Current Assets	220,691	228,808	246,051	243,693	225,011	221,853	218,696	236,948	248,683	271,618	311,950	338,885	376,591	
Employment of Capital	320,691	322,924	334,283	326,041	301,475	292,433	283,392	295,760	301,611	318,662	353,110	374,161	405,983	
SHARE CAPITAL	200,000	200,000	200,000	200,000	200,000	200,000	200,000	200,000	200,000	200,000	200,000	200,000	200,000	
RETAINED EARNINGS	120,691	122,924	134,283	126,041	101,475	92,433	83,392	95,760	101,611	118,662	153,110	174,161	205,983	10
Capital Employed	320,691	322,924	334,283	326,041	301,475	292,433	283,392	295,760	301,611	318,662	353,110	374,161	405,983	10

NOTES TO SHEET 5: BALANCE SHEET

1. The opening fixed asset figure has been assumed.
2. Stocks have been calculated as the quantity purchased in the two previous trading months less the quantity utilised in the current trading month. The opening stocks have been assumed.
3. Trade Debtors have been taken as the sales achieved in the previous two previous trading month and the current trading month.
4. Cash in hand accords with the cash flow shown as at end of each month.
5. Trade Creditors have been taken as the purchases made in the current trading month.
6. Other Creditors comprise Other Costs outstanding for the previous and current trading months together with other costs accrued due to cash flow timing differences in the model.
7. The VAT creditor is accumulated over each successive three months trading period before it is paid.
8. The Corporation Tax Creditor comprises the previous year's annual liability until paid and the cumulative monthly amounts accrued due at the rate of 20% on profits or losses
9. The bank loan monthly repayments include interest but for simplicity these amounts have not been allowed for in the tax payable calculation.
10. Retained Earnings comprise the amount accrued to date together with the profit for each month less the Corporation tax due thereon.

check: The Operating Result for the year gave a profit before tax of £120,691

Retained earnings at the start of the year were £106,615   After deducting Corporation tax at 20%, retained earnings total £85,292

Adding retained earnings for the year and deducting the profit distribution of £80,000   leaves a balance in hand at year end of £205,983

check: The cash in hand carried forward as at the end of the year is £162,044   This is the same as the Net Cash Inflow for the year £50,832   plus cash in hand at the start of the year £111,212

Appendix 6

Example of comparative term loan tables

Examples of a loan of 100 granted for a period of ten years with different repayment methods.

1. Annual repayments of interest and principal in equal instalments.

Years end	Principal (£'000)	Interest due end of year	Debt outstand-ing	Repay-ments end of year	Balance due	Capital released	Release cumulative	Base Profit @ 1.50% pa	Profit on cap release	DCF at 4.5% pa	Present Value
Start	100.00										
1	100.00	6.00	106.00	13.59	92.41	7.59	7.59	4.50	0.34	0.957	4.63
2	92.41	5.54	97.96	13.59	84.37	8.04	15.63	4.16	0.70	0.916	4.45
3	84.37	5.06	89.43	13.59	75.85	8.52	24.15	3.80	1.09	0.876	4.28
4	75.85	4.55	80.40	13.59	66.81	9.04	33.19	3.41	1.49	0.839	4.11
5	66.81	4.01	70.82	13.59	57.23	9.58	42.77	3.01	1.92	0.802	3.96
6	57.23	3.43	60.67	13.59	47.08	10.15	52.92	2.58	2.38	0.768	3.81
7	47.08	2.82	49.90	13.59	36.32	10.76	63.68	2.12	2.87	0.735	3.66
8	36.32	2.18	38.50	13.59	24.91	11.41	75.09	1.63	3.38	0.703	3.53
9	24.91	1.49	26.40	13.59	12.82	12.09	87.18	1.12	3.92	0.673	3.39
10	12.82	0.77	13.58	13.59	-0.00	12.82	100.00	0.58	4.50	0.644	3.27
Totals		35.87		135.87		100.00		26.90	22.60		39.09
								Combined	49.50		

2. Interest only payments with end of term repayment of principal.

Years end	Principal (£'000)	Interest due end of year	Debt out- standing	Repay- ments end of year	Balance due	Capital released	Release cumulative	Base profit @ 1.50% pa	Profit on cap release	DCF at 4.5% pa	Present value
Start	100.00										
1	100.00	6.00	106.00	6.00	100.00	0.00	0.00	4.50	0.00	0.957	4.31
2	100.00	6.00	106.00	6.00	100.00	0.00	0.00	4.50	0.00	0.916	4.12
3	100.00	6.00	106.00	6.00	100.00	0.00	0.00	4.50	0.00	0.876	3.94
4	100.00	6.00	106.00	6.00	100.00	0.00	0.00	4.50	0.00	0.839	3.77
5	100.00	6.00	106.00	6.00	100.00	0.00	0.00	4.50	0.00	0.802	3.61
6	100.00	6.00	106.00	6.00	100.00	0.00	0.00	4.50	0.00	0.768	3.46
7	100.00	6.00	106.00	6.00	100.00	0.00	0.00	4.50	0.00	0.735	3.31
8	100.00	6.00	106.00	6.00	100.00	0.00	0.00	4.50	0.00	0.703	3.16
9	100.00	6.00	106.00	6.00	100.00	0.00	0.00	4.50	0.00	0.673	3.03
10	100.00	6.00	106.00	106.00	0.00	100.00	100.00	4.50	4.50	0.644	5.80
Totals		60.00		160.00		100.00		45.00	**4.50**		38.51

Combined   49.50

3. Equal annual repayments of principal together with interest due.

Years end	Principal (£'000)	Interest due end of year	Debt out- standing	Repay- ments end of year	Balance due	Capital released	Release cumulative	Base profit @ 1.50% pa	Profit on cap release	DCF at 4.5% pa	Present value
Start	100.00										
1	100.00	6.00	106.00	16.00	90.00	10.00	10.00	4.50	0.45	0.957	4.74
2	90.00	5.40	95.40	15.40	80.00	10.00	20.00	4.05	0.90	0.916	4.53
3	80.00	4.80	84.80	14.80	70.00	10.00	30.00	3.60	1.35	0.876	4.34
4	70.00	4.20	74.20	14.20	60.00	10.00	40.00	3.15	1.80	0.839	4.15
5	60.00	3.60	63.60	13.60	50.00	10.00	50.00	2.70	2.25	0.802	3.97
6	50.00	3.00	53.00	13.00	40.00	10.00	60.00	2.25	2.70	0.768	3.80
7	40.00	2.40	42.40	12.40	30.00	10.00	70.00	1.80	3.15	0.735	3.64
8	30.00	1.80	31.80	11.80	20.00	10.00	80.00	1.35	3.60	0.703	3.48
9	20.00	1.20	21.20	11.20	10.00	10.00	90.00	0.90	4.05	0.673	3.33
10	10.00	0.60	10.60	10.60	0.00	10.00	100.00	0.45	4.50	0.644	3.19
Totals		33.00		133.00		100.00		24.75	**24.75**		39.17

Combined   49.50

Interest rate %pa chosen for all	6.00		Front fee: assumed to be 2% flat	2.00
Cost of funds % pa chosen	4.50			
Base profit on capital released	1.50		DCF = discounted cash flow	

4. Comparison of a term loan having an annual review.

Years end	Principal (£'000)	Interest due end of year	Debt out-standing	Fee 1% pa on renewal	Balance due	Capital released	Release cumulative	Base profit @ 1.50% pa	Profit on fee earned	DCF at 4.5% pa	Present value
1	100.00	6.00	106.00	1.00	105.00	0.00	0.00	4.50	1.00	0.957	6.26
2	100.00	6.00	106.00	1.00	105.00	0.00	0.00	4.50	1.00	0.916	5.04
3	100.00	6.00	106.00	1.00	105.00	0.00	0.00	4.50	1.00	0.876	4.82
4	100.00	6.00	106.00	1.00	105.00	0.00	0.00	4.50	1.00	0.839	4.61
5	100.00	6.00	106.00	1.00	105.00	0.00	0.00	4.50	1.00	0.802	4.41
6	100.00	6.00	106.00	1.00	105.00	0.00	0.00	4.50	1.00	0.768	4.22
7	100.00	6.00	106.00	1.00	105.00	0.00	0.00	4.50	1.00	0.735	4.04
8	100.00	6.00	106.00	1.00	105.00	0.00	0.00	4.50	1.00	0.703	3.87
9	100.00	6.00	106.00	1.00	105.00	0.00	0.00	4.50	1.00	0.673	3.70
10	100.00	6.00	106.00	1.00	105.00	0.00	0.00	4.50	0.00	0.644	2.90
Totals		60.00						45.00	9.00		43.88

Appendix 7

Valuation of businesses

Fashion has changed over the years how individual shares are to be valued. There is no single measurement to go by and investors and market analysts have their own favourites. The aspect of valuation to be covered in this appendix is that based on the published financial record of the company. The Inland Revenue have their own procedures for valuing shares when disposals are made.

The more common ratios and other aids used in the valuation of shares will be individually commented on and these are:

- dividend cover and yield;
- asset value;
- price/earnings ratio;
- EBITDA and discounted cash flow;
- value enhancement;
- market conception.

Dividend cover and yield

Dividend cover refers to how many times the (equity) dividend is covered (ie divided into) by earnings available for distribution, each calculated in pence per share, and the yield is the gross annual income as a percentage of the market price of the share that accrues to the company's shares attributable to those shareholders by way of declared distributions of earnings after taxation.

The distribution policy of the company may have been made public through the directors issuing a 'statement of intent' (particularly in respect of newly quoted shares) or it may have to be deduced by comparing the cost of recent years' declaration of the total annual dividends with the earnings (ie the net profit after tax) that is available each year for distribution to the shareholders. Dividends can be declared out of earlier retained earnings not yet distributed but a company cannot distribute to shareholders what it has not yet earned. Comparing the dividend cover, yield and distribution policies of different companies will meet the first valuation criteria. The yield will reduce as the share value increases unless the dividend declarations rise commensurately.

Price/earnings (P/E) ratio

This ratio for quoted companies is the market share price divided by the earnings available for distribution, each designated in pence per share. It is often described as the number of years required to purchase the share as represented by its present price. As the price rises, the ratio will also rise unless earnings rise proportionately. It is a good comparative valuation tool between companies, including acting as a benchmark for unquoted companies of similar size operating in the same field, but adjustments need to be done for 'exceptional' one-off profit and loss items that will distort the earnings for any particular year, such as reorganisation and redundancy costs.

Future trading prospects will affect the P/E ratio and this may be material if there is likely to be an imminent material change in earnings. This is why some P/E ratio comparisons are quoted on next year's estimated earnings. Care should be taken, however, as future expectations may not be borne out subsequently by fact. A half-way stage is to take the most recent 12-months' earnings after the half year trading report has been issued by the company, by adding to the earnings of the second half of the last accounting year to the first half of the current accounting year.

The P/E ratio calculation becomes more complicated if the company has made material acquisitions or sales during the year. The guideline is to account for future earnings from all on-going businesses on an estimated full annual basis. The P/E ratio loses its usefulness, however, should the company report losses.

A surprising feature, perhaps, has been the ambivalence shown for the actual value of a company P/E ratio rather than its comparative value. That is, the demand (or lack of it) for a share determines its share price whether the P/E ratio calculated is overly high or low, given the assumptions that a high ratio may indicate that a share could be overvalued and vice versa. For example, a share on a P/E ratio of 30 with good earnings prospects may still rise to 40 on market demand, regardless of whether 30 or 40 was a true value to place on the share in the first place.

Asset value

A company that is highly cash generative, selling necessity products (eg basic foods) and not being very dependent on fixed assets (ie not capital intensive and having leased premises rather than owned) will have its net worth invested in fast moving stock-in-trade and little by way of trade debtors. Its asset value will bear a relatively close relationship to its true asset worth. If the profitability is good then this added value will give the share a premium (P/E ratio) rating.

Conversely, another company may require a high and continuing specialist investment in plant and machinery to produce its 'widgets'. The second-hand value of this machinery may be much less compared with its cost and book value, particularly if a forced sale is likely. Its true realisable asset value will be much lower than its book net asset value and the share, and other companies in the same field of operations, is likely to have a relatively low P/E ratio.

Further factors to consider are whether the company product(s) manufactured or sold are high tech (ie drugs having a long patent life), 'dirty' (ie rubber manufacture), mature (ie having limited scope for expansion in sales), fashionable (ie out sourcing) and so on. Each category will offer a greater or lesser asset value and expectant P/E ratio.

Sometimes the break up value of a business underpins the share price, especially if much of the asset value is in cash or 'near' (ie easily realisable into) cash. Predators may view the break-up value of the company as an opportunity to acquire the business and sell the unwanted parts while retaining the better parts at little or nil cost after the realisations. Asset values, therefore, have some influence on the comparative values of individual businesses.

EBITDA and discounted cash flow

EBITDA is the **E**arnings of a company **B**efore **I**nterest, **T**axation, **D**epreciation and **A**mortisation'. It is most frequently used when valuing companies for takeover purposes or when valuations are required taking into account trading prospects over a number of future years. It provides the investor with a valuation figure of the worth of its trading earnings but ignores factors which are relevant only to that company and are not truly comparable with other companies, such as the cost and amount of any finance borrowed and the policy adopted for the depreciation/ amortisation of assets.

A prospective buyer, for instance, may wish to repay any borrowings because it is cash rich or may wish to substitute its own cost of borrowing. Furthermore, a valuation comparison may be difficult between companies that have different policies of depreciating fixed assets, which would otherwise lead to a different basis of calculating earnings. It is the comparison of values that will be of interest to the prospective investor, where a change in the basis of accounting, the adoption of the different cost of borrowings and a rationalisation of costs will release savings that will improve the acquiring company's earnings.

Discounted Cash Flow

Discounted cash flow converts a future earnings or dividend or other income or expenditure stream to a present value. In the example following this is calculated to be £2,564,000.

Years	2005	2006	2007	2008	2009
Earnings (£'000's)	2,000	3,000	2,800	3,500	4,200
Discounting factor	6% pa	6% pa	6% pa	6% pa	6% pa
Present value (PV)	1,887	2,670	2,351	2,772	3,138
Calculated as	2,000/1.06	3,000/(1.06 × 1.06)	2,800/(1.06 × 1.06 × 1.06)	Etc	Etc
5 yrs average PV	2,564				

The discounting factor has been assumed as the cost to the company of borrowing funds commercially on the basis that if the rate of 6% pa were lower then the calculation would not lead to a viable proposition. Other discounting rates may be chosen as being more appropriate according to the circumstances, but if 6% pa is the acquiring company's borrowing cost post-acquisition, then this is a representative figure for discounting purposes. The base period shown of five years may also be changed, depending on how long the acquiring company decides to account for and obtain the value attributable to the purchase price (PV) spent. Start-up companies may offer no immediate earnings forecasts. In these cases an estimate is made what might be the likely future level of annual earnings.

Calculations of discounted cash flow are applied to the valuation of new projects and to choose between options of financing the purchase of assets. A similar calculation used is the **internal rate of return (IRR)**. This calculates the discount rate at which the net present value of a stream of values becomes zero. An example of IRR is given in appendix 3, Example 5.

Value enhancement (enterprise value)

This valuation is an adaptation of the original premise that every business is founded on the employment of long-term capital. The capital employed in a business will comprise a mixture of equity investment and long-term loans. As a profit is earned each year and dividends (or drawings in the case of non-corporate businesses) are withdrawn, the net enhancement is left in the business to increase the existing capital.

Enterprise value, therefore, is calculated as the value of the business plus the value of the debt that has been borrowed. It is more perceptual than other measures because it takes into account for quoted concerns the market capitalisation of the business (as given by multiplying the number of shares in issue by their market price) and adding to this the value of the outstanding medium and long-term loans. It is assumed that short-term loans have a maturity of no more than one year (being usually just bank overdrafts) and are used to smooth day-to-day variable working capital requirements.

Market conception

Business valuations sometimes have to rely on the ability of the valuer to imagine what the business is worth. This has been touched on when discussing EBITDA, that is, the value of a business to the acquirer will be different from the value to the seller. Another example of this difference is the value of a portfolio of premises, when an acquirer finds it much cheaper to buy an existing portfolio at a premium value rather than to build premises on 'green field' sites. The selling company, on the other hand, will be relying on the market value of the portfolio as it stands.

Purchasing an unquoted company will be more conceptual than a quoted company. There will be no share price to act as a guide and, if the business being sold is part of a group without separate accounts, its net worth is even more difficult to judge. This difficulty does not aid the bank when a loan has been requested. One format for the bank to follow to calculate a net asset value of the proposed acquisition is:

- ◆ split up the fixed and net current assets from the current balance sheet and formally value the freehold premises;
- ◆ take the past earnings of the unquoted company and adjust them to eliminate any exceptional income/expenditure items and make a charge for the cost of a notional rent of the freehold premises;
- ◆ forecast future earnings on the same basis for an agreed number of years and discount these values back to the present day;
- ◆ add to this present value the market value of the freehold premises
- ◆ deduct the cost of borrowing if any existing loan is to be repaid, and deduct the elimination of any excess borrowing cost where the acquiring company is to borrow at a lower interest rate;
- ◆ the resulting net figure will be the going-concern value to place on the proposed business to be purchased;
- ◆ deduct the cost of loans to be taken out by the acquiring company;
- ◆ this going-concern value can then be compared with the value the acquiring company is paying for the business and will give the gearing of any loans needed to meet the acquisition cost.

The degree of acceptable risk

When purchasing a company partly through commercial finance other factors will need to be taken into consideration apart from the underlying book net asset valuation and the risk that this may prove inadequate security by itself. How will the acquired business be managed? Will the purchase cost be partially recouped fairly rapidly through asset disposals? Will the trading operations dovetail well into the existing business of the acquirer? What will be the strategy for the new business? If the aim is to run the new business autonomously, the risks involved will require an assessment of the following characteristics:

◆ the company should be large enough to have critical mass in its market(s);
◆ the company preferably should not be in a cyclical industry;
◆ the company should have defensive qualities in its own right in the event of a market downturn;
◆ the company should hold a reasonably good chance of value enhancement without jeopardising the parent company.

HM Revenue and Customs

Other than the purchase and sale of a company between a willing buyer and seller where tax rollover relief applies (ie any capital gains are deferred until a subsequent disposal), if shares in a business have to be disposed of that raise a capital gains tax liability, the HM Revenue and Customs valuation may differ from the agreed transfer price. Broadly defined, a P/E ratio and dividend yield and net asset value will be take into account according to the circumstances of the specific case. A critical factor will be the rights of the shares being transferred.

Appendix 8

Example of discount invoicing

This example assumes that the average debts comprising the sales ledger are a base £100,000, which is probably the minimum viable size to discount allowing for the costs involved.

Assumptions:

Sales ledger average debts outstanding each month	£100,000
Average time taken to collect the debts	80 days
Expected time taken by the bank to collect the debts	50 days
Time taken for money to be received by the trader	3 days
Bank overdraft currently costs	8% pa
Invoice discounting proportion of debtors financed	75%
Administrative commission payable	£2,000
Discounting turnover charge	1% pa
Discounting cost of finance	7% pa

Comparison of financing costs by: **discounting**   **overdraft**

Financing of debts:

		discounting	overdraft
By bank overdraft	80/365 x 100,000 x 8% =	£1,753	
By discounting	50/365 x 75% x 100,000 x 7% =	£719	
Add three days to receive funds 3/365 x 75,000 x 8% =		£49	
Sub-totals		**£768**	**£1,753**
Add negotiated administrative fee		£1,000	
Discounting arrangement fee – say waived		£0	
Turnover charge	100,000 x 1% =	£1,000	
Overall costs		**£2,768**	**£1,753**

The example does not reflect the benefit to the trader under the discounting finance option of the credit increasing automatically as debts rise up to the credit limit set. The discounting facility will probably also provide the additional finance up to 100% of the debtor portfolio subject to acceptance of the credit risk attaching to each debtor.

Appendix 9

Farming: schedules of work programme

Accounting for farm arable table:

Note: P = planting; H = harvest with crop yield shown as 1, 2, etc.

For incidence of income see text.

Accounting for farm livestock table:

Note: C = conception; B = birth; S = sale of livestock: M = milking; L = laying. Production per animal per cycle shown as 1, 2, etc.

Beef, pigs and poultry conception would be ongoing but is shown notionally to commence from January.

For incidence of income see text.

Appendix 9: Sheet 1

Accounting for farm arable (Programme of work (typical))

#	Month	Wheat		Barley		Oats		Oilseed Rape		Sugar	Potatoes		Peas	Beans	
		winter	spring	winter	spring	winter	spring	winter	spring	Beet	early	late		winter	spring
1	Jan						P1								
2	Feb		P1		P1		P1				P1		P1		P1
3	Mch		P1		P1		P1		P1	P1	P1	P1	P1		P1
4	April		P1				P1		P1			P1			
5	May														
6	June										H1				
7	July	H1		H1	H1	H1		H1							
8	Aug	H1	H1	H1	H1	H1	H1		H1			H1	H1	H1	H1
9	Sept	P2	H1	P2		P2	H1	P2				H1		P2	H1
10	Oct	P2		P2		P2									
11	Nov					P2				H1					
12	Dec					P2				H1					
13	Jan						P2								
14	Feb		P2		P2		P2				P2		P2		P2
15	Mch		P2		P2		P2		P2	P2	P2	P2	P2		P2
16	April		P2				P2		P2			P2			
17	May										H2				
18	June														
19	July	H2		H2		H2									
20	Aug	H2	H2	H2	H2	H2	H2	H2	H2				H1		
21	Sept		H2	R2	R2		H2	P3							
22	Oct	P3								H2		H2		H2	H2
23	Nov	P3								H2		H2		P3	H2
24	Dec														

Appendix 9: Sheet 2

Appendix 9: farming: schedule of work programme

Life:

#	Month	Beef carcase	Beef dairy	Sheep lambs	Pigs marketed	Poultry eggs	Poultry marketed
1	Jan	C2	C2	B1 early	C2	C2	C2
2	Feb				S1		S1
3	Mch			B1	S1		
4	April			B1 hill	S1		
5	May			S1 early	B2	L1	
6	June			S1	C3	B2	B2
7	July	S1		S1 hill	S2	C3	C3
8	Aug		M1 end	C2 early	S2		S2
9	Sept				S2		
10	Oct	B2	B2	C2	B3		B3
11	Nov	C3	M2 start	C2 hill	C4	L2	C4
12	Dec				S3	B3	B3
13	Jan		C3	B2 early	S3	C4	C4
14	Feb				S3		S3
15	Mch				B4		
16	April			B2	C5		
17	May	S2		B2 hill	S4	L3	
18	June			S2 early	S4	B4	B4
19	July			S2 hill	S4	C5	C5
20	Aug	B3	M2 end	C3 early	B5		S4
21	Sept				C6		
22	Oct		B3	C3	S5		
23	Nov		M3 start	C3 hill	S5	L4	
24	Dec				S5	B5	B5

NOTE: C = conception; B = birth; S = sale of livestock; M = milking; L = laying; with livestock production per animal per cycle shown as 1, 2 etc. Beef, pigs and poultry conception would be on-going but is shown notionally to commence from January. For incidence of income: see text.

Incidence of income chart:

#	Month	Beef marketed	dairy	Sheep lambs	Pigs marketed	Poultry eggs	Poultry marketed
1	Jan		x				x
2	Feb		x		x		
3	Mch		x		x		
4	April		x		x		
5	May		x	x		x	
6	June		x	x		x	
7	July	x	x	x		x	x
8	Aug		x			x	
9	Sept				x	x	
10	Oct		x		x	x	
11	Nov		x		x	x	
12	Dec		x		x	x	x
13	Jan		x			x	
14	Feb		x			x	
15	Mch		x			x	
16	April					x	
17	May	x	x	x	x	x	
18	June		x	x	x	x	
19	July		x	x	x	x	
20	Aug		x		x	x	x
21	Sept					x	
22	Oct				x	x	
23	Nov		x		x	x	
24	Dec		x		x	x	

435

Index